Fighting fo

Fighting for Britain

African Soldiers
in the Second World War

DAVID KILLINGRAY
with
Martin Plaut

JC JAMES CURREY

James Currey
is an imprint of Boydell & Brewer Ltd
PO Box 9
Woodbridge, Suffolk IP12 3DF (GB)
www.jamescurrey.com

and of

Boydell & Brewer Inc.
668 Mt Hope Avenue
Rochester, NY 14620-2731 (US)
www.boydellandbrewer.com

British Library Cataloguing in Publication Data
Killingray, David.
Fighting for Britain : African soldiers in the Second
World War.
1. World War, 1939-1945—Participation, African.
2. World War, 1939-1945—Personal narratives, African.
I. Title 940.5'36-dc22

ISBN 978-1-84701-047-6 James Currey (Paper)

Typeset in 10.5/11.5 Monotype Ehrhardt
by Avocet Typeset, Chilton, Aylesbury, Bucks

Contents

Contents

List of Maps, Tables & Photographic Essays

Maps

Tables

Photographic Essays

Acknowledgements

The idea for writing this book emerged from my research for a doctorate more than 25 years ago. It was further stimulated by work with the Oxford Development Records Project on British soldiers' experiences with the African Colonial Forces, and then given added spur when I was advisor to a BBC Africa Service series broadcast in 1989 that commemorated the 50th anniversary of the outbreak of war. In the making of that programme 'stringers' in different parts of Africa recorded for the BBC the voices of African ex-servicemen who had served with the British colonial forces during the Second World War. Among those who listened to the broadcasts were a good number of former soldiers, and some of their children, who responded by sending the BBC producer, Martin Plaut, accounts of wartime experiences. The result was a substantial quantity of new oral and written material that described the African experience of wartime recruitment, of army life, service on battlefronts from Abyssinia to Burma, and of demobilization and post-war employment and politics. These accounts, often written in a simple and direct form, were at times vivid and gripping, sometimes reflecting the pain of misfortune, in other cases the new opportunities brought as a result of war service.

That collection of unique material served as the basis for this book. It has been supplemented by oral material that I recorded in Ghana many years ago, similar extensive material collected by friends and colleagues from other parts of Africa, and oral and written records in various archival collections, most notably the Imperial War Museum, London; Rhodes House Library, Oxford; and the Liddell Hart Archive at King's College London.

The text of the book has been written by me rather slowly, but throughout the overlong gestation period Martin Plaut has chivvied, encouraged and harried me to keep at it but only as a kindly friend can. And he has performed other important tasks which merit the 'with Martin Plaut' attribution, as part co-parent of the book. Martin has read and helpfully commented on the text, frequently challenging loose statements and unsubstantiated ideas. He has also helped choose and assemble the illustrations. We both wanted photographs to be included but we were determined that they should not be treated as mere illustration but be critically interrogated with a written text.

Writing a book like this relies heavily on the work and efforts of friends and colleagues. In some instances the debts are obvious, arising from published work. In many instances the debt is hidden, with ideas being sparked from reading texts that have little to do with African soldiers in the Second World War. Many ideas have also come as a result of seminar papers and subsequent discussions, conversations, and correspondence. For all of this I am most grateful particularly to my colleagues in the University of London, at my own college Goldsmiths, but also at the School of Oriental and African Studies, the Institute of Commonwealth Studies, King's College, and at the Institute of Historical Research where the weekly Imperial history seminar has met for many years.

It would be impossible to mention all who have helped shape my historical thinking over the years, although I must mention the sustained intellectual stimulation provided by two friends, Richard Rathbone and Andrew Porter. Others to whom I owe a great deal, listed not in order of significance but in alphabetical order, are: David Anderson, Stephen Ashton, Jim Brennan, Anthony Clayton, Festus Cole, the late Michael Crowder, John Darwin, Myron Echenberg, Kent Fedorowich, Albert Grundlingh, Louis Grundlingh, the late Robin Hallett, John D. Hargreaves, Robert Holland, Wendell P. Holbrook, Ashley Jackson, Tony Kirk-Greene, Dick van Galen Last, Nancy Lawler, Eric Lanning, Joanna Lewis, John Lonsdale, Tim Lovering, Wm Roger Louis, Shula Marks, Peter Marshall, Bill Nasson, David Omissi, Melvin Page, John Parker, Timothy Parsons, Andrew Roberts (formerly of SOAS), David Rooney, Terry Ranger, Deborah Shackleton, George 'Sam' Shepperson, Anthony Stockwell, Sarah Stockwell, Martin Thomas, Gardner Thompson, Michael Twaddle, Kenneth Vickery, Suki Wolton, and Peter Yearwood.

I am also grateful for the help and guidance of numerous librarians and archivists particularly in London, Oxford, and Cambridge. A big debt goes to Terry Barringer and her colleagues at the Library of the Royal Commonwealth Society, for many years in Northumberland Avenue, London, and then at Cambridge.

My greatest debt is to my wife Margaret whose clarity of thought and precision of expression has frequently rescued me from ill-thought-out ideas and grievous grammatical and factual errors. Thank you for love and the rich discussions that have taken place on most days over the past 50 years.

Abbreviations

AAPC	African Auxiliary Pioneer Corps
ABCA	Army Bureau of Current Affairs
ACF	African colonial forces
APC	African Pioneer Corps
ADM	Admiralty
ANC	African National Congress (South Africa)
BBC	British Broadcasting Corporation
C-in-C	Commander-in-Chief
CO	Colonial Office
CPP	Convention People's Party (Gold Coast)
DC	District Commissioner
DO	Dominions Office
EA (Div)	East African Division
EAMLS	East African Military Labour Service
EAASC	East African Army Service Corps
FO	Foreign Office
GHQ	General Headquarters
GOC-in-C	General Officer Commanding (-in-Chief)
HCT	High Commission Territories
ICS	Institute of Commonwealth Studies, London
IG	Inspector General
IORL	India Office and Records Library
IWM	Imperial War Museum
KAR	King's African Rifles
Mss	manuscripts
NAAFI	Navy Army and Air Force Institutes
NAG	National Archives of Ghana (Accra; Cape Coast; Tamale)
NCO	non-commissioned officer
NEAS	Non-European Army Services
NMC	Native Military Corps
NRR	Northern Rhodesian Rifles
OC	officer commanding
RAF	Royal Air Force
RAR	Rhodesian African Rifles
RHL	Rhodes House Library, Oxford
RN	Royal Navy
RSM	Regimental Sergeant Major
RWAFF	Royal West African Frontier Force (earlier WAFF)

SADF	South African Defence Force
SCC	Somaliland Camel Corps
SDF	Sudan Defence Force
SOAS	School of Oriental and African Studies
TNA	The National Archives of the UK
UDF	Union Defence Force
VD	venereal disease
WA(Div)	West African Division
WO	Warrant Officer
WOPC	Warrant Officer Platoon Commander
YMCA	Young Men's Christian Association

Introduction

This book is concerned with African soldiers who served in the British colonial forces, and the South African Defence Force, during the Second World War. These men, and a very few women, have not been given the attention that they deserve in the historical literature. Indeed, there are many who will be surprised to know that large numbers of Africans served in the war in the armies of Britain, South Africa, France, Italy and Belgium. To cover all of those African soldiers in one book would be a Herculean task, so the focus here is on those who were black and who came from what rather crudely can be called 'Anglophone' Africa. This ignores white South Africans who fought in the war, but their literacy and the racially discriminatory nature of that country until the 1990s means that they have been documented, with their experiences detailed in numerous chronicles and also by official histories. In contrast black soldiers throughout the whole of Africa have been largely ignored. Official documentation tended to treat them collectively, as units, battalions, regiments and brigades, and as most were nonliterate few individuals produced memoirs or accounts of their war experiences.[1]

The attempt in this book is to tell in their own words the story of African soldiers who fought for Britain and South Africa. Thus the account rests heavily on oral evidence, soldiers' letters, and other sources in which the African rank and file were noted or recorded their experiences of the war years and after. This is 'history from below', a 'people's story', an account of men who so far have been largely forgotten. There are many books by and about ordinary soldiers in European armies in the Second World War, and there are several accounts by Africans who served with the French colonial armies.[2] A good deal has been written on the campaigns in which African soldiers were involved, in Abyssinia, North Africa, the Levant, Italy, and Burma, and although African units are often mentioned their experience has been largely ignored. One or two novels have dealt with African soldiers in the Second World War, the latest being *Burma Boy*.[3]

There is a story of another African soldier, no doubt soon to be written about in various forms for different readerships: that of Hussein Onyango Obama (1895–1979), grandfather of Barack Obama, the 44th President of the United States. Onyango Obama – the name under which he enlisted in the King's

African Rifles – was born in 1895 to Luo parents, his father a farmer living in the village of Kendu, western Kenya. According to his grandson's account he was a restless and curious boy who went to the town of Kisumu to see 'white men for himself'. When Onyango returned to the village he was startlingly dressed in a shirt and trousers. Onyango learned to read and write which 'made him useful to the white man, and during the war [1914–18] he was put in charge of road crews'. After the war, like many Africans, he was attracted by the money wages offered in the town; Onyango walked to Nairobi and became a domestic servant employed by Europeans. With his wages he returned to Kendu, built a hut, bought cattle, married three wives and began a family. In the course of his long life (he died in 1979), he was briefly a Christian and also a Muslim. Although in his mid-forties for some reason Onyango joined up, probably in 1942–3, serving as an army cook and travelling to Ceylon and Burma. 'When he returned, three years later, he came with a gramophone and that picture of the women he claimed to have married in Burma.'[4] Claims are also made that he visited England, returning home with a crystal set that he had bought.

One of Onyango Obama's sons, the intelligent and strong-willed Barack, fell out with his father, left home, but eventually with the help of American mission-aries and via his own success in a correspondence course, gained a scholarship to a university in the United States. Although already married to a Kenyan wife he contracted a short-lived marriage to an American woman, who gave birth to his son, Barack Obama. The rest, as is often said, is history – in this case, world history.

The African soldiers who enlisted during the war years can have had little idea of the global significance of the war in which they were involved. Most men did their duty and returned home unaware of the enormous changes in great-power relations brought about by the years of brutal conflict. What they became all too aware of back in Africa was the economic change brought by war, most noticeably that the money in their pockets had lost much of its value: wartime inflation had eroded their expected and real incomes, and there were shortages of many basic imported goods in the stores. Peacetime returned soldiers to their homes but it also removed them from the protective umbrella of the army's welfare system and placed them back in a labour market where there was a high level of competition for paid employment. For the African continent the war marked the beginning of important changes, but hardly as a result of pressure exerted by ex-servicemen. Rather it came from the forces of social and economic discontent already in place that were further fuelled by the war, and the devel-opment of new political parties that demanded constitutional change. A few prescient voices warned of impending demands for social and economic change as a result of the war, but few thought that political change would be so rapid or that within two decades most African colonies would be independent states and members of the United Nations.

Sources of evidence

African soldiers, the rank-and-file of the wartime armies, have provided the basic sources for this study in the form of oral interviews and soldiers' letters. When the war ended in 1945 what passed for 'African' history was largely the story of European activity in the continent. Thus South African history texts began at 1652, and old Africa hands and historians of colonialism spoke and wrote paternalistically about Africans and either ignored or disparaged their history and achievements. In the late 1940s there were a few scholars interested in the social and economic changes occurring in Africa, and an even smaller number who were beginning to gather evidence on African nationalist political activity. Although the latter credited African ex-servicemen with a significant role in Gold Coast politics, none appeared to have given thought to interviewing veterans of the war to see what they actually thought. For a long time historians were not really interested in the war and postwar experiences of African soldiers; African miners, migrant workers, cocoa farmers, railwaymen and traders held the high ground. An opportunity to collect oral evidence from soldiers was passed by and only taken up in the 1970s. Since then a small number of scholars have collected oral evidence from former soldiers who as the years pass represent a steadily wasting asset.

A good deal has been written on the pitfalls of collecting and using oral evidence. A major problem has been the reliability of the memories of ageing informants about events in a war in which they fought many years before. At best oral evidence has been illuminating, detailed in recall and powerfully descriptive; much of the data gathered from long conversations (and this is a personal experience) has provided a useful supplement, and sometimes a corrective to what was already known from archival research. However, African veterans' experiences provide a markedly different view of the war from that undergone by white officers and NCOs. Their voice thus offers a rich and valid contribution to the history of the Second World War – important and decisive years in modern Africa's recent past. This material has been collected by a number of scholars, usually as research for doctoral theses, so it is scattered, often in private hands and not gathered together in a single archive or library. One or two libraries and archives do have collected taped oral material, for example the Imperial War Museum, London, and also the Liddell Hart Military Archive at King's College London.

Another source used in this book is African soldiers' letters. Most soldiers were nonliterate, so in many cases surviving letters were dictated either to regimental scribes or European officers and the occasional obliging white NCO. Invariably these letters adopted a formal pattern,[5] as did some of the 'memoirs' sent in to the BBC in response to the broadcast on the Africa Service in 1989. Wartime censors kept a number of soldiers' letters and fortunately these have found their way into various national archives, for example in Ghana, Kenya and Malawi, while other letters addressed to Tshekedi Khama were deposited in his personal archive at Serowe, Botswana.

A third source of personal detail on soldiers' war experiences has been the written responses of ex-servicemen who listened to and then responded to the BBC Africa Service 50th anniversary series on Africa's involvement in the war, broadcast in 1989. Letters and notes (most written on lined paper), photocopies of documents, occasional photographs, and in one case a 40,000-word memoir, since published,[6] arrived in Martin Plaut's office. This formed a rich haul of material, which is ultimately to be deposited in the Imperial War Museum.

The activities of the African rank and file do appear at times in official correspondence deposited at the National Archive, Kew. Invariably this is concerned with either bravery or misdemeanour. Thus it is easy to trace the names of African recipients of medals for gallantry. Troublemakers, deserters, and particularly those accused of mutiny also often appear in the official record, and a reading of extensive military judicial proceedings can often provide a wealth of detail on the motives and frustrations of African servicemen. Official archives and documents also include photographs, many taken for wartime propaganda purposes, but occasionally there are images taken of individual soldiers which inadvertently have found their way into War Office or Colonial Office files at Kew. Photographs, as this book demonstrates, are documents which the historian is required to interrogate, 'read', interpret and analyse in exactly the same way as with a written document.

Most military forces, including those in British colonial Africa, kept a personal record of each soldier: an attestation paper detailing recruitment, rank, health and details of service career. In 1979 when I was in Ghana working on a social history of the Gold Coast Regiment for my PhD, I was aware that the Ghana Army had such records. Access was refused by the army – the country was then under a military regime – and so I was not able to even look at this potentially rich source of more than 30,000 documents covering the period 1900 to 1960. And had I got inside that archive what could I have done armed only with notebook and pencil? Recently Dr Alexander Moradi was given access to the archive and, with a grant and this time the support of the Ghana Army, was able to digitally index all the attestation papers. This material, now computerised, is beginning to yield a mass of data – for example, on the relative height of recruits over many decades, or mapping the place and ethnic origin of recruits in wartime and peacetime. There are similar documents in other African national archives that could be handled in a similar way, making it possible to analyse a mass of personal data in a way impossible before the availability of computers.[7]

During the war years the military authorities published newspapers and magazines aimed at African troops. Some were in English, for example *RWAFF News*, described as 'a home newspaper for West African troops serving aboard', which was published in Cairo and Bombay, and the monthly *Jambo* produced for personnel of East African Command 1944–5. Other newspapers such as *Habari Zetu, Heshima, Ulema, Askari* and *Kwetu Kenya* were in Swahili, while a weekly news sheet was published for the Nyasaland Battalion in Chinyanja. *Indlovu/Tlou* was published in South Africa for men of the Military Labour Corps, and later in the war carried a supplement in Setswana. These journals were primarily directed at soldiers serving overseas, while other newspaper catered for home readers. The newspapers contained war news, home news, and also accounts, some written by African soldiers, of their experiences in the army. Two scholars, Katrin Bromber and James Brennan, have recently worked on the Swahili press, sources that until now have been little used.

The colonial armies & campaigns
of the belligerents 1939–45

Over the past 30 years a small number of historians of Africa have studied the armies and police forces of the colonial powers – men in colonial uniform who had been a largely neglected, a subject addressed only by those who wrote regimental histories. All the colonial powers in Africa recruited local indigenous armies, first used to extend and secure territory, and then to ensure internal security and to guard frontiers. Most of these armies were small, often little more than mercenary forces, lightly armed and intended primarily for operations within Africa against other Africans in what the British termed 'savage warfare', in distinction from the 'civilised warfare' fought between European powers.[8] All British colonial forces, including the King's African Rifles (KAR), the West African Frontier Force, and later the Sudan Defence Force, and other smaller armed units such as the Somaliland Camel Corps, were recruited, maintained and equipped for these limited roles of upholding the colonial order. African troops were employed by the British in military campaigns far from their home areas – for example, soldiers from the Central Africa Protectorate and also from Sierra Leone were used in the Asante campaign of 1900, and KAR soldiers from Nyasaland were used for fighting in Somaliland and for garrisoning Mauritius.

The British in South Africa had recruited and used local Coloured and black soldiers in wars to extend and defend the steadily advancing frontier. Coloured soldiers of the Cape Corps helped to suppress the Shona-Ndebele rising in Southern Rhodesia in 1896. However, any suggestion that African troops should be used in a war against white men, as in the South African War 1899–1902, was quickly dismissed. An offer of colonial troops from West Africa was rejected. Despite this the South African War was far from being a 'white man's war', and more than 100,000 black and Coloured people were involved, serving in a variety of roles with both the British and the Boer armies. Some 20,000 Africans also died in British concentration camps.[9] Deep suspicions about and hostility to the idea of arming Africans existed among many Europeans in South Africa. In 1910, when the Union of South Africa was created from the two British colonies of Cape and Natal along with the recently defeated Boer republics of the Transvaal and the Orange Free State, the country's new South African Defence Force (SADF) was solely white. The SADF was a small permanent regular force of 2,000 men, supplemented by young men who undertook four years of 'peace training' (numbering 16,155 in 1935) or enrolled in rifle associations (numbering 110,000 in 1935), while in wartime all white citizens aged 17–60 were liable for military service in the Citizen Force.[10] Thus when South Africa entered the war in 1939 non-Europeans were not factored into the defence system of the Union. While wartime manpower requirements changed that fairly rapidly, as also occurred in the Great War, the official policy remained that Africans might don uniform but only as noncombatants.

In both world wars, Britain resorted to using African troops in Imperial campaigns. In 1914–18 African soldiers were used in campaigns within Africa, the exception being (other than West Africans in specialist roles in Mesopotamia) the employment of nearly 20,000 men of the South African Native Labour Corps on the Western Front. For a large Imperial force the British could draw on the several million men of the Indian Army – paid for by the Indian taxpayer, and since the middle of the previous century used as an 'Imperial fire brigade' – sending battalions to other areas of Asia and also to Africa. By late 1914 Indian troops were facing the Germans on the Western Front. And in the 1939–45 conflict, the Indian Army also served overseas although a primary role was to defend the Indian subcontinent from the Japanese. The successful performance of African troops in the Abyssinia campaign, and the ever-present manpower shortage – and it must be remembered that man for man, African troops were considerably cheaper to employ than Europeans – brought a demand for African regiments to act as Imperial troops outside Africa. From 1940 onwards soldiers from all parts of British colonial Africa, and also South Africa, were employed in both combatant and noncombatant roles against Italian, German and Vichy French forces in the campaigns in Abyssinia, North Africa, the Levant, Italy and Madagascar, and then eventually against Japanese forces in Burma.

The policy of France towards the employment of African colonial troops had long differed from that of most other colonial powers. From the mid-19th century France had recruited North Africans and employed them beyond their home areas – for example, Algerians in the Franco-Prussian war of 1870–71. By 1914 French military policy, following the persistent campaign of Lt-Col Charles Mangin, had endorsed the idea of a *force noire* – a large West African army that could be used to garrison North Africa, thus releasing white regiments for use in defending France in the event of war with Germany. African peasants, whom Mangin saw as 'natural soldiers', would form a reservoir of men that would compensate France for her demographic deficit and military manpower shortage in a European war. Selective conscription was introduced into French West Africa in 1912 and annual drafts provided a steadily growing number of *tirailleurs*. Thus before war broke out in August 1914, France had in place a system whereby colonial troops could be used to fight in France itself. During the 1914–18 war 192,000 *tirailleurs sénégalais* fought for France (more than 470,000 *troupes indigènes* were enlisted from the French colonial empire), many of them being employed in European campaigns – primarily in France against the German invaders. In the latter years of the war casualty rates among *tirailleurs sénégalais* were considerably higher than among metropolitan French troops.[11] During the interwar years tirailleurs fought in Morocco, policed Indochina, and were used to break a dock strike in Marseilles in 1938. In the Second World War France again used colonial troops from her sub-Saharan African colonies in Europe. At the time of the fall of France in June 1940 some 100,000 Africans were mobilised, with 75,000 either being in France or on their way there. Certain estimates put African colonial casualties in 1939–40 as high as 24,000, with 15,000–16,000 being captured by the Germans.[12] The troops rallying to De Gaulle's cause in Equatorial Africa were largely tirailleurs. These soldiers were to play a significant role in expanding Free French control over West Africa, and in providing troops to invade the south of France in 1944 and in the subsequent campaign to free the metropole from German and Vichy control.

In the Belgian Congo the Belgians maintained a colonial peacetime army, the *Force Publique*, of 18,000 men used mainly for internal security. During the First World War Belgian Congo troops were used in the East African campaign. In the war of 1939–45 Belgium surrendered in May 1940, thus isolating her tropical empire from the metropole. The *Force Publique* was strengthened and a contingent joined the British in the fighting in Abyssinia (with the loss of 500 lives). A 13,000-strong expeditionary force went to Nigeria and served alongside British West African units in North Africa and Palestine as garrison troops and guards. A small casualty clearing station served with British forces in Madagascar and also in Burma.

By the late 1930s the British and French perceived Fascist Italy as the greatest potential threat to their African colonies. Italy's use of armoured columns, airpower and gas to defeat Abyssinia in 1935–36 enlarged Mussolini's African empire and also his imperial ambitions. Besides the large and well-equipped Italian armed force pitched against Abyssinia, Italy also had a 60,000-strong colonial army in Eritrea. This was exploitation of the colony's limited resources to the maximum: out of a male productive labour force of only 150,000, more than 40 per cent were under arms. Large numbers of Eritrean troops, and some Somalis, had been permanently deployed in Libya since 1912, but further recruitment for the planned invasion of Abyssinia in 1935 led to the virtual collapse of the subsistence economy of the colony of Eritrea.[13] By 1940 the Italians claimed an army of quarter of a million *ascari* in their enlarged *Africa Orientale Italiana* – a force that far outweighed the British in numerical strength as well as firepower, in East Africa, British Somaliland, and the Sudan, where the Sudan Defence Force (SDF) mustered barely 5,000 men.[14] The SDF, commanded by Gen Sir William Platt and British officers with Egyptian titles of rank, was divided into four units with splendid-sounding names: the Western Arab Corps, the Eastern Arab Corps, the Equatorial Corps, and the Camel Corps. The force of 5,000 French and colonial troops in French Somaliland – mainly in the strategic port of Djibouti, and therefore a focus for an initial Italian attack – posed a threat and a challenge to the Italians. During the war years of 1940–41 the British could rely to some extent on the help of anti-Italian Ethiopian Patriot forces – irregulars who varied in number according to place, time and circumstance. Some 6,000 soldiers of the Patriot forces were incorporated into the British forces during the invasion and reconquest of Abyssinia in 1940–41.[15]

The account in this book is focussed on the various military campaigns involving African soldiers serving with British forces. Although most Europeans think of the Second World War as beginning in 1939, it could be argued that for Africans it started when Italy invaded Abyssinia in 1935 and for East Asians when the Japanese invaded China in 1937. By late 1935 Italian *ascari* were involved in war with Abyssinian troops, and in the following years with Patriot guerrilla forces that contested alien control of the country. This was a messy war, with conflicting loyalties and shifting allegiances, often with difficulty in distinguishing friend from foe. By mid-1940 the war in Europe had spread to colonial Africa as Italy declared war on Britain and France and launched attacks against Egypt and in the Horn of Africa. The campaign in East Africa, which resulted in Italian defeat by May 1941, involved colonial troops from the Sudan,

Somaliland, East and West Africa and Northern Rhodesia, and also South African forces. Within the continent, African troops fought to wrest Madagascar from Vichy French control in 1943. By then the troops' martial and manpower worth had been fully recognised by the British. Large numbers of African soldiers were required as uniformed labour in North Africa and the Levant, and also in the campaign to seize and hold Italy in 1943–44. In the extensive North African campaign of 1940–43, African troops were involved in combat situations involving Italian and German forces; several thousand Africans were captured as prisoners-of-war. Combatants and noncombatants were also employed in the war in Asia, and units from all parts of British colonial Africa fought against the Japanese in Burma – whose terrain was considerably unlike that of their home forests and grasslands. The decision to use African troops in East Asia was taken in early 1942, with the first East African units going to Ceylon early that year. The 11th East African Division was flown to Burma in August 1944 and saw action at Tamu. It was followed by West African troops in two divisions, the 81st in mid-1943 and the 82nd in 1944. The 81st saw action in Burma in December 1943 and it was relieved by the 82nd in January 1945. In the forest terrain Africans sought to outflank Japanese troops and cut their lines of communication.[16]

Altogether, and discounting service in the North African theatre, about one-fifth of the more than half-a-million African soldiers fighting for the British served in foreign campaigns, 120,000 of them in the Burma campaign. Some 15,000 British African soldiers were killed in the war. Overall Africa contributed nearly one million men to the war, drawn from the British, French, Italian and Belgian colonies, and South Africa; the total death toll probably exceeds 50,000.[17] At the end of the war a large number of British African troops remained in Asia, their repatriation delayed by shortages of shipping and the preference given to European troops. The last African units were brought home and demobilised in early 1947. For many African soldiers it had been a long war.

Notes

[1] The first memoir was by Robert Kakembo, *An African Soldier Speaks* (London, 1946). Hama Kim, 'There was a soldier: The life of Hama Kim MM', compiled and written by Ronald W. Graham, appeared as a special issue of *Africana Marburgensia*, 10 (1985). Isaac Fadoyebo's memoirs, which were sent to Martin Plaut of the BBC in 1989, were subsequently published as *A Stroke of Unbelievable Luck* (African Studies Program, University of Wisconsin-Madison, 1999). The most recent memoir is *Can You Tell me Why I Went to War? A Story of a Young King's African Rifle, Reverend Father John E. A. Mandambwe*, as told to Mario Kolk (Zomba, 2008).

[2] See Gregory Mann, *Native Sons: West African Veterans and France in the Twentieth Century* (Durham NC, 2006).

[3] Biyi Bandele, *Burma Boy* (London, 2008).

[4] Barack Obama, *Dreams from my Father* (New York, 1995; London paperback edn, 2007), pp. 396–409. See also the claims made in 'Beatings and abuse made Barack Obama's grandfather loathe the British', *The Times*, 3 December 2008.

[5] Randal Sadleir, *Tanzania: Journey to Republic* (London, 1999), p. 23, provides an example:
'Greetings,
Your letter has reached me safely. I am well; my only fear is for you. How are you? And the cattle and the farm and the crops? Greet my mother, my brothers, my sisters. I have no more news.
Your faithful son,
Mundala Bundala.'

[6] See footnote 1 above.

[7] Alexander Moradi, 'Towards an objective account of nutrition and health in colonial Kenya: a study of stature in African army recruits and civilians, 1880–1980', *Journal of Economic History* 96 (2009), pp. 720–55.

[8] These terms, widely used in the late 19th century, distinguished wars between 'civilised' and 'barbarous' peoples, the former term applying to powers which had agreed to the 'Laws of War' laid down in the Geneva Convention (1886) and the Declaration of Paris (1887). Thus colonial wars, or 'small wars' (Rudyard Kipling's 'savage wars of peace' in 'The white man's burden', 1899), were fought mainly against non-Europeans, peoples who knew no restraint. See further C. E. Callwell, *Small Wars: Their Principle and Practice* (London, 1896). Also Wesseling's 'Introduction' in J. A. de Moor and H. L. Wesseling, eds, *Imperialism and War: Essays on Colonial Wars in Asia and Africa* (Leiden, 1989), pp. 1–11.

[9] See Peter Warwick, *Black People and the South African War 1899–1902* (Cambridge, 1983), and Bill Nasson, *Abraham Esau's War: A Black South African War in the Cape, 1899–1902* (Cambridge, 1991).

[10] Union of South Africa, *Official Year Book of the Union, No. 17: 1934–1935* (Pretoria, 1936), pp. 366–70.

[11] See Richard S. Fogarty, *Race and War in France: Colonial Subjects in the French Army, 1914–1918* (Baltimore, 2008), chs 1 and 2.

[12] Nancy Ellen Lawler, *Soldiers of Misfortune: Ivoirien Tirailleurs of World War II* (Athens OH, 1992), pp. 87 –89.

[13] Tekeste Negash, *Italian Colonialism in Eritrea, 1882–1941: Policies, Praxis and Impact* (Stockholm, 1987), pp. 50–51.

[14] British estimates of Italian military strength in East Africa are given in TNA, WO 33/1636, March 1940, and WO 33/1678, January 1941. See also Brian R. Sullivan, 'The Italian–Ethiopian war, October 1935–November 1941: Causes, conduct and consequences', in A. Hamish Ion and E. J. Errington, eds, *Great Powers and Little Wars: The Limits of Power* (Westport CT, 1993), pp. 167–201.

[15] For the background to this see Daisy M. Miller, 'Raising the tribes: British policy in Italian East Africa, 1938–41', *Journal of Strategic Studies*, 22, 1 (1999), pp. 96–123.

[16] E .E. Sabben-Clare, 'African troops in Asia', *African Affairs*, 44 (1945), pp. 151–54.

[17] This is an estimate; exact mortality figures for the French or Italian colonial forces are not known.

Map 1 *Africa in 1939*

1

Africa 1939

The day war broke out, 3 September 1939, 'was an ordinary day, a day like today', recalled Robert Kakembo from Buganda, when serving as a soldier. 'Most of the tribes in East and Central Africa,' he continued, 'did not know what the trouble was about.'[1] Josiah Mariuki, a Gikuyu, recalled that 'the great war that came in 1939 between the Europeans did not much effect life on the farm'. Early in the war, he wrote, 'there was an ominous rumour that Hitler was coming to kill us all and many people went fearfully down to the rivers and dug holes in the bank to hide from the troops.'[2] Elsewhere in East Africa when people heard of the outbreak of war they immediately thought of the horrors of compulsory labour service during the Great War 25 years before, and some fled into the bush. And a Gikuyu age-group initiated in 1939 'had heard so much about the threat of Hitler and of *mbobomu*, or bombs, that they called themselves "Hitler", to the alarm of the authorities.[3] Literate Africans in urban areas could read in the local press about the likelihood of war and its consequences. In late August the *Uganda Herald* informed readers how to act if Italian bombers attacked the main towns: 'Lie down quietly out of doors and wait till the trouble is over'; and in event of gas, 'urinate on a handkerchief and hold it over your nostrils and mouth'.[4]

While this advice was being read and absorbed, on the other side of the continent the Governor of Nigeria, Sir Bernard Bourdillon, was on tour and out of radio contact on a boat in the maze of waterways that formed the Niger Delta. To alert him that war was imminent and he was needed back in Lagos, the Chief Secretary had a message dropped to his boat by aircraft.[5] On 3 September governors and administrators in colonial capitals from Khartoum to Lagos and Kampala to Maseru were informed by telegram that war had been declared on Germany. In each colony local military or police forces were put on a war footing, German commercial enterprises sequestrated, enemy nationals either detained or placed under restriction, and discussions begun on the future economic and social consequences of belligerence. In Nigeria the Defence Regulations tightened government control over publications and communications.[6] Africans gradually learned of the war and began to feel its impact on their lives as they endured food shortages and compulsory labour, saw men go off to fight, and experienced the gradual effects of price rises. 'I think I must have been naïve about the war,' admitted Mugo Gatheru, looking back at his teenage years. However, he came to fear the prospect of a German victory, recalling the wartime Kikuyu song '*Riria Hitler agatua tukohwo njoki ta cia ng'ombe ...*' ('Should Hitler win the war and come marching towards Kenya, we shall be tied by our necks with yokes, thus carrying and pulling carts like oxen').[7]

Colonial Africa

In 1939 most of Africa was subject to European colonial rule, large areas having been conquered and acquired in the late 19th century and consolidated in the 20th. Political maps showed swathes of territory marked in various colours: British red or pink, generally mauve for the French colonies, and a range of drab colours for the Belgian, Portuguese, Italian and Spanish empires. British territory stretched in a continuous band of colonies from Bechuanaland northwards to Wadi Halfa on the middle Nile, and also included British Somaliland, four territories in West Africa including Nigeria and the Gold Coast, and various small island possessions in the Atlantic and Indian Oceans. White settler minorities, which included a good number of white women, dominated Southern and Northern Rhodesia and also Kenya, largely controlling the best agricultural land and the lines of communication. The population of British Africa was estimated to be in the region of 50 million people. South Africa was an independent Dominion within the Empire with its own small defence force.[8] French colonial territories extended in a continuous swathe from the Mediterranean shores of the Maghreb to the River Congo; reaching across the vastness of the western Sahara desert to the short grasslands of the Sahelian region and to the tropical colonies of West and Equatorial Africa bounded by the Atlantic. Djibouti, on the Red Sea, was an isolated French port colony which controlled the railway into Abyssinia, the land-locked state recently conquered by fascist Italy and incorporated into the latter's East African empire (see below). The large tropical island of Madagascar was also a French possession, along with a number of other small islands in the Indian Ocean. Belgian colonial territory comprised the large, thinly inhabited region of tropical forest and savanna within the Congo river system; the Portuguese held territories in south-western and south-eastern Africa, areas of Angola having only recently been subjugated. To most informed contemporary European observers in 1939 it appeared as if colonial rule in Africa would last for centuries.[9]

At the time when war broke out in Europe in September 1939, only two independent African-ruled states existed; however, both had their sovereignty compromised. One, Liberia, was ruled by an Americo-Liberian oligarchy deriving from slaves 'repatriated' in the 19th century and was economically dominated by United States commercial interests. The other, Egypt, had been notionally independent since 1922 and joined the League of Nations in 1937. However, Egyptian sovereignty was constrained by a 1936 treaty which allowed Britain to have military control of the strategic Suez Canal, 'the jugular vein of Empire', and during the war years Egypt was effectively occupied and governed by the British.[10] Abyssinia, an imperial power in the highlands of north-east Africa and Africa's oldest sovereign state, had been defeated and occupied by

Italy after a brutal war in 1935–6, although a messy guerrilla resistance continued against the Italian occupiers. The Union of South Africa was also independent. Formed in 1910 from four Southern African territories – the two British colonies of the Cape Province and Natal, and the former Boer republics of the Transvaal and Orange Free State – the Union had been recognised by Britain as a Dominion along with other former colonies such as Canada, Australia and New Zealand, along with Ireland, as 'an autonomous state within the British Empire united by a common allegiance to the Crown, but freely associated and equal in status to one another in all matters domestic and external'.[11] However, South Africa was unlike the other Dominions in that it was dominated by a (sizeable) white minority which imposed a harsh system of racial segregation on a majority non-European population.[12]

Most whites in Africa believed that and behaved as if they were superior to Africans. This should occasion no surprise. In 1939 ethnically based discriminatory policies and practices were common in many countries around the world: anti-Semitism was institutionalised in Germany, as well as in Poland and other East European countries, but was also practised more covertly in France and Britain; in the United States, African- and Asian-Americans were discriminated against; and the Japanese proclaimed their racial superiority over the Chinese and other Asian peoples. Ideas about racial superiority lay at the heart of the global imperial enterprise, and overt discrimination was widely practised both officially and privately in the European metropoles. Empire in Africa was a profoundly racist construct, but allied to a strong sense of social class – not least the idea of affinity between white rulers and African 'traditional' rulers. White rulers controlled black subjects and Europeans dominated and determined the affairs of the colonial state and church. This was very evident in many aspects of the social, economic and political life of colonies – in employment, urban housing, the banking system, the allocation of revenues and resources, and in roles and rank within the armed forces and police. In the British colony of Southern Rhodesia a small number of white settlers, outnumbered 25 to one by Africans, had since 1923 enjoyed a degree of political autonomy; much African land had been alienated for exclusive white use and whites controlled most of the vital levers of the economy. A similar economic and social system prevailed in the white-settler-dominated colony of Kenya. However, the British West African colonies, long reputed as being 'the white man's grave', offered little attraction to white settlers, and African farmers and the Colonial Office had been able to resist European pressures to alienate land. Ethnic discrimination, common to the universal human condition, pervaded Africa, and racial minorities such as the Lebanese in West Africa, and South Asians in Southern and East Africa often encountered hostility and abuse from both Europeans and Africans, as indeed did one group of Africans from another.

In the 1930s most officials in the Colonial Office in London saw African management in racial terms, although they often viewed their African charges through liberal spectacles and sought to prevent the extremes of South Africa's system of racial segregation from spreading to the Central and East African colonies. Since the end of the First World War, British official views on colonial rule had embraced the idea of trusteeship and the promotion of the peace and prosperity of subject peoples.[13] Colonies were no longer to be seen merely as overseas possessions to be exploited for their labour and resources. Replacing that predatory idea, at least in principle, was a new view of Britain as a trustee, guiding childlike Africans on the long, slow road to 'civilisation' and modernisation. Certain colonial laws reflected a protective paternalism, for example restricting African access to alcoholic spirits. Nevertheless, the system represented a continuation of an older system that Stocking has referred to as a process of sociocultural evolutionism.[14] A degree of international accountability existed regarding the former German colonies which had been mandated to the victorious powers by the League of Nations at the end of the First World War. Under the mandate system, each power had to provide the League with an annual report on its colonial stewardship.[15] Through the interwar years Germany entertained hopes of regaining her former colonies. In early 1938 this was given some support by the appeasement-minded British premier Neville Chamberlain when he argued for the return of both Cameroon and Togoland to Germany, and – with high-handed disregard for the interests of Africans – for the repartition of Central Africa among the colonial powers and the creation of a new colony in northern Angola for Hitler's Third Reich.[16]

Colonial service

In the 1930s colonial service in Africa offered a lifelong career for many young men and a few young women. Colonial boundaries were assured, and nationalist demands barely ruffled the surface of African politics. British officials little doubted their right to rule Africans and they were confident that not only would there be an African empire to rule for many decades if not centuries to come, but that change in Africa would occur with glacial slowness. The languages of administration were English at the higher levels and various vernaculars at grassroots level. Field officers were expected to learn and competently use the regional *lingua franca* – for example, Swahili in East Africa, Hausa in northern Nigeria, Chinyanja in Nyasaland – and often another local language as well, for daily administrative use. Colonial appointees were recruited mainly from among university graduates who, as cadets, underwent a period of training in colonial administration.[17] However, there was no guarantee that once appointed to serve in a particular colony, an officer would continue to serve there, or indeed even remain in the linguistic area of the initial posting. Nevertheless, the British colonial service by the 1930s–40s attracted adventurous-minded people who by and large had a firm commitment to their work, operated within clear lines of control, and exercised high standards of fiscal and legal probity. Inevitably some colonial officers were dilatory but probably the majority were industrious and competent. Few despised the people that they ruled and there were professional as well as financial inducements to secure a good knowledge of African languages and cultures.

Many contemporary novels and short stories by British writers represented colonial officers as valiant and chivalrous men, steady in a crisis and ever ready to protect white women threatened by 'natives'. However, African views of white administrators were somewhat different – captured in the nicknames given to individuals and in the carvings and the drawings that emphasised the prominent features or behaviour of European officals. The poet Kobina Sekyi, a member of the Gold Coast educated elite, viewed them with a jaundiced eye: 'From Africa is always something new:/The sway of pupil governors; the rule/Of Officers-in-training, blundering through/Affairs of state, uncouth like boys at school.'[18] The prefectorial system that pertained in select secondary schools in Britain was imposed on Africans. In 1939 there were 1,200 European administrative officers in British colonial Africa, excluding those whites who were employed by the government in specialist departments and in artisan roles.[19] Thus it was a colonial system in which the white administrative hand was relatively light, with a limited grid of management mainly concentrated in the towns and in areas of commercial and strategic significance. The structure and pattern of British colonial rule varied from one African territory to another, and often within a single colony, presenting the architects and administrators of colonialism with local challenges of management.

British colonial rule, as with the rule of other powers in Africa, was as Stoler and Cooper neatly put it, 'neither monolithic nor omnipotent'.[20] There were several reasons for this. Although colonies were autocratically ruled, in the interwar years the state had a minimal role, with control thinly spread and often weakly exercised. Under the prevailing system of indirect rule indigenous agents predominated, and across the continent there was little government intervention in social and economic affairs. For example, most education was provided either by Christian missionaries or African agencies. As two scholars have recently stated: 'The more we discover about colonial rule, the more fragmented, contradictory, and malleable it appears to be, dependent on the active participation of some Africans and full of autonomous spaces within which others pursued their own agendas.'[21]

Since the beginning of colonial rule European administrators had of necessity learned to rely on African subordinates as clerks, policemen, soldiers, tax-collectors, carriers, and a host of other minor roles. During the 19th century the British in West Africa had encouraged members of the African educated elite to participate in colonial administration. However, increasingly after the 1860s the development of pseudoscientific racial ideas among new administrators and missionaries led to the introduction of policies of discrimination. Many well-qualified Africans were excluded from positions and roles in government, education, medicine and the church. By 1900 racial discrimination and social segregation had become standard practice in British colonies, most markedly in those colonies with growing numbers of white settlers. By pursuing racist policies in colonial Africa, Britain alienated many Africans who might otherwise have been enlisted as allies in a colour-blind system of rule. In 1938 educated Nigerians urged the appointment of African district officers and assistant district officers (a policy cautiously adopted in the Gold Coast after 1945), but were dismissed out of hand by the Acting Chief Secretary, who contended that 'public opinion would ... be strongly opposed to such appointments' and that it would run counter to the system of indirect rule by chiefs.[22]

Indirect rule

Instead of enlisting members of the educated African elite into the colonial hierarchy, the British authorities had turned to those whom they saw as a better foundation on which to build future colonial rule: the traditional rulers of rural Africa. This idea of co-opting indigenous rulers owed something to policies practised in India, adopted in Buganda early in the century, and applied by Lugard in Nigeria. During the interwar years Lugard's *Dual Mandate* became a standard text for colonial administrative officers, although the system of indirect rule promoted as orthodox policy was revised and pragmatically adapted to the circumstances of different territories. Using chiefs and headmen – those regarded by colonial officials as the natural rulers of the mass of people – the slow business of social, economic and political change could be undertaken at the local level and from the bottom up. 'Native administration', as it was called, resulted in administrative units varying in size and in the form and degree of responsibilities devolved. Indirect rule was an improvised and imposed system designed gradually to educate chiefs across the continent in modern methods of administration and government. No time limit was envisaged for this pragmatic system; its various initiators saw its use continuing up to the distant horizon of the next century, and beyond. There was no hurry to change Africa. As Britain herself had over the centuries slowly progressed towards the modern world, so likewise, it was believed, would Africa. Chiefs would lead their own people under the wise guiding hand of European administrators. Indirect rule had the advantage that it was seen as appropriate to Africa's condition, provided administration on the cheap, and gave African rulers already in place a bottom-up experience of engaging with modern systems of rule.

In order to establish indirect rule, African rulers were appointed to administer their own polities with responsibility for collecting taxes, managing a native treasury and administering native law via courts, a police force and prisons.[23] Africans were often seen by Europeans as predominantly pastoral or rural peoples living 'primitive' lives within nonliterate worlds. Ethnographic and anthropological study might reveal intricacies about how 'backward' societies worked, but also provided – so administrators believed – a guide as to how better to manage African peoples. Convenient ways of doing this were to arrange Africans in hierarchies and allocate them to 'tribes', a term developed and turned into an administrative instrument by whites in Africa. Anthropological research supported 'tribal' nomenclature by recording local histories, legal codes and patterns of custom which delineated Africans into 'Yoruba', 'Igbo', 'Zaramo', 'Temne' and hundreds of other distinct units.[24]

As a result, at the height of colonial rule the vast majority of Africans, who lived in rural areas, were ruled at the day-to-day level by fellow Africans and rarely encountered white officials. However, indirect rule had a decided downside for many Africans. By enhancing the power of traditional chiefs and rulers (and some of these rulers were invented), the colonial authorities often endorsed and even created local tyrants who were able to extort labour and resources from those they were meant to be learning to govern with integrity. Corrupt chiefs were sometimes removed from office, but in certain instances they were either too powerful to sack or the colonial authorities could not manage without them. In northern Nigeria, for example, Muslim rulers were underwritten by British officials and were thus able to accumulate both spoils and power from their sustained feudal position.[25] 'On balance,' argues John Cell, 'Indirect Rule was inefficient and unprogressive', and although 'relatively inexpensive' it 'had no role for educated Africans ... Confined as it was to local authorities possessing little or no connection to central administration, it had no relevance to the political future of independent African states.'[26] By the late 1930s indirect rule was coming under severe criticism from many officials, and also the new Secretary of State for the Colonies, Malcolm MacDonald, who just after the outbreak of war in 1939 said future policy in Africa should take into account how native authorities were to be harmonised with legislative councils.[27]

Colonial economies

The stronger colonial economies relied upon revenues derived from exports of primary products. The Gold Coast exported not only gold but also cocoa, which was grown by African producers; similarly, in northern Nigeria African peasant farmers grew groundnuts for export while in the south a palm-oil industry produced commodities for sale abroad. In Northern Rhodesia European-owned mines yielded copper, which during the 1930s was in high demand due to the expanding world market in electrical products. During the same decade cotton had become Sudan's major export, much of this being grown in the Gezira region.[28] In Kenya coffee and tea were grown by both African and white farmers, although the former were prevented from selling their produce for export on the specious grounds of inferior quality, when in fact the intention of this policy was to protect the incomes of Europeans. Major commercial enterprises engaged in gold-, copper-, diamond- and tin-mining were European-controlled but dependent on substantial African labour forces. Small-scale mining by Africans, particularly of diamonds, often fell foul of colonial laws that gave European companies a monopoly over production and export.

Most African economic life was based on subsistence agriculture. Peasants produced crops for their own consumption with small surpluses for exchange or for sale in local markets, which generated little cash income for the producer and next to no revenue for the colonial state. Like all peasant producers, Africans working their small plots of land were subject to personal misfortune, including periodic droughts and diseases which stifled growth of or killed off crops. Peasant producers were also subject to numerous human diseases which weakened bodies and minds. The results were low levels of productivity and income, poor standards of nutrition, and a never-ending cycle of poverty. The trinity of poverty, ignorance and disease provided a further reason for European officials and observers to believe that it would take a very long time for Africa to transform its economy. In the late 1930s increasing attention was devoted to seeking scientific solutions to certain of Africa's problems – a need made very clear to officials in London by reports on acutely low standards of nutrition in the Northern Territories of the Gold Coast.[29] In South Africa, and later on in Kenya and Southern Rhodesia, substantial tracts of land had been alienated for the exclusive use of white settlers. A major purpose of this was to control African labour and ensure a regular supply of workers for white-owned farms and mines. Large numbers of Africans, especially in Kenya, squatted on white-owned farmlands where they provided family labour, while in the areas reserved for Africans growth in population led to land hunger. Not surprisingly, many soldiers added their voices to demands for a fairer postwar allocation of land and resources.

In British colonial Africa there were few manufacturers of goods, so that the labour force had few industrial skilla. Outside South Africa there was little manufacturing other than the making of soap and beer and some canning of foods for local markets, which employed a relatively small number of workers. Railway workshops, mines and dockyards were some of the few places of employment in sub-Saharan Africa where a modern skilled African labour force could be found. Governments were among the largest employers of wage labour, much of it casual labour, used for road-building and public works. Most manufactured goods had to be imported into colonial Africa – including bulky items such as cement, which was vital for most modern construction work. Banking, trade and shipping, all central to import-and-export economies, were predominantly controlled by European firms which were often able to use their oligopolistic position to dictate market terms and prices. Profits tended to flow out of colonies overseas, to financial interests in Britain and elsewhere. African producers and consumers were thus caught in a commercial web. One response by Gold Coast cocoa producers, repeatedly faced with economic disadvantage in the 1930s, was to resort to a 'hold-up': they refused to sell their cocoa at a low price, if necessary allowing the pods to rot on the trees.

Colonial governments had a limited vision of Africa's future economic potential –but also limited revenue with which to plan any substantial economic development. African colonial economies in the 1930s depended heavily on agriculture and mining, and not manufacturing. Development economics was a child of the 1950s, and in the 1930s serious thought was rarely given to it. Colonial governments built and in many cases ran the colonial railway systems, most lines having been built for imperial economic and strategic reasons. In many colonies the largest individual source of colonial revenue was from indirect taxes, such as duties on imports, licences, postal services, profits, and railway receipts. Few colonies levied income tax. The easiest way to tax African peasants was by levying a hut tax, but this system was deeply resented by peasant producers with limited money incomes. Demands by the colonial state for monetary taxes forced many African subsistence farmers to leave their land and to seek wage labour in towns and mines and on plantations – the very purpose often intended by imposing such taxes.

The depression years of the 1930s led to cuts in colonial budgets and in numbers of colonial officials. By 1939 these economic and administrative misfortunes had hardly been reversed. Investment by colonial governments, as well by private commercial companies, was undertaken on market terms. Successive British governments lacked the means and certainly the will to provide monetary aid to promote colonial economic development. Faced with a stagnating economy in the late 1920s and early 1930s, the London government initiated specific schemes for colonial development – but only in order to stimulate demand for British exports, for which colonies paid from their own revenues. As the governor of Nigeria told the Colonial Secretary in April 1939: 'It is … no exaggeration to say that until a comparatively short time ago any direct financial assistance given by His Majesty's Government to a colony was invariably given, not for the purposes of development, but in order to make up for unavoidable deficiencies in the revenue of the colony concerned.'[30] Nevertheless, by the late 1930s some official thought and research had been devoted to the challenges posed by Africa's economic and social condition. Adding to existing studies of tropical medicine and agriculture, reports were produced on population, scientific research and nutrition.

Local currencies in Britain's African colonies were tied to sterling and managed through currency boards in London. This 'ensured that colonial business continued to be financed through London and also helped Britain to retain a large proportion of the trade itself'.[31] When war broke out the British government immediately tightened the Sterling Area into a more rigid system of exchange control that tied colonial economies ever closer to the Imperial war economy. Although the war shook Britain's global empire to the foundations, especially in Asia, it also proved the economic and military worth of the African colonies. A radical departure from previous investment policy came with the Colonial Development and Welfare Act of 1940 – the vision of MacDonald. This legislation came in response to serious social and political unrest primarily in the Caribbean colonies but also to a lesser extent in several African colonies, and to MacDonald's ambition to move beyond mere trusteeship in Africa. The purpose of the legislation was to allow capital to be invested in economic and social-welfare development, partly in order to contain anticolonial discontent but also to rescue the dependent colonial Empire from the effects of many years of stagnation and neglect.[32] A British administrative officer in 1943 stated: 'Truth is that we have no colonial policy. For years we have drained West Africa of her wealth without putting anything back. We have allowed vested interests to do much as they liked.' To the Colonial Office this was an unpalatable truth.[33]

Communications

For centuries Africa had been a continent inhabited by people looking continually for new lands for pasture or cultivation, by itinerant merchants, and by Muslims who went on the *hajj* to Mecca. The majority of people on these often lengthy journeys travelled on foot. The amount of such human movement increased in the early years of the 20th century as the colonial presence suppressed much lawless activity and made roads more secure, but also because there were new demands for migrant labour in mines and on farms and plantations. The railways in British colonial Africa were built between the late 1890s and 1930, either to serve the strategic interests of the colonial state or in support of European mining, farming, and other commercial concerns – particularly to take export goods to ports. Since colonial railway systems rarely crossed international boundaries they did little to encourage intra-African trade. Cecil Rhodes' ambition at the beginning of the century to see a railway line following a continuous 'all-red route' through British territory from Cape Town to Cairo had not been achieved by the 1930s. By that time Britain did control territory over the full length of the continent, but roads and motor vehicles posed an economic challenge to the railways – even though roads were expensive to build and maintain and few had metalled surfaces. Most rivers, subject to flooding in the rainy season, were crossed by ferries. Invariably railway and major road systems were confined to specific colonies; for example, in West Africa railways did not link British and French colonies. The exception to this was in the case of the landlocked territories of Central and Southern Africa where railways and roads had to cross colonial borders in order to reach coastal ports.

Rapid external communication in the 1930s, for example with London, was either by telegraph or the modern system of radiotelegraphy. A system of telegraph lines linked major towns with the colonial capitals; as the 1930s proceeded, such links were increasingly also made by telephone, although an overseas service was rarely available. As with the transport network, the telephone service rarely extended to neighbouring foreign colonies, except via London and Paris. Most travellers and trade goods entering or leaving British Africa went by ship. Other than Freetown, the West African coast had few natural harbours, and goods and people were moved with some difficulty. At Takoradi 'a deep water harbour within artificially constructed breakwaters' was built by the Gold Coast government in the 1920s.[34] Intercontinental air traffic was still in its infancy in the 1930s, and few African colonies had airfields. A weekly scheduled commercial service to East Africa by flying boats of Imperial Airways – involving a ten-day journey using rivers and lakes – was initiated in the early 1930s; at first this carried mail, then was extended to freight and passengers. By the end of the decade regular services were being operated to South Africa and to Nigeria. However, the volume of freight and number of passengers carried were small. Direct flights to Africa became more common in wartime with the rapid development of aircraft engineering, but transport by sea remained the major means of travel until the early 1960s.

Another form of communication rapidly developed in Africa for wartime purposes was public radio broadcasting. A handful of people in Africa who owned radio sets could listen in to British Broadcasting Corporation re-transmissions in the mid-1930s, while the most developed domestic service was in South Africa where, in 1936, there were 120,000 licensed subscribers. During the war years colonies established local radio services offering news and programmes in vernacular languages, the first such broadcasts being in Afrikaans.

Labour

By 1939 the vast majority of Africans worked in subsistence agriculture, a sector of the economy that was outside the wage system although often permeated by the money economy. Fewer than ten percent of workers in sub-Saharan Africa were employed in wage labour; a large proportion of this small group worked in mines or on plantations. A constant complaint on the part of Europeans in Africa during the interwar years was about the poor supply of African labour. Many Africans were reluctant to leave their land and work as wage-labourers in mines and on plantations, although the regular wages and fringe benefits of military service did attract some men to be soldiers. Tax regimes sought – with varying degrees of success – to force Africans into the money economy. When African labour was available Europeans often saw the potential workforce as lazy and inefficient. In part this represented a failure by white employers to understand the challenges Africans faced when confronted with modern processes of production involving industrial time and regulated methods of work. In the white settler colonies and in South Africa the movement of African labour was restricted by pass laws or registration certificates which prohibited settlement in an urban area without a contract to work. Such contracts often meant the labourer was tied to his work for a set period of service but could be dismissed arbitrarily by the employer. Generally throughout British Africa the conditions of employment were heavily weighted in favour of the employer, while issues relating to the health and welfare of workers were barely addressed. However, across the continent there were many hundreds of thousands of Africans who had either learned new skills or who were eager to acquire them.[35]

In places with a white working class – prime examples being the mines of Southern and Northern Rhodesia – labour relations were characterised by a colour bar, with skilled and semi-skilled work reserved for Europeans. The same situation applied in South Africa, which had a sizeable and at times militant white working class and also had large mining complexes producing gold, diamonds and coal which were heavily dependent on a steady supply of cheap migrant labour. This labour force was periodically recruited on contracts of nine to 12 months, each year numbered several hundred thousand men, and was housed in large, male-only, ethnically segregated compounds owned by the mining companies. Men were recruited from within South Africa and the neighbouring High Commission Territories, but as the price of such labour increased recruiters looked for sources of cheaper workers from colonies to the north, even as far away as Nyasaland and Tanganyika. The aim of the South African government and the mine-owners was to ensure a supply of cheap migrant labour, but that the workers would not settle in the growing towns of the Union. Inevitably some migrant workers did stay on after their contracts expired. Migrant labour was common throughout the British and other African colonies. In some case labourers were encouraged to settle close to the place of work and to become a stable labour force. Some African-controlled agricultural production also relied on migrant workers – for example, that relating to groundnuts and cocoa in West Africa. White farmers in Kenya, keen to secure a regular supply of labour, encouraged land-hungry Africans to squat on European-held lands in return for work; by 1945 more than 200,000 people were in this insecure position.

In most colonies official ordinances regulated labour relations and governments closely monitored the actions of trade unions. In the early years of colonial rule such activity included white trade unions in South Africa and the Rhodesias, although one of the principal interests of these bodies was to ensure African labour did not undercut white wages. White union power successfully secured the placing a colour bar in the mines and on the railways, reserving skilled positions for Europeans. Small African trade unions developed during the interwar years, formed by artisans, clerks and railway, mine- and dock-workers, all of whom held skilled positions and thus positions of relative security enabling them to bargain with employers over wages and conditions of work. The largest unions developed in South Africa where the government attempted to curb their role. A serious strike in response to increased taxes broke out among a wide range of workers on the Northern Rhodesian Copperbelt in 1935. This led to violence and the death of a number of miners, but little change in working conditions. The economic depression of the 1930s pushed down wages and increased labour unrest, and also rural protests, but strike actions such as that by the Dar es Salaam dockworkers in 1939 were unsuccessful because unions were weak and poorly organised and lacked a strong bargaining position. All of this rapidly changed in the early 1940s, with wartime demands for increased output and subsequent growth in the bargaining power of the African workforce. By the late 1930s, in response to increased labour unrest, government labour officers were appointed to direct African labour and working conditions, although during the inflation-ridden war years they were often unable to prevent strikes and labour unrest.

Forced labour was widespread in colonial Africa. Although declared illegal except in time of war and emergency by a League of Nations convention of 1930, it continued to be used by African rulers and also by governments to secure porters or carriers, although the increased use of motor transport reduced the demand for such labour. The system of indirect rule enabled African rulers to use compulsory labour. Often this was for communal work, such as building roads and bridges, but men and women could also be diverted to work for the personal benefit of a chief. Such abuses of labour were common and widespread and almost impossible to police.

Population

The sub-Saharan population grew considerably in the interwar years; Iliffe argues that this 'was the most important consequence of colonial occupation'.[36] Most people lived in rural areas with relatively low population density, the major exceptions being the region of the East African Great Lakes, parts of northern Nigeria, and Zanzibar. Although the urban population increased slightly in the 1930s, most towns in sub-Saharan Africa were relatively small. For example, Nairobi's population in 1936 was 36,000, Lagos in 1939 had 75,000 people, and Salisbury, the capital of Southern Rhodesia, had c. 40,000 people, one-third of them European settlers. There were some towns that pre-dated the colonial occupation, such as Ibadan, Khartoum, Kano and Kumasi, which were predominantly African in shape and structure. Many colonial towns – and not just those in white settler colonies and South Africa – were racially segregated, with separate areas for Europeans and Africans, and this included the educated African elite. Race and colour divided housing and services, while social class imposed a further division on all urban communities. Public utilities such as water, sanitation and electricity supply mainly benefited the European populations; similarly, with policing the security of European commercial and residential areas was a prime consideration.

A view widely held by officials and Christian missionaries, and encouraged by some anthropologists, was that towns were potentially corrupting and thus not suited for Africans. The latter, it was believed, were naturally attuned to rural living, so as far as possible they should be kept apart from the pernicious influences of urban life, with its patterns of occasional work and opportunities for idleness. The future for Africans was in rural production, in societies that were only slowly exposed to the modern world, not in an urban environment that excited ambitions that could not be fulfilled. Influx control aimed at restricting African migration to towns was applied in South Africa but simply could not work, especially in wartime when the growing economy demanded increased African labour.

Nevertheless, towns held a great attraction for many African rural dwellers. Such a situation has been the case throughout recorded history. Towns offered new opportunities, more anonymity, more freedom and an escape from the hierarchies and familiarities of village life, although they also loosened kinship ties. Modern towns also held out the prospect of new kinds of work, wage labour, and access to new relationships and new ideas. It was the last of these from which colonial authorities wished to exclude or 'protect' Africans. And yet towns were often the places that made 'new' Africans, although a widely held European view was that towns also 'ruined' Africans by turning respectful and pliant men and women into people who demanded to be accorded treatment similar to that given to whites. Towns certainly had the institutions that spelt modernity: markets where a great variety of foods could be bought; shops selling a range of imported wares, including kerosene, bicycles and sewing machines; offices; banks; hospitals; schools which offered literacy and numeracy, those vital skills for a modern person; and solidly built houses with permanent supplies of water and electricity. A steadily increasing number of Africans wanted to have access to these facilities and consumer choices, the things they had heard about in their villages and perhaps learned more of in rural mission schools. Such Africans' presence in the towns at times also caused concern to the small African educated elites who were intent on advancing and securing their own position and did not want it challenged, especially by unlettered and pretentious fellow Africans newly sprung 'from the bush'. And despite official attempts to control urban immigration, insanitary slums were an increasing aspect of African towns by 1939.

Education & politics

Modern formal education in British colonial Africa was overwhelmingly provided by Christian missions. The vast majority of schools were at primary level; they were poorly funded, had large classes and offered a basic knowledge of literacy and numeracy. There were few secondary schools for Africans; most that did exist were in the West African colonies. In South Africa, but also in Kenya and Southern Rhodesia, *per capita* expenditure on education was heavily weighted in favour of the white minorities. Africans were only to be educated in vocational skills and in order to serve Europeans, not to compete with them in the workplace. As Hailey put it, education policy was the 'expression of a political determination ... of the place which the African should occupy in the social economy'.[37] By 1939 the West African colonies had a long history of producing a very small but steady stream of secondary-school graduates, overwhelmingly male, some of whom went to Britain and the United States for higher and professional education; however, the East and Central African colonies had very few students who reached Standard IV.

Africans of the educated elite, who were more numerous in West Africa, lived mainly in towns. They were often Christian and certainly self-conscious about their position as 'modern' Africans. These literate Africans – clergy, medical doctors, teachers, and businesspeople – produced and read local newspapers and also engaged in small-town politics. Historians have often referred to them as 'nationalists', although 'patriots' might be a more accurate term. The elite politicians often claimed – with little foundation – to represent the people of the whole colony. Their small local political parties were largely confined to the few towns and acted as little more than intense talking-shops. The parties were 'nationalist' in that African politicians argued for constitutional change within the colony, even within the Empire, and an end to a racially constructed system of colonial administration. The aim at most was self-government, and little thought was given to sovereign independence. However, the racial hierarchy of colonial rule almost inevitably fostered ideas of race nationalism. By the late 1930s there was a growing number of individuals who questioned the future of the colonial state and saw themselves as the rightful inheritors to the colonial rulers.

Military & police forces

All the European powers in Africa raised locally recruited armies for the purpose of internal security and defence of their colonial frontiers. Britain's small colonial forces were not intended for use outside sub-Saharan Africa, although in emergencies policy could change. The Indian Army, long employed to guard the South Asian subcontinent, also provided a valuable imperial force for use in Asia and also in Africa. From late 1914 Indian troops fought in France alongside British battalions. However, during the First World War British African troops fought only in Africa, although the serious manpower crisis of 1918 did mean serious consideration was given to raising a large African army for use in Europe.[38] African military labour was used outside sub-Saharan Africa, in Mesopotamia and also Europe; the 20,000-strong South African Native Labour Contingent served on the Western Front in 1916–18. While Britain was prepared to use African combatants, the South African government, fearful of the consequences of arming and training Africans as soldiers, resolutely opposed such action within its own borders and beyond. It was a predominantly white South African military force that secured the vast area of South West Africa from the Germans by mid-1916.

Among the colonial powers in Africa, the French, long before the outbreak of the First World War, had raised African battalions for employment outside the continent. In 1911 Gen Charles Mangin argued that France's demographic deficit and thus military weakness *vis-à-vis* Germany should be compensated for by the creation and use of *la Force Noire*: a large African army recruited in Africa. Such a policy was pursued throughout the First World War, and thousands of African *tirailleurs* were enlisted mainly from the West African colonies. The result was a large African army that was employed in most major campaigns of the war, although this came at the price of colonial revolts in opposition to French recruiting policies. In the Second World War France again used African troops in Europe; after the collapse of the Third Republic in mid-1940 the bulk of Gen Charles de Gaulle's Free French military force was composed of African troops in equatorial Africa.[39] The other European colonial power that raised a large African army was Italy. Troops recruited from the Italian colony of Eritrea were used in the 'pacification' of Libya, and under Mussolini's regime a large East African army was recruited and used in the conquest of Abyssinia in 1935–36.[40] By the late 1930s the Italians boasted that this force numbered quarter of a million men, causing serious concern to the British. However, when Italy did declare war in May 1940 its much-vaunted colonial military army, isolated by the closure of the Suez Canal, proved far less effective than was feared.

Maintaining the colonial state relied on securing law and order and collecting taxes. The apparatus of police, soldiers, courts and prisons, within a framework of alien law and indigenous legal codes, formed the bedrock of colonial rule. A police or military presence ensured that revenue could be collected and that the colonial state could be upheld and could function. However, rather surprisingly, over a large part of British colonial Africa police forces were small, as were locally raised military forces. In the late 1920s and early 1930s, in response to economic recession, military and police forces were actually reduced in size, with policing of rural areas becoming largely the responsibility of 'native administrations' under the system of indirect rule. In the late 1930s the Nigerian central government police numbered fewer than 5,000 men, and in the Gold Coast there were fewer than 2,000 policemen. Many police forces were armed but increasingly the official aim was to have an unarmed constabulary. Racial discrimination permeated the police and armed forces. With a few exceptions, all officers were Europeans, the rank-and-file being Africans. Many African policemen were former soldiers, although by the late 1930s literate and numerate men were increasingly required to service modern branches of policing such as detection work in the urban areas.[41]

In the whole of its sub-Saharan African empire, Britain had local armies that in 1935 numbered only 15,000 men. Other than white officers to lead the African

Table 1
Africa: Colonial military forces, 1938

Britain	
Royal West African Frontier Force	4,400
King's African Rifles	2,900
Sudan Defence Force	4,000
Somaliland Camel Corps	460
Northern Rhodesian Regiment	450
Southern Rhodesia	3,000*
Mauritius	200
South Africa	3,358* (Regulars); 14,631* (Active Citizen Force)
Egypt (British Army)	23,000

* European-only forces

Map 2 *British military forces in Africa, September 1939*

colonial forces and a few specialist non-commissioned officers seconded from the British Army, there were no regular British troops south of Khartoum. The African forces comprised three main formations: the Royal West African Frontier Force (RWAFF), responsible for the four West African colonies; the King's African Rifles (KAR), charged with defending the four East African territories and Nyasaland; and the Sudan Defence Force (SDF), stationed in the Anglo-Egyptian Sudan. Other, smaller African armed forces existed in Somaliland and Northern Rhodesia. Kenya and Southern Rhodesia also had forces recruited from among local white settlers. The Nigeria Regiment, part of the RWAFF, in 1935 had six battalions of infantry and one battery of 3.7in howitzers, plus minor support services; in the Gold Coast there were four companies of infantry and a single artillery battery. The KAR in 1939 had expanded slightly to seven battalions, totalling 6,450 men. Many of these forces were little more than lightly armed *gendarmeries* – unshod infantry that marched with accompanying light artillery carried on the heads of porters. From the late 19th century, when the majority of colonial military forces were established, recruiters sought to enlist men from what were believed to be martial races. Consequently, colonial armies drew most of their recruits from specific ethnic groups that were labelled 'martial'.[42] South Africa's regular Defence Force, created in 1912, was effectively a 'burgher' army composed of 2,000 white men. Policy in the Union was not to arm non-Europeans; their employment was restricted to noncombatant military labour roles, as had been the case during the First World War. Although white South African military forces had been used in the 1920s and 1930s to deal with disturbances, their major employment was to put down the white miners' rising on the Rand in 1922. When South Africa entered the war in 1939 its armed forces comprised a Permanent Force of 3,350 officers and men plus a part-time force of 14,600; fewer than 1,000 men in the Seaward Defence Force[43]; and the South African Air Force, comprising a training school, a single squadron with older aircraft, and a small reserve.

African colonial forces had three purposes in peacetime: to aid the civil power when required, which meant supporting the police in maintaining law and order; defence of the colony's borders; and providing aid to neighbouring colonies when requested. The process of British colonial conquest and pacification had largely been achieved by 1912 (a few 'unsettled' regions remained), and generally there was little violence that threatened colonial order during the interwar years. Islamism, a source of anxiety before and during the First World War, caused little concern in the 1920s–30s. In only a very few instances was the colonial military called out to aid the civil authorities in dealing with small-scale risings, riots, strikes, communal disturbances of one kind and another, and crises (sometimes merely the product of vivid official imaginations).

The official intention was for African colonial forces to operate only within the colonies from which they were recruited. Neither in training, equipment nor interior economy were they suited for employment in a modern war against a European army or for operations outside Africa. They were not designed to serve as Imperial troops even in the way that the French used colonial *tirailleurs* to supplement their European army. For Imperial purposes the British relied heavily on the Indian Army. During the First World War African colonial troops were used within Africa, playing an important role in conquering Germany's

West African colonies and also in the longer-drawn-out campaign to defeat the Germans in East Africa. These conflicts involved some elements of modern warfare, but were essentially fought between mainly African armies led by European officers. Fighting was fierce at times, but perhaps no more so than in some of the campaigns of 'savage' wars, as they were often called, that had been fought against African opponents. The fighting took place within African grasslands and forests and rarely took the form of trench warfare, with heavy artillery and modern technology, encountered in the European theatres.

However, the rise of fascist dictatorships in Europe led to increased international tension and forced the British to rethink how they might employ African colonial troops in a modern war. The major threat in Africa, as perceived by the British and South Africans, came from Italy, which by 1934 already had a locally recruited Eritrean army of some 60,000 soldiers organised in two divisions.[44] The conquest of Abyssinia by Italian forces in 1936 altered the strategic landscape of north and east Africa. Italy had a large African army and a large number of military aircraft in its new East African empire; these posed a serious threat to the small and lightly armed KAR. Consequently, steps were taken to modernise the KAR so it could better face an Italian invasion. The KAR acquired lorries in order to become more mobile, and increasingly trained selected units in certain techniques of modern warfare. Similar action was also taken with the SDF and RWAFF. During the war Britain relied heavily on the manpower of the Empire, with more than half the 103 divisions being provided by India, the Dominions and the African colonies.

The value of the African empire

A number of questions might be asked about Britain's African colonial empire in 1939. What was the economic value of the colonies to Britain? Did the colonies have any strategic value? And how was Britain able to maintain effective control over such a vast area of the continent with such a light administrative and military presence?

Britain had gained its African empire in a variety of ways. In economic terms the most valuable area was South Africa, but by the 1930s the Union was an autonomous and self-governing Dominion and not at the beck and call of London. The commercial value of the dependent territories north of the Limpopo River varied greatly and, for our purposes, can be assessed on the overall value of their trade balance with Britain. In 1938 Britain's trade balance with the four West African colonies was equal, with approximately £17.9m worth of exports and imports flowing in each direction. The value of exports from the East and Central African colonies outstripped those of imports by some £3.4m. Each colony was required to pay for all administration and economic and social development costs out of locally raised revenue. New ideas about funding colonial development and welfare were being discussed in London in the very late 1930s, but these did not materialise until after 1940. At the end of a decade marked by economic depression, Britain had not, on balance, reaped substantial fiscal returns from its African colonial empire. Certainly, some African exports were significant to the British economy: vegetable oils and cocoa from Nigeria and the Gold Coast; copper from Northern Rhodesia; tea and coffee from Kenya; and cotton from the Sudan. However, these were products of relatively fragile economies that were heavily reliant on a narrow range of cash crops and mineral ores which, given the volatile global prices of the 1930s, returned little real benefit to African producers or workers. Only slowly did colonial and economic theorists come round to the view that expanding the market in Africa for British imports required considerable, sustained investment in the economic and social wellbeing of potential African consumers.

Empire was not only about fiscal profit. Britain's African colonies formed part of an extensive global empire that included white Dominions, vast areas of Asia, and territories in the Americas and the Pacific. Imperial possessions confirmed Britain's status as a great world power – what one historian rather grandly referred to as an imperial 'superpower'[45] – but global commitments resulted in military overreach and thus vulnerability. The demands of home defence, particularly against German and Italian ambitions, competed with the needs of Middle Eastern and Indian security and the serious threat from Japan in East and South-East Asia. As politicians and officials in London sought to balance this difficult strategic equation, they gave relatively minor significance to Africa south of the Sahara other than a role in providing important bases for the Royal Navy.

The principle prevailed that once colonial territory had been acquired it was not easily to be given up. Keeping territory meant it would not be possessed by another, perhaps potentially hostile power. Africa's long coastline did, as noted, provide a few highly important strategic naval bases: at Freetown on the Atlantic coast, Simonstown at the Cape, and Durban and Mombasa on the Indian Ocean. The Suez Canal, a vital waterway which Britain had secured by treaty, was guarded by a military presence. In 1939 London could be fairly confident that the white Dominions (other than the Irish Free State) would align themselves with Britain in the event of conflict with major European powers or Japan. When the crisis came in September 1939, of the extra-European Dominions South Africa initially proved the least reliable, although the Union's Parliament did quickly align the country with Britain against Germany. Some of those who opposed South Africa's support for Britain in wartime formed the pro-Nazi Afrikaner-nationalist *Ossewabrandwag* organisation, which engaged in acts of sabotage. On the other hand, the African National Congress – then a relatively small body that denounced racial segregation – supported the war effort as a means of securing equal rights; in the words of its president Z. R. Mahabane, 'I fight as a subject of King George for a place in his household, and I will not be content with a place in his stables.'[46] African colonies also proved their strategic value after 1939 by supplying men and resources for the British war effort, manpower being the focus of this book. Britain's beleaguered wartime economy relied on the African colonies for crucial materials: gold, diamonds, bauxite, palm oil and a variety of foodstuffs. In the 1930s the value of empire was weighed not merely by its current fiscal performance in peacetime but by what it might contribute at a future date and in wartime.

A further question is how the British, with a small number of administrators and a limited armed presence, were able to rule such a large area of Africa seemingly with ease. The question is of added relevance to contemporary Africa, given its several 'failed states' and widespread disorder and violence. During the years after the end of the First World War serious unrest in Britain's African colonies occurred rarely. There were some riots and strikes and occasional outbursts of rural violence – often local disputes involving African rulers – but no concerted attempt to challenge colonial rule.[47] Since the 1890s the colonial powers had attempted (with considerable success) to control the flow of modern precision firearms into Africa. However, there were weak spots potentially allowing an influx of guns and ammunition – most seriously the porous Horn of Africa, the closest part of sub-Saharan Africa to Asia. The Italian invasion of Abyssinia had also resulted in the flow of a large number of modern firearms into that area, and had stirred regional insecurity. In any military contest the balance of fire-power rested with the colonial rulers and the disciplined firepower of their small but well-ordered armies, equipped with modern weapons such as repeater rifles, machine-guns and small artillery pieces, and with a monopoly over the supply of ammunition. African colonial armies, supported by armed police, had the prime task of maintaining internal security, which meant where possible avoiding armed conflict. In most cases when trouble threatened, demonstrations of military power such as marches to show the flag accompanied by occasional examples of disciplined firepower, were sufficient to warn Africans not to step out of line. In addition, aircraft of the Royal Air Force provided a cheap and fairly efficient way of policing vast, thinly inhabited areas, while the spectacle of a large warship armed with huge guns in a harbour further emphasised to coastal peoples the might of the British Empire. The various colonial powers also had an interest in cooperating with each other in curbing anti-colonial activity.

As argued above, the system of indirect rule adopted by the British during the interwar years provided local administration on the cheap. African chiefs and rulers, who owed their continued position of authority to the British, were charged with the day-to-day business of governing Africans within their jurisdiction. African rulers had power delegated to them and in the process became partners with the colonial power in upholding the colonial state. It was a system of divide and rule. If African rulers stepped out of line they could be summarily dismissed and replaced with a more pliant ruler. Thus, African rulers often served as the watchmen of the colonial state, as well as being the recipients of blame from those they ruled if things went sour. Indirect rulers had an interest in upholding law and order, or at least in maintaining a system that did not challenge the colonial order, because on that their position and role depended. At the same time the British colonial administrative system depended on a large number of Africans who served as clerks, officials, messengers, and policemen.

Britain's touch was fairly light; colonial rule had only recently been established and for many Africans in appeared to provide certain tangible benefits. Not least of these was the *pax Britannica* – the new imposed system of law and order, which within the new boundaries encouraged easier movement of people and goods. Compliant indigenous rulers were often beneficiaries of colonial rule. The leaders of the new educated elite, invariably products of missions, were frequently active Christians who embraced new ideas, enjoyed the benefits of commerce and modernisation, and expected future entitlement to a role in government. However, this participation in government was not forthcoming because the British imperial system was rooted in race, with white rulers and black subjects. Government in colonial Africa was not racially inclusive, at least not until this was forced on the British after 1945, and then on terms and under timings not of their own choosing. In South Africa and the colonies of white settlement, especially Kenya and Southern Rhodesia, the lines dividing the races were strongly drawn. After 1948 London acceded relatively easily to demands for constitutional change in most of its African colonies; in the colonies of white settlement extensive violence preceded acceptance by whites that the African majority was entitled to govern.[48]

Besides military force and African ruling-class allies, there was another aspect of colonial rule in Africa in the 1930s which was implicit but amorphous: the assumed superiority and power exercised by whites over blacks. The Empire was based on race and many, perhaps most, Europeans in Africa, whether they were officials, settlers, or involved in commercial activities, thought, and indeed invariably *knew*, that their whiteness conferred on them a sense of superiority. This gave many Europeans, men and women, the confidence that they were there to rule and to be obeyed by Africans. This cerebral but often unconsciously exercised white arrogance meant European rulers believed that they could command; there is considerable evidence that this approach appears to have succeeded. Such an image was projected in the popular media in Britain. For example, the film *Sanders of the River*, screened in Britain in 1935, had an opening scene with a map of Africa to remind viewers where it was, plus the following legend, read out in a sonorous male voice: 'Africa – tens of millions of natives, each tribe under its own chieftain, guarded and protected by a handful of white men, whose work is an unsung saga of courage and efficiency.'[49] This notion of assumed authority and African passivity should not go unchallenged. There is a great deal of evidence to indicate that Africans saw through this assumed veneer. Strikes, riots and challenges to white authority steadily grew in the late 1930s throughout Africa, not only heralding greater challenges to colonial rule to come during wartime, but also a strong sense that Africans were not fooled into believing that Europeans were their superiors.[50]

Conclusion

On the outbreak of war in September 1939 Britain had an African empire more than 3,600,000 square miles in size, comprised of 16 territories with a total population of some 50 million. African Colonial Forces (ACF) at the time numbered fewer than 15,000 men; most of them were clearly not up to the task of even guarding such a vast area in wartime, let alone playing a larger role in the war effort. Britain's primary concern in colonial Africa in September 1939 focused on the strategic value of the Suez and the Cape routes. Sub-Saharan resources were also of significance, much more so after the loss of Malaya in early 1942. The major military threat in Africa came from the very large Italian forces in East Africa, and to meet this, the King's African Rifles had been expanded after 1938. Military thinking about the use and employment of African troops had moved on slightly since the First World War but the expectation was that African colonial forces would be used exclusively within Africa and that such operations would require substantial support from a large labour corps. The course of the war in Europe, the role of African troops in defeating the Italians in East Africa, the military and labour demands placed on Africa for the North African campaign, and the Japanese threat to India in 1942–43 determined that African soldiers would play a much more prominent role overseas than was demanded of them in the Great War.

Notes

[1] R. H. Kakembo, *An African Soldier Speaks* (London, 1946), p. 7. Kakembo's manuscript, completed in July 1944, was written in his spare time while he was in the army.

[2] Josiah Mwangi Kariuki, *'Mau Mau' Detainee* (Oxford, 1963; Penguin edn, 1964), p. 32.

[3] Muga Gicaru, *Land of Sunshine* (London, 1958), p. 114.

[4] 'Nemo', in *Uganda Herald*, 30 August 1939, quoted by Gardner Thompson, *Governing Uganda: British Colonial Rule and its Legacy* (Kampala, 2003), p. 71.

[5] Robert D. Pearce, *Sir Bernard Bourdillon: The Biography of a Twentieth-Century Colonialist* (Oxford, 1987), p. 249.

[6] Nnamdi Azikiwe, *My Odyssey: An Autobiography* (London, 1970), p. 320.

[7] Mugo Gatheru, *Child of Two Worlds* (London, 1964), pp. 68–70.

[8] On the evolution to Dominion status, see Andrew Stewart, *Empire Lost: Britain, the Dominions and the Second World War* (London, 2008), pp. 9–13.

[9] There are a number of excellent studies on colonial rule in Africa: see Andrew Roberts, ed., *The Colonial Moment in Africa: Essays on the Movement of Minds and Materials, 1900–1940* (Cambridge, 1990); Frederick Cooper, *Africa since 1940: The Past of the Present* (Cambridge, 2002); A. Adu Boahen, *African Perspectives on Colonialism* (Baltimore MD, 1987); Mahmood Mamdani, *Citizen and Subject: Contemporary Africa and the Legacy of Late Colonialism* (Princeton NJ, 1996); and Crawford Young, *The African Colonial State in Comparative Perspective* (New Haven CT, 1994).

[10] Steven Morewood, 'Protecting the jugular vein of Empire: The Suez Canal in British defence strategy, 1919–1941', *War and Society* 10, 1 (1992), pp. 81–107.

[11] Andrew Stewart, *Empire Lost* (London, 2008), p. 9.

[12] According to the 1936 census South Africa's population consisted of 2m Europeans, 6.5m Africans, 769,000 Coloureds, and 219,000 Asians. In the period 1936–46 African, and non-European, annual population growth exceeded two per cent while European growth was 1.7 per cent.

[13] The American Protestant theologian and political thinker Reinhold Niebuhr wrote: 'No nation has ever made a frank avowal of its real imperial motives. It always claims to be primarily concerned with the peace and prosperity of the people whom it subjugates.' In *Moral Man and Immoral Society – A Study in Ethics and Political Philosophy* (New York, 1952), p. 105.

[14] George Stocking Jnr, *Victoriana Anthropology* (New York, 1987), pp. 169–79.

[15] The British Mandated territories comprised part of western Togoland, areas of Cameroon adjoining the eastern border of Nigeria, and Tanganyika. From 1945 the Mandated territories continued to be administered by the European colonial powers but were retitled 'Trust Territories', reporting to the United Nations.

[16] See Ronald Hyam, *Britain's Declining Empire: The Road to Decolonization 1918–1968* (Cambridge, 2006), pp. 43–45.

[17] Ralph Furse, *Aucuparius: Recollections of a Recruiting Officer* (Oxford, 1962).

[18] 'Sonnet' quoted by Samuel Rohdie, 'The Gold Coast Aborigines abroad', *Journal of African History* 6, 3 (1965), p. 389.

[19] To this number should be added the 125 in the separate Sudan Political Service, and also the more than 50 officers of the Native Affairs Department in Southern Rhodesia. See John W. Cell, 'Colonial rule', in Judith M. Brown and Wm Roger Louis, eds, *The Oxford History of the British Empire. Vol. VI: The Twentieth Century* (Oxford, 1999), p. 232.

[20] Ann Laura Stoler and Frederick Cooper put it neatly in 'Between metropole and colony', in Cooper and Stoler, eds, *Tensions of Empire: Colonial Cultures in a Bourgeois World* (Berkeley CA, 1997), p. 6.

[21] John Parker and Richard Rathbone, *African History: A Very Short Introduction* (Oxford, 2007), p. 109.

[22] A. E. Ayendele, *The Educated Elite in the Nigerian Society* (Ibadan, 1974), p. 102.

[23] See T. O. Ranger, 'The invention of tradition revisited: The case of Africa', in Ranger and Olafemi Vaughan, eds, *Legitimacy and the State in Twentieth-Century Africa* (London, 1993), pp. 162–211.

[24] Leroy Vail, ed., *The Creation of Tribalism in Southern Africa* (London, 1989). But see further Thomas Spear, 'Neo-traditionalism and the limits of invention in British colonial Africa', *Journal of African History*, 44, 1 (2003), pp. 3–27.

[25] W. R. Crocker, *Nigeria: A Critique of Colonial Administration* (London, 1936). Crocker was a colonial administrative officer in northern Nigeria.

[26] Cell, 'Colonial rule', p. 242.

[27] S. R. Ashton and S. E. Stockwell, eds, *British Documents on the End of Empire. Series A, Vol. 1: Imperial Policy and Colonial Practice 1925–1945* (London, 1996), pp. 295, and, for the background, xlviii–lii. Lord Hailey, in his mammoth *An African Survey* (London, 1938), expressed misgivings about indirect rule, which were made more explicit in conversations with senior officials in London; by 1942 he stated categorically that indirect rule was going 'nowhere'.

[28] Strictly speaking the Anglo-Egyptian Sudan was not a colony but officially administered jointly by Britain and Egypt. In effect, Britain had controlled the Sudan since 1924; the territory had its own Sudan Civil Service, subject to the Foreign Office in London.

[29] Sabine Clarke, 'Specialists or generalists? Scientists, the Colonial Office and the development of the British colonies 1940–1960', PhD thesis, London, 2005; Michael Worboys, 'The discovery of colonial malnutrition between the wars', in D. Arnold, ed., *Imperial Medicine and Indigenous Societies* (Manchester, 1988), pp. 208–25.

[30] Sir Bernard Bourdillon to Malcolm MacDonald, 5 April 1939; see Ashton and Stockwell, *Imperial Policy and Colonial Practice, Part II*, p. 70.

[31] P. J. Cain and A. G. Hopkins, *British Imperialism: Crisis and Deconstruction 1914–1990* (London, 1993), p. 207.

[32] M. Havinden and D. Meredith, *Colonialism and Development: Britain and its Tropical Colonies, 1850–1960* (London, 1993); also W. M. Macmillan, *Warning from the West Indies: A Tract for the Empire* (London, 1936).

[33] TNA, CO554/1233/33738, 11 and 15 October 1943. However, Britain's economic relationship with its African colonies is more complex than the often-argued idea of fiscal exploitation; see Hailey, *An African Survey* (2nd edn, 1945), ch. 20 on public finance.

[34] *The Gold Coast Handbook 1937* (London, 1937), p. 82.

[35] Frederick Cooper, *Decolonization and African Society. The Labor Question in French and British Africa* (Cambridge, 1996).

[36] John Iliffe, *Africans: The History of a Continent* (Cambridge, 1995), p. 241.

[37] Hailey, *An African Survey*, p. 1208.

[38] David Killingray, 'The idea of a British Imperial African army', *Journal of African History* 20, 3 (1979), pp. 421–35.

[39] Myron Echenberg, *Colonial Conscripts: The* Tirailleurs Sénégalais *in French West Africa, 1857–1960* (London, 1991); John Chipman, *French Power in Africa* (Oxford, 1989); Anthony Clayton, *France , Soldiers and Africa* (London, 1988); Gregory Mann, *Native Sons: West African Veterans and France in the Twentieth Century* (Durham NC, 2006); and Richard Fogarty, *Race and War in France: Colonial Subjects in the French Army 1914–1918* (Baltimore, 2008).

[40] Black pan-Africanists and white South Africans strongly criticised the colonial powers' use of African troops: Marcus Garvey's poem 'The Brutal Crime', published in his *The Blackman* (London), December 1935, p. 4, talks of 'Askari, grinning soldiers/Like April fools at summer play,/Did shoulder arms for Italy/To give the beast of Rome the day. When blacks fight blacks in white men's wars/They're fools for all their valiant pain,/For they shall never hope for right/In whatsoever is the game.' In the penultimate line of the last verse of this doggerel, he refers to African soldiers as 'traitorblacks'. The second verse of George Padmore's ironic poem 'Enlist Today', published in I. T. A. Wallace-Johnson's *African Standard* in Freetown, 28 July 1939, stated: 'Your country needs you/For the rebuilding of your shattered homeland – /By the tyrants of foreign nations/Who would use you as their catspaw/While they starved you to subjection.'

[41] David M. Anderson and David Killingray, 'Consent, coercion and colonial control: Policing the Empire, 1830–1940', in Anderson and Killingray, eds, *Policing the Empire: Government, Authority and Control, 1830–1940* (Manchester, 1991), pp. 1–15.

[42] Risto Marjomaa, 'The martial spirit: Yao soldiers in British service in Nyasaland (Malawi), 1895–1939', *Journal of African History*, 44, 3 (2004), pp. 413–32.

[43] D. Oakes, ed., *Reader's Digest Illustrated History of South Africa: The Real Story* (Pleasantville NY, 1988), p. 347.

[44] See Tekeste Negash, *Italian Colonialism in Eritrea, 1882–1941* (Stockholm, 1987).

[45] Anthony Clayton, *The British Empire as a Superpower 1919–39* (Basingstoke, 1986).

[46] Address to ANC annual conference, December 1939; I owe this reference to Dr Stephen Gish.

[47] Millennialist movements did cause unrest in Central Africa immediately after the First World War; in 1924 Sudanese troops mutinied in Khartoum; the 'Women's Riots' occurred in southern Nigeria in 1929; a brief revolt took place in the Sierra Leone Protectorate in 1931; and in the 1930s there was increased labour unrest, but not such as to challenge colonial rule or cause great alarm in colonial

capitals or in London.

48 The idea that Britain ruled its overseas empire benignly is belied by severe responses visited on opponents or critics in India (1858), Jamaica (1865), India (1919), and in Africa by the more than 1,000 Africans executed during the Mau Mau emergency in Kenya (1952–60); see David Anderson, *Empire of the Hanged: The Dirty War in Kenya and the End of Empire* (London, 2005).

49 Quoted by Jeffrey Richards and Anthony Algate, *Best of British* (Oxford, 1983), p. 10.

50 All too often the private and public behaviour of whites in the colonies exposed their moral and intellectual qualities to African scorn; see Piers Brendon, *The Decline and Fall of the British Empire 1781–1997* (London, 2007; paperback edn 2008), pp. 345–46.

2
Recruiting

In early 1942 the 16-year-old Isaac Fadoyebo thought he would not be able to get a suitable job in Nigeria. Many years later he wrote: 'I simply saw military service as a good job. Without consulting my parents and caring less about the consequences I took a plunge into the unknown by getting myself enlisted in the army at Abeokuta.'[1] As with many other Africans who served in the Second World War, Fadeyebo was a volunteer, eager for paid work, the chance of adventure, or perhaps to wear a uniform to impress young women. There were other men who found their way into the army by means not of their choosing. 'The chief picked out some men and sent them to Bawku ... The chief told me to go and do something there and I was put in the army,' said Agolley Kusasi, recalling 40 years after the event how, as a 19-year-old farmer in the northern Gold Coast, his chief had sent him to join the Gold Coast Regiment in late 1939.[2] Unaware of the real reason for which he was being sent to Bawku, Agolley Kusasi found himself with other young men enlisted in the army and sent away for training and eventually war service in Burma. He did not return home to his family until 1946. About the same time as this young man was forcibly enlisted, the district commissioner recorded that 'both Bawku market and Bawkumaba's court was [*sic*] noticeably affected by the recruiting campaign, people being afraid to come into Bawku'.[3] Throughout Britain's African colonies during the war years several hundred thousand men were recruited for military service, most enlisting voluntarily but some as a result of varying degrees of pressure, including force.

In September 1939, Britain's African Colonial Forces (ACF) were small and inadequately equipped for a modern war, but only deemed necessary for use in Africa. Through the 1920s colonial defence plans for West Africa assumed any future conflict would be with France, although this was assessed as 'very unlikely'.[4] However, the Abyssinian crisis of 1935–36 turned the spotlight onto the potential threat from Italian policies, mainly in the Horn of Africa. British colonial defence plans were subsequently amended and local military forces restored to the levels from which they had been reduced in the early years of the economic depression. However, even though Italy had now conquered Abyssinia, officials in London still thought military conflict with Mussolini's fascist state over colonies was unlikely to occur.[5] The position was to be guarded and watchful, but not fearful. With the outbreak of war in September 1939 the military situation altered; then in 1940 it changed to a drastic degree for Africa, with Italy's declaration of war in May followed by the collapse of France in June and the creation of the Vichy regime in July. Italy launched attacks against the British in Egypt, and from her recently extended east African empire against the Anglo-Egyptian Sudan, British Somaliland and Kenya. At the same time the British colonies in West Africa found themselves placed under increasing threat as the substantial French colonial forces, previously allies, now came under the control of administrations loyal to Vichy. France's post-Armistice force in West Africa numbered 33,000 *tirailleurs* in the *Armée d'Afrique*, later covertly increased to 100,000, plus aircraft and warships.[6] In a bid to meet these problems the ACFs were expanded rapidly, with recruitment drives for African soldiers. Recruiters increasingly employed all the means at the disposal of the colonial state, continuing with the traditional means of persuasion through the field administration and chiefs, and later making use of radio broadcasts, film and other propaganda material to persuade men to enlist. Expansion was relatively rapid. For example, the King's African Rifles in 1939 had only seven battalions; this had grown to 28 by 1942, and by 1945 to 43 battalions with a range of specialist corps. However, while conscription across Africa was generally avoided, it would be quite wrong to infer that all recruitment was voluntary.

A certain number of recruits were required as combatants and literate men were needed for the newly created specialist corps such as engineers, signals and transport, but the majority of men were needed as uniformed military labour to undertake all those unsung and unglamorous activities associated with warfare such as construction, handling supplies, and garrison and guard duties. As the war proceeded the distinction between combatants and noncombatants became blurred, and men who had been recruited to labour corps often found themselves trained in arms and playing a direct role in the fighting. By late 1945 more than 500,000 Africans had been through the ranks. Men – and a few women – were drawn from across the continent to serve in the war effort. Military service often resulted in dramatic social dislocation which in many cases had an enduring effect not only on the men who enlisted but on the societies from which they were drawn. However, it is important to remember that the Second World War was by no means the first occasion when Africans had been called to arms by their imperial masters. From the earliest days of colonial rule, recruitment into local militias had been an integral part of British administrative policy and it was against this background that Africans heard once more in 1939 that they were required to fight for 'King and Country'.

Although the Second World War has long been claimed by historians to have been a crucial watershed in the recent political history of Africa, only in the last 20 years have scholars turned their attention to analysing the experience of the colonies at war.[7] A certain amount has been written specifically on military recruiting,[8] although several significant colonies have been ignored. The semi-official histories of the RWAFF and the KAR, and the official history of the Bechuanaland Pioneers, mention recruiting only in passing.[9] Documentary material in the British National Archives, Kew, and the official archives of various African states has proved a rich and fruitful source for such histories, although oral evidence – that other vital source, once readily available from

1 *Gold Coast family listening to the radio*

A junior British officer, Lt H. J. Clements, was employed to make an official record of West African civilians and troops in wartime. Many of his photographs were carefully staged. This one, taken in May 1943, attempts to identify a middle-class African family living in the Gold Coast capital, Accra, with concern for the war effort. It is similar to a number of wartime photographs of British families gathered round the radio, the difference being that the African family unit is larger. In the late 1930s British Broadcasting Corporation relay and rebroadcasting services were established in the Gold Coast, Nigeria and Sierra Leone. By 1938 there were 2,000 radio subscribers in the Gold Coast, 80 per cent of them Africans even though wireless sets were expensive to buy. The radio or 'wireless' service expanded in wartime, forming a valuable part of the propaganda machine under the direction of the Ministry of Information. Broadcasts were made in vernacular languages as well as English. There was a limited range of programmes including war news, which was also broadcast on public loudspeakers.

(Source: Imperial War Museum WA 451)

numerous ex-soldiers – is clearly now a rapidly wasting asset 60 or more years after the end of the war.

The First World War

While colonial armies had been necessary to maintain law and order in Britain's nascent African empire, it was the First World War that first saw the mobilization of really large numbers of men, particularly porters and labourers to support military operations. The measure of force required to secure a sufficient number of labourers for the long-drawn-out campaign in East Africa, especially from 1916 onward, and the harsh experiences of many Africans, cast a long shadow that affected recruiting in the 1940s. Forced recruitment of labour for war service was not new. In most African military campaigns during the 19th century the British impressed men and women as porters to serve on the extended lines of supply. Tropical campaigns in areas infested by tsetse fly meant horses and cattle could not be used for transport, so military equipment and supplies had to be head-carried by porters. For example, in the Asante campaign of 1873–74 more than 20,000 carriers were required for the advance on Kumasi, and the smaller-scale campaigns of 1895–96 and 1900–01 required similar numbers. Carrying for military campaigns was predictably unpopular and a substantial part of the labour force had to be conscripted.[10]

In the First World War thousands of labourers were conscripted in West Africa for service in the African campaigns.[11] The British in their lengthy Sinai campaign against the Ottoman Empire imposed a huge labour exaction on Egypt which, in the words of one general, amounted to 'a new form of corvée'.[12] But the heaviest and most oppressive demand for labour was in East and Central Africa where the long-drawn-out campaign against Von Lettow-Vorbeck, with his guerrilla tactics, resulted in more than one million men and women being forced to serve as porters by the British, Germans, Belgians and Portuguese. Nearly 200,000 carriers came from the East African Protectorate (present-day Kenya) alone.[13] They were, as the war memorial in Kenyatta Avenue, Nairobi, proclaims in Swahili, 'the feet and hands of the army'. But to many Africans this was the war of *thangata* – a Chichewa term indicating that it was 'work which was done without real benefit'.[14] Porters died of disease, malnutrition and overwork, and rarely as a result of direct military activity. The total death rate may have been as high as ten per cent. Whole areas were stripped bare of young and able men, with women, children and the elderly left to struggle to produce food and to keep community life together. In the words of the Nyasaland nationalist John Chilembwe, the carriers were 'poor Africans who have nothing in this present world, who in death, leave only a long line of widows and orphans in utter want and dire distress, [who] are invited to die for a cause which is not theirs'.[15] It was an appalling experience which left an enduring scar on African attitudes to involvement in future wars fought by their colonial masters.[16] For many black South Africans the sacrifice of war was marked each year on 21 February, Mendi Day. This commemorated the loss in 1917 of the SS *Mendi* which, while carrying men of the South African Native Labour Contingent to the Western Front, was struck by another ship and sank in the icy waters of the English Channel with the loss of 600 lives.[17]

Peacetime recruiting

Throughout the colonial period the majority of recruits to colonial armies were drawn from those areas that had been identified as traditional recruiting grounds. Certain regions provided large numbers of soldiers, sons often following fathers into the ranks. Some villages became effectively 'soldier villages'. These often peripheral areas of colonies were for the most part poor and remote from any modern economic development. They were invariably regions with marginal rainfall where drought brought food shortages or famine. The results were low levels of health and high levels of malnutrition, a point graphically made in the Colonial Nutrition survey of the late 1930s. There were few if any schools (either mission or government), limited health facilities, and little means locally of earning cash wages.

Before the advent of the lightweight motor lorry in the 1920s, small sums of cash might be earned via employment as a carrier or porter. A further and more enduring way of acquiring cash incomes was for men to migrate to distant places where there might be opportunities for paid work on farms or mines, or doing other work. Thus the Northern Territories of the Gold Coast, a region with a relatively large population but a poor transport infrastructure that was distant from the economic development in the Colony and Ashanti, saw a steady haemorrhage of young men bound for the cocoa farms and goldmines of the south. Soldier work provided another form of paid employment, more selective and requiring a much smaller number of men compared to other forms of wage labour. This did not always mean that colonial armies had a ready supply of suitable soldiers. Up to the late 1930s large areas of colonial Africa had a shortage of labour and various means were used, such as taxation, to force men onto the market. In 1932 the Officer Commanding the Gold Coast Regiment reported that 'recruiting has been unsatisfactory for years ... [it] is unpopular because other work is better paid, often less onerous, and easily procurable'.[18] Also in the interwar years many former soldiers were disgruntled over wartime gratuities, and popular knowledge of this acted as a deterrent to enlistment.

British peacetime recruiting, unlike that of the French or Italians in Africa, was on a voluntary basis. Of course, 'voluntary' does not mean that all men entered the ranks as free volunteers. The influence of chiefs, the need to find money with which to pay taxes, and dire poverty drove some men into the colonial armies. In Uganda men who joined the KAR were exempted from the terms of the Poll Tax Ordinance, 1914. Some men also joined up because the army offered a degree of anonymity – enlistment under a false name was one way to escape the past and also to protect oneself from witchcraft.[19] But as a policy the British sought only volunteers. There were several ways to obtain soldiers. Men could always enlist at the local headquarters or barracks, although in the early years of colonial rule recruiting expeditions were sent out to find suitable soldiers. The West African forces in the late 19th century regularly replenished their ranks using men brought back by expeditions that had gone into the 'Hausa' country of northern Nigeria or to the market centres of northern Gold Coast. The formal delimitation of African frontiers meant that other methods had to be tried. 'Bringing-in' money, usually a few shillings, was paid for every man that was brought in as a recruit. Sometimes it was earned by soldiers, but it was also earned by traders who at the turn of the century preyed upon escaped slaves. Occasionally a small detachment of soldiers, accompanied by a military band, went on a route march through a district in an attempt to attract men to the colours.

The most common method of recruiting was via the chiefs. This generally worked well, although local rulers had to carefully balance their supposed loyalty to the colonial rulers who sustained them and the interests of the people they ruled. With increased demand for soldiers in wartime, a growing number of chiefs started refusing to help or were slow in supplying men, fearing that their communities would be stripped of their youngest and fittest members. Under the British system of indirect rule (steadily introduced as orthodox administrative policy in the interwar years) chiefs were paid salaries and thus acted, and were often seen by their people to be acting, as servants of the colonial state. The position of the chief was thus compromised and his popularity could be severely challenged when demands for recruits became heavy. All too often men sent by chiefs to the army proved to be sick, lame or too old. Nevertheless, for the whole of the colonial period the vast majority of soldiers enlisted by the British came via chiefs. In West and East Africa in both world wars recruiting durbars or *barazas* were held, at which chiefs assembled their people in the presence of the governor or his representative, and amidst all the pomp and ceremony, men were urged to come forward to join up. On attestation, each recruit swore an oath of allegiance – Muslims on the Qur'an, 'pagans' upon their fetish or by licking a bayonet and swearing fealty to the king. The term of engagement was usually six years; men could re-engage and many served for more than 25 years in the ranks. Officers favoured time-served men. Soldiers took time to train and a stablilised army was a guarantee of economy and efficiency.

Martial races

Colonial administrators developed a firm idea of the kind of man required as a soldier; they were not willing to take just anyone into their armed forces. Raw recruits had to meet certain requirements and from very early on British officers, often influenced by ideas gained while in service in India, identified particular African ethnic groups as 'martial races'. Early recruiting patterns helped establish and give flesh to such ideas.[20] From the mid-19th-century onwards Europeans in West Africa began to identify the Hausa as the archetypal martial race – steady, amenable to discipline, sturdy in battle, and able to march great distances with few provisions. Sir John Glover referred to them as 'the Sikhs of Africa'.[21] The British and Germans, and also the Belgians in the Congo Free State, sought to recruit Hausas as soldiers. In the late 19th and early 20th centuries Britain's West African soldiers were invariably referred to as 'Hausas', even though many were not. The Hausa language became and remained the *lingua franca* of the West African Frontier Force. Similarly, the French had a preference for Susu and Bambara recruits and the language of the latter, Bambara, was adopted as the language of command for the *tirailleurs sénégalais*.

The Belgian *Force Publique* in the Congo drew on Lingala speakers, while a good part of the regular Italian colonial army, used in the conquest of Libya and later Ethiopia, was recruited from Eritrea. In East Africa officers of the KAR identified as 'martial races' the Kakwa from the southern Sudan; the Acholi, Lango, Nubi and Teso and those from the West Nile district of Uganda; and in Kenya the Kalenjin, Nandi, Luo and Kamba. In Tanganyika the Nyamwezi were identified as having martial characteristics, along with the Yao, Ngoni, Sukuma and Hehe. In Nyasaland there was a preference for Yao, Ngoni, Chewa and Nguru recruits. In 1938 the 400-strong Northern Rhodesian Regiment was made up of more than one-third Bemba and nearly one-fifth of Ila men.[22]

The idea of martial races was a construct in the minds of Europeans, although such perceptions could change.[23] Judgements about martial worth, loyalty and disloyalty, and whether one group rather than another was amenable to military discipline were often subjective and superficial. Many recruits were identified as members of 'martial races', but in fact came from peoples which did not have a particularly martial tradition or history. In fact, many of those peoples singled out as 'martial' in the 19th century for their resistance to the British did not provide sources for recruitment either because they were viewed with suspicion by the colonial authorities (so were not used), or because they were very reluctant to join colonial military forces. And those who were recruited often came from ethnic groups that had actually been conquered by their neighbours. For example, in the Gold Coast the Asante, who had overcome their northern neighbours, were the main protagonists of the British throughout the 19th century. Only in 1896 was Asante occupied, and even then it was still not subjugated until after the revolt of 1900. If any society did have a claim to be martial then it was Asante. However, the British chose to recruit from the northern peoples who had been dominated and despised as *odonkos* – slaves – by the Asante, and the British refused even to consider Asantes for the army until well into the First World War. The same was true of Uganda, where Acholi and Langi were recruited into the KAR rather than the dominant Baganda.[24]

For the most part Britain's peacetime colonial armies were composed of mercenaries and men drawn from peripheral areas of the colony or from neighbouring territories. Thus, 60 per cent of soldiers in the Gold Coast Regiment up to the Second World War were actually drawn from peoples living across the frontier in the French colony of Upper Volta, or beyond. The 'reliable alien' became heavily dependent upon the military system he joined, and invariably was an outsider in the areas where he was stationed. Various theories were formulated to explain relative martial valour in Africans. Inevitably the Indian paradigm had a considerable influence. Martial qualities, it was argued, resulted from race and religion, terrain and climate, or pastoral lifestyle as against cultivation. Coming from 'open country' and having familiarity with horses, it was argued, produced the qualities sought in soldiers. Wolseley wrote of pastoralists as brave and accustomed to war, claiming that Muslims made better fighting men than 'idolaters'; 30 years later Lugard was of the opinion that 'the nilotic tribes – known as "Sudanese" and "Blacks" – though not intelligent ... [were] more dependable'.[25] Opinions varied over the value and the reliability of African Muslims as soldiers, especially during the First World War when the Ottoman Empire was an enemy and fears of a Mahdist *jihad* were abroad. In the KAR many officers thought being a grain-eater equated with having martial qualities – grain supplemented by occasional meat made a man more robust, while banana-eaters tended to work less hard, were inclined to be lazy and were likely to get drunk on *posho*.[26]

Europeans required recruits with a 'simplicity of character' who in a short time would transfer their loyalty from a chief to a white officer.[27] It may well have been the case, as Mazrui suggests for Ugandan recruits, that men drawn from acephalous societies were more able to make the transfer of loyalty to a body such as the army.[28] By the start of the 20th century, racial theories about martial qualities became an accepted part of the official military mindset. During the recruiting campaign in West Africa in 1917, Col A. Haywood talked of 'fighting tribes' and 'tribes who are cowardly by nature and totally unfitted to become soldiers'.[29] In 1923, as Inspector-General, he divided West African peoples into 'recruitable' and 'non-recruitable' tribes, arguing that 'the fighting spirit is weak amongst the people of the forest belt'.[30] During the Second World War an officer with the RWAFF described the 'Hausa' of the 81st Division in eugenic terms as people who live 'in a healthy but poor country and the principle of the survival of the fittest has resulted in making them a remarkably tough race'.[31] The idea of martial qualities became an established orthodoxy among most European army officers serving in Africa and ideas about martial hierarchies persisted well after the Second World War in both East and West Africa.

What this clearly meant was that certain groups of people were not wanted as soldiers. The best source was men from societies untouched by modern ideas of government or commerce, nonliterates who would provide a clean slate upon which could be written new military codes of discipline. 'The blacker their face, the huskier their voice, the thicker their neck, the darker their skin and the more remote parts of Africa they come from – the better soldier they made', wrote an officer of the KAR in 1940.[32] To many Europeans an origin of perceived simplicity marked out the ideal African soldier. An 'inherent dislike of the unknown and the lack of intelligence which precludes quick thinking' and 'a dog like devotion to his leaders he can trust and admire' were the qualities that Gen Sir Hugh Stockwell saw in the West African troops of the 82nd Division in battle in Burma in 1945.[33] In peacetime, Africans who had been in contact with modern ideas and methods were invariably rejected by the military, except in the case of the small number of clerks and storekeepers. Vulgar Europeans on the coast sometimes referred to them as 'trousered apes' or 'savvy boys', and they were viewed as tainted by a thin veneer of 'civilization' and devoid of martial qualities.[34]

After the Second World War the term 'martial races' was deemed inappropriate by senior military officers, although there were many officers in the British and French colonial forces who continued to act as if the spirit of Wolseley and Mangin still ruled. Postwar recruiting continued to focus on the traditional recruiting grounds. With the increase in nationalist political activity in West Africa it was even argued that the best way to keep the army and police free of 'left-wing influences' was to continue recruiting northerners into these organisations.[35] The result of such an ethnically based pattern of recruiting through the colonial period was that at independence a high percentage of recruits still came from the traditional recruiting areas. This was the case in most colonies irrespective of the European power that had controlled them. For example in 1960, three years after Ghana's independence, the vast majority of the country's soldiers continued to come from the north or from beyond the national borders, while the few African officers were overwhelmingly from the south of the country.[36] The ingredients for potential rivalry and conflict within the armed forces were clearly manifest.

Recruits for the colonial armies were medically examined and only those of certain height (ideally 5ft 8in), physique, and standard of health were accepted. When recruits were readily available the medical standards were high; when recruits were more difficult to secure or were needed in large numbers, as at certain times during both world wars, the medical standards were lowered. The minimum height and chest measurements would be adjusted by officers during the course of a recruiting campaign if insufficient men were being attested. Many of the men sent in by chiefs as potential recruits in wartime were rejected as medically unfit. Those with leg lesions, Guinea worm, partial blindness or more serious physical ailments were sent home, sometimes at government expense. Even then officers complained that their commands contained soldiers who were of poor physical standard. In the Second World War malnourished men were enlisted and then built up in three months on an army diet. The age of the recruit was of little consideration; physical appearance was the usual guide. And the minimum age of 18 for recruits laid down in 1942 was rarely observed. Kwame Asante, who joined the army in the Gold Coast in 1942, was only 17: 'I was accepted because I was tall. There were many boys in the army who were only 15.'[37] Thirteen-year-old John E. A. Mandambwe was enlisted in Nyasaland in 1939, having been deemed suitable for the army because he was tall enough to reach the 'line carved in a doorpost'.[38]

Recruiting for the Second World War

It was against this background that recruitment began in 1939. The British hoped the traditional recruiting grounds would provide sufficient men of suitable martial character to form the backbone of the necessary force. These soldiers might be supplemented by other, less overtly suitable recruits, so as to make up the rest of the force. Chiefs would assist in the process, as they had done in the past, and the entire effort could pass off with the minimum of fuss and without the use of conscription. In some colonies most men enlisted voluntarily. For example, in Uganda the authorities had powers to conscript, but this was little needed for combatant units and even for labour corps other than the East African Military Labour Service. Thompson's measured assessment is that 'there appears to have been little difficulty in recruiting for armed service', although he adds that 'hardship and want' undoubtedly helped propel men into the ranks, especially from the poorer areas of the colony.[39]

The path of conscription was one which the Colonial Office in London and the various British colonial administrations were reluctant to tread. French conscription policies in the First World War had led to serious outbreaks of rebellion in West Africa. British pressures to secure soldiers and labour had also resulted in unrest. At the approach of recruiting parties peasants fled into the

Table 2
Wartime recruits: British colonial and South African forces

The actual number of men who served in African colonial forces is not always easy to calculate. Certain men served for a short term, some re-enlisting. The figures below are rounded up to the nearest ten.

East Africa (KAR)	323,480
Kenya	98,240 (30%)
Tanganyika	86,740 (27%)
Uganda	76,160 (24%)
Nyasaland	28,890 (9%)
West Africa (RWAFF)	
Nigeria	121,650
Gold Coast	96,000
Sierra Leone	21,400
Gambia	4,500
High Commission Territories	
Basutoland	21,460 (+3,000 in NMC)
Bechuanaland	11,000
Swaziland	3,600
Northern Rhodesia	14,580
Southern Rhodesia	14,300 (African),
	9,927 (European)
Mauritius	5,000
Seychelles	1,500
Sudan (SDF)	25,000
South Africa	211,000 (European),
	123,000 (non-European)
[Egyptian Army	100,000]

bush; whole villages decamped across international colonial borders; and men forcibly enlisted often deserted at the first opportunity. Consequently, conscription was seen as a costly and inefficient way to obtain reliable men in wartime that also posed a threat to the internal political security of a colony. Although Britain's Parliament did not exercise great interest in colonial matters there were always alert members, and missionary and humanitarian lobbies that had a long and relatively successful tradition of protest against forced labour in the colonies dating back to the 19th century.[40] Britain was a signatory of the League of Nations Convention of 1930 banning forced labour, and strong in condemning other colonial powers for ignoring it. The convention did leave a loophole in that colonial powers were permitted to forcibly recruit manpower in time of emergency, including war.

However, during the First World War men had not come forward to the colours in sufficient numbers, and this was a pattern repeated after 1940 when even larger numbers of men were required for war. Rapid growth in war-related industries and services in all parts of colonial Africa also demanded labour, some of it literate and semiskilled, and such work often offered higher-paid or otherwise more attractive employment than the army. The various modern corps of the African armed forces, created after 1941, such as engineers, signals or education, could only function with a nucleus of literate men, and in many instances such men could only be obtained through conscription. Consequently, conscription was adopted as policy in the West African colonies, albeit reluctantly. In the East and Central African colonies, where there were white settler minorities, labour was also conscripted for private farm employment.[41] A broader Imperial argument was advanced to justify conscription in Africa: if it was acceptable for military and labour manpower to be conscripted in the United Kingdom, then why not impose a similar system in the colonies which equally were involved in a war against Nazi racism?

However, most Africans viewed the prospect of military service from a rather different perspective. For a start, soldiering was not considered the most desirable of professions. Soldiers, and often policemen, were generally despised by the majority of Africans, especially in those areas of a colony where they were aliens. They were disliked as armed representatives of colonial rule and for the way in which they flaunted their uniformed authority to demand preference and privilege. Literate Africans looked down on them not only as foreigners but also for their non-literacy. And predictably, soldiers competed for local women, were often indifferent to local sensitivities and occasionally clashed with that other rival group clothed with colonial authority, the police. Then there was the experience of the First World War. Stories of experiences in 1914–18, just over 20 years before – of the sea, strange lands and food, as well as the likelihood of injury and death – compounded African fears about service away from familiar surroundings. On the other hand, military service offered adventure, a chance to see the world – however poorly perceived – beyond the village, to earn money, and to prove manhood. The latter ideal was frequently exploited by recruiters. Recruiters in the Second World War had to deal with a deeply ingrained hostility that stemmed from the earlier world war and the popular belief that men had been needlessly sacrificed, wages not fully paid, and obligations not properly met. And there was much genuine grievance to fuel these feelings.

Recruiting such large numbers of men posed major problems for colonial administrators and imposed serious strains on African societies. The old peacetime 'voluntary' system of small-scale enlistment from the traditional recruiting areas and ethnic groups was soon shown to be inadequate. The army and other activities associated with the war required labour, and this could only be found if heavy pressure was placed upon chiefs and people to supply men. In peacetime, and even during the First World War, the British had denounced French policies of conscripting troops in their West African colonies. Faced with the dilemma of how to raise sufficient men in 1939–45, the British resorted to a variety of practices that ranged from outright conscription to methods that forced men to enter the army or provide their labour for wartime service.

West Africa

From 1940 onwards West Africa supplied more than 200,000 soldiers and labourers for military service in the East African campaign and North Africa, and after 1943 for operations in Asia. Not all recruits served the full length of the war, but by July 1945 there was a total of 164,850 West Africans in the armed forces; 92,000 – the majority – came from Nigeria, 47,000 from the Gold Coast, 21,400 from Sierra Leone, and just under 4,500 from the small colony of Gambia.[42] Altogether Nigeria provided 121,652 men for the armed forces, and some 30,000 served overseas,[43] while the Gold Coast contributed 96,000 men. At the start of the war the Royal West African Frontier Force numbered 8,000 men. There were three periods of major military recruitment: in late 1939–early 1940 with the initial expansion of the RWAFF for service in East Africa to counter possible Italian aggression; throughout 1941 and until November 1942 when the Vichy-held colonies in West Africa were seen as a potential threat; and in 1943–44 for the Asian expeditionary force.

The recruiters soon turned their attention to areas of each colony which formerly had not provided men for the army. For example, in Nigeria until 1942 recruiting only took place north of a line marked by the towns of Okuta, Jebba, Keffi, Jalingo and Yola; similarly, in the Gold Coast Ashanti and the southern part of the colony only became the focus of recruiting in late 1940 after the army began to need more men, particularly literate tradesmen and artisans for the new technical corps. The peacetime Sierra Leone battalion of the RWAFF enlisted mainly Kono and Mende men (Temne were regarded as 'truculent and intractable') who were referred to contemptuously by Krios as 'Joe Khaki'. The idea that the army was no place for 'educated' men changed after 1940.[44] The major increase in ethnic diversity within the Nigerian and Gold Coast regiments forced a linguistic change from the established *lingua franca*, Hausa, to English as the language of command and instruction, although this was already in use in the Sierra Leone regiment and the Gambia battalion. West African recruiting was reported in the British press, and cinema audiences watching *Pathé News* in early 1941 would have seen an item that described Gold Coast troops as 'bronze giants of nature. Every man strips to display muscles calculated to make Joe Louis look to his biceps'. The commentator went on to say: 'They are not conscripts, but volunteers who have found the Union Jack worth living under, and worth fighting for'.[45]

Chiefs played a vital role as wartime recruiters but in the process often undermined their own authority by incurring popular displeasure. Salifu Moshi remembered that in late 1941, as an unemployed labourer, he was 'collected by truck' in Bolgatanga, in the northern Gold Coast, not realising until shortly afterwards that he was being put into the army.[46] Of course, the quota system provided a means of conscription. Admittedly this method was not as drastic as those employed by the French, where occasionally villages were surrounded and men impressed. Nevertheless, for the individuals caught up by this system the experience was equally appalling. Pressure was put on chiefs to provide their quota and they forced men to enlist. In Borgu, northern Nigeria, the district office complained that one district head 'has mixed up recruiting with the compulsory registration of adult males and that he proposes to adopt press-gang methods'.[47] Men in Tivland, central Nigeria, enlisted for various reasons – some to avoid being conscripted for the tin mines, and others because of economic hardship, although Aond'aaka's micro-study of Gboko suggests that young men mainly joined up for adventure. Igbado Tyober was influenced by First World War veterans who told of 'how they had with their own hands killed whitemen', Ujih Anula left school 'to go and see things for ourselves', while Yongu Jongur Kuji, who was often in fights, was told by people 'that if I was so strong why was I afraid to go and join my mates in the army. To disprove their allegations I left and enlisted.' Yaro Nevkaa joined up because he was 'thrown in awe' by seeing a recruiting team of 'soldiers in full military regalia'.[48]

The close alliance of chiefs with government was clearly seen in recruiting durbars such as those held in the southern Gold Coast in 1940 and 1941. At Cape Coast in January 1941, for example, the assembled people were exhorted to enlist by the Governor, chiefs, members of the educated elite and representatives of the ex-servicemen's association. The regimental band played stirring music and an aircraft dropped leaflets over the town.[49] Recruiting bands in the Gold Coast sang songs to attract men to the colours. One song included a pun on the Akan word *barima* ('brave man' or 'warrior') which sounded like 'Burma':

> Barima ehh yɛn ko ooh!
> Barima ehh yɛn ko ooh!
> Yɛn kɔ East Africa, Barima
> Bɛsin, na yɛn kɔ!
> Brave men and warriors let us go [enlist]
> Brave men and warriors let us go [enlist]
> Let us go to East Africa and Burma
> Come let us go [enlist]![50]

In a number of cases the younger relatives of chiefs were commanded by their seniors to enlist as an example and inspiration to other recruits to come forward. In the Gold Coast the Gonja chief at Daboya 'forced his son' to join the armed forces, while Nana Ofori Atta, the ruler of Akyem Abuakwa, sent three of his many sons into the army.[51] Faced with such pressure in societies where the word of the chief was effectively law, it was difficult for 'commoners' to do other than obey. 'Nana Ofori Atta said that anyone who wanted to help the Akyem State should join up, so I volunteered,' said Kofi Anane, a farm labourer in Kibi who enlisted in 1942.[52] Chiefs broadcast messages of support over the radio and also promised recruits rewards for enlisting. To further encourage recruitment, and to assure enlisted men that their welfare was not being forgotten, chiefs from all the colonies went on officially organised visits to soldiers on overseas postings in North Africa and Asia.

A conscription ordinance was introduced in the southern Gold Coast in late 1941 in order to secure motor drivers and artisans, and extended to Ashanti and the Northern Territories in 1942. Similar ordinances were introduced in the three other British West African colonies. The Compulsory Service Bill in the Gold Coast was opposed by the three provincial councils representing African opinion in the colony. The conscription law, argued Nana Ayanamain at the Central Province Council:

2 Africans looking at a wartime recruiting poster, Accra, Gold Coast, 1942

Undoubtedly this official photograph was taken (again by Lt Clements) to encourage enlistment and also show the transformation that could occur when African peasants and workers – the onlookers – joined up and became smart, modern soldiers. The purpose was to indicate the progress that could be made by becoming a soldier: gaining a uniform, smartness, a weapon to hand, and proven loyalty to the ruling system. Although Clements's photograph was in black-and-white, wartime posters were often in colour, which boosted their eyecatching potential. The Ministry of Information set out to produce and display the relatively few printed posters in colonial Africa in such a way that they would have maximum effect. It is impossible to know how many men enlisted as a result of this kind of propaganda.

(Source: Imperial War Museum WA 14)

3 *West African recruits swearing the oath of allegiance*

All recruits to the African colonial forces were required to swear an oath of attestation that they would loyally serve the British king. Muslims might do this on the Qur'an, Christians on the Bible. However, men who belonged to neither world religion or who were nonliterate were often required to lick a bayonet or an item they believed to have religious significance. These 'pagan' soldiers, pictured by Clements at the Accra Recruiting Centre in June 1942, have joined the Gold Coast Regiment and are being sworn in by licking the bayonet.

(Source: Imperial War Museum WA 13)

went to the root of the question of the constitutional status of the Gold Coast. In view of the fact that the Gold Coast were a free people and that the country had never been conquered or ceded to the British Government he did not see the necessity for introducing such a law into the country, particularly as the chiefs had endeavoured to do their best in providing recruits.[53]

The system in Ashanti whereby recruiting was undertaken through the chiefs was described by Kofi Genfi II:

We went to Kumasi. The man in charge of the recruitment was one Captain Sinclair, a D.C., in charge of recruitment. He was allotted three trucks, to go to the villages. The Asantehene allotted every village chief, allotted a certain number of men. It worked like this: The Asantehene set a quota then he called the District Chiefs and allotted each of them a certain number. Then the District Chiefs called their village chiefs and gave them each a number of men that had to be ready on a specific day. It was the job of Sinclair, he had the list, he knew how many men from each village there would be. He would take the trucks to each village and bring the men.[54]

Conscription was universally unpopular and resulted in widespread opposition, avoidance of recruiters and an increase in desertion from the ranks. In the southern Gold Coast town of Winneba, serious opposition to conscription occurred in August 1941. Rioting broke out and the police were forced to fire on the crowd, killing six men. Other anti-conscription riots took place in the Gold Coast in late 1942 and mid-1943.[55]

The process of conscription was often arbitrary. In Bathurst, Gambia, in early 1943, 400 'corner boys' were rounded up one night on the orders of the Governor, Sir Hilary Blood, and taken by lorry to the local army camp where more than half were enlisted. Within the next ten weeks some 100 had deserted.[56] In Accra, one man recalls how he was 'snatched' from the street by soldiers on 28 February 1942 while on a trip from Koforidua to visit his brother.[57] In Sierra Leone, men arrested for illicit mining in the diamond and gold mining areas were sent to the army. And able-bodied men brought before the courts accused of offences against the law were sometimes offered the choice of military service as an alternative to prison. Commercial companies also helped with recruiting. An employee at the diamond mine at Akwatia, Gold Coast, remembered that in 1939 'at that time, the mines all be closed. We were told to all report for our pay. The mines be closed. But when we reached there, it be army.'[58] Another man, a railway worker, said: 'We were working on the railway near Kumasi when in 1940 we were told: you don't join army, you don't work. A white man came and gave the orders.'[59] A case long remembered by educated men in southern Nigeria was the treatment of boys from King's College, Lagos, in 1944. Housed in temporary school buildings, the boys protested at the conditions. Seventy-five were arrested and although the magistrate threw out the case, eight boys were conscripted into the army.[60]

It is not possible to compute the number of men who were forcibly enlisted and those who, for a variety of reasons, voluntarily joined the army in West Africa. The army had an attraction for many youngsters and this was played on by recruiters. Soldiers visited schools and regaled classes with accounts of their adventures in the East African campaign against the Italians. The Italian invasion

4 *Nana Sir Osei Tutu Agyeman Otuumfuo Prempeh II, KBE, the Asantehene,*
inspecting the Kumasi Home Guard, October 1942

The Asantehenes, rulers of the West African state of Ashanti, had opposed British control over their territory. Following the British military occupation of Ashanti in 1896, Prempeh I was exiled to the Seychelles islands in the Indian Ocean. Ashantis campaigned for him to be restored, but when this eventually happened in 1924 it was only as ruler of the capital Kumasi. His nephew became Prempeh II in 1931 and died in 1970. Prempeh II helped to promote the economic and political interests of Ashanti while also cooperating with the British. In 1941 he was appointed an honorary lieutenant-colonel, had charge of the Kumasi Home Guard and served as Zone Organiser. He assisted in recruiting Ashanti for the army. This photograph, taken by Clements in October 1942, shows Prempeh inspecting the Kumasi Home Guard, an action that preceded a drive to raise more recruits in Ashanti for the Gold Coast Regiment.

(Source: Imperial War Museum WA 185)

51

5 *The Emir of Kano en route to a march-past of troops, July 1943*

This photograph was taken by Clements outside the mud walls of the city of Kano, northern Nigeria, in mid-1943. African troops were often paraded before traditional rulers in a bid to raise the soldiers' morale. Nigerian soldiers of the RWAFF were to march past the Emir of Kano, Abdullahi Bayero, the central figure mounted on a horse, who was *en route* to join Maj-Gen E. B. B. Hawkins on the saluting base. Traditional rulers, subject to the colonial authorities, often played a crucial role in wartime recruiting by encouraging men to enlist.

(Source: Imperial War Museum WA 577)

of Abyssinia in 1935–36 had been met by indignant condemnation from many literate and urban West Africans. It was not only a protest at Fascist aggression but also at French and British pusillanimity.[61] For many Africans the Second World War began in 1935. When Italy entered the war in May 1940, a number of Africans volunteered to fight because they saw the war as an African cause. Ambitious young men intent on improving themselves, such as S. K. Boeteng, also joined up:

> I was in Accra. I was a volunteer. I joined voluntarily by myself ... I thought it would serve me ... It is good, Discipline. You discipline your life. I was a stenographer then. I decided to join. In those days there were certain privileges with the army. You could take correspondence courses at half the rate. They had a big library. The army was the place for an ambitious young man. And I was ambitious ... You must understand. We had discipline. We were a unit with doctors, stenographers, teachers.[62]

A number of West Africans made their own way to Britain, sometimes by arduous routes, in order to enlist. James Adewale, who was a tailor in Nigeria, gave up his job and set out for Britain in 1943:

> I left Lagos by land for Half-Assini in the Gold Coast then to Grand Bassam to Abidjan in the Ivory Coast. Then to Bobo Diolasso and on to Bamako and finally to the port of Dakar in Senegal. The journey between Lagos and Dakar took me ninety-two days. I then got a job on the British ship *S.S. Nigos* as a galley-boy. Since the ship was undergoing minor repairs at the port, we stayed there for five months before we finally sailed off to Liverpool. There I was paid off and sent to what they called 'Operation pool' where I was recruited compulsorily and sent off to London. It was made clear to me that the alternative of going to war was prison; I was put on a ship in London heading for Normandy with war materials. On our way back from Normandy we ran into enemy mines and our ship was blown up. Fortunately, I was one of the lucky survivors of that incident.[63]

Robert Ngbaronye, a 22-year-old Igbo from southern Nigeria, a teacher and then a student at Yaba College, saved enough money to get to Freetown where he stowed away on a ship bound for Liverpool, initially in order to study medicine. He got into Britain because 'I am a British subject', and having heard a broadcast by P/O Peter Thomas, another Nigerian, he had joined the RAF.[64] For John Henry Smythe from Sierra Leone, who flew with 619 Squadron RAF, the impulse was both a quest for adventure and also a moral one:

> At that age you are adventurous. The world of flying itself was attractive. And then our tutor at school, Victor King – the late Victor King, brought the book *Mein Kampf* to the school, and we had the opportunity of reading it through and through. And we saw what this man [Hitler] was going to do to the blacks, if he gets into power ... We read the book in Sierra Leone ... And he attacked the British and the Americans for encouraging the blacks to be doctors and lawyers and so forth. It was a book that would put any black man's back right up and it put mine up.[65]

Nearly 50 West Africans were recruited into the wartime RAF, some seeing active service as aircrew, and a handful being commissioned; many more West Indians served in the RAF, 500 as aircrew and 6,000 as ground crew.[66] Undoubtedly their presence in the wartime RAF greatly helped to breach the colour bar that the Army and Royal Navy wished to reintroduce once the war was over.

Colonial recruiting propaganda often emphasised that the war was being waged against German and Italian racist ideologies. Many British propaganda posters and leaflets were crudely simple;[67] the broadcasts from the rapidly expanding radio services tended to be more polished. Selected soldiers, newly returned from the front, broadcast accounts of their military activities linked with an appeal for further recruits. The newly established government information services worked closely with army recruiters; loudspeaker vans and mobile film shows toured each colony to encourage support for the war effort and to show films of African soldiers in training and in action against the Italians.[68]

Patriotic ideas undoubtedly influenced some young men to join up. Abdul Aziz Braimah volunteered for the Gold Coast Regiment because 'it was in our interest' to fight against Germany.[69] John Borketey, also from the Gold Coast, joined up 'to help my country', while Paul Gobine, from the Seychelles, enlisted out of a sense of loyalty.[70] One Sierra Leonean who served in Burma said: 'I joined the war because I felt it was a place for a young man of my vintage to go and get some experience and to see what I could do to contribute to the war effort of my country.' However, when pressed he retorted that

> our boss was involved ... the colonial power. And when the boss is involved – or when the head of the household was in trouble – everybody had to go to his support. And that is why Africa had to rise to go to the support of our colonial bosses ... If we had not gone to the Second World War to fight against the Japanese we would all be speaking Japanese today.[71]

Invariably such patriotic notions were influenced by other pressures. C. Amenyah, interviewed in 1980, said of his enlistment into the Gold Coast Regiment at Suhum in 1941:

> At that time I had no work. I wanted to learn a trade. Nana Ofori Atta [the influential ruler of Akyem Abuakwa] called for men to go and fight Hitler who wanted to take our land. If you are in your state and someone threatens, you must rise to defend. My younger brother joined [the] army first. Nearly the entire football team left from here for the army.[72]

Employment and opportunism pulled men into the ranks. Although the war did increase the number of wage-labour opportunities, this was an erratic process. At times job openings abruptly disappeared – for instance, as government demand contracted or mines closed. Marshall Kebby, of Lagos, left college in 1942 only to find that the government had frozen all clerical posts and that the commercial firms wouldn't employ anybody. 'So I didn't want to waste my time', he said, 'I simply went up to Enugu to join the army ... That's all ... There was no idealism whatsoever. I just wanted a job ... I just wanted a military career. I had no idea of what the place [war] was about. No idea whatsoever. I just joined.'[73] The army did offer reasonably well paid work, especially for literate men, clerks, and skilled artisans. C. Amenyah, who has already been quoted, said that his idea of joining the army was not to be a footsoldier on one shilling a day but to be a clerk. Explaining this he said that

> no southerners who had education would accept less than a shilling a day; that was one of the reasons why southerners were reluctant to join the army at that time. When war broke

54

out the pay was increased to a shilling a day for infantrymen; and then, they separated tradesmen: tradesmen had additional pay. That attracted us [southerners] to come in as clerks, as mechanics, as drivers and so forth.[74]

Ibrahim Funtua, a Fulani boy from northern Nigeria, had accompanied his father on the *hajj* to Mecca in 1930. His father died and Ibrahim returned home many years later, having wandered in Arabia and the Middle East, not only an orphan but also without inheritance. 'Dispossessed and rootless' he joined the Nigeria Regiment in 1938, where his linguistic skills acquired during his wanderings in Africa and the Middle East – to his Hausa and Fulani he had added Arabic, English, French, Italian, Swahili and Amharic – were effectively ignored.[75]

A good deal of encouragement for the recruiting programmes of colonial governments came from the indigenous press in West Africa. Even radical newspapers critical of colonial rule – such as the *West African Pilot*, edited by the Nigerian nationalist Nnamdi Azikiwe – lent its support to the drive for recruits. A more cautious newspaper, the *Ashanti Pioneer*, stated in an editorial on West Africans in Burma in early 1944:

> The brave West African lads have enlisted for service overseas to fight against the King-Emperor's enemies; they are doing battle to purge the world of EVIL THINGS represented by Nazism and Fascism, the worst and most dangerous aspects of human nature which deny elementary rights of human beings to a people outside the Aryan race, especially the black race which is generally regarded as the 'service' race for the dominant races of the world.[76]

Chiefs, the educated elite, and also the institutions that had grown up around the colonial administration and its services, were mobilised to find recruits. In Sierra Leone Wusu Bundu Sanu was encouraged to enlist by the secretary-general of the Ex-Servicemen's Association:

> One day in the year 1942 I was sent to Makeni town, seven miles from my home town, and on my way back I met a soldier who was going on leave. He asked me to carry some of his loads, and these were instructions I had to carry out. Since then I made up my mind that I must one day join the army. Two months later an army officer met us in school to recruit young men to be trained as signallers. I was the first boy to accept the offer, and went to Makeni the next day to be enlisted in the Sixth Brigade, Recce Company.[77]

The influence of family and friends also helped to push young men into the army. In 1940 Hama Kim was a 13-year-old boy living in Kano with his uncle, a soldier in the Northern Nigeria Regiment. The glamour of soldier life was all around him but at his first attempt to enlist he was rejected as being too young. However, Kim's enthusiasm was rewarded: he was taken under the wing of the regimental sergeant-major and within a year he had been accepted as an army band boy. However, Kim did not join the band but stayed in Kano with the RSM and somehow contrived to mix with the other recruits in the barracks and to be signed up.[78] Hama Kim went on to serve through the war. Many years later, after independence, he became a major in the Nigerian Army.

6 *Gold Coast recruits at bayonet drill, late 1942*

Most African combatants in the Second World War served in infantry battalions – the standard units of pre-war colonial armies in British Africa. Infantry marched and were armed with rifle and bayonet. Many wartime recruits underwent a period of combatant training, including bayonet drill, whatever the subsequent branch of service to which they might be directed. Bayonet practice often involved charging an imaginary enemy – a sandbag swinging by a rope from a wooden frame. This may have helped develop a sense of aggression, but employed a largely redundant weapon. The bayonet for the standard-issue SMLE rifle in 1939 had a 17in blade. By 1943 this had been modified to 8in and was being cheaply produced as a socket bayonet, rather like a spike, useful for opening cans of condensed milk. For most of the 20th century the bayonet had limited value in modern battle conditions, and was most commonly used when the enemy was in flight. This official photograph was taken by Clements.

(Source: Imperial War Museum WA 252)

7 *Adamu Sokoto in training with the Northern Nigeria Regiment, 1943*

Adamu Sokoto was a Hausa-speaking farmer from Sokoto, northern Nigeria. He became attached to the army as a 'barracki boy' – employed by several soldiers to wash their clothes and perform other menial tasks. When he was old enough he enlisted in 6 Battalion, Northern Nigeria Regiment. This photograph is one of a series taken by Clements in early 1943 to show Adamu Sokoto undergoing his 12 weeks' basic training. In this image he is receiving Bren-gun instruction from a white officer. British propaganda books and films often showed Africans progressing from peasant recruit to fully trained and cheerful soldier. Such visual images could be used for recruiting purposes in Africa, showing that army service offered opportunities and status. The Bren, adapted from a light machine-gun developed at the Czechoslovak city of Brno, was widely used by the British Army during the Second World War. With its rapid rate of fire, removable barrel and weight of only 20lb it was an ideal infantry weapon.

(Source: Imperial War Museum WA 373)

East Africa, Nyasaland, & the Indian Ocean islands

Between September 1939 and October 1945 a total of 324,000 men from the East and Central African territories (Kenya, Uganda, Tanganyika, Nyasaland and Northern Rhodesia) served in the armed forces, either in the KAR or the Northern Rhodesian Regiment. More than 210,000 served outside the colonies in the Ethiopian campaign, North Africa, in the operations in Madagascar, and in Asia. The largest number came from Kenya (98,200), followed by Tanganyika (86,740), and then Uganda, which supplied 76,100 men, some 10 per cent of the total adult male population of the colony. From Nyasaland more than 30,000 men joined the KAR during the war years, while others enlisted in Northern and Southern Rhodesian forces. Additionally, in 1941, many Ethiopians were enlisted into battalions commanded by British and Ethiopian officers for operations against the Italians, with the manpower drawn from the *c.* 6,000 Ethiopian refugees in Kenya and the Sudan, many of whom had been soldiers in Haile Selassie's army.[79] Mauritius and the Seychelles together provided more than 6,000 men for service with the Royal Pioneer Corps mainly in the Middle East, while Mauritius also conscripted 8,000 men to a local Civilian Labour Corps.[80]

Memories of forced recruitment as carriers for the Great War caused some people to flee their homes when they heard rumours of war.[81] East African recruiting for a new conflict was overshadowed by images of the harsh conditions of 1914–18. As with the RWAFF, recruiting for the KAR occurred in three waves: for the defence of the East African colonies and after May 1940 for the campaign against the Italians in Somaliland and Ethiopia; in 1941–43, to provide soldiers for operations in Madagascar in May 1942 and to supply reinforcements, mainly in the form of pioneers, for the Eighth Army in North Africa; and finally, for the Asian campaign against the Japanese. Although wartime recruiters sought soldiers from ethnic groups other than those designated in peacetime as martial races, they rarely enlisted Maasai who were thought to be ill-disciplined and incapable of being trained. The Chaga, who lived on the slopes of Kilimanjaro, were the best-educated of Tanganyika's ethnic groups, with funding for this having come from income derived from profitable cash crops, particularly coffee. However, the Chaga were reluctant to enlist in the army in wartime – a time when more money could be made from farming and trade.

At the outbreak of war in September 1939 the KAR consisted of seven battalions; it was primarily an infantry force with a small motorised unit. Recruits were drawn mainly from specific areas and from groups thought to possess martial qualities. The potential enemy, the Italian colonial army, included a reported 200,000 *ascari* along with a substantial number of artillery pieces, tanks and armoured cars. The Italian air force, the *Regia Aeronautica*, also had bombers and fighters at stations in Italy's new East African empire. However, even though the Italians had proclaimed the total conquest of Ethiopia, guerrilla resistance continued to tie down a substantial part of the colonial army.

The first period of the war was referred to in Swahili as *mpakani*, 'at the borders'.[82] The old peacetime system of voluntary recruiting was soon abandoned in favour of quotas imposed on chiefs through district commissioners, supported by the police. Bildad Kaggia, who served in the KAR, wrote that the colonial rulers 'used every method of persuasion to force chiefs to reach their quotas', and 'the chief[s] used the power of conscription to get rid of anybody they did not want in their locations'.[83] The authorities in East Africa distributed leaflets in vernacular languages urging people to 'volunteer' for the army. There were also livestock sales, which greatly increased in the war years, and chiefs were leaned upon to produce men or money from the sales of livestock for the war effort.

In Nyasaland, which had been drained of manpower at the time of the First World War, Batison Geresomo recalled:

> When we heard about the conflict in the year 1939, we were not sure of how this conflict could be as to whether they will be taking everybody by force or not. When the conflict was about to come, the white man came in all the districts of Malawi to recruit soldiers. Some were taken by the chiefs' force and some went on their own wish. There wasn't any promise to be given to us after the fighting.[84]

According to another Malawian who was conscripted in 1940, 'the DC's messengers were sent on ceaseless errands during that period'.[85] And for Chama Mutendi Kadanse his military service began when

> all the chiefs were alerted about the raging war by the district commissioners who requested them to contribute in form of personnel. Thus in my area [of Northern Rhodesia], recruitment of soldiers was conducted by a Mr Whitemore, then DC of Kasama. After that all the recruits were taken to Lusaka ... That is how I came to be recruited.[86]

The young schoolboy John E. A. Mandambwe was drafted. 'It was not my choice to go,' he said, and even though his father wrote to the authorities urging that his son be released from military service, this was refused.[87]

Men volunteered for the army for a variety of reasons. Wellington Odera, a Luo with Standard VII schooling, enlisted in August 1940 because the army offered regular employment; he became a dresser in the Medical Corps.[88] In the congested African reserves in Kenya there was high unemployment, and rural labour, if it was available, paid a mere 14 shillings per month. Gikuyu men from Nyeri enlisted in the thousands. The army immediately offered 20 shs, rising to 28 shs when a man was posted to a battalion, and there was the prospect for some of earning as much as £4.10shs along with food, clothing and other fringe benefits. John Muriuki, a primary-school teacher earning 25 shs a month, enlisted as a medical dresser and was able to earn as much as 90 shs per month while serving in Burma, Ceylon and India.[89] Another incentive in Kenya, although it is difficult to assess its significance, was that recruits were exempted from paying the head tax and also from arrest for debts and other minor infringements of the legal code. However, the demand for recruits in Kenya did not go unchallenged. Elija Masinde, founder of the *Dini ya Msambwa* ('Cult of the Spirits of the Dead') movement, which rejected European civilisation and sought the expulsion of Europeans from the country, in 1943 opposed the conscription of Africans for the war, arguing that it was a European war and of no concern to Africans.[90]

Some recruits were propelled by popular rumours about the war and the enemy, or by fear of being conscripted for agricultural labour. Hamis Makiti

Lashau came from the Kilimanjaro region of Tanganyika. According to his son, he

> heard that Hitler was fighting with Britain. Hitler wanted to rule Britain. People were told that Germans would come to fight in East Africa. They were much worried. Also he told me that King Edward of England was a man who didn't like war. Because of this his people didn't like him and King George was elected to replace him. He had heard that Hitler fought Poland. He told me Mussolini of Italy and Japanese were helping Hitler. He didn't expect whether Hitler can defeat Britain. In recruiting, normally the government (under the English governor) directed their chiefs to select people who will join KAR and to fight in the war. But also you may join voluntarily. My father decided to join the army voluntarily. [He] enlisted at Arusha to join the war.[91]

A Ugandan who had become a regimental sergeant-major by 1944 said there were three reasons why Ugandans volunteered for the army:

> It is clear that the majority of the African soldiers came into the Army not to fight for King George VI or to defend the Empire. No. The King and the Empire meant and still mean nothing to them. The men you see in the forces came to help a certain kindly lady missionary or a good District Commissioner whose wife plays with their children. When their friend and lady told them that back in England her or his mothers were in trouble, a fierce bully was threatening to take them slaves, and that if they joined the Army they might help to avert that threat and danger to their beloved ones ... the appeal to save the mother and other relations of their beloved lady missionary kindled a fire in the minds of the Africans, which still burns after five years of weary war ...
>
> There was another kind of African who joined the Army because he knew what German conquest of the world meant. This type of African had read or heard of what Hitler wrote in his famous book 'Mein Kampf', regarding Africans, and take it from me those men bore and still bear Hitler a grudge for having written the following words: 'From time to time our illustrated papers publish the news that in some quarters of the globe a Negro has become a lawyer, a teacher, a pastor, or even a grand opera singer ... This is sin against reason itself; it is an act of criminal insanity ...' The Africans who knew these words came not only to fight for the preservation of the Empire but to frustrate the accursed man's ideals and save themselves and their children from cruelty and permanent bondage.[92]

Then there were those who came into the army later just to get a job and money. In the Seychelles, Paul Gobine had enlisted out of loyalty, but others joined up because life was dull in the islands and military service was a way of escaping poverty.[93]

There were also other, more pressing reasons. Failure of the rains in 1939–40 brought drought and acute food shortages to the Akamba of Kenya; want, and pressure from chiefs, forced men into the army and that period is still known as 'the famine of the Italian'.[94] Young men were often encouraged to enlist by the glamour of marching soldiers and bands, as this Malawian recruit explained:

> The DC's based soldiers marched in our villages in their full uniform. They were always smartly dressed and they gave us tinned beef plus biscuits. They sang while marching so we were greatly attracted to join them with a covetous mind. We never knew it was the white man's clever way of curbing us into the war and they never revealed where we would go. They chose only those of us who were physically fit ...
>
> Every village was combed through. We were kept at the DC's headquarters for a few days before being transferred to Zomba. Zomba was the only place where military training

could be undertaken. It was the headquarters for King's African Rifles and the capital of the then Nyasaland. It was in Zomba where we were told that we had been recruited with a purpose of serving in the British Army force as infantry soldiers.[95]

At the start of the war the army selected recruits after a simple physical fitness test. Recruits were chosen on the basis of height, eyesight, an adequate right forefinger – the trigger finger – and a reasonable standard of health. Many men were rejected because they suffered from various physical ailments, many associated with diseases or malnutrition. If a recruiting *safari* went well potential recruits might be more thoroughly sifted and only those with the highest physical standards taken. However, as the war progressed and conscription agents scoured the countryside, physical and medical standards were reduced; the army received recruits of a poorer standard and relied on the training period with good food and medical attention to build up their strength and health.

Recruiters in search of literate and numerate young men visited schools and in some cases established close links with headteachers who encouraged students to join up. But school students could also be conscripted. 'I remember how unhappy I was when on 25.10.40. I was conscripted out of school to serve in the army, the King's African Rifles,' wrote Mussa K. Kilwelo from Dar es Salaam.

Apart from my bitterness to forcibly cut short my schooling by government order, I was also disgusted to leave my homeland and family to go to strange countries. But all the same I had no alternative but to endure the hardships ... My general comment is that by forcibly joining the army my life is different from the life I would be having now had I completed my schooling.[96]

However, James Mpagi from Kampala, as a young teacher in training, saw military service from a more glamorous viewpoint:

When I was still at school the war broke out, during September 1939; we being young boys we thought perhaps war was something very simple, we had very little idea; perhaps the same thing as if people were quarrelling for a cow or [between] neighbouring villages ... When I went to college, I found many teachers, many of them Europeans. Soon after many Europeans and Africans joined the war. One of the Europeans came back after only a short time of nine months. He was a major. Wonderful, we thought, that in the Army getting high ranks was not very difficult. So many of us joined too; that was 1940 ... I promptly approached the warden of the college. I told him that I wanted to join the war as a teacher. He said good, but remember war is war. There are a lot of difficulties. Still I know you will be able to do well, he went on. But never try to smoke, and try to see that you do not drink beer and other strong drinks and never forget your Creator. Good bye! I soon went to Kampala; next morning I got a ticket for the way to Nairobi, a distance of about 600 miles from my home, I reported to the details camp, where they had to send to the EAAEC a place for the Army teachers. East African Army Education Corps near Nairobi. When I arrived at the place there were very many people. Very educated young men from all over East Africa, Central and South Africa. We were many indeed. We were given uniforms and all the things wanted in the Army.[97]

Another Ugandan saw the army as opportunity: 'My father had no money to send me to school, but I am lucky to get education free of charge in the army', and in addition there was travel abroad and the chance to learn new languages.[98]

Between July and October 1940 conscription for noncombatant labour was introduced in East Africa to replace the existing quota system imposed on districts and operated by district commissioners through the native authorities. In early 1941 the second major period of recruitment for the KAR began. Middle East Command asked the East African colonies for a supply of 'trained and disciplined labour' for pioneer service in North Africa. This resulted in the creation of the African Auxiliary Pioneer Corps (AAPC), which was to serve outside the colonies. The first units in this new force came from the ranks of the East African Military Labour Service (EAMLS) which had carried out pioneer work during the East African campaign, and was to remain in East Africa. The AAPC was an integral part of the British Army, its ranks composed of men recruited from other British territories such as Palestine. For many men, forced recruitment remained as a bitter memory. Martin K. Lwambura recalled that

> personally and without my consent I was arrested on 12 March 1941 in Kampala city. Me and several other people spent the night in custody and on the following day were packed into a train like firewood, and transported to Ruiru in Kenya. From Ruiru I was taken to the depot in Nanyuki. At Nanyuki we underwent military training such as how to shoot a gun and so on. We were provided with military uniforms, identify [sic] cards, kit bags and foodstuffs.[99]

Martin Lwambura spent the next five years serving in Somalia and in North Africa.

The authorities did not experience great difficulty in early recruiting for the AAPC, even when service involved a period overseas, and a steady flow of men came from the traditional recruiting grounds; indeed, many men were also eager to transfer from the EALMS to the AAPC. For many men in Kenya, reasonably well-paid military service with all the attendant advantages of food, clothing and medical care proved more popular than peasant labour in the congested reserves or work on settler-owned farms. Nevertheless, there was spasmodic resistance to recruitment. In the Kahama district of western Tanganyika in 1941, young men joined a forbidden dance organisation known as *puba*, dressing in women's clothing, wearing ornaments, braiding their hair and aping female actions until they were banned from doing so by the Native Authority.[100] The KAR sent 'A Message to the Peoples of Uganda', stating: 'The men of your tribe in the newer battalions of the KAR are beginning to feel themselves soldiers. They are stronger, heavier and smarter than when you last saw them in the villages. They are well fed and well exercised.'[101] However, faced with a farm-labour shortage in 1941, Kenyan whites successfully petitioned the government to briefly suspend recruiting for both the EALMS and the AAPC. In Uganda, conscription was used in order to spread 'the implementation and impact of call-up'; local food production had to be considered and the authorities did not wish to deplete certain areas of able-bodied men.[102]

As the military situation in North Africa became more critical in early 1942, white troops were increasingly required for combatant roles and Africans for noncombatant and support services. However, these differences did become blurred and many Africans who were recruited for pioneer or noncombatant duties found themselves being trained in the use of firearms and operating in frontline positions. Recruiting in Kenya resumed in April 1942 when East Africa Command was asked to provide for North Africa a further 18 companies of pioneers for garrison duties and three more companies of cooks and servants. In 1942, the Ministry of Information and East Africa Command published an illustrated booklet, *A Spear for Freedom*, in Swahili, Chinyanja, Luganda and English.

The foreword, by A. G. Dickson, stated: 'These pictures tell how an African villager became a Pioneer ... a Corporal in the Army of His Majesty the King'. The model soldier is Kisarishu, a Warusha whose home is on the slopes of Kilimanjaro. His village is visited by askaris who tell him about army life and show their uniforms, which makes Kisarishu think of 'adventure', and so he enlists in the EAMLS. The attractions of military service are shown in a sequence of photographs of Kisarishu wearing shoes and uniform, having a shower (indicating plentiful water), and receiving regular pay and food. He learns new skills, such as ironing clothes with a charcoal iron, and takes a lead in communal activity, with soldiers eating together using knives and forks, participating in healthy physical exercise and competitive sports, singing songs, and travelling by train and lorry. Soldiers are always shown with smiling faces, even when wielding pickaxes while clearing land for an airfield or building a road in Abyssinia. The caption states: 'These men are helping to make a new camp for the Army. They seem to enjoy the work.' In one photograph, Kisarishu is shown reading a copy of *Baraza*, the army newspaper, thus indicating that he is literate. Soldiers have the opportunity to learn to be a 'personal servant' or to become a 'fundi', an artisan, which is illustrated by a recruit being instructed to use a sewing machine. Kisarishu 'volunteers' to serve as a combatant in North Africa, so he receives rifle training and practises using the bayonet and throwing grenades. 'All the Pioneers have been given the British soldiers' uniform – it is sometimes cold in the North', states the text. A final illustration shows 'TML 87264 Corp. Kisarishu s/o Kitambos, of Arusha, Tanganyika, now serving in the A.A.P.C. (E.A)'.[103]

The increased demand for recruits meant that the authorities had to go outside the traditional recruiting grounds and use new recruiting means. In Kenya a large number of pioneers had been drawn from among the Luo, Nandi and Luyia of Nyanza province in western Kenya, while in Uganda the recruits had come largely from the Toro, Teso, Soga and Gwere. By early 1942 the Kenya authorities agreed to the conscription of civil labour for white-owned farms, so that Kenya in particular, but also Tanganyika, became large areas of recruitment for all kinds of wartime labour. In central Tanganyika during 1942–43 rainfall was below average, which led to food shortages. Production of food, already hit by wartime conscription, hit women and children and drove even more men into migrant-labour contracts.[104]

The military recruiting organization developed new strategies to attract men to the ranks. Recruiting *safaris*, composed of convoys of trucks accompanied by African soldiers, showed off modern armaments and displays of medals and screened films such as Guy Johnson's *War Came to Kenya* and *With Our African Troops in Action*. The mobile propaganda units emphasised 'patriotic duty' and the many and varied benefits to be derived from military service. Wartime propaganda that stressed Nazi ideas of racial superiority often had a strong local echo for some Africans, particularly in the white-settler-dominated territories of Kenya and Southern Rhodesia. The veteran Zimbabwean nationalist Ndabaningi Sithole provides a striking story of British recruiters appealing to African hostility to Germany:

'Away with Hitler! Down with him!', said the British officer.
'What's wrong with Hitler?', asked the unsuspecting African.

'He wants to rule the whole world,' snorted the British officer.

'What's wrong with that?'

'He's German, you see,' said the British officer, trying to appeal subtly to the African's tribal consciousness.

'What's wrong with his being German?'

'You see,' began the British officer, trying to explain in terms that would be conceivable to the African mind, 'it is not good for one tribe to rule another. Each tribe must rule itself. That's only fair. A German must rule Germans, an Italian, Italians, and a Frenchman, French people.'

But the extremely wary British officer did not say, 'A Briton, Britons'. What he said, however, carried weight with the Africans who rallied in thousands under the British flag. They joined the war to end the threat of Nazi domination.[105]

Numbers of recruits increased although service in the pioneers was never as popular as that in the infantry. There were acute memories of the harsh conditions under military labour during the Great War 20 years before, which acted as a strong deterrent to enlisting in the EAMLS or the AAPC. Conscription had to be resorted to and chiefs responded by sending in men who were medically unfit for labour. Desertions increased and on several occasions there were problems in disciplining men and embarking them for overseas service.

The third major recruiting period for the KAR was for the campaign in Asia and lasted from 1943 until the war's end. By mid-1945 more than 46,000 East and Central African troops were serving in Asia. Some of these troops were required for porter-borne operations in jungle terrain, but a good number were infantrymen trained to use mortars and machine-guns, or as signallers, drivers and medical orderlies. Gaining new skills for these tasks required a measure of literacy and numeracy, which were developed by the army through the new education corps. Expectation of reward often figures prominently in reasons for enlistment – a result of deliberate misinformation, vague promises, misunderstandings and/or rumours. This was obviously the case with Usiwa Usiwa, from Blantyre in Nyasaland, who served as a lance-corporal in the KAR:

I made two trips to Zomba (from Mulanje – my home about 130 kms away) before I was finally enlisted as a soldier, in 1943 when the war was already on. I expected to die any time as war was associated with death. We were promised much money, enough to make a whole village rich at the end of the war, but this was cheating. They gave me about £50 in 1946 when I left the army. We were asked either to stay in the army or leave for home. I chose to go home.[106]

Likewise, Samson Muliango from Lusaka, who was told by his white employer 'that he wanted me to join the war', expected financial and material rewards for military service. 'During the recruitment, the Northern Rhodesian Government promised us all as a reward farms and lots of money if only we fought for the British Army during the reign of King George VI.'[107]

The Anglo-Egyptian Sudan

When Italy entered the war in May 1940, the Sudan Defence Force (SDF) numbered 4,500 men, with six motor machine-gun companies hastily created in 1936 after the Italian invasion of Ethiopia. There were no tanks or artillery. The SDF was organised on a territorial basis, with North, West and East camel corps, each recruited from among local men who knew the region in which they operated. One-quarter of the SDF was constituted by the Equatorial Corps, based in southern Sudan. This was entirely a black African force officered by Europeans in which the language of command was English and the practice of Islam was discouraged. Each unit of the SDF was designed to be self-sufficient and to be able to live off the country. Clearly the force was no more than a gendarmerie, ill-equipped for modern warfare. However, in support were three British regular battalions totalling 2,500 men based at Khartoum, Tabara, and Jabait outside Port Sudan.

A substantial proportion of the SDF was required for garrison duty within the Sudan and so was not available for operations on the southern frontiers in the event of an Italian attack. The vast region of the Sudan assumed a new strategic significance for its raw materials and later as a supply line up the Nile valley to Middle East Command in Egypt. The Sudan had a superior and effective system of intelligence-gathering which also sowed false information among the Italians. Following Italy's declaration of war the strength of the SDF was quickly increased to 6,000 men, albeit largely untrained, and these were supported by Indian troops and whatever other forces Gen Sir William Platt could assemble in the Sudan. Among the new SDF units was the Frontier Battalion, which guarded the border with Italian-occupied Ethiopia and carried arms to the Patriot forces fighting the Italians. Most men were new recruits although some were old soldiers. Governor-General Sir Stewart Symes was not only on friendly terms with the Duke of Aosta, the Italian governor-general, but also unsympathetic to the use of African troops in a war with Italy. Gen Archibald Wavell, GOC Middle East Command, demanded the removal of Symes and Churchill personally directed that he should go; in October 1940 he was replaced by Gen Sir Hubert Huddleston, a man of very different mettle.

Further men were recruited for the SDF, including the Frontier Battalion – five companies each of 250 men that were employed in escorting arms to the Ethiopian Patriot forces. There were also irregular forces engaged in guerrilla warfare, harassing the invading Italian forces in the south and operating across the frontier into Ethiopia and Eritrea. One example involved E. E. Evans-Pritchard, the Government anthropologist, commanding a force of Anuak irregulars. The war in the Sudan was over by the spring of 1941. Although the SDF had increased to 30,000 men by early 1943 – with units including a new artillery regiment, armoured cars, signals and engineers – the soldiers were for the most part employed within the Sudan or on garrison duty in Libya and Eritrea.[108]

Southern Rhodesia

The peacetime army in the colony consisted of 3,000 white men. When war broke out the view of the settler government, endorsed by Whitehall, was that whites would provide officers and NCOs for the colonial armies and that Southern Rhodesian Africans would not be recruited for military service but remain as labour on farms and mines producing for the war effort.[109] As in South

Africa, some whites viewed the prospect of arming Africans with alarm. Opposition to the war spread among Africans by pacifist African Watch Tower preachers, who proclaimed that it was the hand of God punishing white oppressors, was swiftly dealt with.[110] The movement was banned – as it had been in neighbouring Northern Rhodesia, where the authorities had said it was undermined recruiting for the KAR.

By mid-1940 the Southern Rhodesian government reluctantly agreed to recruitment for an African regiment of 700 men, to be called the Rhodesian African Rifles (RAR). The RAR was led by white officers and NCOs many of whom had served with the local police force – the British South Africa Police – and in the Native Department.[111] During the First World War, at which time Africans were also recruited, and until 1980, the territory's military was racially segregated at nearly every level: wages were 'racially graded ... the army cemetery was racially segregated and access to amenities such as showers and barracks swimming pools controlled'.[112] However, by mid-1941 only 900 men had enlisted in the RAR, of whom just over 300 were discharged, for various reasons. Men avoided recruiting parties; some among the Shona claimed that they were not warlike. The officer in charge of recruiting among the Ndebele suggested that chiefs should call upon their men to enlist. A good number of recruits were in fact 'alien' Africans from neighbouring colonies. By late 1941 some 2,000 men had enlisted at the recruiting centres in Salisbury (now Harare) and Bulawayo. And when the first batch of recruits arrived at the Salisbury centre they had to build their own pole-and-dagga huts before training began.[113] The business of getting the RAR off to war was slow. Other than a detachment sent south to Durban to escort Italian prisoners-of-war, the principal role from 1940 to 1943 was garrison and guard duties within the colony. Inevitably morale was low and men deserted, often attracted by higher wages elsewhere.[114] The unit's commanding officer said the lack of action caused unrest because civilians taunted the soldiers, saying 'you are only "uniform" soldiers, not real soldiers, and are afraid to go and fight; if not, why has the Government not sent you to help the King, there is a lot of fighting going on and yet you "women" stay here'.[115]

However, conscription was ruled out; instead, more intensive recruiting was attempted in August 1943 in order to maintain troop levels for the 1st Battalion, which had relocated to East Africa prior to shipping to Ceylon.[116] The tour of Ndebele lands yielded few recruits; similar attempts the following year in Mashonaland also met with a poor response. Although 8,200 Africans joined the RAR between mid-1940 and mid-1945, more than half were later rejected as medically unfit; of the accepted recruits, just over 2,000 actually came from Southern Rhodesia; the others originated in neighbouring colonies. From Ceylon the RAR went to Burma, where it accompanied the advance against the Japanese. True to its segregationist ideology, the Southern Rhodesian government created a separate Coloured Transport Company which provided mechanics and drivers for the campaign in Abyssinia and thereafter for the convoys that ran between Nairobi and Juba. Coloureds, or 'Euroafricans' as some like to be called, enlisted in part to demonstrate their loyalty and rights to citizenship in a society that demeaned them. For Joe Culverwell, a Coloured Southern Rhodesian, wartime propaganda had a powerful effect. He joined up as a freely enlisted man in a Southern Rhodesian transport company.

Don't forget the propaganda that was being proliferated from the BBC. The BBC had a very powerful station to Africa then, you know ... Hitlerism and referring to black people as baboons, etc., and so forth, and what he was going to do. And so we thought, not a damn, we were going to defend our country if that was the last. That was the motivation for it ... I know, stupid as it may sound now, we were very, very loyal Britishers ... That was over 40 years ago, and we were proud because everything we did was British. We had British coinage ... the same films that they showed; the same songs. Noel Coward was enjoyed by us just as much. So, we were really, possibly brainwashed into being little brown Britishers, so to speak ... But the majority of my friends felt like me. They felt very loyal to the crown, very British.[117]

The Southern Rhodesian government refused to adopt conscription for military recruitment. Many whites opposed recruiting, fearing that it would reduce the labour supply; a few white farmers actively discouraged Africans from enlisting. The authorities were concerned about 'racial balance' in the armed forces – that blacks should not outnumber whites. There was another immediate consideration for the government: not to reduce the labour available for the colony's aerodrome-building programme. At the start of the war Southern Rhodesia, with its good climate and flying conditions, was selected by the Royal Air Force as one of the locations for the Empire Air Training Scheme. Eleven aerodromes were required. The 15,000-strong 'Labour Corps' used in their construction was enlisted, mainly from the Reserves, in ways similar to military recruitment in other colonies. Native Commissioners were given district quotas and chiefs and headmen were then told to produce men. Tribal messengers, acting as policemen, rounded up the labour. There was widespread resistance to this additional system of coerced labour (*chibaro* or *cibbalo*), with which so many Africans in Southern Rhodesia had been long familiar. Africans feared they would be put into the army and sent out of the colony; rumours were widespread. Men fled to the bush and deserted when opportunity arose.

However, the largest forced conscription of civil labour was for food production following the passing of the Compulsory Native Labour Act in June 1942. The drought of 1940–41 reduced food output, and much of this conscripted labour was for white-owned farms. African labour was rounded up by officials via chiefs. Timothy Siamaimbo, from the maize-growing district of Tonga, was caught among the first batch of conscripts in 1942: 'The *cibbalo*: He caught us – Bwana Price, the Makabuka D.C. He came into this village with his messengers. The messengers caught us ... there were many of them – six on this side, six on that side.'[118] The official figure for the total number of conscripts, for a system that continued well after the war had ended, was 33,145. Together with aerodrome labour the total for wartime conscript labour is somewhere between 50,000 and 100,000 men. A similar system of compulsory labour for wartime food production was introduced in Northern Rhodesia; this continued until 1952.[119]

Army recruiters had to compete in this very unfavourable climate. Native commissioners and chiefs hectoring African men and calling them cowards for refusing to enlist rarely worked. A major disincentive, certainly until August 1942, was that army wages – even for senior African ranks and tradesmen – could not compete with the wages offered in the mines and towns of the colony and in South Africa. Sgt Jeleman said he had dropped income by enlisting:

Before entering the R.A.R. I was a compound Police Boy on the Shabani Mines where I earned £4.17.–, and rations. I was able to support my family and my deceased father's family. I was allowed to my *kraal* to plough after my father died and had no difficulties supporting my families. On my present rate of pay (1s 4d per day) I am quite incapable of supporting my family ... I have to buy grain for them as I cannot go and plough myself, and they also require clothing, etc ... I would point out that since March 1941 I have had to sell 8 head of cattle to keep my family.[120]

Another reason for African reluctance to join up, occasionally mentioned by the more perceptive native commissioners, was African political consciousness and antipathy to lending support to a white regime which was largely based on racial discrimination.

The High Commission Territories

The three southern High Commission Territories (HCTs) – Bechuanaland, Swaziland and Basutoland – were closely integrated with the economy of the Union of South Africa. All three territories provided a regular supply of migrant labour principally for the farms and mines of the Union. However, wartime military recruitment disrupted this supply of labour and source of remittances; it also heightened competition for labour between the civil and military authorities in Central and Southern Africa.[121] Early in the war the British allowed the Union to recruit men from the HCT for the South African Native Military Corps (NMC), established in June 1940. Although some rulers – for example King Sobhuza of Swaziland, with the support of his council – agreed to this, they were very anxious to resist political incorporation into the Union and any extension of its racist policies, and they were eager to identify with the United Kingdom. In Bechuanaland the High Commissioner urged the local rulers (*dikgosi*) to aid recruiting for the NMC, but found little success.

Following the British defeat at Tobruk and the demand for more labour by Middle East Command, in 1941 the British created the African Auxiliary Pioneer Corps (AAPC, later the African Pioneer Corps). Recruiting for the AAPC received the support of most senior traditional rulers in the HCTs. Bechuanaland contributed 10,000 men, half of them coming from the Bamangwato Reserve.[122] This area yielded up 20 per cent of its adult male population for the military; at the same time 10,000 men from the area were working as migrant labourers in South Africa, which gives a fuller picture of the consequences of the war for this part of southern Africa. In Kweneng, a small Tswana state in the south of the Bechuanaland Protectorate, military recruitment and labour migrancy to South Africa had by 1945 stripped the area of 35 per cent of its adult males.[123]

Recruitment was often done through traditional age regiments and men were encouraged to enlist to serve their rulers. Several chiefs also enlisted to serve as NCOs, thus retaining a measure of chiefly rule within the ranks of the AAPC. Opposition to military service grew and inevitably took the form of hostility to chiefs. In Bangwato recruiting took place in two phases: in April 1941, when 5,000 men were enlisted, and in June 1942 when a similar number of recruits were secured. Tshekedi Khama, chief of the Bangwato, and Bathoen II of the

Bangwaketse, the other major chief in Bechuanaland, strongly supported Britain's war effort and aided recruiting for the AAPC. During the second phase of recruiting Tshekedi suspended organised-labour recruiting from South Africa and pressured tax evaders to enlist.[124] Both rulers, and many other chiefs, regarded Britain as an imperial protector – a view dating back to the days of Queen Victoria (widely known in Setswana as *Mmamosadinyana*, 'Mrs Little Woman'), who aided them against the Boers , the 'bad whites', and who continued to oppose South Africa's attempts to incorporate the High Commission Territory into the Union. For Tshekedi, there were also other motives: he hoped to develop the economy of his reserve and reduce its dependency on South Africa, and also to increase control over his own people.[125] Chiefs and the colonial administration, aided by members of the London Missionary Society, supported the recruiting campaigns. The administration demanded that recruiting be voluntary, but in practice it clearly was not and often an official blind eye was turned to what was going on. Chiefs regarded it as a traditional right for men to obey their call to arms and the difference between a conscript and a volunteer was often blurred. Sebatso Masimego of the Bakwena recalls the traditional responsibility:

> Regimental service is compulsory. When a regiment is called by the chief to perform a duty it is a matter of no one has to resist, if that man resists he must be punished. It is a law. When a regiment is called the Batswana believe it is by the orders of the law. The Chief has the right to issue such an order.[126]

Recruiting policies varied from one part of Bechuanaland to another. Sixteen-year-old Julius Segano volunteered in December 1942:

> I joined the Army here at Lobatsi. I was not in any way forced like some of our tribes when the Chiefs got them to join – we are in a detribalized place so I was just attracted to join because we found it to be so thrilling. No one who joined from here was forced.[127]

Other men hid from recruiters, their relatives concealing their whereabouts and feeding them covertly.[128]

In Swaziland, the recruiting campaign of 1941 was carried out via the traditional political system. Traditional war messengers, using the traditional war-cry *ingene!* ('the enemy's army has come!'), were sent throughout the country. By October 1941 Sobhuza had successfully recruited 1,000 men and with little coercion. The general expectation of recruits was that they would only serve for a short time. Jachoniah Dlamini, who served in the Swazi Regiment in 1942–46 and saw action in North Africa and Italy, recalls:

> I heard on the news that the Germans were fighting with Poland and there was never any thought that in some way Swaziland would be involved in this conflict. At this time ... we were called by the King of Swaziland and informed that he was raising a regiment to help the British war effort and he called for volunteers to go and fight. There was never any talk of rewards as we were doing this for King and country.[129]

A similar story is told by Volinda Maseko:

> The King called all the chiefs to the kraal at Lobamba where he told them that men were required for the war to help the British. Following this, chiefs went to their kraals where they held meetings in which they told their subjects to come out and enlist for service in the war.[130]

Another man, Ngongolozi Mzinyane, recruited in southern Swaziland, said: 'I was from Johannesburg where I was working in the mines, and on my arrival home I found that the chief was calling all men for enlistment for war service and I joined voluntarily.'[131]

However, the 1942 recruiting programme was coercive, being referred to in Siswati as *emabanjwa* – 'those who were caught'. One veteran remembers:

> During those years it was not safe for a man to walk along the road in broad daylight. Many men were grabbed along the roads to be drafted to the army. Government vehicles were speeding up and down the roads hunting for men … To avoid the government vehicles we … used the footpaths which were inaccessible to vehicles…. the safest routes were those which cut across forests and mountains.[132]

Recruiting gangs are reported also to have worked at night. One man recalled that 'for those of use who were not willing to go to war it became almost impossible to sleep in our houses and still remain safe from the recruiting gangs'.[133] A woman remembers that 'during the war when they wanted men, my late husband could not stay or sleep with us in the house. He stayed in the bush for over a month only coming into the house on rare occasions … My husband was really living like an animal those days.'[134] To avoid recruiting gangs men went to extreme measures and used cunning. One of Simelane's informants tells of a man who tied himself in a tree deep in the bush and was found by another man out hunting when he was near to death. Another chose a 'less dramatic' refuge – the house where 'lived a very old woman (Mrs Ndlela) all by herself. For about two months I slept in Mrs Ndlela's house. No recruiter thought of her house because it was known that she was old and on her own. I was happy to beat the recruiters this way'.[135] One man feigned a broken leg:

> My uncle wrapped my left leg in pieces of cloth, built two crutches for me. He then went to the Chief to report that I broke my leg in a hunting expedition. Throughout the recruiting campaign I was hopping around on my crutches.[136]

The total number of men recruited in Swaziland for the AAPC throughout the war was 3,386. The second recruiting campaign of 1942 had secured men but had also revealed deep divisions between the interests of the Swazi monarchy and those of ordinary peasants.

In Basutoland the war was remembered as *Ntoa ea Hitlara* ('Hitler's War'). Although this small country sent nearly 25,000 men to the war, this did not happen without criticism locally. Early on in the war an educated Sotho, Emmanuel B. N. Qhobosheane, wrote to the editor of *Moeletsi*, pouring scorn on Sotho who enlisted: how, he asked, could their sticks and spears stop the white man's aeroplanes?[137] Military recruitment was through the chiefs. By and large they supported Britain's war effort but they also campaigned to keep their men separate from the racist institutions of South Africa and from joining the Union

Defence Force. There were three recruiting campaigns, in 1940, 1941 and 1942.[138] The first two campaigns involved voluntary enlistment (*boithaopi*), although that did not stop 1,300 men deserting *en masse* in November 1941, probably as a result of rumours that families were to pay poll tax. The recruiting campaign of 1942 involved conscription, known as *kholhola-koqo* (literally 'swept up in a torrential storm'), and men recruited for the mines were directed into the military.[139] Altogether Basutoland contributed 21,463 men to the AAPC; an additional 2,500 men living in South Africa joined the NMC. Total war deaths were about 1,000.

South Africa

Throughout the 19th century non-Europeans, especially members of 'Cape Coloured' contingents, played an important role in the military history of South Africa. The South African War, 1899–1902, involved large numbers of combatant Africans, most of whom fought for the British. Although the Union Defence Act 1912 stipulated that the small permanent Defence Force and the potentially larger Citizen Force should be confined to 'citizens of European descent', in late 1915 a Cape Coloured battalion was raised which saw combatant service in East Africa, Egypt, Palestine, and on the Western Front. Black Africans were also employed during the First World War, but only as noncombatant military labour.[140]

There was a very strong feeling among white South Africans that Africans should not be involved in the armed forces in any capacity. However, demand for labourers in uniform soon swept away most such reservations and the Non-European Army Services began recruiting in June 1940. There were three branches: the Cape Coloured Corps, the Indian and Malay Corps (both recruited via the Director of Recruitment), and the Native Military Corps (NMC, which recruited through the Native Affairs Department). Official policy was that Africans should only serve in noncombatant roles in the armed forces. Early recruiting posters even showed Africans in uniform carrying assegais and knobkerries. This policy was largely adhered to within the borders of the Union although some black South African soldiers acting as guards did handle firearms. The noncombatant policy was undoubtedly a contributory factor to the relatively poor response to the recruiting campaigns from mid-1940 to March 1943. Some Africans refused to enlist, deterred by personal memories of the rigours of the Great War and the lack of recognition given to ex-servicemen by the state. Walter Nhlapo wrote to a newspaper: 'Our brothers faced shot and shell and bore the perils of war,' yet there was 'no cenotaph ... to honour our fallen dead.'[141] Eventually, in February 1944, Union Prime Minister Jan Smuts announced that from now on Coloured soldiers would be permitted to carry arms. During the war more than 123,000 Africans, Coloureds and Asians served in the Union Defence Force; non-Europeans constituted 37 per cent of the Union Defence Force.

The authorities hoped to secure a large number of recruits from among the Zulus, who continued to be regarded as an archetypal martial race. However, the 'disgustingly poor response' after two-and-a-half years of intensive recruiting was 803 men. The magistrate at Richmond reported that as a result of his persistent efforts to enlist Zulus he had only 'two old boys of between 65 and 70 [who] said they would like to go to wash dishes'.[142] Rural areas proved to be the best source of recruits for the NMC, providing 80 per cent of enlistments, although the response varied from one area to another. The most fruitful response came from the northern Transvaal, but this was a region that had experienced severe drought followed by famine. Men were propelled into the army by need rather than by any strong desire to serve traditional rulers or the country that treated them as a servile underclass. The northern Transvaal village where 20-year-old Nelson Koza lived with his wife and child was visited by the recruiters in 1940. The chief urged men to enlist. The young men shouted; the women stood silent. Koza and 14 other men enlisted and went away to fight; a year later Koza was captured in North Africa. He died in an Italian prisoner-of-war camp.[143] As May Santon recalled, even in Cape Town her husband, whom she had only recently married, enlisted because 'there was no work, there was no work for the men'.[144]

The Native Affairs Department, in co-operation with the military authorities, used a wide variety of means to encourage men to enlist in the NMC. Posters were placed in beerhalls, railway stations, cinemas and clubs, and on buses and trams. The advantages of military service were proclaimed in press advertisements, radio broadcasts and films. A common aim, particularly in the case of the specially commissioned films, was to depict 'the building up of a Native soldier from civilian life to that of a finished soldier'.[145] Chiefs and headmen were also used, but with a mixed response. In order to present military service in a more vivid way, selected black soldiers were recalled from the Middle East to help in enlisting their kinsmen. L/C M. Mqali described in a letter his attempts to enlist his friends:

> I met them, they took no notice about this which when I spoke the thing you sent us to people that we should ask them to join in when we have gone for leave they answered in the form of a question as this how can you join because when you have joined the children are troubled. Others asked me why I have not ploughed and yet I have joined for the Government.[146]

Army marches, bands and displays also brought only a limited response; few men were recruited by these means.

Even when men did wish to join up it was not always made easy for them to do so: the disdainful attitude of white officials acted as a further discouragement. One prospective recruit said:

> I applied at the Drill Hall for my service, they gave me a form to fill in and after filling the form in, they told me to take it to the Labour below ... When I reached the place they told me to go to the pass office. Then I went to the pass office ... they told me there is no depot there. Then I went back to the Drill Hall and asked one of the miltery [sic] police ... and he told me to return to the coloured exservice men ofice [sic]. Then I was told that they dont take native on in there regement [sic]. So I like to know ... were [sic] am I go to.[147]

So why did more than 70,000 men enlist in the NMC, and why was recruiting relatively poor over much of the country? The nature of South African society, with its institutionalised and legalised racial discrimination, appears to have distanced many Africans from the state. Some educated Africans put it in stark political terms. 'Why should we fight for you?' declared an African at a meeting in the Eastern Cape.

We fought for you in the Boer War and you betrayed us to the Dutch. We fought for you in the last war. We died in France, in East Africa and in West Africa, and when it was over, did anybody care about us? Why should we fight for you again? What have we to fight for?[148]

Racial discrimination was invoked again and again by many Africans as a reason for not enlisting. The refusal by the authorities to arm Africans deterred recruits. The Acting Paramount Chief of the Zulus, Chief Mshiyeni ka Dinizulu, whose support had been paid for by the Government, was angered at the official condemnation of Zulus as cowards because they had refused to enlist. He retorted: 'I desire to have established a Zulu Military Regiment trained in the manipulation of Big Guns, war tanks, armoured vehicles, motor cycles – all for combating the armed forces of the enemy. All necessary weapons and vehicles will be made available.'[149] Inequality of pay was another grievance and a barrier to recruitment. Whites received twice as much pay as men enlisted in the Cape Coloured Corps and the Indian and Malay Corps, while African recruits were at the bottom of the pile with 2s 3d *per diem*:

If you can pay me £8. 10s. in the military service I will join. But there is always a cloud before me – three pounds seven shillings six pence per month – I fint [*sic*] it a very meagre subsidy to a man with a family. This worries my mind every time but I wish to defend our country and our things – this I find as my bounden duty.[150]

Attempts at 'patriotic' appeals for 'king and country' had little impact on men when military wages were so low.

Overall there was a poor response to the call from the men who would have made the most likely recruits – those in the 20–30 age group. They preferred the higher wages to be found in mine work. The army had to be content with older recruits, mostly from the reserves where average monthly farm wages were as low as 15s plus mealie-meal in kind. For rural workers the higher wages offered by the NMC, and the improved food and welfare services, provided a strong attraction. Of course the NMC, whether in South Africa or on overseas service, carried the discriminatory policies of South African society with it. As Dr A. B. Xuma, president of the African National Congress, put it:

It is the consensus of opinion among African people of all classes in the Union, both urban and rural, that the condition of service for the African soldiers and the pin-pricks and humiliation he is subjected to at times, apparently to put an inferiority complex in him, tend to discourage the African people from joining the Native Military Corps and cognate units … We cannot maintain these peacetime discriminations in the army, and expect the victims of such discriminations of their friends and relatives to rush in their thousands to the army to defend them.[151]

Racial policies were sometimes softened, but also made more obvious to NMC men, when they served overseas alongside British colonial battalions where the lines of racial discrimination were less strongly drawn. And rumours of harsh treatment overseas percolated back to South Africa and further hindered recruiting. Another reason why men refused to come forward as recruits was that they feared that this was a means for the government to tax them.

A number of literate Africans joined the NMC. This was done from a mixture of motives. Some hoped to learn a trade; others saw army service as adventure, education and conferring prestige. 'I think it was out of a quest for adventure,' said Frank Sexwale, who joined the NMC in 1941. 'We read books about other countries. And when this war started we found that it was an opportunity to get around and see places we had read of and places we had been told about. So that's adventure.'[152] Sexwale also went on to refer to a pan-African motive that inspired some men to join up:

> We were reading about the Abyssinian campaign. You know where there was war in Abyssinia between Mussolini and the Ethiopians. And when it came up to us to get involved in war, we said "this is the opportunity, let's get into it and see what we can do for our country".[153]

Sexwale was a volunteer: 'I just walked into the army myself, without being persuaded to do so. This was 13 August 1941.'[154] So was B. C. Mcanyangwa, who applied to enlist in January 1945, so that he 'would be the only African teacher that has joined up in Aliwal North out of African male teachers'.[155]

Propaganda that stressed patriotism persuaded some prospective recruits but invariably motives were laced with political, social or economic expectations. J. Sephiphi said his motive for enlisting, like that of many others, was that 'we wanted to go and fight for the country thinking that maybe we'd get a better life when we came back'.[156] Sgt R. Moloi joined up

> because I did not want to be a slave in this country; because these people told us that this enemy is a very bad enemy – he is a bad man – Hitler – when we can win this war we would be slaves, especially as black people ... We cannot allow this man to come here and give us a certain rule that we don't know – rather live under present Government than Hitler's Government – the devil you know is better than the devil you do not know.[157]

Such invested hopes were sadly disabused with the postwar political changes in South Africa and the victory of the National Party in the election of 1948.

Military recruitment was also extended to the mandated territory of South West Africa, which the Union treated as a province. Under the terms of the League of Nations mandate, this former German colony could have a military force sufficient for territorial defence which could be enlarged in time of emergency. Recruiting in South West Africa began in December 1941. During the war some 7,000 Africans enlisted. The majority came from the northern area of Ovamboland, a region which had traditionally served as a labour reserve. Gordon argues that 'economics was undoubtedly the major factor' in recruiting targets being met. The Kuanyama region close to the Angola border suffered from 'severe population pressure' and the north generally was experiencing drought which, combined with army wages of 1s 6d per day for a private, made military enlistment an attractive proposition. Attestation took place at Ondangua (Ondangwa) and Windhoek and men then went to a holding camp at Tsumeb before being moved to South Africa for training. Recruiting methods were similar to those employed in other colonial territories – film shows, martial parades with a band, and the pressure of chiefs – and brought more than 1,000 recruits to the colours by early 1942. Most were destined for service with the Native Military Corps; few saw active service, with most employed in labour roles within South Africa.[158]

Recruitment in South West Africa continued into 1943, but not without official concern. Recruiting teams in Kavongo got out of hand with assault, rape and theft being committed; respect for traditional authority diminished. In December 1942 the Administrator reported that it was said: 'We are soldiers. We can kill people if we wish to. There is no law for us. We are not afraid of the husband of any woman who we may wish to sleep with.'[159] In January 1943 Smuts ordered the suspension of all recruiting in South West Africa. There were also official fears that soldiers were developing new attitudes and an independence of attitude. In August 1944 the mine-labour recruiting body WENELA was officially asked to find employment for 1,800 soldiers 'at once'.

Conclusion

During the course of a long and costly war the British, and the South Africans, were able to recruit large numbers of Africans for military service despite the reduction in the number of colonial field administrators. In all the colonies, most enlisted men can be classified as volunteers – overwhelmingly so in Uganda, less so in Kenya and Tanganyika, and comprising perhaps 70 per cent in Nigeria and the Gold Coast, although there were economic forces which drove men into the ranks. Sometimes there was the desire to earn a better wage, but hardship and poverty also acted as powerful stimuli. The colonial authorities, and the South Africans, relied to some extent upon chiefs to act as recruiting agents. Thus the distinction between 'volunteer' and 'conscript' is not always easy to make. Undoubtedly many 'volunteers' enlisted because they were told to do so by chiefs or because of dire physical need. Some 90 per cent of African soldiers were nonliterate and most were drawn from areas subject to indigenous authorities that were often only on the fringes of the money economy; all these facts indicate the soldiers' relative lack of personal autonomy in such matters. Among the volunteers motives ranged along a trajectory not unlike that influencing British men to enlist in the wartime armed forces: emotional response to national need; a sense of adventure; a new departure; opportunities for advancement; escape from an unwelcome situation. Although the colonial state in its varying manifestations was not a strong edifice, it is nevertheless remarkable that in a time of serious emergency it was able to mobilise so many men with relatively little unrest. The colonial state may have lacked profound rigidity, but those men who formed the 'thin white line' of administration in each colony clearly demonstrated a high degree of self-assured confidence in what they were doing.

75

Notes

[1] Isaac Fadoyebo, *A Stroke of Unbelievable Luck* (African Studies Program, University of Wisconsin-Madison, 1999), p. 17.

[2] Interview with David Killingray, Accra, 5 May 1979.

[3] NAG (Accra), ADM63/5/8, Navrongo informal diary, 13 September 1939.

[4] TNA. CO820/2/8191, Sir Samuel Wilson to Col S. S. Butler, IG WAFF, secret, 17 March 1928.

[5] See David Killingray, 'The colonial army in the Gold Coast: Official policy and local response, 1890–1947', PhD thesis, University of London, 1982, pp. 97–101.

[6] Anthony Clayton, *France, Soldiers and Africa* (London, 1988), p. 129.

[7] An early but unpublished study is by John Shuckburgh, 'Colonial civil history of the war', 5 volumes, unpublished MS, 1949 (copies in TNA, Kew; Rhodes House Library, Oxford; and the Institute of Commonwealth Studies, University of London). See further Ali Mazrui, *UNESCO History of Africa and the Second World* War (Paris, 1981); Nicholas Westcott, 'Impact of the Second World War on Tanganyika, 1939–49', PhD thesis, University of Cambridge, 1982; John Paul Rozier, 'The effect of war on British rule and politics in the Sudan 1939–45', DPhil, University of Oxford, 1984; David Killingray and Richard Rathbone, eds, *Africa and the Second World War* (Basingstoke, 1986); Michael Crowder, 'The Second World War: prelude to decolonization', in Crowder, ed., *The Cambridge History of Africa. Volume 8: from c. 1940 to c. 1975* (Cambridge, 1984), pp. 8–51; Mary Ntabeni, 'War and society in colonial Lesotho 1939–45', PhD thesis, Queen's University, Kingston, Ontario, 1996; Ashley Jackson, *Botswana 1939–1945: An African Country at War* (Oxford, 1999); Ashley Jackson, *War and Empire in Mauritius and the Indian Ocean* (Basingstoke, 2001); M. W. Daly, *Imperial Sudan: The Anglo-Egyptian Condominium 1934–1956* (Cambridge, 2003), chs 6 and 7; Gardner Thompson, *Governing Uganda: British Colonial Rule and its Legacy* (Kampala, 2003); and Ashley Jackson, *The British Empire and the Second World War* (London, 2006), ch. 9.

[8] Wendell P. Holbrook, 'The impact of the Second World War on the Gold Coast: 1939–1945', PhD thesis, Princeton University, 1978; David Killingray, 'Military and labour recruitment in the Gold Coast during the Second World War, *Journal of African History* 23, 1 (1982), pp. 83–95; O. Shiroya, *Kenya and the World War Two* (Nairobi, 1985); Killingray, 'Labour mobilisation in British colonial Africa for the war effort, 1939–46', in Killingray and Rathbone, *Africa and the Second World War*, ch. 3; L. W. F. Grundlingh, 'The participation of South African blacks in the Second World War', DLitt et Phil thesis, Rand Afrikaans University, 1986; Hamilton Sipho Simelane, 'Labour mobilization for the war effort in Swaziland, 1940–42', *International Journal of African Historical* Studies 26, (1993), pp. 541–71; Ashley Jackson, 'Motivation and mobilization for war: Recruitment for the British Army in the Bechuanaland Protectorate, 1941–46', *African Affairs* 96 (1997), pp. 399–417; David Johnson, *World War II and the Scramble for Labour in Colonial Zimbabwe, 1939–1948* (Harare, 2000).

[9] H. Moyse-Bartlett, *The King's African Rifles: A Study in the Military History of East and Central Africa* (Aldershot, 1956); A. Haywood and F. A. S. Clarke, *The History of the Royal West African Frontier Force* (Aldershot, 1964); R. A. R. Bent, *Ten Thousand Men of Africa: The Story of the Bechuanaland Pioneers and Gunners 1941–1946* (London, 1952).

[10] David Killingray, 'Labour exploitation for military campaigns in British colonial Africa, 1870–1945', *Journal of Contemporary History*, 24, 3 (1989), pp. 483–501.

[11] David Killingray and James Matthews, '"Beasts of burden": British West African carriers in the First World War', *Canadian Journal of African Studies*, 13, 1–2 (1979), pp. 5–23.

[12] P. G. Elgood, *Egypt and the Army* (Oxford, 1924), p. 314.

[13] See Geoffrey Hodges, *The Carrier Corps: Military Labor in the East African Campaign, 1914–1918* (Westport CT, 1986); for the broader context, the best and most recent study is Edward Paice, *Tip and Run: The Untold Tragedy of the Great War in Africa* (London, 2007).

[14] Melvin E. Page, 'The war of *thangata*: Nyasaland and the East African campaign, 1914–1918', *Journal of African History*, 19, 1 (1978), p. 87.

[15] George Shepperson and Thomas Price, *Independent African: John Chilembwe and the Origins, Setting and Significance of the Nyasaland Native Rising of 1915* (Edinburgh, 1958), p. 235.

[16] D. C. Savage and J. Forbes Munro, 'Carrier recruitment in the British East African Protectorate, 1914–18', *Journal of African History*, VII, 2 (1966), pp. 313–42; G. W. T. Hodges, 'African manpower statistics for the British forces in East Africa, 1914–18', *Journal of African History*, 19, 1 (1978), pp. 101–16; Hodges, *The Carrier Corps*.

[17] N. Clothier, *Black Valour: The South African Native Labour Contingent and the Sinking of the* Mendi (Pietermaritzburg, 1987). B. P. Willan, 'The South African Native Labour Contingent, 1916–1918',

Journal of African History, 19, 1 (1978), pp. 61–86.

[18] TNA, CO820/13/13828, Thomas to Cunliffe-Lister, 10 March 1932, enclosure 2, 'Memorandum on recruiting policy' by Col Wilson.

[19] A. W. Cardinall, *The Natives of the Northern Territories of The Gold Coast* (London, 1921), p. viii.

[20] These notions perhaps owe something to the work of the ethnographer J. C. Prichard. In his *The Natural History of Man* (London, 1843), he divided Africa by an imaginary line marked by the 'Mountains of the Moon'. The northern 'more civilized' area contained the Muslim states, the southern area the 'pure Negro type'. Prichard described the Hausa as 'acute, intelligent and industrious'. See Mary Hammer, 'Black and white? Viewing Cleopatra in 1862', in Shearer West, ed., *The Victorians and Race* (Aldershot, 1996), pp. 57–59.

[21] John Glover, 'The Volta expedition during the late Ashantee campaign', *Journal of the Royal United Service Institute*, 18 (1874), p. 324.

[22] L. H. Gann, *A History of Northern Rhodesia: Early Days to 1953* (Salisbury, 1963), p. 326 fn 1.

[23] See further Cynthia H. Enloe, *Ethnic Soldiers: State Security in a Divided Society* (Harmondsworth, 1980), especially chs 1 and 2; J. Bayo Adekson, 'Ethnicity and army recruitment in colonial plural societies', *Ethnic and Racial Studies*, 2, 2 (1979), pp. 151–65; A. H. M. Kirk-Greene, '"Damnosa Hereditas": Ethnic ranking and martial race imperative in Africa', *Ethnic and Racial Studies*, 3, 4 (1980), pp. 393–414; Ali A. Mazrui, *Soldiers and Kinsmen in Uganda: The Making of a Military Ethnocracy* (London, 1975), and *The Warrior Tradition in Modern Africa* (London, 1977); David Killingray, 'Imagined martial communities: Recruiting for the military and police in colonial Ghana, 1860–1960', in Carola Lentz and Paul Nugent, eds, *Ethnicity in Ghana: The Limits of Invention* (Basingstoke, 1999), pp. 119–36; Timothy Parsons, '"Wakamba warriors are soldiers of the Queen": The evolution of the Kamba as a martial race, 1890–1970', *Ethnohistory*, 5, 46 (1999), pp. 671–701; Risto Marjomaa, 'The martial sprit: Yao soldiers in British service in Nyasaland (Malawi), 1895–1939', *Journal of African History*, 44, 3 (2003), pp. 413–32.

[24] A similar policy was pursued by the French in Madagascar. The least favoured recruits – *les médiocres* – for the *Régiments Tirailleurs Malgaches* were the Hova and Merina, peoples who fiercely opposed the French in the late 19th century; see Chantal Valensky, *Le Soldat Occulté: Les Malgaches de l'Armée Francaise, 1884–1920* (Paris, 1995), ch. 2.

[25] Garnet Wolseley, 'The Negro as soldier', *Fortnightly Review*, December 1888, pp. 699–700; F. D. Lugard, *The Dual Mandate in British Tropical Africa* (London, 1922), p. 574.

[26] Jennifer Warner, 'Recruitment and service in the King's African Rifles during the Second World War', unpublished MLitt thesis, University of Bristol, 1985, pp. 55–78.

[27] C. E. Cookson, 'The Gold Coast hinterland and the Negroid races', *Journal of the Royal African Society*, 60 (April 1915), p. 307.

[28] Mazrui, *Soldiers and Kinsmen*, p. 35.

[29] TNA, CO445/42/27100, Haywood to Adjutant-General, War Office, 2 May 1917.

[30] TNA, CO537/954/33394, memorandum on 'Manpower: Native races of Africa', by Col A. Haywood to Devonshire, secret, 3 July 1923.

[31] India Office Records and Library (IORL), British Library, London, L/WS/1/1328, 'Note on 81st Division', by Lt-Col Cantlie, War Office Liaison Officer, 31 May 1943.

[32] RHL, Mss. Afr. s. 1715, Box 5, G. H. Cree, who served with the KAR, 1931–45.

[33] Liddell Hart Archive, King's College London, Gen Sir Hugh Stockwell, 5/3, 'The 82nd West African Division in battle'.

[34] Derogatory terms used with reference to coastal peoples and southerners punctuate many of the printed and documentary accounts from West Africa in the period 1860–95. Both the terms above were used by European informants who had served with the RWAFF in the 1930s.

[35] TNA. CO968/400. Central Security Council meeting, 29 August 1952.

[36] Martin Staniland, 'The "military participation" of Ghanaian ethnic groups', *Research Review* (Legon, Ghana), 8, 2 (1972), pp. 29–31.

[37] Kwame Asante, interview with David Killingray, Accra, April 1979.

[38] Mario Kolk, *Can You Tell Me Why I Went to War? A Story of a Young King's African Rifle, Reverend John E. A. Mandambwe* (Zomba, 2008), p. 16.

[39] Thompson, *Governing Uganda*, ch. 6.

[40] Nicholas Owen, 'Critics of Empire in Britain', in Judith M. Brown and William Roger Louis, eds, *The Oxford History of the British Empire. Volume IV: The Twentieth Century* (Oxford, 1999), pp. 188–211.

[41] Killingray, 'Labour mobilisation'; Kenneth P. Vickery, 'The Second World War revival of forced labor in the Rhodesias', *International Journal of African Historical Studies*, 22, 3 (1989), pp. 423–37; David Johnson, 'Settlers, farmers and coerced African labour in Southern Rhodesia, 1936–46', *Journal of African History*, 33, 1 (1992), pp. 111–28.

[42] TNA, CO98/97, 'Demobilization and resettlement of Gold Coast Africans in the armed forces (1945)'.

[43] N. J. Miners, *The Nigerian Army 1956–1966* (London, 1971), p. 239 fn 7.

[44] Felix Cole, 'The Sierra Leone Army: A case study of the impact of the colonial heritage, 1901–1967', MA, Fourah Bay College, University of Sierra Leone, 1987, ch. 2. I am grateful to Dr Cole for letting me read his thesis.

[45] 'Troops from the Gold Coast', *Pathé Gazette*, 20 January 1941.

[46] Quoted by Wendell P. Holbrook, 'War and tradition in the Gold Coast, 1939–1945', p. 8. I am grateful to Dr Holbrook for a copy of his unpublished paper.

[47] J. F. A. Ajayi and M. Crowder, eds, *History of West Africa: Vol. 2* (2nd edn, London, 1987), p. 667–68.

[48] D. C. Dorward, 'An unknown Nigerian export: Tiv benniseed production, 1900–1960', *Journal of African History*, 16, 3 (1975), p. 447; J. I. Tseayo, *Conflict and Incorporation in Nigeria: The Integration of the Tiv* (Zaria, 1975), p. 125; Akaatenger John Aond'akaa, 'Military recruitment and its impact on the Tiv, 1914–1970: The case of Gboko', BA History project, University of Jos, July 1971, pp. 25–27. I am grateful to Dr Peter J. Yearwood for a copy of this project.

[49] Killingray, 'Military and labour recruitment', p. 91.

[50] Kwabena O. Akurang-Parry, 'Africa and the World War II', in Toyin Falola, ed., *Africa. Vol. 4: The End of Colonial Rule. Nationalism and Decolonization* (Durham NC, 2002), p. 53.

[51] Holbrook, 'War and tradition in the Gold Coast', pp. 10–11.

[52] *Ibid.*, p. 14.

[53] TNA, CO98/91, Central Province Council minutes, 5 June 1941.

[54] Nancy Lawler, *Soldiers, Airmen, Spies and Whisperers: The Gold Coast in World War II* (Athens OH, 2002), p. 90.

[55] Holbrook, 'The impact of the Second World War on the Gold Coast', pp. 199ff.

[56] RHL, Mss Afr. S. 1734, Box IV, J. A. L. Hamilton, and personal letter to Killingray, 24 April 2002.

[57] Wendell Holbrook, 'Oral history and the nascent historiography for West Africa and World War II: A focus on Ghana', *International Journal of Oral History*, 3, 3, (1982), pp. 162–63; other examples are provided by Holbrook in 'War and tradition in the Gold Coast, 1939–1945', unpub. paper sent to author.

[58] Quoted Holbrook, 'Oral history', p. 161.

[59] *Ibid.* p. 166, n. 38.

[60] Chief Enahoro, *Fugitive Offender* (London, 1956), pp. 68–70.

[61] S. K. B. Asante, *Pan-African Protest: West Africa and the Italo-Ethiopian Crisis 1934–1941* (London, 1977).

[62] Nancy Lawler, 'We don't like you Mr Hitler', unpublished paper, interview, Kumasi, 30 March 1994.

[63] BBC Africa Service. James Adewale.

[64] *West Africa*, 18 September 1943, p. 827. See Roger Lambo, '"Achtung! The Black Prince": West Africans in the Royal Air Force, 1939–46', in David Killingray, ed., *Africans in Britain* (London, 1994), pp. 145–63.

[65] BBC Africa Service. John Henry Smythe.

[66] Lambo, 'Achtung!', p. 160.

[67] See Peter Clarke, *West Africans at War 1914–18, 1939–45: Colonial Propaganda and its Cultural Aftermath* (London, 1986), ch. 3.

[68] Rosaleen Smythe, 'Britain's African colonies and British propaganda during the Second World War', *Journal of Imperial and Commonwealth History*, 14, 1 (1985), pp. 176–85.

[69] IWM, London, Department of Sound Archives, No. 18429/1-3, Al Haji Abdul Aziz Braimah.

[70] *Ibid.*, No. 18428, John Borketey, and No. 18366, Paul Gobine.

[71] BBC Africa Service, El Hadji Abu Bakkr Magba-Kamara, 4th Infantry Bde, Recce Company.

[72] Holbrook, 'Oral History', p. 158.

[73] BBC Africa Service. Marshall Kebby, interviewed by Elizabeth Obadina, Lagos, Nigeria, 1989.

[74] Holbrook, 'Oral History', p. 158.

[75] R. T. Kerslake, *Time and the Hour: Nigeria, East Africa and the Second World War* (London, 1997), pp. 103–4.

[76] *Ashanti Pioneer* (Kumasi), 18 February 1944, quoted by Yasu'o Mizobe, 'African newspaper coverage of Japan (the Japanese Army) during World War II: The case of *The Gold Coast Observer* and the *Ashanti Pioneer*, 1943–1945'. Unpublished paper, 2007.

[77] BBC Africa Service. Wusu Bundu Sanu, who, in the early 1990s, was chairman of the Ex-Servicemen's Committee, recorded, Freetown, Sierra Leone, 1989.

[78] Ronald W. Graham, compiler and editor, 'There was a soldier: The Life of Hama Kim MM', *Africana Marburgensia* 10 (1985), p. 14.

[79] David Shirreff, *Bare Feet and Bandoliers* (London, 1995), pp. 10, 31, 41 and 67. IWM, London, Sound Archive, No. 4414/7, Col Alexander Tancred Curle, 'Recruitment of Ethiopian refugees for irregular

units in East Africa, 1940'.

[80] Ashley Jackson, *War and Empire in Mauritius and the Indian Ocean* (Basingstoke, 2001), ch. 4.

[81] John Iliffe, *A Modern History of Tanganyika* (Cambridge, 1979), p. 250.

[82] *Ibid.*, p. 370.

[83] Bildad Kaggia, *Roots of Freedom 1921–63* (Nairobi, 1975), p. 21.

[84] BBC African Service. Batison Geresomo, recorded Ntchisi, Malawi,1989.

[85] BBC African Service. Mustafa Bonomali, recorded by A. M. Mwamkengenge, Salima, Malawi, 1989.

[86] BBC African Service. Chama Mutendi Kadanse, recorded Ndola, Zambia, 1989.

[87] Kolk, *Can You Tell Me Why I Went to War?*, p. 17.

[88] Meshack, "'For your tomorrow, we gave out today"', pp. 129–31, provides examples of literate Luo men who volunteered for the army.

[89] Derek R. Peterson, *Creative Writing: Translation, Bookkeeping and the Work of Imagination in Colonial Kenya* (Portsmouth NH, 2004), pp. 165–66.

[90] Bethwell O. Ogot, 'Mau Mau and nationhood: the untold story', in E. S. Atieno Odhiambo and John Lonsdale, eds, *Mau Mau and Nationhood* (Oxford, 2003), p. 14. See also Hal Brands, 'Wartime recruiting practices, martial identity and post-World War II demobilization in colonial Kenya', *Journal of African History* 46, 1 (2005), pp. 103–25.

[91] BBC African Service. Hamis Makiti Lashau, as told to his son, recorded Moshi, Tanzania, 1989.

[92] R. H. Kakembo, *An African Soldier Speaks* (London, 1946), pp. 8–9.

[93] IWM, London, Sound Archive, No. 18366, Paul Gobine.

[94] S. K. Mutiso, 'Indigenous knowledge in drought and famine forecasting in Machakos District, Kenya', paper presented to African Studies Association of the UK, Stirling, 8–10 September 1992, p. 5.

[95] BBC African Service. Mustafa Bonomali, recorded by A. M. Mwamkengenge, Salima, Malawi,1989.

[96] BBC African Service. Mussa K. Kiwhelo, recorded Dar es Salaam, Tanznia, 1989.

[97] BBC African Service. James Mpagi, recorded Kampala, Uganda, 1989.

[98] Quoted by John Iliffe, *Honour in African History* (Cambridge, 2005), p. 231.

[99] BBC African Service. Martin K. Lwambura, recorded Kampala, Uganda, 1989.

[100] K. Brown, 'The military and social change in colonial Tanganyika: 1919–1964', PhD thesis, Michigan State University, 2001, p. 364. On dance as protest during the First World War and after, see T. O. Ranger, *Dance and Society in Eastern Africa* (London, 1975).

[101] Quoted by Thompson, *Governing Uganda*, p. 106.

[102] Thompson, *Governing Uganda*, pp. 107–10.

[103] *A Spear of Freedom* (Nairobi, 1942). Alec Dickson, of the Cameron Highlanders and the East African Intelligence Corps, served for most of the war in Africa; later he founded the volunteering charity Voluntary Service Overseas. See H. C. Swaisland, 'Alexander Dickson', in H. C. G. Matthews and Brian Harrison, eds, *The Oxford Dictionary of National Biography* (Oxford, 2004), vol. 16, pp. 114–15.

[104] Gregory H. Maddox, 'Gender and famine in central Tanzania: 1916–1961', *African Studies Review* 39, 1 (1996), p. 96.

[105] Ndabaningi Sithole, *African Nationalism* (London, 1959, new edition 1968), p. 48.

[106] BBC African Service. Usiwa Usiwa, recorded Blantyre, Malawi, 1989.

[107] BBC African Service. Samson Muliango, recorded Lusaka, Zambia, 1989.

[108] R. O. Collins, 'The SDF and the Italian-Ethiopian campaign in the Second World War', unpublished paper delivered at conference on Africa and the Second World War, School of Oriental and African Studies, University of London, 1984; H. D. Jackson, *The Fighting Sudanese* (London, 1954); General Sir William Platt, *The Campaign against Italian East Africa, 1940–41* (Khartoum, 1951). Daly, *Imperial Sudan*, ch. 6, 'The Sudan during the Second World War'.

[109] See Johnson, *World War II and the Scramble for Labour*, p. 10ff.

[110] See Lawrence Vambe, *From Rhodesia to Zimbabwe* (London, 1976), p. 125.

[111] Christopher Owen, *The Rhodesian African Rifles* (London, 1970).

[112] J. K. Seirlis, 'Undoing the United Front? Coloured soldiers in Rhodesia 1939–1980', *African Studies* 63, 1 (2004), p. 75.

[113] Peter McLaughlin, 'Collaborators, mercenaries or patriots? The "problem" of African troops in Southern Rhodesia during the First and Second World Wars'. Unpublished paper presented at African History Seminar, School of Oriental and African Studies, University of London, 6 February 1980.

[114] J. F. MacDonald, *The War History of Southern Rhodesia* (2 vols) (Salisbury, 1947); Owen, *Rhodesian African Rifles*.

[115] Quoted by Johnson, *World War II and the Scramble for Labour*, p. 24.

[116] MacDonald, *War History of Southern Rhodesia*; *Vol. 1*, pp. 94–95; *Vol. 2*, pp. 444, 574 and 583.

[117] BBC African Service. Joe Culverwell, recorded Harari, Zimbabwe, 1989.

[118] Kenneth P. Vickery, 'The Second World War revival of forced labour in the Rhodesias', *International Journal of African Historical Studies* 22, 3 (1989), p. 434.

[119] Kusum Datta, 'Farm labour, agrarian capital and the state in colonial Zambia: The African Labour Corps 1942–1952', *Journal of Southern African Studies* 14, 3 (1988), pp. 371–92.

[120] Quoted by Johnson, *World War II and the Scramble for Labour*, p. 24.

[121] Isaac Schapera, *Migrant Labour and Tribal Life* (London, 1947), was based on an investigation carried out in July–September 1943 and is a study of Bechuanaland 'during wartime', p. v.

[122] R. A. R. Bent, *Ten Thousand Men of Africa* (London, 1952); B. Gray, *Basutho Soldiers in Hitler's War* (Maseru, 1953); D. Kiyaga-Mulindwa, 'Bechuanaland and the Second World War', *Journal of Imperial and Commonwealth History*, 12, 3 (1984), pp. 33–53.

[123] Brian Mokopakgosi III, 'The impact of the Second World War: The case of Kweneng in the then Bechuanaland Protectorate, 1939–1950', in Killingray and Rathbone, *Africa and the Second World War*, pp. 160ff.

[124] Diana Wylie, *A Little God: The Twilight of Paramountcy in a Southern African Chiefdom* (Hanover NH, 1990), pp. 119 and 176–77.

[125] According to Neil Parsons, Thomas Tlou and Willie Henderson, *Seretse Khama 1921–80* (Gaberone 1995), p. 56, Tshekedi's harsh wartime recruiting policies added to his unpopularity and contributed to his political downfall in 1949.

[126] Ashley Jackson, 'Watershed in a colonial backwater? The Bechuanaland Protectorate during the Second World War', unpublished DPhil thesis, University of Oxford, 1996, p. 51. Ch. 1 of the thesis is on recruiting. See also Jackson, 'Motivation and mobilization for war: Recruitment for the British Army in the Bechuanaland Protectorate, 1941–42', *African Affairs*, 96 (1997), pp. 399–417.

[127] Jackson, 'Watershed in a colonial backwater', p. 62.

[128] Jackson, 'Supplying war', p. 737.

[129] BBC African Service. Jachoniah Dlamini, recorded Mbabane, Swaziland, 1989.

[130] Hamilton Sipho Semelane, 'Labour mobilization for the war effort in Swaziland, 1940–1942', *International Journal of African Historical Studies* 26, 3 (1993), p. 552.

[131] *Ibid.*, p. 552.

[132] *Ibid.*, pp. 558–59.

[133] *Ibid.*, p. 560.

[134] *Ibid.*, p. 560.

[135] *Ibid.*, p. 561.

[136] *Ibid.*, pp. 561–62.

[137] Mary N. Ntabeni, 'War and society in colonial Lesotho 1939–1945'. PhD thesis, Queen's University, Kingston ONT, p. 124.

[138] Mary Nombulelo Ntabeni, 'Military labour mobilisation in colonial Lesotho during World War II, 1940–1943', *Scientia Militaria: The Journal of South African Military Studies*, 36, 2 (2008), pp. 36–59.

[139] Ntabeni, 'War and society in colonial Lesotho', pp. 21, 123–4, and 138ff.

[140] S. Horwitz, 'The non-European war record in South Africa', in Ellen Hellman, ed., *Handbook on Race Relations in South Africa* (Cape Town, 1949), pp. 534–38; Peter Warwick, *Black People and the South African War 1899–1902* (Cambridge, 1983); M. Roth, '"If you give us our rights we will fight": Black involvement in the Second World War', *South African Historical Journal* 15 (1983), pp. 85–104; John Keene, ed., *South Africa in World War Two* (Johannesburg, 1995); H. J. Martin and N. Orpen, *South Africa at War: Military and Industrial Organization and Operations in Connection with the Conduct of the War, 1939–1945* (Cape Town, 1975); Albert Grundlingh, 'The King's Afrikaners? Enlistment and ethnic identity in the Union of South Africa's Defence Force during the Second World War, 1939–45' *Journal of African History* 40, 3 (1999), pp. 351–65.

[141] *The Star* (Johannesburg), 16 February 1939, quoted by Peter Walshe, *The Rise of African Nationalism in South Africa: The African National Congress 1912–1952* (London, 1970), p. 263. Nhlapo also wrote a poem, 'The unknown African soldier', *The Bantu World*, 4 May 1946, p. 10.

[142] Grundlingh, 'The participation of South African blacks in the Second World War', p. 74.

[143] Jennifer Crwys-Williams, *A Country at War 1939–1945: The Mood of a Nation* (Rivonia, 1992), p. 383.

[144] Karen Daniels, 'Life in Claremont: an interview with May Santon', *African Studies*, 60, 1 (2001), p. 54.

[145] Louis Grundlingh, 'The recruitment of South African blacks for participation in the Second World War', in Killingray and Rathbone, *Africa and the Second World War*, p. 182.

[146] Grundlingh, 'The recruitment of South African blacks', pp. 184–85.

[147] Grundlingh, 'The participation of South African blacks in the Second World War', p. 83.

[148] Baruch Hirson, 'Not Pro-Boer, and not Anti-War – just indifferent: South African blacks in the Second World War', unpublished paper presented at the conference on Africa and the Second World War, School of Oriental and African Studies, University of London, May 1984, p. 13.

[149] Grundlingh, 'The participation of South African blacks in the Second World War', p. 76.

[150] Grundlingh, 'The recruitment of South African blacks in the Second World War', p. 191.
[151] *Ibid.*, pp. 191–92.
[152] BBC African Service. Frank Sexwale, recorded in South Africa, 1989.
[153] *Ibid.*
[154] *Ibid.*
[155] Grundlingh, 'The participation of South African blacks in the Second World War', p. 80.
[156] *Ibid.*, p. 80.
[157] *Ibid.*, p. 80.
[158] R. J. Gordon, 'Impact of the Second World War on Namibia', *Journal of Southern African Studies* 19, 1 (1993), pp. 156–57.
[159] *Ibid.*, pp. 159–60.

3
Army Life

It seems a good thing to have a war, bwana.
People are better fed, better clothed and better
paid than ever before.[1]

For many young men the Second World War was a time of adventure and opportunity. Despite regimentation, occasional danger and much boredom, they could look back on their 'good war' as the most exciting time in their lives. They left home and familiar surroundings, met different people, travelled to other countries, saw new sights, and underwent a range of novel experiences. This was true for many Africans who enlisted in the British colonial armies, and who entered a life very different from their civilian one. Men who had never worn boots or eaten with utensils, had never seen a tarmac road or a motor vehicle, let alone the sea, or had never travelled aboard a vast ship, were thrust from the bush via the barracks into a startling new world. However, the 'good war' is a reflection for fortunate survivors. The dead lacked a voice and those whose lives were shattered had bitter regrets; for example, a wounded Tswana sergeant wrote from a hospital in the Middle East in 1945: 'I never get sleep out of the pains from my knees. I now feel that I am a cripple who will not do anything in life.'[2]

Initial training

For African recruits the first encounter with army life was invariably being taken, sometimes by lorry, to an assembly point or camp. There men were formally enlisted by a recruiting officer, often with the help of an African NCO who acted as interpreter. An attestation form was completed detailing the soldier's name, ethnic origin, home, next of kin, physical appearance, weight and height. Literate men signed the form, nonliterates provided a thumbprint. Recruits swore an oath of loyalty.[3] In West Africa this involved 'pagans' licking a bayonet and saying, usually in Hausa: 'If I should break this oath, may this bayonet devour me', while Muslims and Christians swore on the Qur'an or the Bible.[4] Soldiers were given a uniform; in the KAR this consisted of a light khaki tunic and "long shorts" (to keep out thorns), a khaki slouch hat, with the battalion number on it in Arabic numerals, and boots, the latter just introduced and worn unwillingly on the parade ground only. Heads were closely shaved against lice.[5]

The army meant regimentation, with daily activities commanded by the alien clock and by the sound of bugle and whistle. New and unfamiliar rules had to be learned and obeyed. Marshall Kebby, a Nigerian private with the Royal West African Frontier Force, recalled:

> At five o'clock the bugle would blow. Then at six o'clock you are on the parade field, doing physical training. You come back and you take your breakfast … Then you go on parades, either parades or you go on training … In the afternoon you break off and go and have your meal. After that you have your rest. After rest go back and march about – just march about. Then evening you finish up. Can go to the canteen, drink tea till night. Then till following morning. That's all. Can't go to cinema or anything. It wasn't anything to write home about. Military life? Useless! True![6]

Large numbers of recruits arrived at training centres barefoot and in the scanty garb of peasants. The army provided a new and altogether unusual welfare umbrella, providing clothes, food, housing, medical attention, training and some formal education. For men who had worked as migrant labour for large mining companies some of this was familiar, but certainly not on so grand a scale. Military service in the war years provided a wider range of benefits to more Africans than had any previous institution or system. In the war years many recruits – both volunteers and conscripts – were not just poorly clothed but also in poor physical health and suffering from malnutrition.[7] The high rejection rates for volunteers all over the continent indicate this. In its quest for manpower the army accepted selected men in poor physical condition (and below the required height) in the confident belief that their health could be improved within a few months by means of an army diet, drugs and physical care.

During the early years of the Second World War the period of initial training lasted between seven and nine months – longer than in peacetime, since a more technical army required more time 'to turn the African villager into a trained soldier'.[8] Andrea Pangla, interviewed by Meshack Owino, explained: 'You marched to the latrine, you marched to the mess, you marched to the barracks.'[9] As the war progressed training time steadily increased. By 1942 recruits in West Africa were receiving on average 408 periods of individual training in drill, bayonet, rifle firing and use of grenades, and 204 periods of collective training, mainly route marches, but officially this was thought sufficient only for an African campaign. Rapid recruiting for the two West African divisions for the Asian campaign put great strain on the training camps and thinly spread African NCOs and British junior officers, with the result that the 81st Division went into action in April–May 1944 'in an extremely untrained condition'.[10] Gen Francis Nosworthy, the C-in-C West Africa 1943–45, argued that 'the West African soldier is slow to absorb new ideas and I consider therefore that nine months of uninterrupted training in favourable conditions of weather and ground are required to rest the Division and fit it for employment for all types of operations'.[11] As a result the training programme in West Africa became both more intensive and extensive. By early 1945 recruits were receiving three months in one of the training centres, six months in a training battalion, then a further two months in a holding company where the soldier was 'kitted-up' for overseas service –a total of 11 months. Intensive and uninterrupted training was regarded by many senior British officers as essential: 'the African learns soldiering like a parrot', argued Gen Montagu Burrows, and six weeks' leave and six weeks' transit to India would 'make him forget a great deal of what he had learnt'.[12]

In peacetime African soldiers lived in 'lines' – rows of huts self-built in local style using wood, mud and thatch. The families or women friends of soldiers lived with them and cooked and kept house. The lines often resembled tidy villages, with smells of cooking, washing hanging out to dry, and children running about. The wife of a senior NCO, often the regimental sergeant-major, was 'queen of the barracks' and saw to order and discipline among the women in the lines. The position of *sarakin marguri*, as she was known in Nigeria, was officially marked by a medallion, a red sash and payment of five shillings a month. She dealt with matrimonial matters and 'woman palaver', and also served as instructor in childcare and guardian of sanitary standards.[13] A casual system of this nature was possible with relatively small armies that mainly served within a colony. However, wartime expansion brought change. Wives and children were sent home and the rapidly expanding army became an all-male institution. The transition was bitty but by the early 1940s most soldiers lived in barracks and ate institutional food served by army cooks. In the Middle East thousands of soldiers lived in large tented encampments. Bildad Kaggia from Kenya remembers that in Egypt 'the depot was in the desert and the headquarters was housed in tents. For the first time I slept under canvas and tasted life in the desert.' Later he was moved to Ismailia, where 'our new camp was fully provided with hot-water taps, modern baths and kitchens. We regarded Ismalia as more than a home … [it] was paradise.'[14]

The first aspect of army life encountered by recruits the world over was regimentation. Soldiers had to learn new notions of discipline and order cast in the framework of industrial time.[15] For many African recruits, particularly those from rural areas where life and production had been governed by sun and season, this was a very new experience. However, many soldiers – often to the surprise of their British officers – learned this elementary part of army life fairly quickly. Comfort and self-interest dictated obedience to and close observation of the new rules. As so often with colonial rule, indigenous subordinates enforced European commands. African NCOs cajoled new recruits, bellowed, threatened, punished by fist and threat of fine in order to induct them as rapidly as possible into the skills of the soldier. The method differed little from that of any other army. Obedience to order was paramount. Instruction was by rote, first to determine left from right and then to impose regimented order through repeated drill.

Race & rank

Race was a determining element in the command and order of the British African colonial forces. Officers were white men, and the few senior white NCOs were addressed as 'sir' by all Africans, even by those who held the same rank. The South African Defence Force reflected the discriminatory patterns of white dominance that pervaded the Union. Coloured soldiers could visit 'the British

Club, the New Zealand Club, the Australian club … there's only one club you couldn't enter, that's the Springbok Club. There was a lot of apartheid in the army', recalled one Coloured Cape Town veteran.[16] Non-Europeans could never become officers in the SADF, and in the pre-1939 colonial armies the highest rank to which any African could aspire was that of warrant officer. Practice at that time was for African troops always to be led by a white man, whether officer or NCO. The war years, and the recruitment of educated Africans, challenged colonial policy and practice and brought change in the Sudan and West Africa but less so in East, Central and Southern Africa.

Despite being excluded from commissioned rank, senior African NCOs held positions of considerable influence in the colonial forces. European officers and NCOs relied heavily upon them for day-to-day management of the force. Senior NCOs occupied key positions, acting as arbiters, negotiators and translators between officers and the rank-and-file, explaining soldiers' actions and arranging terms and conditions that could often be to their own advantage. Regimental sergeant-majors, in the peacetime force invariably soldiers of long service, were highly trusted by officers; they were men to whom first referral was often made in dealing with disputes involving the rank-and-file. The quartermaster-sergeant – the 'quarterman' as he was often called in the RWAFF – was always a literate soldier and occupied an important management position. His command over stores and supplies gave him certain powers to decide entitlements and the quality of provision to officers and also NCOs of whatever colour.

Colonial military policies closely reflected those of the British Army. According to the King's Regulations in 1938, King's commissions in the armed forces could only be given to those of 'pure European descent', which excluded even black Britons born and brought up in the United Kingdom. This racist policy was challenged by the UK-based League of Coloured Peoples before September 1939, with change urged by the Colonial Office on a reluctant Army Council. The result was that from 1940 onwards a handful of black British Army officers were appointed, mainly to specialist corps, but only for the duration of the war.[17] For the War Office, as also for the many senior officers who had served with the African colonial forces, the sticking-point was that black officers might have to command white soldiers in combat. Social class and culture also played their part: how would an African officer behave in the mess? There were deep racial and cultural prejudices to be surmounted, although in the parallel case of the Indian Army such obstacles had been partly overcome with the appointment of Indian officers, since 1919.

By the late 1930s the appointment of African officers in the RWAFF was under consideration – especially in the Gold Coast, where demands for this were made in the Legislative Council and in the local press. There was the example of African officers serving in the *tirailleurs* of neighbouring French colonies, and if an African could be appointed a judge in the Gold Coast, then why not an army officer? By 1939 an officer-cadet training scheme, endorsed by the Colonial Office and generally supported by senior officers, was agreed for the RWAFF. In 1942 the first West African officer was commissioned: Seth Anthony, a graduate of the prestigious Achimota College. He had joined up on the outbreak of war and by December 1939 had become a sergeant. Two years later he recalled: 'I was summoned to GHQ, West Africa, and on arrival marched before the GOC-in-C who told me he was sending me to Britain to train as an officer. I think it all lasted for less than a minute.'[18] Anthony proved to be a popular officer, not least because he was good at sports, and he went on to see action and serve with distinction in Burma. He ended the war as a major. One African veteran of the Burma campaign remembered that men liked to serve under Anthony because he was believed to have 'powerful juju'.[19] However, while a few other Gold Coast men were considered for commissions or appointed as cadets, most were rejected; only one other officer, T. K. Impraim, was appointed. He went to Britain in 1944 and was awarded his 'pip' the next year.

Although the wartime KAR recruited men suitable for officer training – for example Robert Kakembo, a Ganda graduate from Makerere college – policy tended to reflect the local colour bar and the hostility to African advancement from white settlers in Kenya. However, wartime exigencies demanded that African NCOs be given wider and more responsible roles, and the new rank of warrant-officer platoon commander (WOPC) was created in 1942. WOPCs led platoons in action in Burma with considerable success. A few Ugandans with diplomas in medicine from Makerere were given the rank of lieutenant in the East African Medical Corps;[20] so also were some African chaplains and, for purposes of political symbolism, members of the Kabaka's family.[21] In the forces of the High Commission Territories the highest rank that could be held by an African was RSM, and most such ranks were given to chiefs or senior men of royal households. Tshekedi Khama, touring Batswana forces in the Middle East in 1942, protested 'that they can only go as far as Sergeant Major'.[22] Although the question of commissions was discussed in 1944, the military authorities were keen not to antagonise the South Africans. In 1944 two warrant officers had applied for commissions, and in 1945 so did RSM Theko Makhaola, a senior Sotho chief, on the basis of the 'vast responsibilities I have ... shouldered'.[23]

African soldiers could not escape the racial bounds of military service. They might be diminished when the soldiers served in diluted units alongside British troops, but colour and race were the determinants as to what they could and could not do, and where they might or might not go. Many African soldiers, perhaps the majority, simply accepted the racial divisions associated with military service. This was simply a palimpsest of the colonial order. However, they frequently protested about racist slurs that came from whites. This did occur, despite many commanders' attempts to prevent thoughtless or spiteful behaviour or speech that was tied to stereotyped and deeply ingrained attitudes and prejudices. Some Southern Rhodesian junior officers brought into the RWAFF as an emergency measure also brought racist language and attitudes, to the distress of many existing officers; in 1940 Gen Sir George Giffard, the then commander of British forces in West Africa, refused South African officers as their 'peculiar ideas of the treatment of natives ... will be ... little short of disastrous'.[24] Africans' letters and 'political intelligence' reports are littered with complaints from soldiers who had had demeaning or pejorative terms such as 'monkey', 'boy' and 'munt' used with reference to them. This abuse came mainly from white soldiers, especially those who were white settlers, but also from Asians and a variety of other Africans encountered while overseas.[25]

When Seth Anthony's commission was announced there was disquiet among some of the regular African rank-and-file who thought *all* Gold Coast Regiment

8 *Capt Seth Anthony in Burma, 1944*

Anthony (1913–2008) was the first African to be commissioned as an officer in the British colonial forces during the Second World War. Until 1939 King's Regulations stated that non-Europeans could not command white soldiers. Anthony attended Achimota College and trained as a teacher, joining the Gold Coast Territorial Force. On the outbreak of war he was mobilised into 5 GCR and promoted to sergeant. Two years later he was sent to Britain for officer training at Sandhurst. On his return to the Gold Coast as an officer his presence caused a sensation – large crowds turned out to greet him and even small boys knew his name. Anthony saw action in Burma with 81 (WA) Division in 1943–45, returning home in 1946 as an acting major. Created an MBE, he came to Britain for the victory celebrations, then served as a district officer – the governor stating 'that if he is good enough to command troops in the field, he should be good enough to run a District'. Later Anthony joined the diplomatic service and served as Ghana's High Commissioner to Ottawa and London. Lt T. K. Impraim, another West African, was commissioned at war's end but saw no action.

(Source: author's collection)

officers should be white men. But more generally Africans objected to the imposition of racial barriers to promotion. Edward Broadbent, whose early colonial career in Nigeria was interrupted by military service, wrote from Asia that West African troops in India

> have observed hundreds of Indian commissioned officers who live on terms of equality with their British colleagues; they know of only one African commissioned officer. This must inevitably encourage them to desire similar opportunities and wider educational facilities which will enable them to realise these ambitions.[26]

Gaining the knowledge and the confidence to voice criticisms took time. Bates wrote of his KAR battalion in Gondar, Abyssinia, being joined by a French detachment which included a Senegalese officer named Marie-Joseph: 'to start with ... our askaris were a little surprised ... Our C.O. was also a little surprised.'[27] By the middle of the war there was a good number of African voices demanding to know why Africans could not also be officers. Lovering, in his study of Nyasaland troops, says that the failure to promote Nyasas to commissioned rank 'engendered a specifically national response' of 'specific bias against Malawians', men complaining 'we cannot become Officers like Uganda askari', and 'our fellow Africans are being awarded and promoted' whereas 'our limit of promotion is only the rank of Regimental Sergeant-Major'.[28] Africanisation was slow and uneven. Eliud Mathu, appointed to the Kenya Legislative Council in 1944, asked questions about commissions for Africans. When the war ended there were only two African officers in the African colonial forces south of the Sahara, and the rank of *effendi* lieutenant, the equivalent of a Viceroy's Commission in India, was agreed by the civil–military committee in East Africa in September 1946. In contrast, by August 1942 there were more than 400 indigenous officers in the Sudan Defence Force.[29] The Royal Air Force, which required mechanical and navigational skills, enlisted some 50 West Africans, several of whom became officers.[30]

Punishments

Breaches of rules by soldiers were punished in various ways. Arbitrary punishment came from African NCOs who enforced their authority with blows, canings and extortion – all actions that were illegal but often winked at by British officers. Official punishments entailed confinement to barracks, fines and whipping. Imprisonment was reserved for the most serious crimes and was often seen as an inappropriate punishment in wartime. To lock up a trained soldier needed at the front when manpower was scarce represented poor military economics. Summary corporal punishment had the great advantage of giving a short sharp shock, immediate and inexpensive in terms of time and labour. European proponents argued that Africans responded better to physical punishment, which they were also more able to withstand, and that on active service it was essential that a commanding officer should have the authority to beat and flog. Corporal punishment had been used in the British African colonial armies since their establishment in the 19th century. It varied in form according to the crime.

Caning, often known among West African soldiers as 'six for arse', was frequently administered by African NCOs for all sorts of minor offences. A soldier would be taken behind a hut and beaten with a stick on his back or buttocks. The 'child-like' African, so it was widely argued particularly in white settler societies, needed to be schooled with a stick.

Whipping, or flogging as opponents tended to call it, was more brutal and had been suspended in both the KAR and RWAFF by 1934; by the end of that decade caning could only be awarded by courts-martial. Whipping had been reserved for more serious crimes – theft, rape, desertion, or assault of white officers and NCOs. It involved the offender being stripped, stretched on the ground and beaten on the back of the body with a leather whip before the paraded battalion. The few eyewitness accounts emphasize the brutality of the process.[31] When war broke out in 1939 'alleged military necessity' brought back a wider use of caning in the face of strong opposition from the Colonial Office, sundry voices in Parliament, and the concerted condemnation by the African elites in the colonies.[32] When questions on corporal punishment were raised in the House of Commons by the MP Reginald Sorenson and reported in the press in the spring of 1944, E. Y. Boateng, then a student in Cambridge, wrote to the MP: 'I was in the West African army for 3 years and 9 months, saw action in Kenya, Italian Somaliland and Ethiopia. I think I may be of help to you if you need any informations [sic].'[33] In the South African Defence Force corporal punishment was not officially permitted for non-European troops during the war.[34] However, in the Sudan Defence Force the 'traditional punishment' of whipping remained. This was up to 25 lashes 'on the damp buttocks (covered only by a damp cloth) with a hide whip' administered by the *bash-shawish* (sergeant major), the punishment preceded and followed by a medical inspection.[35]

In the Second World War the African Colonial Forces, now under War Office direction and thus subject to the Army Act, developed methods of punishment more in keeping with a modern military system. Institutionalised violence remained as an uncomfortable reminder of a past system; it also teetered on the edge of legality as it was allowed by local ordinance but not permitted by the Army Act. More commonly, defaulting soldiers now could be fined, confined to barracks, reduced to the ranks, dismissed from the service, sent to a military prison, or pursued by a new military police corps.[36] However, old attitudes and systems of disciplinary action died hard and throughout the war there were many instances of soldiers being knocked about by NCOs, both white and black, and of harsh and arbitrary treatment that would not have been tolerated in the British Army. For example, one method of punishment in the RWAFF involved defaulters drilling with a sandbag or large stone on their heads. A Gold Coast Regiment battalion commander was severely reprimanded in 1940 for punishing soldiers by making them carry rolls of barbed wire on their heads instead of sandbags.[37] Marshall Kebby, a Nigerian who served with the RWAFF, remembers one incident which nearly provoked a riot:

> There was a time when a white officer sat on the back of an African soldier to deliver a lecture on aircraft recognition. Only once. And I took it up immediately. I went to the commanding officer and reported ... The commanding officer took it very seriously, because that kind of thing could make the black man shoot the white man in the battlefield

... What that officer did was bad, and the commanding officer called him and chastised him.[38]

Languages of command

In the peacetime colonial armies the language of command was a local vernacular or lingua franca. Men who joined up came from many different language groups but often spoke languages other than their native tongue. Swahili had for long been the language of command in the East African battalions of the KAR, although different varieties of the language were used in the different colonies.[39] It was logical to use Swahili in that it already served as a trade lingua franca, having spread extensively over east and central Africa in the 19th century, and was also used by colonial administrators in Tanganyika and Kenya. In the KAR battalions recruited from Nyasaland, Chinyanja was the language of command, while officers appointed to the Somaliland forces were expected to learn to speak Somali, which at that time had not yet been reduced to writing. From the early years of colonial rule in Nigeria and the Gold Coast the military forces had used Hausa, also a trade lingua franca widely used in areas from which most soldiers were recruited. The Sudan Defence Force used what was known to European officers as 'Bimbashi Arabic',[40] while the South African Defence Force used both English and Afrikaans. Wartime expansion brought a change in language policy in both the KAR and the RWAFF. Increasingly English was adopted as the language of command, used alongside Swahili, Hausa, or whatever other language. This change in policy was necessary as the African Colonial Forces were inducted in new technologies, served under mixed commands, and had officers and NCOs drawn from among conscripts. Some European officers and NCOs did learn an African language – indeed, they were encouraged to – but this was often not a requirement as it had been for Europeans seconded in peacetime to the African colonial forces.[41]

Africans joining the army might have their initial entry helped by men who spoke their own language. After that they were invariably on their own and had to rapidly gain a working knowledge not of only the old vernacular languages of command but also some basic English. A former Nyasaland soldier recalled that

> at first not all African soldiers could understand English language. As a result the Army Education Corps introduced basic English lessons. We used to call it "Churchill Basic English course", because it was the wish of the Hon. Sir Winston Churchill that basic English should be taught to all H. M. forces throughout the British Empire.[42]

More astute men saw great advantage in learning the language of their colonial masters. Language and literacy skills offered greater chance of promotion and higher pay in the army and held out the prospect of wider opportunities for civilian employment. In the KAR men who learned English received an 'E' badge, worn on the shoulder of their uniform. A modern army system required literate men as clerks, engineers, radio operators and signallers, and for a wide range of new services. As the war progressed the army sought recruits among school-leavers who had a basic level of literacy in English. In order to develop these skills, the Army Education Services were created. A central function was to teach English and to encourage literacy and numeracy. At the same time a good many Africans also received their first introduction to the world of political ideas and debate in classes run either by educated African NCOs or more likely by European conscripts, some of whom had ideas that were critical of the colonial order.

Training in new skills

The army also taught men new skills. The purpose was to take raw recruits and turn them into a disciplined force that would do what it was told. The teaching of literacy, numeracy and technical skills was incidental to this higher purpose. Military training was all about prosecuting war even if much of the effort may not have seemed to add up to that. As a large part of the African Colonial Forces was engaged in labouring services, instruction was given in how to wield a pick and shovel, handle supplies in crates, unload ships and move bulky objects. Certain soldiers objected that they had not joined the army to be mere labourers. Most did receive training in arms and it is interesting to reflect that for many Africans their first personal experiences of the mechanical world involved being trained to look after and use a carefully machined precision instrument, namely a rifle. The rifle's parts were given names by African soldiers – for example, in northern Nigeria 'the trigger of the rifle was the "scorpion" because of its curly tail, the butt was the "backside", and there were other nicknames even more indelicate'.[43] Literate men probably gained most from army training, being preferred as lorry drivers, signallers, radio engineers and medical orderlies. The late Robin Hallett used to tell a story about his car breaking down somewhere in rural Nigeria in the late 1950s. A man dressed in an old army greatcoat was herding cattle nearby. He wandered over and offered to see what was wrong with the car. In a short time the engine was running. 'And where,' asked the grateful but somewhat surprised Hallett, 'did you learn about cars?' The reply was 'Driving in the army, sir.'[44]

Basic military training required one to learn simple rules of command: how to stand still at attention, dressing-off in line, marching in order, leading with the left foot and so on. Long hours were spent on the parade-ground under the eye of African NCOs, rehearsing elementary drill until soldiers could respond to orders without faltering. Drill and marching in order were means to an end but also a way of employing soldiers when there was little for them to do. Great emphasis was placed on accuracy in shooting at a target, although in the early years of the war rifle practice had to be limited due to the shortage of live ammunition. Soldiers were trained to recognise the fact that weapons had to be well cared for and kept intact. For those trained to serve artillery or use machinery, great stress was placed on safety. As in all armies, a good number of accidents – some fatal – occurred due to faulty equipment or carelessness in handling the mechanical paraphernalia of war, although it is not possible to quantify the relative number of accidents suffered by African troops compared to those of soldiers in British units. The number of casualties away from the frontline points up the dangers of army life for many Africans. One aspect of military activity for which

9 *Training drivers for the East African Army Service Corps, Nairobi*

This Ministry of Information photograph, taken in mid-December 1943 at the Motor Transport Depot in Nairobi, Kenya, shows African soldiers learning to become drivers. They are being trained on wooden mock-ups of lorry cabs which include a steering-wheel and a gearstick. To prevent learners from looking down when changing gear a small stone was placed on each of their heads. Lorry transport was introduced into the KAR in the late 1930s. During the war large numbers of African soldiers learned to drive, many serving on the long supply lines that enabled military material to be ferried along the Nile valley, and on campaigns in Africa and Asia. After the war some soldiers used their earnings to buy ex-army lorries and set up as civilian transport owner-drivers. And all over Africa ex-soldiers used the mechanical skills they had learned to establish various kinds of repair shops.

(Source: Imperial War Museum K 4943)

92

African troops were thought ideally suited was jungle warfare. This was considered urgent in 1941–42 because it was thought that West African troops might have to be used against Vichy France. When that threat faded the new enemy became the Japanese in the forests of Burma. Hama Kim of the Nigeria Regiment was sent with his battalion to Baiguma in Sierra Leone in late 1942 to train in forest warfare. There the training involved 'hand-to-hand combat, unarmed combat, bayonet training and more exotic pursuits like learning how to build rafts for river crossings'.[45]

Food & rations

The task of feeding and supplying a growing army of recruits with adequate and appropriate foodstuffs presented severe challenges to commanders. Soldiers from different parts of the continent were used to different diets. For example, Sierra Leone troops generally ate rice as their basic food while men from southern Nigeria wanted a non-grain diet. There were also differences in main diet within a single territory, for example between men from the Northern Territories of the Gold Coast and those who came from the Colony in the south. Muslims could not be served pork and sensitive commanders had to recognise the particular dietary demands of Ramadan. Yet men from widely different backgrounds were often to be found in the same battalion or even company, and the exigencies of war might scatter them further, diluting them with soldiers from other armies from Africa or Europe.

The army became a major purchaser of meat, rice, grains and other food crops as it took over responsibility for feeding troops. Early on in the war Gold Coast troops received food similar to that given to civil prisoners in jail. With time, the army organised its own catering system; cooks were trained and soldiers fed on a company basis.[46] Traditional foodstuffs were supplied but gradually these were supplemented by imported rations and soldiers were introduced, often for the first time, to tinned meat, bread and tea.[47] Soldiers, as ever, complained about their conditions and particularly about food. W. S. Mewabeni Mphahlele, serving with the South African forces in the Middle East, wrote that 'we are only supplied with two blankets even though it be winter' and there 'are times when I would give the lunch we are supplied with to eat to pigs'.[48]

Scales of rations for African and European troops were calculated separately. In the Middle East it was emphasised that Africans should not receive European-type rations 'owing to the adverse effect it might have on the return of troops to West Africa'.[49] Nevertheless, on overseas postings access to European foodstuffs became fairly common and African soldiers from all parts of the continent became regular consumers of a wide range of foodstuffs that a few years before had been totally foreign to them. One example is bread. This became standard fare for many soldiers. The army trained bakers and at war's end some set up in business to meet the demands of returned soldiers and also in response to changing consumption patterns.[50] New foodstuffs were associated with new ways of eating. Tin plates and mugs, mess-tins and cutlery, tables and chairs, all became fairly commonplace to African soldiers as a result of war service. The dietary and cultural impact of military life was considerable. As one African stated in late 1945: 'A great mass of consumers have been created by the Army. European boots, clothes and food have become part of the African soldiers' everyday life during the last six years'.[51]

King David, and much later Napoleon, knew that soldiers required full stomachs in order to march and fight. In the East African campaign of 1914–18 the British, by neglect, indifference and undoubted logistical difficulties, brought many of their soldiers and carriers to the verge of starvation.[52] The Cameroon campaign was bad but conditions there did not reach the 'near scandal' situation in East Africa. By 1939–40 both the administrative and the transport infrastructure of Africa had been expanded and supply services greatly improved. Even so, supplies of food were frequently disrupted in the East African campaign of 1940–41 and in certain areas officers and men were on the verge of protein deficiency.[53] When motor and camel trains could not get into Ethiopia, soldiers of the SDF were forced to live off the country as best they could and were even reduced to killing and eating exhausted and dying camels.[54] Nevertheless, for the most part in the 1939–45 campaigns the British military machine, and especially its commissariat services, worked fairly efficiently. Supply services in the Asian campaign were better organised than in East Africa, although the old problem of distributing rice to grain-eating troops caused temporary discontent. In Burma fighting troops had their rations supplemented by United States Army 'K' rations. At that stage in the war the British authorities were acutely aware of the need to maintain high protein and calorific standards for all troops. In April 1944 the Directorate of Medical Services denounced as inadequate a daily ration scale of 3,856 calories for East and West African soldiers in Asia: 'The average African is a man of great physique and requires a diet of high calorific content to maintain him.' African troops' allocation was increased to 4,300 calories a day.[55]

Uniforms

The army also clothed soldiers and provided them with equipment that was often new and novel. Plans for mobilisation of the African colonial forces in 1937–38 resulted in changes to uniform and equipment. In August 1939 soldiers of the RWAFF were issued with long-sleeved blouses, long shorts, slouch hats, boots and gasmasks. Rapid expansion of the armed forces was held up in 1940–41 in East and West Africa because of a shortage of materials for making uniforms and building encampments. Whether or not African soldiers should wear boots was an old question. In peacetime African soldiers went barefoot; indeed it was argued by many European officers, often vehemently, that Africans performed best without boots and that if such were issued they would only be an encumbrance that was likely to be discarded or sold at the first opportunity. A dispute over the failure to issue boots to the Sierra Leone Regiment in Freetown led to a brief mutiny in 1939. The year before, a Colonial Office committee had endorsed the opinion of Gen Giffard, then Inspector-General of African Colonial Forces, that boots and socks were 'necessary in a war in the future'. From August 1939 onwards all troops received boots, which became an accepted part of regulation equipment.[56] David Shirreff, who served with the KAR, stated that the War Office decision to put Africans into boots was taken due to fear of mustard-gas attacks by the Italians, but he said boots slowed up his soldiers who 'until then in their sandals ... could have matched any Italian colonial battalions in marching'.[57] By 1945 most African soldiers were clothed in the regular olive-green or khaki battledress of the British Army.

Pay & savings

Receiving regular payment of money was another feature of military service. Army wages were generally higher than those paid for unskilled civilian employment, thus offering alternative employment for more money. Regular wages were new to many recruits who did not come from a society having a formal money economy. All soldiers had a paybook – possibly the first item of printed material many nonliterate soldiers had ever handled, let alone owned. Private soldiers in the RWAFF received one shilling a day, those in the KAR ninepence. There were additional payments for proficiency and technical skills. Marriage and overseas allowances were introduced in 1940.

However, disparities in basic pay led to problems when men from different parts of Africa served alongside each other or Africans served alongside European troops. In the Middle East and India African soldiers became keenly aware of the low level of their pay compared to the two shillings a day, plus overseas allowances, received by British troops. In their home colonies men spent their money in the markets around army camps; in North Africa and Asia there were fewer opportunities to leave camps and cantonments and most money was spent in the NAAFI or in officially sanctioned stores. Coins, which came in low denominations, were preferred to paper money as they were easier to recognise and were durable, and when they had a hole in the middle they could be strung around the neck for safekeeping. They were also more convenient for gambling games. As wartime inflation eroded purchasing power soldiers also demanded increased pay.

The military authorities in Africa pursued a paternalistic policy towards African soldiers and their pay. They were concerned that soldiers' dependants should be supported and that men should not return home penniless without anything to show for their years of service. The idea that Africans should be encouraged in habits of 'temperance and economy' was an old one. Army savings would also help set up ex-soldiers when they returned to civilian life. In peacetime armies men were encouraged to open post-office accounts, but given the high levels of non-literacy and the lack of post office facilities it is not surprising that only a few did so. Under a deferred-pay scheme soldiers let the army save a small weekly sum from their wages. Until 1943 most deferred pay was kept by the paymaster and gained no interest. In December of that year an Army Savings Scheme was introduced in the RWAFF, largely with the purpose of ensuring that soldiers discharged at the end of the war would have savings in addition to deferred pay. In 1945 it was estimated that the average savings of soldiers from the Northern Territories of the Gold Coast amounted to about £35 each.[58] A relatively small number of soldiers serving overseas also opened post office savings accounts; some 3,700 men from the Gold Coast took out accounts and by 1945 they had saved £158,523, roughly £40 each.[59]

Payment of separation allowances or allotments to wives began in West Africa in November 1941. Initially these were distributed each month by district officers. They totalled ninepence, made up of three pence from the private soldiers' pay and a further six pence from the government.[60] In certain areas the distribution of allotments became a time-consuming task. As one district officer at Juaso, in the Gold Coast, put it: 'Some 800 women sit, chatter, spit and generally make a mess outside the office from 8.30 am. to 5 pm.; unlike road or sanitary labourers they are quite uncontrollable and many dispute the sum they are paid.'[61] Payments were made to agreed relatives or 'nominated wives' and in the Northern Territories of the Gold Coast it was reported that money went towards 'bride-price instalments' and 'laying up of cattle'.[62]

In West Africa, the definition of a 'wife' for purposes of being able to receive a separation allowance was 'a woman who has reached the age of puberty and who is deemed to be the wife of a soldier according to the native law and custom of the area in which the soldier/or his wife originate or is domiciled'.[63]

Soldiers serving overseas were often very anxious about whether payments were getting to the right people. An African journalist predicted trouble if men returned home and found that wives, seducers or relatives had defrauded them. In Navrongo in the Northern Territories of the Gold Coast, half the complaints made by ex-servicemen to the district officers were about disbursal of payments.[64] A soldier from Bechuanaland serving in North Africa wrote to his chief, Tshekedi Khama:

> Chief I have a grave complaint especially due to what is happening down there at home. Chief, since I joined the army, I decided to register my uncle's name so that he should be the recipient of my salary but I have not since heard from him. He does not even bother to inform me as to whether he is receiving such money or not. I had told him that he should always give something to my wife in the form of clothing. However, I am not only hurt but also alarmed to hear that my wife goes about in poor clothing ... I am now suggesting that such money be scraped off from my uncle Mothibedi.[65]

Other letters to Tshekedi Khama from soldiers in the Middle East complained about fathers who had failed to reply and doubts whether money that had been sent them was being spent as instructed. Some soldiers asked Tshekedi himself to look after their allotments and ensure that they were handled properly. N. Morekwe, a private also serving in the Middle East, complained in an undated letter that his children were 'not receiving proper attention' although money had been sent to his wife, and he asked Tshekedi to look after his allotment and let his wife only have four shillings. And about a wife suspected of adultery, Pte Rahakwena asked his chief: 'Please question her on her behalf my honour as to why she fails to inform me as to whether the money I send her does fall her hands or what [sic]. How does she expect me to know if she does not write?'[66]

Hygiene & health

Concentrating men in barracks or encampments made hygiene and sanitation a high priority for the military authorities. A healthy army was vital for the war effort and every attempt had to be made to improve and maintain the health of soldiers and reduce the prospect of illness. In peacetime conditions soldiers either built their own 'swish' huts or, in the more permanent cantonments such as those in Nairobi and Kumasi, lived in huts constructed of concrete and brick.[67] Sturdier and better-built barrack accommodation was provided at large military camps during the Second World War.[68] Modern ideas of order and sanitation were instilled in soldiers and enforced from the first day onward, so as to regulate disposal of rubbish and human waste, and spitting. Regular inspections of accommodation by NCOs and medical officers aimed to ensure that sanitary regulations were obeyed. Whether this actually succeeded in teaching men about sanitation can be questioned. No doubt some soldiers did learn, for the military took strenuous measures to inculcate ideas about sanitation, but in all probability many soldiers regarded the measures imposed to ensure health and hygiene as just another part of the new world of military order that painted stones white, polished boots and raised flags to the sound of bugles.

The army provided a medical service probably unique in British Africa, that was certainly more efficient and comprehensive than systems operated by large mining corporations for migrant labour in southern Africa.[69] Medical officers had the difficult task of improving the health of recruits, many of whom enlisted suffering from sores, skin ailments, tuberculosis and the debilitating effects of tropical diseases such as bilharzia and malaria. Malaria was endemic throughout tropical Africa, and in Nigeria in 1944 a quarter of all recruits were infected with bilharzia. Good feeding and the use of certain drugs improved the health and physical fitness of most men within three to six months. However, the relatively high number of deaths from natural causes in wartime among African compared to European soldiers seems to indicate the Africans' generally lower standard of health and physical fitness. Maintaining health was a constant struggle, particularly in regions where disease was endemic. Modern medicine was one way in which the military authorities extended their control over soldiers. Strong efforts were made to discourage resort to indigenous medical methods and practitioners and to encourage reliance only on modern medicine. Battling against indigenous methods (which might actually sometimes be efficacious) was an uphill struggle. So were attempts to encourage regular taking of prophylactics against malaria by issuing tablets on parade. Malaria was a serious problem among West African troops in the Gambia in 1941 and also in Madagascar in 1942, but at the time many soldiers failed to take quinine or atebrin even though officers signed certificates stating that regulation doses had been strictly adhered to.[70]

Keeping men healthy and particularly free of that scourge of all armies, venereal disease, was particularly difficult in encampments sited near large urban centres. Incidences of syphilis and gonorrhoea increased globally during the Second World War; in East and Central Africa some medical officials feared that soldiers would spread the disease in 'epidemic' proportions. The military authorities favoured greater control and intervention, placing much of the blame on prostitutes and continuing a debate that had existed from the early colonial years on how African male sexual behaviour could be controlled and the spread of sexually transmitted diseases arrested.[71] Venereal infections followed African armies. In an attempt to deal with the high levels of VD among KAR troops in Ethiopia, the Royal Army Medical Corps organised a brigade brothel and gave out to askaris thousands of captured Italian condoms. The response from one soldier was 'Do Europeans like wearing shoes in the bath?'[72] The problem became particularly serious, officers estimating in 1941 that more than one-third of the 900 men in 1/6 KAR were infected. Faced with this problem, Michael Blundell's policy in Addis Ababa was both ruthless and drastic. He had the local prostitutes in Addis Ababa rounded up, taken by lorry 20 miles out of the city and there stripped naked. However, within a short time the women had returned to their old haunts.[73] In May 1941, a total of 5,461 askaris in East Africa Command (EAC) were treated for VD; in the period August 1941–January 1942 there were 15,000 recorded cases, equivalent to the loss of a whole division. In the first quarter of 1944 the problem had become even more serious, with EAC having a VD infection rate of 471.8 per 1000.[74] In Africa, the Middle East and Italy it was difficult to keep soldiers isolated from the civilian population and VD remained a major disabling infection; in India military cantonments were more rigorously isolated, largely to avoid confrontations with civilians, and thus VD was a less serious problem.

The African Colonial Forces enjoyed the services of a relatively large number of medical officers.[75] However, perceptions of sickness varied, and medical officers ignorant or with limited knowledge of tropical illnesses sometimes proved ineffectual in coping with the ailments of African soldiers. One Tswana soldier serving in North Africa wrote home:

> I have a great complaint about people here, but we have no one to lodge our complaints to. Some of our people are sick but if their illness is reported, the 'whites' say they are not ill but pretending. After telling one so, he dies. One example is about your servant's son, Titeo Mangope who was driven away that he was not ill. We took him to the hospital on the 24-6-43 and on the 25th he died.[76]

For many soldiers the war provided levels of healthcare that they would not have experienced had they not enlisted. Military hospitals, often with limited facilities, could not maintain the racially segregated systems of the colonies so that African and European soldiers found themselves receiving treatment in the same ward. 'I was in the British hospital,' wrote a wounded black South African soldier:

> I have enjoyed the best time which has never [sic] been enjoyed by any person in South Africa. We were dining on one table, getting the same type of food, sleeping in one ward, one cinema, same showers and same 'equality' of opportunity without slightest distinction. You must always come in touch with the Tommies and Anzacs, they have no animosity for other people.[77]

Welfare service, wives & families

Welfare services for African soldiers barely existed before 1943. The army traditionally provided basic medical care and helped a few time-served soldiers to find work. The systematic development of welfare services only began well into the Second World War when the greatly expanded African Colonial Forces were under War Office direction and large numbers of men, distant from home, were housed in camps throughout Africa, the Middle East and south Asia, often for long periods involving enforced idleness. By then the military authorities had become much more conscious of the need for a welfare role and increasing demands for such services were being made, particularly by articulate African soldiers. The first welfare officers were appointed in early 1942 to help African soldiers with legal and domestic matters. In mid-1943 the Colonial Office, spurred by reports of low morale among British troops in India, discussed welfare provision for African troops who were about to go to Asia. Maj W. Tadman was appointed the welfare officer to West African troops in India and in the following year Capt D. H. Barber became public relations officer for all African troops in the Middle East.[78] A large part of Barber's time was taken up with questions of leave, repatriation and allowances – the major concerns of African troops.[79] With only a small staff and slender resources, welfare departments were limited in what they could provide. At the battalion level 'family problems' were left largely in the hands of the few padres and Muslim clerics (*mallams*) that accompanied each battalion or with sympathetic officers. Barber records the 'lengthy business' of discussing with soldiers the death of a child, an unfaithful wife and houses destroyed by fire, and occasionally writing to a district commissioner to see what might be done.[80]

African soldiers serving overseas rarely received leave. Home leave presented major logistical problems for all soldiers, whatever their race or origin, whereas local leave was more likely to be given to European than to African soldiers. Long absence from home, often for several years, created deep anxieties and severe personal problems for many African servicemen. Homesickness was widespread and exacerbated by lack of news from home. A majority of soldiers in the African military forces were nonliterate; few had received any schooling, although some learned to read and write in the army. Soldiers serving overseas were encouraged to send letters to their wives and families; contact with home was vital for morale and a free army postage scheme existed. Nonliterate soldiers were aided by literate men some of whom carried on 'a flourishing amanuensis business'.[81] The white platoon commander with the KAR also typically 'spent several hours every Sunday writing letters home, dictated in Swahili, for his men'.[82] At home wives were similarly encouraged to reply, with school students and literate neighbours enlisted to act as scribes aided by officially issued model letters.[83] However, military mail services were irregular and it was not uncommon for a letter to take many months to make its slow way from North Africa or Asia to some remote village in the interior of Africa. Letters were lost in the post, failed to be delivered because the address was indecipherable, were held up by the censors, or remained in official hands.[84]

Concerns about wives and children, family matters and property such as cattle, wells, and land were conveyed in poignant terms in the letters written home. 'Chief I am asking myself the following question every day', wrote a soldier from Bechuanaland,

is that person whom I regarded as my wife present or has she decided to venture for green pastures in other areas ... I am saying this because I am not receiving any letters from her. I send her money but she does not even write to inform me if at all she receives such money.[85]

Another soldier, also from Bechuanaland, wrote from the Middle East: 'Since my departure my wife has found another man and they are in fact staying together. This causes me great pain when taking into consideration the fact when I departed she was a decent wife of mine.'[86]

Adultery on the part of wives was a common complaint by troops overseas, although many soldiers frequently consorted with prostitutes. Some soldiers heard via the family that their wives had become pregnant in their absence. Pte Wale Mokakapadi, writing to his chief, expressed his anger at the culprit:

> Greeting to you my Lord. I have heard that the son of Ratarki has impregnated my wife. I felt it was best that I should inform you in case you were not told. I do not want you to take any action. I wish God will bless me and I manage to come home so that I can retaliate.[87]

Pte Letshulo Hulela urged Tshekedi to 'please sentence this gentleman' who has made his wife pregnant. 'The woman is mine and I have worked very hard and painfully for her. My in-laws made me pay through hard labour hence I request that you charge the gentleman in question *Phuhi*.' [a fine] [88] Another soldier, originally from Southern Rhodesia but conscripted in Bechuanaland, heard from his father that his wife, who had not had any children, was now pregnant: 'So, Sir,' he wrote, 'I am disappointed to learn of my wife's pregnancy during my absence. I am therefore handing these people to you Sir. Any punishment which you give to them to me will be okay.'[89] From Tshekedi's reply to an unnamed soldier in early 1943, it is clear that marital infidelity was a common problem:

> I received your letter about your wife's pregnancy but I have now written so many letters to others that you people are going to come back and it is then that these family cases can be settled. So I say the same words to you.[90]

After the war adultery cases were heard in indigenous courts. In Ghana, extant records of the Asantehene's court include the Soldier's Adultery Fee Orders. One case concerns John Mensah, of the Gold Coast Regiment, who married his wife 'according to the native custom from the parents for the past twelve years'. However, he stated:

> I left for Gold Coast for Burma on active service. I paid the head dowry of two bottles gin and £3 to Kwami Mensah, the grandfather of the said wife. When I returned from Burma, I suspected my wife for having had sexual connection with somebody. I therefore approached the parents of my wife and suggested to them to allow her to swear to me a fetish to renew her allegiance to me … At this stage, the wife of mine confessed to me in the presence of her parents that the Defendant had sexual connection with her.[91]

Mensah was unsuccessful in attempting to claim a £9 6s adultery fee from the defendant, but proceedings such as this occupied the time of 'native courts' during the latter years and immediately after the war.

The welfare of children and other family members was another major concern of soldiers at the front. Pte N. Morekwe feared that his children were 'not receiving proper attention' from his wife, while Tebalo Kwafiela, of Sesoma, complained that he had heard recently that 'his father has suddenly abandoned his children'.[92] Money sent home by Pte Nksholetsang Nkosho, he told Tshekedi, was for the education of his child, and his wife's parents, who had removed the child from school, should be compelled to return him there: 'This child is to attend school in Serowe ... I have realized that an uneducated person is like a donkey. Educated people have positions in life and so I wouldn't like my child to be donkey-like.'[93]

Letters from Tswana soldiers to Tshekedi asked for permission to build a house, for help over property disputes, about the loss of cattle, about tax that was owed and about theft of stock: 'We are fighting here and they've taking womens field [*sic*] and their tobacco. I want that field. A Kalanga does not own any land,' demanded Pte N. Olebetse on learning of his mother's death. Pte Ogaketsa Rantoka wanted his chief to secure his possessions and he hints at a family conflict:

> I have cattle, sheep and goats together with 14 plates, 6 utensils used for cooking and a cooking pot. Chief I have received a letter informing me of the fact that all my property has been shared away among strangers. My request is that you call upon such people to bring back my property especially members of Bagwasi family.[94]

Most letters dwell on family and social concerns similar to those mentioned above and also on opportunities for employment after the war.[95] An educated but unnamed corporal with the NEAS wrote:

> After the war does it mean that they will all get the one and a half penny jobs? This question has rather worried many of us. We feel we should be treated by employers on the same basis as European soldiers. Can't you persuade the chief bodies of employment to reserve decent posts for African soldiers? It seems to us that by the time we return to civil life, we shall have to start from the bottom.[96]

Sport & leisure

Physical exercise and sport were closely related to health and welfare. Physical training was regarded as similar to drill, another form of disciplined exercise which had the advantage of improving standards of fitness, and also served as a way to occupy soldiers' spare time and release some of their energies. Learning to swim, as was done by Waruhui Itote in Ceylon, proved useful to soldiers faced with crossing rivers in Burma.[97] By 1944 more than 100 West African physical training instructors had been produced and 'PT' became an essential part of military life.[98] Organised team games were seen as centrally important in encouraging battalion or regimental *esprit de corps*.[99] The army organised competitive sports such as football, athletics, wrestling and boxing, the particular sport adopted often reflecting the interest and encouragement of officers.[100] Sport was also seen as a means of social control. For example, Blundell used football and intercompany competitions as a means of controlling unrest in his East African labour battalion.[101] Boxing was popular in West Africa and Roy Ankrah, the boxer nicknamed 'Black Flash', started his career when he joined the Gold Coast Regiment in 1941,[102] but it was generally discouraged in the KAR 'due to the risk of blows falling on spleens, often enlarged as a consequence of malaria'.[103] The

KAR had its own game, *Karamoja*, which involved two teams of any number of men whose object was to carry a football to the opposing goal, but who had to drop the ball when touched by an opponent.[104]

Soldiers also played games in their own time. Jachoniah Dlamini, of the Swazi Regiment, said that 'when off-duty we generally played football, engaged in traditional Swazi dancing or played *it Juba*, a traditional African game that some westerners liken to chess'.[105] Ngaraito Makiti, from Tanganyika, explained to his son that when off duty in Asia 'they were playing different games, music, singing … but he told me there was nothing like resting as such … Only after the war they were able to go to town, drinking, etc.'[106] Soldiers of 8999 Company East African Pioneers, from Uganda, had dances and hymn-singing in the dining tent at the ordinance depot at Kanatra where they were stationed in 1942.[107] Dancing was a common past-time and popular European officers might be invited to sit and watch the entertainment.[108] Other indigenous games included *bao* or *owerri*, played by two or more men with pebbles in scooped hollows in the sand. Jacobs, who served with the SDF, describes two indigenous games, *beyut*, a form of musical chairs with piles of sand serving as chairs, and *yalla ya ra'is* ('Run away, headman'). In the latter

> The men squat in a circle facing inwards. One man selected as a searcher goes a few yards away and whilst his back is turned one of those in the circle is chosen as the *rais* or leader. The men then at the instigation of and copying the leader start making gestures at the same time chanting '*Y Allah ya rais*'. The searcher then returns to the middle of the circle and tries by observation to spot the *rais*. The *rais* will change gestures frequently, the remainder of the circle of course following suit.[109]

Games and sports often ignored frontiers and had a universal appeal. They also needed someone to initiate and organise. Perhaps most soldiers, as Blundell commented on his East African *askari*, were 'best left alone to play draughts, gamble with a greasy pack of old cards, or gossip in the evening'.[110] Many Africans also learned to smoke cigarettes, encouraged by the abundant supply of cheap tobacco provided by the army.

Boredom and idleness made up a good part of soldiers' lives. Army life consisted of long periods of enforced inactivity interspersed with times of intense physical activity. Indolence could breed discontent and it provided headaches for the military authorities. With small armies men might be left to their own devices. In the large tented encampments of North Africa and India, far from home, with seemingly endless amounts of time rarely interrupted even by local leave, new devices and schemes were required to fill enforced leisure time. Exercise and training could fill some of the time but not all of it. Soldiers produced their own amusements, ranging from gambling to Bible study. The military authorities, as in all modern armies, had to help devise various ways to occupy soldiers' time; they provided canteens, film shows, radio broadcasts, literacy and English classes and other education programmes, they supplied books and magazines, produced regimental newspapers, and provided local leave and also brothels.[111] Rest camps for African troops were opened in 1944 close to some of the major cities, that near Jerusalem being among the most popular.

For many soldiers alcohol was an important accompaniment to leisure. In East and West Africa this could usually be obtained from local people who brewed it legally or otherwise. Josiah Kariuke says that his mother brewed 'Nubian gin' which attracted men from miles around and earned money to pay for his education. 'During the early years of the war', he wrote,

> many soldiers would come out from Lanet and Nakuru to drink in our hut. There were Europeans, Africans, and coloured South Africans all together. They frequently became very drunk and began to abuse and fight each other. One coloured soldier was badly hurt and we hid him in the nearby forest where he spent three days unconscious. We soon had a gramophone and other luxuries from the money earned in this way.[112]

In some companies men brewed their own beer. Wartime Army canteens also sold bottled beer although, says Barber, in North Africa when supplies became short whites were reduced to one bottle a week while Africans were restricted to one every five weeks. Thoughtless commanders who failed to ensure regular supplies of beer and cigarettes for their men were likely to be confronted with unrest.[113] Some soldiers, for example devout Muslims and Christians, did not drink alcohol, but many men learned to enjoy commercially processed beer and carried that taste and a demand for the product into civilian life after the war. Attempts were made to control soldiers' drinking by putting towns 'out of bounds', banning spirits and policing the amount of alcohol brought into camps. However, if soldiers wished to drink they invariably found ways to do so despite the best efforts of officers, NCOs and the military police. In Italy in 1943 a report warned of African soldiers from the HCTs being exposed to the heady mix of cheap drink and readily available sex, 'temptations to which these men are subjected in Sicily and Italy are serious ... The people are large producers of potent wine ... [and] the women of Sicily and Italy display a deplorable lack of any sense of moral decency.'[114]

Armies concentrate human skills and provide both time and occasion for their development. A few musical and theatrical groups formed to entertain soldiers in wartime continued as commercial groups after the war. Most African battalions had bands, and wartime expansion brought talented musicians together to play popular music. In 1943–46 an African theatre existed within the RWAFF and put on concerts for troops in India. Bob Vans was the leader and with six other Ghanaians the groups played at camps and hospitals, performing in West African Pidgin English. Vans was influenced by African-American comedians and on demobilisation he formed with other Ghanaian ex-servicemen a group known as the Black Jokers.[115]

Life in the army, and particularly overseas, served as a startling educative process for large numbers of soldiers drawn from rural areas. Ships and aircraft, other modern machines, new places and peoples, offered them a view of an amazing world to which they rapidly adapted. To ride on a train for the first time, to feel the rolling and stomach-churning motion of a large ship at sea, and to fly in an aeroplane were memorable if slightly terrifying experiences. 'It was heart touching,' recalled Justice C. Banda from Malawi. 'For the first time we flew from Burma to India by planes. And from Bihar, India, to Bombay by electric train. At Bombay it was our last view of India. We left ... bound for East Africa on February 1946.'[116] For many West African soldiers bound for the Middle East or Asia the first foreign country they saw was South Africa as the troop transport

10 *East African troops seeing the sights of Colombo, c. 1943*

The British agreed to commit East and West African troops to the campaign in Asia in late 1942. Once the threats from Italy and the Vichy regime were removed, and following the United States landing in North Africa in November 1942, the way was clear to use African forces in India and Burma. Ceylon served as a staging post and training base for Africans due to be transferred to Burma. In India and Ceylon Africans encountered the wonders of large Asian cities. The official caption on this photograph reads: 'From a safe distance, Askaris admire the seemingly miraculous powers of an Eastern snake charmer.' The city is Colombo and the photographer is unknown, as is the actual response of the African onlookers. Of course, many British soldiers sent to south Asia during the war often viewed new and unusual sights with equal amazement.

(Source: Imperial War Museum IND 3008)

104

11 *Black South African troops on leave in Jerusalem, 1942*

The majority of black soldiers enlisted in the South African forces were non–combatants. The men in this photograph had been employed on rock cutting and tunnelling in the construction of the Syria–Palestine railway. Alongside them worked soldiers recruited from the High Commission Territories. Local leave to Jerusalem was arranged for 100 men at a time. Accompanied by officers, they stayed in a local leave camp for a week, and had conducted tours of the city. For many Africans of Christian background a visit to Jerusalem, the 'Holy City', was a highlight. A 'Sergeant Gladstone' took this photograph on 4 October 1942 – of soldiers on the roof of the Palace of Pontius Pilate looking across the Old City to the Mosque of Omar. These soldiers have become incidental tourists, seeing sights and hearing sounds far removed from anything they can have imagined in their home villages. Nevertheless, most men soon adapted to their new surroundings.

(Source: Imperial War Museum E 17666)

sailed into Cape Town or Durban; for East Africans the first foreign port was Aden, Port Suez or Bombay.

Foreign countries left memorable impressions on young minds. A soldier from Nyasaland said 'it was a privilege to join the army and to visit strange foreign lands. Because to almost all of us thought those countries were in heaven. It was an adventure in true sense and as tourists in disguise.'[117] For those African soldiers who were unused to large towns, the noise, bustle and particularly the poverty of Egyptian and Indian cities came as a great surprise. Jachoniah Dlamani thought 'Rome had too many people and was too big', although 'the people unlike the Arabs, treated us very kindly'.[118] Cpl Agba, one of several West African soldiers who wrote essays for their officer on their impressions of a visit to Calcutta, said 'the most important thing that I saw, its that the Begars are too much than [sic] the richest men in the town'.[119] L/C Israel Agwu, of the West African Army Service Corps, wrote of an outing to Calcutta that he had

> been to different townships and never atal [sic] been to a city, definetly [sic] this is my first of its kind ... In the Market, despite from different articles which were new to my sight, I thought I was in another world ... In general, Calcutta is thickly populated in so much that I think some people can miss their way home. Had we not been guarded by a good officer I am sure that we should have missed our way in the city ... In Calcutta there are so many tribes and different nations.[120]

Big cities came as less of a surprise to men from southern Africa with knowledge of migrant labour conditions and compounds. Encountering a variety of languages seemed to pose few problems for Africans, many of whom inhabited multilingual worlds. Bildad Kaggia, who had lived in Nairobi, said of his time stationed in Egypt that

> a striking feature ... was the widespread poverty and unemployment. The great number of people who lived on the streets and spent their days begging, stuck in my mind. At night they just spread their mats on pavements, or on the grass, to sleep. They would follow and not leave you until you gave them something.[121]

Foreign lands and different cultures provided unusual sights, sounds and experiences. Southern African troops in Italy were surprised to see German female prisoners-of-war. In Ceylon, said Justice Banda, 'the people ... were very clean, self-sufficient in food and very friendly towards strangers. Their civilization was far more advanced than ours.' When his battalion moved to India, he observed that

> although the people did not cooperate among the Hindus, Muslims and the untouchables, but they were all friendly towards African soldiers. Same as it was in [Ceylon] language was not difficult because some of the Indians and Africans spoke English. As we went further north to the Assam province, the people we found too were very friendly, tidy and healthy. Their women very similar to those at home in ... carrying loads on their heads just as good as Nyasaland women did ... We were also amazed to see our friends Indians using buffaloes for ploughing in their rice paddy gardens.[122]

Leave

African troops in the Mediterranean area and in Asia rarely received home leave – a cause of unrest. Local leave was limited; Barber relates that in North Africa 'during the first three years an African was lucky if he got as much as one week's leave a year'.[123] A report on Bechuana troops in Italy said that

> as much liberty as possible is given on the off duty days. Parties are taken on lorries to visit other Bechuana Companies in the vicinity and others are marched off to a neighbouring town where, at first, the focus of interest was the ancient Roman ruins.[124]

As far as possible the military authorities tried to regulate African contact with local people, partly to minimise conflict over women but also to prevent soldiers being exposed to alternative ideas about race relations. A South African Coloured veteran, Adam Jacobs, recalled that in Cairo military policemen of the SADF patrolled areas of the city popular with soldiers to ensure that black and white soldiers did not patronise the same establishments.[125] The leave camps in Beirut, Cairo and Jerusalem provided controlled environments, as did the YMCA clubs with their supply of carefully selected books and magazines and vernacular newspapers from home which were sometimes censored.

Visits to Jerusalem and the Biblical sites were very popular with Christian soldiers. A Nigerian soldier who visited Jerusalem wrote home that 'I have got my own share of privileges in making my pilgrimage to the Holy City' where he went 'for Easter Service at Christ Church on Mount Zion'.[126] Kaggia, with his mission-school background, was selected to attend a church leaders' course in Jerusalem. In his autobiography he described his strong sense of excitement at going to the 'Holy Land':

> I shall never recapture the feeling that I had that morning when I boarded the train heading for Jerusalem, the 'Holy City', the city of David, the city paved with gold. This vision of Jerusalem was in my mind as the train moved swiftly towards the city. To me there was little difference between the Jerusalem in Palestine and the Golden Jerusalem in heaven. The heavenly Jerusalem was always more real to me than the Jerusalem that existed in Palestine. I felt I knew the heavenly city.[127]

At the rest camp Kaggia and other literate soldiers were each given a copy of a booklet entitled *Walks Around Jerusalem*, specially written for African troops and with a foreword by Lt-Gen Sir Wilfred Lindsell stating: 'This book is a gift to you from the Middle East Forces so that you may learn about all the wonderful places which you will see, and so that you may remember them.' During his time at the rest camp, Kaggia toured the city, attended lectures on 'the holy places and their history' and went on 'excursions in and around Jerusalem, Bethlehem, Jericho and in TransJordan ... and these places made a deep impression on me'.[128] African soldiers in Italy seemed to have mixed fairly freely with local people, to the extent, says Modise Thebe, that 'Italian women willingly invited [African] men into their beds in exchange for money and gifts'.[129] Tswana troops leaving Naples were cheered by the crowds on the quayside, and when Jachoniah

Dlamani had ten days' leave he 'visited the Vatican and was blessed by the Pope'. He told us: "I thank you for not bombing Rome because it took time to build and it is a place for religion." I was very impressed by the Pope.'[130] In Italy African soldiers encountered people who despite years of fascism seemed untainted by racially rigid views. Soldiers from the HCTs, one officer reported, were in camps relatively near to towns where they 'have met a very different European who is ready to treat them as equals and have little colour consciousness'.[131]

In Ceylon some East African troops received home leave but soldiers' contentment had to be balanced against shipping space. For some Africans in India, according to Justice Banda, there were organised visits to towns. 'The army used to arrange to take us to lunar parks, movies, magicians, and to the Indian halls to see Indian culture and dances.' It was not always supervised and 'while off duty we had the pleasure to visit Indian towns too. There we had time to move around. Instead by taxis, it was on elephant back, something which is unknown in Africa up to now. It was jolly good indeed.'[132] L/C J. B. F. Hocquarto, from the Gold Coast, described the journey by train into Calcutta, the high buildings of the city, going up in a lift, a visit to the zoo and a film show. At the end of the day, after a meal 'twas now dark and what to do was to excercise [sic] the whole limbs by strolling to the station to catch the sunset train going to where my temporary staying was'. His companion, Israel Agwu, commented on the zoological gardens: 'It is no exageration [sic] if I say that a Rhinoceros can last the whole of SGTC for a fortnight meal.'[133] India contained much to see with 'tamed poisonous snakes and monkeys [that] dance to the tune of flutes played by Indian owners. Quite amazing,' recalled Justice Banda, looking back nearly 50 years. He also remembered 'the pleasure of seeing Mount Everest from a far distance, the holy river Ganges where Hindus sacrifice, and Brahmaputra – the river we sailed on our way to Burma when we landed at Bay of Bengal from Ceylon'.[134] However, for other soldiers their recollection was of the military police arresting 'you if they find you wandering about, [and] put you in prison'.[135]

Sexual relations

Sex and soldiers are almost inseparable. The all-male military institution, long absence from wives and girlfriends and confinement to encampments all encouraged a climate of sexual hunger and hope. Predictably, accounts of homosexual relations are rare; perpetration of a homosexual act was a serious offence under military law. Military camps have always served as a magnet for prostitutes and African encampments were no exception. 'Generally, the army enjoys the goodwill of women anywhere,' said Pius Osakwe of the RWAFF, and 'we did not experience colour prejudice in love affairs.'[136] According to Ngaraito Makiti's son, 'the Burma women love the Africans. He told me about having some affairs with them'.[137] A former corporal who had seen action in Burma also said that

a soldier in every society gets the cream of almost everything. Likewise for women, the girls we met could not turn down our love proposals because every time we had money which were often spent on them. In most towns were given food by our concubines but not openly.[138]

Wherever there were soldiers with money, women were to be found. 'The best moments came during off-duty period,' said Samson Muliango. 'We normally left the camps and go into town to enjoy ourselves especially in bars which were crowded with Somali girls who always wanted a soldier.'[139]

Official policy tried to discourage casual sexual liaisons by soldiers. The concern was threefold: to keep soldiers free of venereal disease; to avoid serious conflicts with local people; and to prevent Africans mixing on equal terms or having sexual relations with women who were either light-skinned or white. This last, a serious breach of the colour bar, was very important to whites from settler colonies and South Africa. Chama Mutemi Kadansa, who served with the Northern Rhodesian forces, recalls that:

> Twice a week we used to be taken to town halls to be entertained by dancing girls known as *Saimanga*. Close contact with women was strictly forbidden in order to stop soldiers from getting venereal disease which would eventually weaken them. If a soldier dared to sleep with a woman, he would be severely reprimanded. To this effect, daily medical check-ups were being taken by medical Dressers.[140]

Soldiers were told futile and silly scare stories by white officers, such as: 'We were to stay away from the local women [in North Africa] as we were told that the Germans had poisoned the women, which would result in your penis falling off if you engaged in sexual intercourse with them.'[141] To prevent soldiers going to local 'unclean' brothels, official army brothels were created. Jacobs, who served with the SDF, jokingly said that the brothel that he set up in Massawa, Eritrea, 'was *perhaps* his most valuable contribution to the war effort. At least the women were regularly inspected.'[142] Faced with 'astronomical' figures for VD in his KAR battalion in Abyssinia, Darrell Bates 'started a brothel. All the girls were, to put it mildly, volunteers, and there was no difficulty at all in finding recruits. I used to inspect it on Thursdays, and the M.O. went there on Tuesdays and Fridays. It was run on the best public-school-lines.' Although the battalion VD rates fell from 35 per cent to eight per cent, the authorities in Nairobi ordered the brothel closed.[143]

Brothels were opened in India for African troops although one commanding officer, a devout Roman Catholic, had some of them closed down. In India, where occasional serious clashes with civilians occurred over women, it was reported that women were 'a problem without a solution'. The Indian authorities, already facing civil unrest, were extremely anxious to minimise further disorder involving African soldiers. Brothels provided a solution but, as one officer said, he could make no suggestion 'acceptable in the eyes of the Government of India or the Church'.[144] Rivalry over women often led to violent fights and deep resentment between soldiers from different units or ethnic groups. In Nairobi in 1941–42 men of the Gold Coast Regiment, known locally as 'Golgos', gained a fearsome reputation for violence off the battlefield. From their camp at Kabete in western Nairobi they fought local men and other soldiers, even white soldiers, over rights to prostitutes in Pumwani. Some soldiers kept a live-in woman, known as *malaya*, as cook and sexual companion.[145] Similar clashes took place close to all large army encampments and involved soldiers in search of sexual pleasures in towns. Samson Muliango recorded an incident in a small Somali town near to the border with Ethiopia:

> Two of my drivers while off duty left the camp into town to drink and look for women. After some hours they came into the camp running and crying towards me. Both men fell in front of me. One hard [*sic*] a stab wound on the chest the other had all his manwood [*sic*] cut off. The fight was between soldiers and civilians in the town.[146]

Competition for women could turn into racial violence with white troops. Joe Culverwell, a Coloured volunteer with the Southern Rhodesian forces, said that in North Africa

> we used to fight with the South Africans at least three or four times a week. Because this was the first time – particularly in Egypt – that we mixed up with white girls. You know, they sent out millions of WAACS from England, and the South Africans didn't like it. So we used to have at least, at least three times a week, fights with them. And of course the Rhodesians never approved of it either.[147]

However, Culverwell further states that unit loyalty would override race. Because he was then attached to the Argyll and Sutherland Highlanders, even wearing a kilt, men from that regiment would join with black soldiers to fight the white South Africans.

Sexual relations across the colour line challenged racial concepts regarding the sanctity of white womanhood and the notions of white superiority upon which colonial rule was based. This posed a potential threat to colonial order, and certainly to white supremacy in South Africa, as officers with SADF and High Commission troops never tired of pointing out. In Europe, stated an official report,

> mixing with the white population on almost equal footing has made an impression on the mind of the African – and if care is not taken, might have unfortunate repercussions not so much in his homeland, but in the neighbouring European states where 70% of these *men find* employment.[148]

The South African military authorities in particular tried to keep their non-European troops away from any women that were not black-skinned. This was difficult almost anywhere and impossible in North Africa and Italy during wartime. The concern was deep – for example, with a UDF hospital orderly in North Africa who tried to smuggle in photographs of Africans who had associated with 'strong white girls here',[149] or the censor in Nairobi who retained the letter from a Ganda soldier serving in Ceylon who wrote that 'We are having enjoyment with white ladies. We pay 7½ rupees to have a go with them.'[150] On one occasion West African troops *en route* to the Mediterranean were forbidden by their officers to disembark at Rabat because they might associate with prostitutes in the town, a ruling which led to a short-lived mutiny.

Inevitably some love affairs between African soldiers and women they met while on overseas service endured. Ras Makonnen mentions a Gold Coast soldier who married an Ethiopian woman and settled down with her in Kenya, while Hama Kim said that some West Africans who were stationed in India for some time married Indian girls and brought them back to Nigeria: 'Even when I was in Sokoto, one was there with his wife. They have so many children already. He was Yoruba, of course.'[151] Although Italian women were reported to be fearful of African troops, Paul Gobine, who served with the Seychelles Pioneers in Italy, said many years later that 'my first child was born in Italy'.[152] Love affairs between Africans and white women – and there were certain opportunities, given the large number of Women's Royal Army Corps personnel serving in the Mediterranean theatre – were effectively prohibited, so that those that did occur took place in secrecy. Marshall Kebby recounts an affair between a white woman officer and her Nigerian batman while they were serving in a military hospital in India. 'She was a nurse … it appears that this boy was in love with this woman. He was in love with his mistress. So an officer happened to know this, and then he revealed it to his co-officers and they set a sort of trap.' The soldier was caught, says Kebby, the woman disavowed him, and he was sentenced to three years in prison. 'Why should a man be jailed for having something to do with a white woman – after all the white men here [in Nigeria] were having lots of things to do with our own girls here? Why?'[153]

Religion

In peacetime most soldiers in the small colonial armies were either Muslims or believed in indigenous religious ideas and practices. Muslim clerics, *mallams* or imams, had long been associated with the Nigerian and Gold Coast regiments where they acted as teachers, advisors and counsellors. In 1942 selected imams were appointed to the RWAFF, one per brigade with the rank of warrant officer, specifically to help discipline young men from Muslim areas. Indigenous beliefs, often held syncretically alongside Islamic or Christian ideas, had long played a powerful part in soldiers' lives.[154] In several of the letters addressed to Tshekedi Khama, BaTswana soldiers expressed their fear of supernatural powers that could affect their health or even life. For example, N. Morekwe feared 'being killed by my wife together with her new boyfriend'.[155] Certain soldiers were recognised, even by European officers, for their influence with supernatural power, such as the '1st Battalion JUJU-Man, Pioneer W. A. Sowar of Teshie' of the Gold Coast Regiment.[156] Indigenous religious ideas that potions, charms or talismans would protect a man from death in battle were widespread in many parts of Africa. The 'Maji Maji' rising against the Germans in East Africa in 1905–7 took its name from the medicine – the *maji* ('water') that people took to ward off the white man's bullets. Large numbers of African soldiers carried talismans (as did many Europeans). John Mandambwe recalled that before going into battle in North Africa with a Chinyanja-speaking friend he swallowed an *nzama* bean and part of its root, assured by an older soldier that although 'bullets could come to us, hitting us anywhere, they could not penetrate us anymore'.[157]

Wartime expansion and the need to recruit literate, mission-educated men greatly increased the number of Christians in the army. According to Gen Sir William Platt, in 1939 the RWAFF was composed of 70 per cent Muslims, 25 per cent 'pagans' and only two per cent Christians; by 1945 Muslims constituted one-third of the force, pagans 20 per cent, and Christians 47 per cent.[158] Platt does not provide any source for his figures although other individuals, using evidence that could have come from paybooks which indicated religion, made estimates for specific companies. Thus Barber says that in 8999 Pioneer Company from Uganda, 80 per cent of the men were Christians and only 10 per cent Muslim, while a chaplain with the Bechuanaland troops calculated that the Bakwana company, 'unlike all other companies', was 'nearly all "heathen" or "pagan"'.[159] In the tented encampments of North Africa and the Middle East, Christian groups flourished. Bildad Kaggia ran a Bible class, and the BaTswana troops were reported as having 'brought their Christianity with them. Each company has its own church, with a leader, a band of communicant members and a larger number of catechumens. They engage in Bible teaching, collect money for church work at home'. The 12 companies numbered nearly 4,200 men of whom more than 3,400 were Protestant Christians.[160] Derek Peterson argues that the large number of Christians enlisted in the KAR 'turned the army into an extended catechuminate'.[161] Silvanus Wami, a Kukwa from Koboko who was of the *bolokele* ('the revived'), enlisted in the wartime KAR; later he became chaplain to the Uganda Army and succeeded Janani Luwum as Archbishop of Uganda.[162] Certainly the number of soldiers baptised increased rapidly in the war years, although there is little evidence to indicate what impact, if any, individual Christian soldiers had on their fellows.

African padres were appointed to the KAR and RWAFF from 1940 onwards. The Rev. Musa Miwanuha from Tanganyika, who had served with the KAR during the First World War, was ordained and served as a padre with the Pioneer Corps in North Africa. There were four other clergymen and two catechists also serving in North Africa.[163] The first European padre with the RWAFF was appointed in mid-1941, largely at the instigation of Gen Giffard; there had been a strong resistance to such appointments for fear that it would antagonise Muslims within the force. By 1942 six African clergy had been appointed to the RWAFF, with the rank of lieutenant.[164] Many of the men recruited from Bechuanaland had nominal links with the London Missionary Society, and the LMS school at Tiger Kloof in South Africa provided several graduates to serve as chaplains. Gabantlwe Modukanele, a veteran of the First World War, had trained as an evangelist at Morija in Basutoland and at the Tiger Kloof Bible school; he and Odirile Modukanele were ordained and sent to Egypt, where they were joined in 1942 by Andrew Kagasa. All three men proved active and diligent pastors to African troops.[165] For some African Christians the height of their wartime experience was to visit Palestine and be baptised in the waters of the Jordan.[166]

Education & literacy

Military expansion in wartime also meant a great increase in the number of literate men serving in the African Colonial Forces. For example, by late 1942 there were estimated to be 10,000 literate men serving in the Gold Coast Regiment and 20,000 with the Nigerian Regiment, mainly employed in the signals, service or engineer corps.[167] Army training and trade schools were established in both West and East Africa with the purpose of upgrading artisans, clerks and mechanics and equipping them with specific skills for military roles. In order to attract students from schools, the military authorities in East Africa set up basic educational schemes at recruiting depots. The largest was at Maseno in western Kenya, first established in late 1942, which provided a four-month programme to train 450 boys aged 16–17 years for the signal and medical corps. The curriculum consisted of simple mathematics and basic English. The scheme proved popular with students and with their parents, who appreciated the provision of free education. In West Africa the military created a similar system of trade schools. However, in neither East nor West Africa did the Army have enough English teachers and thus Africans had to be trained by the Army for that role. Men who graduated as teachers or instructors were given the rank of sergeant. In the KAR 40 per cent of Kenyan instructors were Gikuyu – from an ethnic group officially regarded as non-martial. African instructors had a considerable influence on African troops; besides teaching practical skills that enabled soldiers to manage military life, they also served as role models for younger men and purveyors of new political ideas, while also acting as a brake on possible insubordination.

Planning for educational corps for African troops began in late 1941. The South Africans approved the setting up of an Army Education Service in February.[168] Gen Platt, GOC East African Command, believed that an educational system that explained the war aims of the Allies to African soldiers would be good for morale and reduce discontent. The purpose of wartime education was military and utilitarian, and it was largely free of civilian control.[169] Such Army educational provision as existed in the war theatres of the Middle East and Asia was very closely associated with concern for the welfare and morale of soldiers. Literacy and other classes, it was argued, would help to keep soldiers away from bars and brothels. In mid-1943 it was reported from the Middle East 'that nothing is being done at present regarding educational training. There are some potential teachers in the ranks but at present there are no books and there is no policy. The men are being worked too hard that there is no time for education.'[170] A start was made on supplying African soldiers with selected books, newspapers and magazines, and with free army newspapers. For example, *Habari Zetu* was published by East African Command for soldiers in Abyssinia, and the weekly *Heshima* for the 11th (EA) Division in Ceylon; *Jambo* and *Askari* circulated in East Africa. The *RWAFF News* was produced in both Bombay and Cairo. These newspapers, as Katrin Bromber argues, formed part of a wider propaganda scheme 'to secure the individual and collective discipline of the *askaris*'.[171] Army newspapers were primarily directed at literate soldiers, although there were many occasions when literate men would read the news to their nonliterate comrades. Army newspapers and the official military education programme had a propaganda purpose in helping soldiers to develop new ways of thinking, although not *what* and *how* they thought. Broadened horizons and exposure to new ideas risked fostering in soldiers a critical questioning of the colonial racial order. Official propaganda took various forms: radio broadcasts in vernacular languages, visits by chiefs to the Middle East and to Asia, the screening of carefully selected films, and encouragement to soldiers to write home. Army service provided many Africans with new educational opportunities; Africans became 'voracious readers' and some men took correspondence courses with the Pelman Institute in Bombay.

Army education services for African troops only got into their stride in the latter years of the war.[172] Nevertheless, by 1945 many African soldiers had learned to read and write in vernacular languages as well as English, although there were instances of older soldiers opposing formal education because they thought it would challenge traditional ideas of hierarchy and indigenous authority systems. Gerald Hanley observed that 85 per cent of the men in his artillery battery in Burma had learned to read and write in the vernacular within six months.[173] A large part of the education of soldiers was due to self-effort, through reading, correspondence courses and contacts with other soldiers. According to an anonymous 'Military Observer', in 1942–45 non-literacy among African troops serving in the Middle East had been reduced from 85 per cent to 30 per cent.[174] As D. A. Thandabantu of the NEAC wrote: 'I am very thankful to the Lord Jehovah that I am now able to write Sesotho language which I could not do the time I left my Shangaan place'.[175] Some military officers viewed army education as a destabilising influence. Noticing growing unrest in the 11th (EA) Division during training in Ceylon in 1943, a senior officer reported that African soldiers 'remain children at heart and are finding it difficult to digest their newly acquired knowledge', and that 'many of them … have rather lost their heads and are inclined to be unduly touchy and take an exaggerated view of their newly acquired dignity'.[176]

Censorship of soldiers' letters home was standard practice, a means for the authorities to gain an insight into the fears and ambitions, doubts and political attitudes of Africans. Soldiers' reading material was also censored, but not with the same purpose or rigour. Fairly strenuous measures were taken to prevent African soldiers looking at 'pin-up' pictures of white women in magazines and also seeing films and live shows in which scantily-clad white women appeared. *Heshima* contained pictures of African pin-ups, which was acceptable. African welfare clubs and YMCA centres in towns, such as those in Jerusalem, were supplied with a range of vernacular-language newspapers, books and magazines and also games such as draughts. In Nairobi Africans soldiers were not allowed to enter private cinemas. When questions were asked in the House of Commons about restrictions being placed on the films that African soldiers could watch, the Colonial Secretary replied that the Film Censorship Board passed certain films for exhibition to non-Africans only in accordance with the film censorship rules of 1930.[177] Black troops in the South African Defence Force stationed in North Africa were not allowed to attend a UDF concert which included white women. In addition the South African military authorities, intent on maintaining the racial policies of the Union, exercised firm social control over non-European troops by placing a ban on all alcohol other than that provided with official rations, and firm restrictions on free movement outside camps. Africans had to be protected, one official argued, from situations where they might be 'subjected to insistent temptations by an impecunious people to whom the presence of our simple-minded and well-meaning Natives are a God-send'.[178] Of course, it was impossible for such restrictions to be constantly maintained, and many black soldiers in North Africa, the Middle East and in Italy went to bars, mixed with white women and questioned the rules guarding racial contact at home.

Conclusion

Army life exposed African soldiers to a wide range of new experiences. Overseas service in particular, which for some men lasted for several years, introduced soldiers to new peoples and cultures and a range of new ideas about food, dress, culture and behaviour. The army provided an opportunity and the time for men to observe and sometimes to absorb parts of this experience. A vital question is the extent to which this experience of army service change the way soldiers thought, and whether those new ideas and experiences influenced their attitudes and actions when they returned home. The evidence is thin. Clearly such experiences must have had some influence – providing a wider idea of the world, of how other people lived, and different mental maps from those they may once have held in a rural African village. However, a bit of extra knowledge of the world does not mean that attitudes were changed to any great extent. Military life and provision were after all geared to military service. The world outside was very different and a living still had to be earned, crops grown, children cared for, relations maintained. Undoubtedly many African soldiers, perhaps most, slipped back into the rural world from which they had come. They had returned from the war with tales to tell but with relatively little to show as tangible evidence of their years of military service.

Notes

1. An anonymous East African soldier recorded by Andrew B. Doig, 'The Christian church and demobilization in Africa', *International Review of Missions*, 35 (1946), p. 182.
2. ICS. Crowder papers. Box 17. Sgt Ontwetse M. Molefi, 1966 Coy Bechuana APC, to Tshekei Khama, 31 January 1945.
3. A good description, from Nyasaland, is in Mario Kolko, *Can You Tell me Why I Went to War? A Story of a Young King's African Rifle, Reverend John E. A. Mandambwe* (Zomba, 2008), pp. 19–30.
4. R. T. Kerslake, *Time and the Hour: Nigeria, East Africa and the Second World War* (London, 1997), p. 80.
5. Randal Sadleir, *Tanzania: Journey to Republic* (London, 1999), p. 23.
6. BBC Africa Service. Marshall Kebby, interviewed by Elizabeth Obadina, Lagos, Nigeria, 1989.
7. In the 1920s–30s nutrient deficiency was slowly recognised as a barrier to development; see Michael Worboys, 'The discovery of colonial malnutrition between the wars', in David Arnold, ed., *Imperial Medicine and Indigenous Societies* (Manchester 1988), pp. 208–25. On diet and its inseparability from culture, see Audrey Richards, *Land, Labour and Diet in Northern Rhodesia: An Economic Study of the Bemba Tribe* (Oxford, 1939), and the issue of *Africa*, 9, 2 (1936), on 'Problems of African native diet'.
8. TNA, CO323/1787/4, Eden to Lloyd, 3 July 1940, encl. WO 'Note on the raising of African troops', July 1940.
9. Meshack Owino, '"For your tomorrow, we gave our today": A history of Kenya soldiers in the Second World War', PhD thesis, Rice University, 2004, p. 425.
10. TNA, WO172/6590, War Diaries, HQ West African Division, 81st Division, G Branch, secret, May–Dec. 1944, 81st Div. Ops. Instruction 31, secret, by Maj-Gen C. G. Woolner, 19 May 1944.
11. TNA, WO173/996, War Diaries, West Africa, GS GHQ, secret, 1944.
12. TNA, CO820/55/34542A. Report by General Burrows on tour of the Gold Coast, top secret, 1 March 1945. Maj-Gen Hugh Stockwell, who commanded the 82nd West African Division in Burma, said of his troops that 'there are very many who are very "bush" and who in consequence take a long time to reach the required standard. The training takes far longer with Africans than other soldiers and has continuously to be repeated to ensure it is not forgotten.' Liddell Hart Military Archives, King's College London, Stockwell 5/3, 'The 82 West African Division in battle'.

[13] See further David Killingray, 'Gender issues and African colonial armies', in David Killingray and David Omissi, eds, *Guardians of Empire* (Manchester, 1999), pp. 221–48.

[14] Bildad Kaggia, *Roots of Freedom, 1921–1963: The Autobiography of Bildad Kaggia* (Nairobi, 1975), pp. 24–25. See also Kolk, *Can You Tell me Why I Went to War?*, p. 35.

[15] Cf. Keletso E. Atkins, *The Moon is Dead! Give us our Money! The cultural origins of an African Work Ethic, Natal, South Africa 1843–1900* (London, 1993), ch. 4.

[16] Kevin Greenbank. '"You chaps mustn't worry when you come back": Cape Town soldiers and aspects of experience of war and demobilisation 1939–1953', MA thesis, University of Cape Town, 1995, interview: 'J. H.', p. 17.

[17] David Killingray, 'Race and rank in the British Army in the twentieth century', *Ethnic and Racial Studies*, 10, 3 (1987), pp. 278–90; this article provides the essentials but now requires revision.

[18] Letter to David Killingray, January 1981.

[19] Wendell P. Holbrook, 'War and tradition in the Gold Coast, 1939–1945', unpublished paper, p. 24.

[20] See John Iliffe, *East African Doctors* (Cambridge, 1998), p. 86.

[21] Timothy H. Parsons, *The African Rank-and-File: Social Implications of Colonial Military Service in the King's African Rifles, 1902–1964* (Oxford, 1999), pp. 105–10. Michael Kawalya Kagwa, son of Sir Apollo Kagwa, was a lieutenant in Ethiopia, recalled by the Governor of Uganda in 1945 to take the post of *katikiro* (chief adviser) in Buganda; see David Apter, *The Political Kingdom in Uganda: A Study of Bureaucratic Nationalism* (Princeton NJ, 1961; new edn, 1967), pp. 230–31.

[22] Ashley Jackson, 'African soldiers and Imperial authorities: Tensions and unrest during the service of High Commission Territories soldiers in the British Army, 1941–46', *Journal of Southern African Studies*, 25, 4 (1999), p. 652.

[23] TNA, DO35/1435/Y1069/19, 'Grant of commissions in His Majesty's Forces to Natives of HCT.' Memorandum. See further Jackson, 'African soldiers and Imperial authorities', pp. 651–53.

[24] TNA, CO820/43/34396, secret; WO 216/55, Giffard to Lt-Gen Sir Robert Haning, secret and personal, 3 January 1941.

[25] Timothy J. Lovering, 'Military service, nationalism and race: The experience of Malawians in the Second World War', in R. Ahuja, *et al.*, eds, *The World in World Wars: Experience, Perception and Perspectives from the South* (Leiden, forthcoming).

[26] *West Africa*, 11 November 1944, p. 1100.

[27] Darrell Bates, *A Fly-Switch from the Sudan* (London, 1961), p. 115.

[28] Lovering, 'Military service, nationalism and race', ms. copy sent to author.

[29] K. D. D. Henderson, *The Making of the Modern Sudan: Life and Letters of Sir Douglas Newbold* (London, 1953), p. 257.

[30] Roger Lambo, 'Achtung! The Black Prince: West Africans in the Royal Air Force, 1939–46', in David Killingray, ed., *Africans in Britain* (London, 1994), pp. 145–63.

[31] John Nunneley, *Tales from the KAR* (London, 1998), pp. 65–67 and 170–71.

[32] This is discussed at length in David Killingray, '"The rod of empire": The debate over corporal punishment in the British African Colonial Forces, 1888–1946', *Journal of African History*, 35, 2 (1994), pp. 201–16.

[33] House of Lords Record Office, Sorenson Papers, SOR/65/A; E. Y. Boateng to Sorenson, 6 April 1944.

[34] L. W. F. Grundlingh, 'The participation of South African Blacks in the Second World War', unpublished DLitt thesis, Rand Afrikaans University, Pretoria, 1986, p. 280.

[35] B. L. Jacobs, 'Going Backwards', ts. Memoirs, p. 73, ms. in private hands.

[36] V. R. McMahon, 'The military police in West Africa', *The Red Cap: Journal of the Corps of Military Police*, (BAOR), 1, 7 (1946), pp. 12–13.

[37] David Killingray, 'The colonial army in the Gold Coast: Official policy and local response, 1890–1947', PhD London, 1982, p. 247.

[38] BBC African Service. Marshall Kebby, interviewed by Elizabeth Obadina, Lagos, Nigeria, 1989.

[39] Mungai Mutonya and Timothy H. Parsons, 'KiKAR: A Swahili variety in Kenya's colonial army', *Journal of African Languages and Linguistics*, 25 (2004), pp. 111–25.

[40] 'Bimbashi Arabic is to classical Arabic what pigeon [*sic*] English is to the Queen's English, limited in scope, eloquent in initiative, colourful, ungrammatical, simple, wonderfully understandable and magnificently effective. The Arabic as spoken by the non-Arab companies [such as] the Equatorial Corps was delightfully bimbashic.' John Orlebar, ed., *Tales of the Sudan Defence Force* (privately printed, 1981), p. 55.

[41] An undated wartime information sheet for British soldiers on *The African in the Nigerian Regt* stated: 'If you can learn to speak an African language you will find that your labours have been well rewarded in increasing his [the African soldier's] confidence and respect towards you.' Copy in author's possession.

[42] BBC African Service. Justice C. Banda from Malawi, who served with the 21st East African Brigade in Ceylon, India and Burma, recorded Blantyre, Malawi, 1989.

[43] John Morley, *Colonial Postscript: Diary of a District Officer 1935–56* (London, 1992), p. 108.

[44] Personal information: Robin Hallett (1926 –2003), historian of Africa who taught in Nigeria 1956–59.

[45] 'There was a soldier: The life of Hama Kim MM', compiled and edited by Ronald W. Graham, *Africana Marburgensia*, 10 (1985), p. 17.

[46] F. A. S. Clarke, 'Recollections: 1940–41', *West African Review* (September 1950), pp. 1057–60.

[47] Interview: David Killingray with Agolley Kusasi, formerly of the Gold Coast Regiment, Accra, 5 May 1979.

[48] Joel Bolnick, '*Sefela sa Letsamayanaha*: The wartime experiences of Potlako Kitchener Leballo', Wits History Workshop, 6–10 February 1990. See also D. H. Barber, *Africans in Khaki* (London, 1948), p. 95; Barber, an officer with the East African Pioneers in North Africa, mentions that food was often of poor quality and that there were 'tribal' difficulties over foodstuffs.

[49] TNA, CO820/55/34542A, 'Notes on colonial and local troops', conference, February 1945.

[50] Peter Kilby, *African Enterprise: The Nigerian Bread Industry* (Stanford CA, 1965), p. 9.

[51] Moses Danquah, 'African soldiers and what they will want in their post-war life', *West African Review* (December 1945), p. 36.

[52] David Killingray and James Matthews, 'Beasts of burden: British West African carriers in the First World War', *Canadian Journal of African Studies* 13, 1–2 (1979), pp. 17–19.

[53] T. Farnworth Anderson, 'The diet of the African soldier', *East African Medical Journal*, 20, 7 (1943), pp. 207–13.

[54] Orlebar, *Tales of the Sudan Defence Force*, p. 74.

[55] TNA, WO203/813, 'Rations: Asia 1944'. This compares starkly with the mere 1,000 calories given to carriers in Tanganyika in 1917–18: see TNA, CO445/44/24800, Lugard to Long, 8 April 1918.

[56] TNA, CO820/32/34220. Report on conference at Colonial Office, to Macdonald, secret, 11 June 1938; IWM, London, PP/MCR/68, Brigadier Ian Bruce, 'They put us in boots' (ts); Morley, *Colonial Postscript*, pp. 97–8, describes paying allowances in the 'Igala backwoods' of Nigeria in 1941.

[57] David Shirreff, *Bare Feet and Bandoliers: Wingate, Sandford, and the Patriots and the Part they Played in the Liberation of Ethiopia* (London, 1995), p. 21.

[58] TNA, CO968/142/14516/41A, C. T. Edwards to J. Goepel, 2 July 1945.

[59] TNA, CO 98/81, Gold Coast, Post Office Report, 1946–47.

[60] Morley, *Colonial Postscript*, p. 104, for an account of Nigerian soldiers learning to put on socks and boots in 1940.

[61] 61 NAG, Accra, BF1765, vol. 1. Acting Chief Commissioner Ashanti to Colonial Secretary, 14 May 1943. In June 1943, a total of 23,047 allotments were being paid in the Gold Coast, 25,597 in December 1943. By February 1945 the figure was 37,500. Travelling paymasters with vans were introduced in December 1943 and visited 187 centres to distribute payments throughout the colony. See also TNA, CO 98/87, Burns to Legislative Council, 13 March 1944; RHL, Oxford, Mss Afr. s. 1495; A. A. Tournay, 'Payments to dependants of Gold Coast soldiers overseas, 1944–45'; and 'How the soldier's wife gets paid', *The Empire at War*, 26 September 1945.

[62] RHL, Oxford, Mss Afr. s. 1207, H. W. Amherst, District Diary, Lawra, 29 December 1942.

[63] NAG, Accra, BF4695, 'Demobilization and Resettlement Committee (WAWC 221), 1945'; and TNA. WO 172/6590. War Diary, HQ West Africa, 81st Division, 'G' Branch, secret, May–December 1945.

[64] Gerald Plange, editor, *Daily Echo* (Accra), to Campbell (public relations officer in Department of Information) from Burma, 28 June 1945; NAG, Accra, BF5602, 'Complaints: GCR soldiers in Asia, 1945'.

[65] ICS, Crowder papers, Box 17, Pte Manaheng Lesotho, MEF, to Tshekedi Khama, 4 February 1944.

[66] ICS, Crowder papers, Box 17, Pte Rahakwena, 1985 Bechuana Company A, Pioneer Corps, Middle East, to Tshekedi Khama, 20 February 1945.

[67] See Isola Olomola, 'The history of Nigeria's military barracks', *Nigeria Magazine*, pp. (1980), pp. 112–19.

[68] For an example from the Gold Coast see 'Life at Labadi Camp', *Gold Coast Independent*, 14 October 1939, p. 966.

[69] Mark Harrison, *Medicine and Victory: British Military Medicine in the Second World War* (Oxford, 2004), covers the major campaigns but has little to say on the African forces.

[70] TNA, WO106/4649, 'West African troops: Asian malaria', meeting at War Office, 26 January 1943.

[71] Megan Vaughan, *Curing Their Ills: Colonial Power and African Illness* (Cambridge, 1991), pp. 144–49; also 'Syphilis in colonial east and central Africa: The social construction of an epidemic', in Terence Ranger and Paul Slack, eds, *Epidemics and Ideas: Essays in the Historical Perceptions of Pestilence* (Cambridge, 1992), pp. 290–98.

[72] Sadleir, *Tanzania*, p. 29.

[73] Michael Blundell, *A Love Affair in the Sun: A Memoir of Seventy Years in Kenya* (Nairobi, 1994), p. 75.

[74] Luise White, *The Comforts of Home: Prostitution in Colonial Nairobi* (Chicago, 1990); Timothy Parsons, *The African Rank-and-File: Social Implications of Colonial Military Service in the King's African Rifles, 1902–1964* (Oxford, 1999), pp. 160–66.

[75] F. A. E. Crew, *Medical History of the Second World War: Army Medical Services*, 5 vols (London, 1953–66); also V. Z. Cope, *Medical History of the Second World War: Medicine and Pathology* (London, 1952).

[76] ICS, Crowder papers, Box 17, letter to Tshekedi Khama written on behalf of Cpl M. Thebe, 20 June 1944.

[77] A. J. Hlope to Director Non-European Army Services, undated, quoted by Grundlingh, 'Participation of South African Blacks', p. 239.

[78] TNA, CO820/55/34458C, 'Welfare African troops in Far East', 1943–44, secret. See also D. H. Barber, *Africans in Khaki* (London, 1948), pp. 45 and 84. Welfare initiatives among East African troops were inspired by a series of strikes and mutinies in AAPC companies.

[79] TNA, CO820/55/34542A, 'Duke of Devonshire's visit to West African troops, Far East', February–March 1945. See also TNA, WO172/9561, War Diaries 82nd WA Division, Conference 17–18 May 1945, 'Welfare requirements'.

[80] Barber, *Africans in Khaki*, p. 51.

[81] Shepperson, 'The obsequies', p. 56.

[82] Sadleir, *Tanzania*, p. 23.

[83] An example of a model letter, from a Meru wife to her husband away at the war, is in a Meru-language reading primer written by the Methodist missionary E. Mary Holding, *Kamincuria Metho* ('The Little One That Opens Eyes') (East African Literature Bureau, Nairobi, 1951), mentioned by Lynn M. Thomas, 'Schoolgirl pregnancies, letter-writing and "Modern" persons in late colonial East Africa', in Karen Barber, ed., *Africa's Hidden Histories: Everyday Literacy and Making the Self* (Bloomington IN, 2006), p. 204, fn 12.

[84] NAG, Accra, BF692 SF11, five bulky files containing *c.* 600 letters from soldiers in Asia appealing for postwar employment.

[85] ICS, Crowder papers, Box 17, Pte Rahakwena, Pioneer Coy, Middle East, to Tshekedi Khama, 20 February 1945.

[86] *Ibid.*, Private Osehile Keritetse to Tshekedi Khama, 27 July 1945.

[87] *Ibid.*, letter to Thsekedi Khama, 19 May 1944.

[88] *Ibid.*, letter to Tshekedi Khama, 1 January 1945.

[89] *Ibid.*, Sgt S. Motswaio, African Pioneer Corps, to Tshekedi Khama, 23 September 1944.

[90] *Ibid.*, Letter from Tshekedi Khama, 8 March 1943.

[91] Asantehene's Appam Court D, Record Book 31, 17 May 1946, p. 552. I owe this reference to Dr Jean Marie Allman. See also J. N. Matson, *A Digest of the Minutes of the Ashanti Confederacy Council 1935–1949* (Cape Coast, nd, *c.* 1951).

[92] ICS, Crowder papers, Box 17, N. Morekwe to Tshekedi Khama, undated letter; Tebalo Kwafiela to Tshekedi Khama, 31 January 1945, in a letter written by a letter-writer.

[93] *Ibid.*, Nksholetsang Nkosho to Tshekedi Khama, 11 December 1942. See also Barber, *Africans in Khaki*, p. 73, for an account of a Muslim soldier whose ambition was to be a lance-corporal so that he could earn more money to pay for his son, who was at a Roman Catholic school in East Africa.

[94] ICS, Crowder papers, Box 17, Sgt O. B. Matshaba to Tshekedi Khama, 13 May 1942; Ogaketsa Rantoka to Tshekedi Khama, nd.

[95] See further Owino, '"For your tomorrow, we gave our today"', pp. 468–74.

[96] Letter to Margaret Ballinger, 1942, quoted in Grundlingh, 'Participation of South African Blacks', p. 333; ICS, Crowder papers, Box 16, *Newsletter* of 1981 (Bechuanaland) Company, AAPC, May 1942 (probably written by a European) mentions sea-bathing and football.

[97] Waruhiu Itote, *Mau Mau General* (Nairobi, 1967), p. 26.

[98] H. A. Tomalin, 'Physical and recreational training in West Africa', *Mind, Body and Spirit: Journal of the Army Physical Training Corps*, 21 (June 1946), pp. 21–22.

[99] Anthony Clayton, 'Sport and African soldiers: The military diffusion of western sport throughout Sub-Saharan Africa', in W. J. Baker and J. A. Mangan, eds., *Sport in Africa: Essays in Social History* (London 1987), pp. 114–37.

[100] Prof B. L. Jacobs, interview with David Killingray, Beckley, East Sussex, 10 January 1996.

[101] Blundell, *A Love Affair with the Sun*, p. 50.

[102] Roy Ankrah, *My Life Story* (Accra, 1952), pp. 2–3, which was republished on the day of his state funeral in Accra, 28 May 1995.

[103] Anthony Clayton and David Killingray, *Khaki and Blue: Military and Police in British Colonial Africa* (Athens OH, 1989), p. 245.

[104] This game is described by Maj T. R. King: RHL, Oxford. Mss. Afr. s. 1715, Box X.

[105] BBC African Service. Jachoniah Dlamani, recorded Mbabane, Swaziland, 1989.

[106] BBC Africa Service. Ngaraito Makiti, interviewed by his son Estos Hamis, Dodoma, Tanzania, 1989.

[107] Barber, *Africans in Khaki*, pp. 53–54.

[108] Nunneley, *Tales from the KAR*, pp. 62–64, for an account of a KAR *ngoma* in Somaliland, 1941.

[109] B.L. Jacobs memoirs, 'Going backwards forwards', p. 75, ms in private hands.

[110] Michael Blundell, *So Rough a Wind* (London, 1964), p. 58.

[111] On radio broadcasts to Nigerian troops see Peter B. Clarke, *West Africans at War 1914–18 and 1939–45: Colonial Propaganda and its Cultural Aftermath* (London, 1986), pp. 51–52.

[112] Josiah Mwangi Kariuke, *Mau Mau Detainee* (Oxford, 1963; Harmondsworth, 1964), p. 33.

[113] Barber, *Africans in Khaki*, p. 42; Kaggia, *Roots of Freedom*, pp. 35–36.

[114] TNA, DO35/1183/Y1069/1/1, Col E. Collins to High Commissioner, 13 October 1943.

[115] E. J. Collins, 'Comic opera in Ghana', *African Arts*, 9, 2 (1976), p. 52.

[116] BBC Africa Service. Justice C. Banda, from Malawi, who served with the 21st East African Brigade in Ceylon, India and Burma, recorded Blantyre, Malawi, 1989.

[117] Ibid.

[118] BBC Africa Service. Jachoniah Dlamani, recorded Mbabane, Swaziland, 1989.

[119] RHL, Oxford, Mss. Afr. s. 1734, Box 2, file 108, M. L. Crapp, 'Accounts by African soldiers of a visit to Calcutta', written by Cpl Agba, 14 December 1943.

[120] *Ibid.*, M. L. Crapp, 'Accounts by African soldiers of a visit to Calcutta', written by L/C Israel Agwu, 14 December 1943.

[121] Kaggia, *Roots of Freedom*, p. 25.

[122] BBC Africa Service. Justice C. Banda, from Malawi, who served with the 21st East African Brigade in Ceylon, India and Burma, recorded Blantyre, Malawi, 1989.

[123] Barber, *Africans in Khaki*, p. 54.

[124] ICS, Crowder papers, Box 16, 1981 (Bechuanaland) Company, AAPC, *Newsletter* for May 1942. See further Jackson, *Botswana 1939–1945*, pp. 92–97.

[125] Neil Roos, *Ordinary Springboks: White Servicemen and Social Justice in South Africa 1939–1961* (Aldershot, 2005), pp. 57–58.

[126] Quoted by Clarke, *West Africans at War*, p. 53.

[127] Kaggia, *Roots of Freedom*, p. 29.

[128] *Ibid.*, p. 29.

[129] Deborah A. Shackleton, 'Recipe for "failure": Integration of Botswana soldiers within British units during the Second World War', paper presented to 37th conference of the African Studies Association of the United States, Orlando FL, November 1995, p. 17.

[130] BBC Africa Service. Jachoniah Dlamani, recorded Mbabane, Swaziland, 1989.

[131] TNA, DO35/1183/Y1069/1/1, report 9 January 1944.

[132] BBC Africa Service. Justice C. Banda, from Malawi, who served with the 21st East African Brigade in Ceylon, India and Burma, recorded Blantyre, Malawi, 1989.

[133] RHL, Oxford, Mss. fr. s. 1734, Box 2, M. L. Crapp, 'Accounts by African soldiers of a visit to Calcutta', written by L/C J. B. F. Hocquarto and L/C Israel Agwu, 14 December 1943.

[134] BBC Africa Service, Justice C. Banda, from Malawi, who served with the 21st East African Brigade in Ceylon, India and Burma, recorded Blantyre, Malawi, 1989.

[135] Quoted in Lovering, 'Military armies, nationalism and race', ms. copy sent to author.

[136] BBC Africa Service. Pius Osakwe, RWAFF, recorded 1989.

[137] BBC Africa Service. Ngaraito Makiti, interviewed by his son Estos Hamis, Dodoma, Tanzania, 1989.

[138] BBC Africa Service. Mustafa Bonomali, translated from Chichewa by A. Mwamkenenge, Malawi, 1989.

[139] BBC Africa Service. Samson Muliango, recorded in Lusaka, Zambia, 1989.

[140] BBC Africa Service. Chama Mutemi Kadansa, C Company, Northern Rhodesia 22 Brigade, who served in Kenya, Madagascar and Burma from 1939 to 1945, recorded Ndola, Zambia, 1989.

[141] BBC Africa Service. Jachoniah Dlamani, recorded Mbabane, Swaziland, 1989.

[142] Interview: Jacob with David Killingray, 10 January 1996. Also Orlebar, *Tales of the Defence Force*, p. 79.

[143] Darrell Bates, *A Fly-Switch from the Sudan* (London, 1961), pp. 106–7.

[144] TNA, CO 820/55/34458/C, Tadman to Rolleston, 14 September 1944, writing about a leave camp established at Ranchi.

[145] Luise White, *Comforts of Home*, pp. 168 and 179–81; TNA, CO 820/55/34458/C, Tadman to Rolleston, 14 September 1944, writing about a leave camp established at Ranchi.

[146] BBC Africa Service, Samson Muliango, recorded in Lusaka, Zambia, 1989. For other similar conflict in Somaliland, see Owino, '"For your tomorrow, we gave our today"', pp. 458–60.

[147] BBC Africa Service, Joe Culverwell, recorded Harari, Zimbabwe, 1989.

[148] TNA, DO 35/1183/YI069/1/1, 'Report on African and colonial troops employed with British Forces', 3 January 1944.
[149] Grundlingh, 'Participation of South African Blacks', p. 393.
[150] Parsons, *African Rank-and-File*, p. 166.
[151] Ras Makonnen, *Pan Africanism from Within* (Nairobi 1973), p. 12. BBC Africa Service. Hama Kim, recorded Kano, Nigeria, 1989.
[152] IWM. 18366, Paul Gobine from the Seychelles.
[153] BBC Africa Service, Marshall Kebby, interviewed by Elizabeth Obadina, Lagos, Nigeria, 1989.
[154] See the instance of KAR soldiers who feared that a white lieutenant had put a curse on them in Louis Leakey, *By the Evidence: Memoirs, 1932–1951* (New York, 1974), pp. 121–22.
[155] ICS, Crowder papers, Box 16, N. Morokwe to Tshekedi Khama, nd.
[156] Kenneth Gandar Dower, *Abyssinian Patchwork* (London, 1949), p. 63; see also George Youell, *Africa Marches* (London, 1949), pp. 10–11, and the short novel by K. A. Bediako, *A Husband for Esi Ellua* (Accra, 1967).
[157] Kolk, *Can You Tell me Why I Went to War?*, p. 35–6.
[158] William Platt, 'The East African Force: The War and the future', *Journal of the Royal United Services Institute* 93 (1948), p. 113.
[159] Barber, *Africans in Khaki*, p. 10; ICS, Crowder papers, Box 16, S/133/2/1, circular letter No. 7 from Capt the Rev A. Sandilands, c/o Deputy Chaplain-General GHQ MEF, 7 December 1942.
[160] Kaggia, *Roots of Freedom*, p. 28; Rev A. Sandilands, 'About the Bechuana of the AAPC', *Chaplains' Magazine*, January 1943, copy in ICS, Crowder papers, Box 16.
[161] Derek R. Peterson, *Creative Writing: Translation, Bookkeeping and the Use of Imagination in Colonial Kenya* (Portsmouth NH, 2004), p. 165.
[162] Kevin Ward, 'Archbishop Janani Luwum: The dilemmas of loyalty, opposition and witness in Amin's Uganda', in David Maxwell and Ingrid Lowrie, eds, *Christianity and the African Imagination: Essays in Honour of Adrian Hastings* (Leiden, 2002), p. 220.
[163] Barber, *Africans in Khaki*, pp. 9 and 104–6.
[164] R. H. Bassett, 'The chaplain with the West African forces', *Journal of Royal Chaplains' Department*, 49 (July 1950), pp. 21–24; G. Holderness, 'A chaplain with the West African division in Burma', *Journal of the United Services Institute of India*, 74, 315 (April 1944). See also *RWAFF News*, 19, 1 August 1944.
[165] See further Jackson, *Botswana 1939–1945*, pp. 115–20.
[166] Bill Deans, an American missionary in the Congo, was commissioned in the *Force Publique* as a padre; he baptised 18 African soldiers in the Jordan. See 'Staccato drumbeats from Zaire: Newsletter of Mr and Mrs William A. Deans, 6 November 1992'. In author's possession.
[167] TNA, CO 820/49/36018, report of Conference of West African Labour Officers, 23–25 November 1942.
[168] Michael Cardo, '"Fighting a worse imperialism": White South African loyalism and the Army Education Services (AES) during the Second World War', *South African Historical Journal*, 46 (2002), pp. 141–74.
[169] See further Timothy H. Parsons, 'Dangerous education? The Army as school in colonial East Africa', *Journal of Imperial and Commonwealth History* 8, 1 (2000), pp. 112–34.
[170] TNA, DO 35/1183/Y, 1069/1/1, 'Report of meeting in office of deputy director of O & PS (CT), 28 June 1943'.
[171] Katrin Bromber, 'Do not destroy our honour: Wartime propaganda directed at East African soldiers in Ceylon (1943–44)', unpublished paper, Centre for Modern Oriental Studies, Berlin. Available online at: <www.sasnet.lu.se/EASASpapers/22KatrinBromber.pdf>, accessed 9 August 2008. See also John Iliffe, *Honour in African History* (Cambridge, 2005), ch. 13.
[172] Education programmes began in the British Army in the 1860s, and an Army Education Corps was established in 1920; see T. H. Hawkins and L. J. F. Brimble, *Adult Education: The Record of the British Army* (London, 1947). On East Africa see East African Command, *The Story of the East African Army Service Corps* (Nairobi, nd. *c.* 1944); E. V. H. Hudson, 'The East African Education Corps', *Army Education*, 25, 2 (1951).
[173] Gerald Hanley, *Monsoon Victory* (London, 1946), p. 150.
[174] ICS, Crowder papers, Box 16, 5.133/2/2, 'Fight against illiteracy: Education progress among Africans (by a military observer) late 1945'.
[175] Grundlingh, 'Participation of South African Blacks', p. 147.
[176] TNA, WO 172/3985, 11th (EA) Division Progress Report, No. 4, October 1943.
[177] House of Commons Debates, 25 June 1941, vol. 372, cc 1025–6.
[178] Quoted in Grundlingh, 'Participation of South African Blacks', p. 243.

4

Indiscipline, Strike & Mutiny

Diégo Suarez, December 1943

The men of the 1st Infantry Battalion, Mauritius Regiment, who landed at Diégo Suarez as part of the Madagascar invasion force on 20 December 1943 were already deeply dissatisfied. The week-long voyage had been stormy and most of the soldiers had been very seasick. There was widespread and deep resentment at the racial discrimination within Mauritian forces, which were segregated into white and non-white units. Whites were primarily combatants and paid more than non-whites who were mainly employed as military labour. All officers were white, a mixture of upper-class francophone and anglophone Mauritians, and all attempts by non-whites to gain a commission had been rebuffed. And for many of the recruits in the 1,000-strong regiment that went ashore there was a double sense of betrayal: they had been enlisted for service only in Mauritius and were now being sent abroad, while no white units had been sent overseas. This rankled deeply. An added and deep anxiety was for the welfare of the womenfolk back home, now subject to the attentions of the Nyasaland troops of 17 KAR, who had recently arrived to garrison Mauritius.

John Harrison, then a lieutenant in the British Army but later a distinguished social historian, remembers that the Mauritian troops 'landed on the quay at Diégo Suarez late in the morning, when the sun was at its hottest, and had to parade there in full kit for over an hour. Some fell down from sheer exhaustion and were insulted by their Anglo-Mauritian officers.' Lt-Col Jimmy Yates, a regular officer, refused transport and decided that his men should march the 12 miles to the camp at Orangea. Harrison continues: 'The march was a disaster, as the troops were in no fit state and kept falling down on the road or in the ditch. Witnesses said later that at least one Anglo-Mauritian officer kicked the men while ordering them to get up.'[1] At Orangea the tented camp in a forested area was poorly cleared and prepared. One man set fire to 'a bit of the forest, the fire spread and half the camp was destroyed before the fire was brought under control'. The final breaking point came over an apparently insignificant event the next morning. Company commanders ordered physical training at 6.30am.

121

The battalion baulked, some soldiers refusing to assemble while others staged a sit-down strike on the parade ground.[2]

The unrest was swiftly quelled with the help of soldiers of the KAR who were ordered to round up the mutineers. More than 350 soldiers were arrested and eventually 500 were tried. At the field courts-martial, two men were sentenced to death, subsequently commuted to 15 years' imprisonment, and 24 men received sentences ranging from seven to 14 years.[3] The Mauritius Regiment was disbanded and the men sent to join the Mauritius Pioneers serving in the Middle East. By 1946 all but six of the mutineers had been released from prison. Mutiny by soldiers on active service in wartime was regarded as a serious affair by the British. A Colonial Office official called it 'a stupid hot-headed act', while a post-war petition by Mauritian ex-servicemen, pleading for the release of all the convicted men, argued that 'under the goad of instigation from malicious sources, they might have had the sense of soldiership benumbed and hence stooped to a participation in a rash act'.[4]

Hotheadedness or rashness may indeed have characterised the action of some of the disgruntled soldiers at Diégo Suarez, but essentially the battalion went on strike – a demonstration of discontent by recruits whose only effective means of protest was the withdrawal of their labour. Their 'mutiny' was typical of the kind of action taken by African soldiers throughout the war. Strictly speaking these were mutinies or mutinous acts, but the vast majority were little more than strikes or protests arising out of the hardships of military conditions.[5]

Dissenters in uniform

The military environment is always characterised by discipline and an extensive system of social control over the lives and actions of soldiers.[6] This is necessary not only because soldiers work and live in close proximity to each other, but because they very often have access to firearms and are required to perform military duties. Discipline to varying degrees of intensity is always central to military life, but much more so in wartime and in active-service conditions. Indiscipline could be defined by the authorities in various ways, possibly including individual disobedience to commands, kit being dirty or missing, cases of drunkenness, theft or murder, clashes with civilians and police, and collective insubordination or mutiny. Contracting venereal disease, which rendered a soldier unfit for duty, was considered an offence during the Second World War. Punishments varied according to the perceived seriousness of the offence. Individual soldiers could demonstrate their opposition to military life not only by defying direct orders but by also selling their kit and military equipment, pilfering stores, and neglecting duty. Cases of petty indiscipline, the usual day-to-day occurrences, were dealt with by officers and NCOs, often in an informal way. Serious offences came before courts-martial and on active service before field courts-martial.

The small size and voluntary nature of peacetime African colonial armies meant there were few serious breaches of discipline. Punishment was frequently physical and immediate – often a caning administered by an NCO. Soldiers could also be given extra duties or fined. Serious offenders sentenced to terms of incarceration were invariably sent to civil prisons. However, wartime expansion of the army created a range of new problems. A body of volunteers, conscripts and reluctantly enlisted men had to be fashioned into a disciplined force as rapidly as possible, often by officers who had limited or no first-hand experience of commanding African troops. Increased numbers of soldiers and a much greater volume of war material and other supplies provided new opportunities for theft and other criminal activities by both soldiers and civilians. Coercive measures were increased, enforced by a new system of military police and military prisons.

Corporal punishment, often referred to as 'flogging' and largely abandoned by the East and West African forces by the late 1930s, was reintroduced in wartime. Many officers argued for its retention as a vitally effective means of maintaining discipline and control in wartime conditions.[7] It was not used in the South African Defence Force. Acts of indiscipline on the battlefield were always treated as serious breaches of the military code. Desertion, dereliction of duty, casting away arms, or acts crudely described in the First World War as 'cowardice' continued to be firmly dealt with during the 1939–45 war. However, the harsh ideas about moral conduct in the face of battle had changed during the interwar years and 'cowardice' in the face of the enemy ceased to be a capital offence.[8]

Absenteeism & desertion

Being 'absent' by failing to report for duty or overstaying leave is a common offence by soldiers in most armies. In the British African forces it was sometimes difficult to distinguish 'absenteeism' from desertion. Often soldiers did not turn up when they were required. Some operated on their own timescales and had difficulty adjusting to notions of industrial time. And actions that could be construed as 'being absent' or 'deserting' arose from various motives, as they do with soldiers in all armies: family and domestic troubles, drink, delayed transport, miscalculation and so on. Absenteeism and desertion could also be a form of resistance to military service itself, perhaps in response to the hostility of an officer, a breach of a soldier's sense of honour, or fear of going overseas. Men forcibly enlisted into the wartime African colonial forces were more likely to desert than volunteers, although this was not always the case. Desertion was a common response by soldiers dissatisfied with their treatment in the army and the material conditions of the lines in which they lived. For a soldier drawn from an area that was a traditional source of migrant labour, service in the army was seen as little different from working for a civilian employer in a mine or on a farm. If conditions were harsh or pay inadequate then a man might go and look for work elsewhere. For men tied to the rhythms of rural production, times of planting and times of harvesting assumed great significance. It was not uncommon for men to 'desert' because they were required at home for essential rural labour tasks.

There are accounts of men deserting because they had not been placed in the service of their choice – for example, deserting an infantry or auxiliary unit and then enlisting under another name in a service corps where the pay was higher. The idea that men could switch from one military unit to another continued in India. General Hugh Stockwell reported in August 1944 that a small outbreak of desertion or absenteeism among native West African troops has been found to be due ... to a belief ... that if they can get to Calcutta they will be able to join units of the USAAF as labourers or servants. Steps are being taken to refute this idea.[9]

When it was announced that units were due to go overseas the number of deserters also increased. For example, the rate of desertions began to grow steadily among the troops of 1 Battalion (Somali) KAR in late 1943 as soon as it became known that they were destined for south-east Asia. Some of the troublemakers were weeded out and transferred to 2 Battalion (Somali) KAR, which later moved to Moshi in Tanganyika. Desertions continued and in the end the battalion was temporarily disbanded.[10]

A good deal of research has been undertaken on levels of desertion among African soldiers in the Gold Coast colony.[11] Desertion rates in that colony were relatively high in wartime with 15 per cent of the total force listed as deserters in mid-1943. Men recruited from the Northern Territories, and who had been sent by chiefs to the army, were marched in handcuffs to Tamale for fear that they might desert. Soldiers often served in their home colony without any qualms, but the prospect of overseas service inevitably increased their desire to escape from military service. As a result convoys and troop trains with men *en route* to the coast and bound for overseas service were closely watched. Desertion was also high among men from Ashanti and the coastal towns, particularly among conscripted lorry drivers. In July–August 1942 large-scale sweeps for deserters were made by the army and police through the towns of Koforidua, Angona-Denkwa, Anum and Somanya. During January–August 1942 there were 2,400 desertions from the Gold Coast Regiment; 600 of these deserters were apprehended. By 1943 the highest proportion came from Ashanti with 42 per cent; nearly 20 per cent of deserters came from the coastal regions. A year later one in seven of all Gold Coast troops was listed as a deserter and the figures climbed as reinforcements became due for service overseas in the Asian campaign. However, the traditional recruiting grounds of the north, despite enforced enlistment, registered relatively low desertion rates of only seven per cent by early 1944.

There were more subtle forms of protest than desertion which, if the soldier was fortunate, might not earn him any punishment but provide financial return or some ease. Selling kit, stealing stores, avoiding work, neglecting orders, and feigning stupidity – sometimes known as 'dumb insolence' – have all been part of the strategy adopted in protest against coerced, unrewarded or poorly paid labour. Of course, theft and idleness by soldiers should not always be interpreted as opposition to military service. All armies have a proportion of thieves, rogues and misfits, but it is important to recognise that such activities could also express opposition to conscription into the army or protest against poor conditions.

Mutiny

Once African military units were overseas it was more difficult for soldiers to desert. Where could they go? However, on overseas service the many hardships, long hours of inactivity and great distance from home all helped foster discontent and unrest. Few African soldiers received leave from overseas postings. Many of the mutinies and disturbances in the African colonial forces occurred either when soldiers were told they were to move overseas, or while they were actually serving overseas.

The Army Act 1879 defined a mutiny as a 'collective insubordination, or a combination of two or more persons to resist or induce others to resist lawful military authority'.[12] With such a broad definition, it was possible for the military authorities to interpret a wide range of military offences as 'mutiny'. Soldiers' protests, strikes, riots, collective desertion and striking an officer or NCO could all be considered mutiny if the military authorities so wished. Generally, the military authorities did acknowledge the strains and tensions endured by African troops. A sense of proportion often prevailed and many minor acts of collective insubordination were dealt with wisely. It was also recognised that thoughtlessness and insensitivity on the part of officers and harsh treatment of African soldiers could lead to unrest teetering on the edge of mutiny. In a report on the colonial military forces written for the Colonial Office in 1946, E. E. Sabben-Clare listed the major mutinies and commented: 'sometimes, however, it is impossible not to sympathise with the soldiers who caused them'.[13] Most mutinies were little more than strikes, the withdrawal of labour and a temporary refusal to obey the commands of officers.[14] In one or two mutinies immediate discontents coalesced with demands related to race and rank, pay and opportunities, and these can be more broadly interpreted as having a political flavour although rarely is this prominent. Most soldiers, and few among those who actually mutinied, had anti-colonial ambitions. The official response to mutinies was to play down the significance of the disturbance; collective reprisals were avoided, but examples were made of ringleaders, especially NCOs, in order to send a strong warning to the rank-and-file. In serious cases, as with the Mauritius Regiment in December 1943 and the Somaliland Camel Corps in June 1944, the battalion or regiment was disbanded and the men dismissed or relocated to other units.

There is a long record of mutiny by colonial or semi-colonial forces. The memory of the Indian revolt of 1857–58 helped to frame British perceptions about the reliability and dependendability of 'native' troops, as well as immediately changing British recruitment patterns in India.[15] By contrast revolts or mutinies by soldiers in British colonial Africa were generally small, localised affairs that were easily dealt with, and even if they gave the authorities a nail-biting moment they rarely if ever posed a real threat to the colonial order. Two mutinies can be seen as exceptions to this. The first was that by Sudanese troops in Uganda in September 1897, which seriously threatened the nascent British administration in the Protectorate.[16] The second occurred during the British attempt to force Egyptian troops to evacuate the Anglo-Egyptian Sudan in late 1924; the 11th Sudanese Battalion mutinied in Khartoum and was besieged in the military hospital where the men fought to the death. Three Sudanese officers were executed for their part in the mutiny.[17]

But for the most part mutinies tended to be small-scale and often focused on specific grievances.[18] The possibility that African colonial troops might mutiny and turn their arms against their officers and perhaps against the colonial regime, hovered in the minds of some army officers and administrators. One official in East Africa early in the century warned,

> the smart soldier for all his veneer of cleanliness and discipline should not disguise the old African nature ... pleasant and kindly as the soldier may appear one must look on every one as a potential murderer, bully, ravisher, slave dealer and thief. It is only fear and discipline that prevents him from being all these things ... One must be ever on the watch with one's native soldiery.[19]

In South Africa the fear of armed Africans shaped military policies in both world wars. Whereas in the First World War the Cape Coloured Corps was armed and served in combatant roles, in the Second World War the authorities rejected persistent appeals for the corps to be other than a noncombatant body.[20] Similar fears also possessed many white settlers in Southern Rhodesia and Kenya, although in both colonies African troops were recruited as combatants for both world wars.[21]

Nevertheless, in most British colonies various strategies were adopted to reduce the risk of African soldiers using their arms against the regime. Many regiments had internal security schemes to guard against any such eventuality. Firearms and ammunition were closely controlled and the armourer-sergeant was invariably a senior European NCO. To avoid collusion between soldiers based on ethnic ('tribal') or religious background, mixed battalions were created. Military units were deployed within a colony principally to safeguard internal security, but policy was also shaped to ensure that Africans could not act decisively against the colonial authorities. Unlike most armies in post-independent Africa, colonial forces were small infantry forces without armoured vehicles; indeed in the majority of cases before 1939 they had few vehicles of any kind and thus lacked a mobile capacity. Peacetime colonial armies also lacked modern communications systems, or if they existed they were used only by Europeans. This ensured that mutinies, if they occurred, were more likely to be localised and thus more easily contained. As an extra surety most colonies also had an armed European volunteer force; in some cases this included whites-only machine-gun units. White rifle associations also existed, and many whites in Africa, whether officials or in commercial employ, had gained some experience of military service during the First World War. The Defence Act of South Africa required all white men aged 17 to 60 to undergo military training.

Military men generally believed that the quality of European army officers and NCOs was the crucial element in the control of African soldiers. Select officers carefully and they would become role-models – father figures – for the African rank-and-file. However, in wartime such an ideal was impossible. Officers came from wherever they could be found. In peacetime a staff officer in the Colonial Office screened all applicants to serve in the RWAFF and the KAR. The outbreak of the Second World War changed all that. The colonial forces were rapidly expanded and officers sought wherever they could be found. A constant complaint by RWAFF commanders was about the poor quality of officers – men who knew nothing about West Africa or its people and had attitudes which made them antipathetic to commanding African troops. This was particularly the case with many Southern Rhodesian and South African whites with emergency commissions who served in West Africa, and of East African whites who encountered RWAFF troops in various overseas campaigns.[22] Gen Hugh Stockwell, commanding the 82nd (West African) Division in Burma in 1944, thought many of the officers under his command were of poor quality.[23]

The structures of the South African Defence Force invariably reflected the racist society that it sought to defend. White officers often addressed African and Coloured soldiers in derogatory terms. When black South African troops served alongside British colonial forces, for example in East and North Africa, the differences in treatment and attitude were starkly obvious to the rank-and-file of both forces. This was the experience of Joe Culverwell, a Coloured Southern Rhodesian soldier, who volunteered enthusiastically to fight 'for King and country' at the outbreak of war.

> In the British army – all the British units I belonged to – they never showed any discrim-ination at all. I belong to the Argyll and Sutherland Highlanders and I actually wore a kilt. A khaki kilt! [Laughs] We always used to go out drinking together, visiting the night-spots and the lowspots together. Because this was the first time – particularly in Egypt – that we mixed up with white girls. You know they sent out millions of WAACs and all that crowd from England. And I must say some of the girls rather favoured us. I suppose it was a novelty, as far as they were concerned. But the South Africans didn't like it, so we used to have at least, at least three times a week fights with them. In fact, one South African captain, he threatened me that if he saw me, [with a white girl] ... so I went to tell these Argyll and Sutherland Highlanders what he told me. And of course they came back and we knocked the daylight hell out of him and got confined to barracks for it![24]

Indeed, differences in levels of pay between West and East African troops stationed in the same theatre were also a cause of discontent which sometimes helped fuel unrest.

The colonial authorities thought that the rapid expansion of the African colonial forces after mid-1940 might lead to disciplinary problems. Taking men, whether by enlistment or conscription, and exposing them to a military regime almost inevitably risked a measure of discontent and open dissent. The exigencies of wartime meant hastily built and inadequate barrack accommodation, remote training camps, separation from families, new and wrong foods (such as meat improperly prepared for Muslim troops or meat for men who were prima-rily rice-eaters), the absence of women and the sudden transfer of troops over-seas. All these caused problems which had to be fielded by overstretched and often ill-experienced officers. As Sabben-Clare wrote in his report to the Colo-nial Office, with wartime expansion, it was 'not surprising, therefore, that the list of disturbances and mutinies in Colonial forces during the war is larger than one would have wished'.[25]

What follows is an account of the various mutinies that took place in the African colonial forces during the war. As has already been indicated, the term 'mutiny' is capable of wide interpretation. It was not as a rule taken to include the frequent riotous clashes between soldiers and civilians which occurred at one time or another near most army camps. Civilians often resented the presence of soldiers, especially the competition they posed over resources and most espe-cially over sex. Soldiers had a tendency to use their uniforms and their collec-tive weight to intimidate civilians and many of the disputes inevitably involved women.[26] On foreign postings soldier–civilian rivalries were often exacerbated by interethnic antipathy. Very serious clashes occurred in mid-1944 between West African troops and Indian civilians near the Ranchi rest camp, in which six Indians were killed and several women raped.[27] In Asmara at the end of the war, a drunken brawl resulted in Eritrean civilians stoning soldiers of 3 Battalion, Sudan Defence Force. When troops in the barracks heard the accounts they seized their guns, went into the town and in an hour and a half murdered nearly 40 people and wounded more than 70. At the subsequent court of inquiry 69 soldiers were charged, eight with murder. Sentences ranged up to 15 years.[28]

The problem with writing about mutinies, even those by African troops which occurred 50 or more years ago, is that records of courts-martial or courts of inquiry are either not extant or still closed to public scrutiny.[29] It is also clear that for reasons of wartime security the authorities covered up many incidents of unrest by African soldiers, such as the mutiny by 25 East African Brigade in early 1942 described below. Dissent and insubordination probably occurred with greater frequency than is often imagined, especially in certain units and particularly among Somali troops. Gen Sir William Platt, who took over East African Command in December 1941, wrote:

> There have been numerous incidents in almost all Somali units, and some amongst Somali personnel attending courses at Command School … They have generally taken the form of refusals to obey orders, sit-down strikes, shouting, desertion with weapons, untrustworthiness as guards, collusive theft, occasional stone throwing and drawing of knives, but little physical violence, none against Europeans.[30]

Another difficulty encountered in writing about protests by African soldiers is that most information is derived from official reports. There are very few African voices offering accounts by mutineers and dissidents; some African evidence is available but invariably from 'prosecution' witnesses at courts of inquiry.[31] Without the 'view from below', which of course must be treated with equal caution, any scholarly analysis of reasons and motivation can only be very tentative.

Mutiny by British African colonial troops was generally small-scale. Certainly no British mutiny was of the dimensions and significance of that by French *tirailleurs* at the barracks of Thiaroye, near Dakar, in December 1944, or the mutinies by battalions of the *Force Publique* in the Belgian Congo earlier that same year.[32] However, the protests, strikes and other acts of collective insubordination, which were a not uncommon feature of British African colonial military life during the Second World War, are as worthy of study as African labour relations and disputes, to which historians have directed considerable attention. Indeed, there are many similarities with labour unrest: most wartime mutinies and protests by soldiers, in all armies, arose due to grievances over matters which touched soldiers' personal lives and essentially were concerned with questions of pay and working conditions.

As many of the incidents that occurred during the war were small disputes unlikely to be recorded except perhaps in the daily war diaries kept by each unit, there is no formal checklist available of all mutinies or disputes involving African soldiers. From the evidence available it is possible to categorise the reasons for mutiny, and this has been done below. Given the racial policies and nature of South Africa, it seemed sensible to look separately at unrest and acts of insubordination in the South African Defence Force. Soldiers mutinied due to conditions of service, which includes issues relating to food, clothing, accommodation, work tasks, and questions to do with wives and children; racial discrimination; relations with officers and NCOs; reactions to service overseas; battlefield conditions and stress; and as a result of inactivity and assumed official neglect, this often being the case at the end of the war in military encampments in Asia and the Middle East and on troopships returning to Africa.

British African colonial forces

Soldiers' disquiet at the conditions of military service was a constant source of potential unrest. In rapidly expanding military forces that required the services of literate Africans, but continued to be segregated on racial lines with white officers and black rank-and-file, differences in pay and general conditions of service became more obvious. Educated Africans resented the racial discrimination inherent in the army and particularly the attitudes of many white South Africans and colonial settlers. One former KAR soldier recalled a confrontation with a white South African officer who wanted him to be his servant: 'I did not feel good about this. I refused because I joined the army to be a soldier not a servant.'[33] However, often the causes of unrest were the everyday matters that were simply endured most of the time but at some point, for one reason or another, assumed unbearable proportions.

On such incident, in late January 1939, involved 150 soldiers of the Heavy Battery, Sierra Leone Battalion, who, led by Emmanuel Cole, refused to go on parade. This small-scale mutiny occurred in response to general conditions of service but in particular because the authorities refused to issue soldiers with boots. The soldiers strongly resented discrimination whereby they would not be provided with clothing similar to that received by British troops. The leader of the mutiny has entered into the panoply of Sierra Leone's national heroes.[34] At his court-martial he was reported as saying:

> I told him [Lt Meade] that my money was not sufficient to meet my demands. I told him also that I am buying starch and coal every week together with brasso and kiwi polish to clean my uniform ... I told him this month's money was not correct, that Lt. Meade paid me £1.6s.7d. leaving a balance of 4s.10d and when I went to report him he told me to shut up and then asked me to go and complain to Major Kummit. I did so. Before Major Kummit asked me a word, Lt. Meade said "all the bushmen here want to follow Cole".[35]

In the Gold Coast in late 1939, lorry drivers protested at being moved away from their families to Teshie Camp, just outside Accra. With shouts of 'I want my wife' and 'Don't put your uniform on', the soldiers paraded in old clothes and pyjamas. After 1 Battalion GCR was called to the camp the mutinous protest, a not very serious affair, ended with the ringleaders receiving light prison sentences.[36] More serious in the eyes of the military authorities was the refusal of East African Pioneers to do road work; the men thought they had joined up to fight, not to build roads and dig latrines in the Northern Frontier District. In the ensuing disturbances one soldier was killed and 70 soldiers injured.[37] Michael Blundell described the first three months after he had taken over command of the battalion as living on a volcano: 'I never knew whether an order would be obeyed or not. The remittances to families had gone astray, their clothing was in a shocking condition, and equipment almost non-existent ... The men were bitter and felt they had been cheated.'[38] The ringleaders were sent to Nairobi for court-martial presided over by Robin Wainwright, the local district commissioner. He wisely listened to the men's complaints, dismissed all the charges and sent them back to their units.[39] Another incident was the protest by a unit of East African signallers, largely formed from among literate men, who refused an order to have their heads shaved; the demonstration was led by Cpl W. Itote, the future Mau Mau 'General China'.[40]

Conditions-of-service disputes were ever-present. As preparations to move overseas became apparent to African troops the rate of desertions increased. In some cases the news led to riotous behaviour, as at Aba and Calabar in Nigeria in October 1943, and outright refusal of troops to embark on a ship.[41] Lack of leave and long service overseas without leave compounded the sense of grievance and added to tensions. A company of Sudan Defence Force troops at Kafra, smouldering with discontent at lack of leave, mutinied in August 1941. A few weeks later a second company also went on strike.[42] In early 1942 some 100 men of the 25th East African Brigade, then stationed at Massawa on the Red Sea coast and destined for the Burma campaign, refused to embark without first receiving leave. The men had been on active service away from home for more than two years (white officers had recently had leave), and also senior Nandi NCOs felt that a number of Nandi young men should return home for circumcision before further campaigns. A Kikuyu signaller named Robin (or Reuben) from 2/3 KAR was a principal instigator of the strike. The press was forbidden to report the mutiny, and officers and mutineers played football together to cool feelings. Courts martial were convened and a number of senior NCOs were convicted, a few given the death penalty and others immediately flogged. The deputy judge advocate-general and his co-judge were so distressed at the sentences awarded that they appealed to Gen Sir William Platt, the C-in-C, who reprieved the men and arranged for them to rejoin their units.[43]

Certain ethnic groups were recognised by the British military authorities as being difficult to manage. The Somalis headed the list. 'An intense pride of race and religion', and a clan structure plus a strong sense of individualism, inhibited training and notions of military discipline.[44] On the night of 5–6 June 1944, 'massed rioting' occurred among soldiers of the Somaliland Camel Corps (SCC) stationed at Burao in British Somaliland. Unrest had been stimulated by proposals to move the SCC to Kenya for re-equipping as an armoured-car regiment and fears among the Somalis that they were to be 'East-Africanised'. Somali troops thought of themselves as distinct, even 'Asian' rather than African, and this was to some extent reflected in the dress and regulations of the corps. Somali soldiers had little time for Swahili-speaking East African troops.[45]

A few days before the mutiny around 100 askaris had gathered at a sheikh's tomb outside Burao; the military authorities saw this religious ceremony as 'a cloak for a political meeting at which grievances would be discussed' and evidence that the mutiny was planned. Two months earlier, senior warrant officers and NCOs had sent their commanding officer a letter asking that men of the SCC 'be treated better', that due consideration be given to askaris' property if the corps went overseas and concluding: 'We are not cowards, and will face all war difficulties. We are also bravely willing to play our part of the war anywhere.'[46] The day before the mutiny a number of army trucks had arrived at Burao, driven by East African soldiers. This set rumours circulating that 'Swahili troops were coming to force Somalis to obey orders'.[47] The first indication of the 'bad mutiny' for the British officers was the sound of a shot and the shouted warning of Orderly Sergeant Mohammed Wais: 'These people are mad, for God's sake don't go near the square or you will be shot.' The mutineers entered the fort, broke open the magazine and released prisoners from the guardroom. 'Undesirables' from the town joined the mutineers in looting. However, the incident was soon dealt with. Armoured cars were brought up and the mutineers either surrendered or fled, later to be rounded up. Various punishments were handed out to the mutineers and the SCC was disbanded.[48] In Gen Platt's view 'there is no truly dependable and loyal core on which the SCC can be re-built'.[49]

Disputes arising from long absence from home and the tedium of military service increased particularly in the latter part of the war or after victory. Many months after the war in Europe had ended nearly 30,000 soldiers from the High Commission Territories were still scattered throughout the Middle East and Italy. Four companies of Basuto pioneers in Palestine stopped all work in November 1945. The soldiers' objections were threefold: slowness of repatriation, their employment as guards amidst the Arab–Jewish conflict, and excessive and unnecessary discipline. A month later a 'notorious mutiny' occurred at a military prison and detention barracks when the detainees attacked the white and black staff with sticks and stones. British troops were called in and, in suppressing the disturbance, shot and killed four Basuto soldiers. By then sit-down strikes and large-scale indiscipline had become common among Basuto companies and they were officially labelled as 'a liability and not an asset'.[50] Explanations to Batswana troops that repatriation was slow because shipping was in short supply were greeted with '*maaka a makgoa*' ('the lies of the whiteman').[51] In March 1946, three Basuto of 1943 Company were killed and several others injured when troops put down a mutiny in a military prison and detention barracks in the Middle East.[52] Discontent grew at the slow pace of repatriation and a warning was given by an official of 'serious mutiny'. As Germany collapsed in the spring of 1945 two leave drafts in South Africa refused to re-embark for the Middle East. The authorities were reluctant to use force and agreed that the drafts should remain in South Africa but be deprived of further leave.[53]

During the war many incidents of unrest occurred as a consequence of ethnic abuse and/or rivalry. Food could serve as the catalyst for mutiny, as in early 1945 when Gold Coast troops in the 37th General Hospital, Accra, refused to obey instructions, rejected 'native chop' and demanded 'white man's food'.[54] The military authorities made great efforts to keep African soldiers away from white prostitutes and also to reduce the incidents of 'women palaver'. At issue were notions of white superiority but also the need to control venereal disease and limit tensions with local communities. African troops, who were barred from watching live entertainments in which white women appeared and from seeing films featuring scantily-clad white women or biracial love scenes, often turned verbal objections into violent clashes. In early 1944, West African troops being moved by ship from the eastern Mediterranean westward expected to be going home. They were put off temporarily at Rabat in Morocco but not permitted to leave the dock area because their officers feared that they might consort with prostitutes in the city. The troops were not prepared to accept this and they began to march *en masse* into Rabat, only to be confronted by armed white South African troops.[55]

Breaches of the white–black sexual divide were treated seriously. Marshall Kebby, a Nigerian who served in the war, described how after the war an African soldier had a sexual relationship with a white military nurse at the 46th West African General Hospital in Dakka, India. The man was arrested and sentenced to three years' imprisonment by a courts martial. 'On the day he was to be taken away by the military police', says Kebby,

> they called the whole troops to come and witness our man being taken away by the military police [Gurkhas] ... So, we went on muster parade. As the boy was being taken away he said 'How can you ...', he spoke in our language, 'You mean you will stand here and watch while I am being taken away by the military police, to go and suffer three years imprisonment for a crime I did not commit? It is true I was in love with the woman, but I was obeying her orders. You know that whatever I did was at her own request.' So we said, 'At her own request!' OK. Then the troops rioted. On that day we killed anybody we could get hold of. Raped anybody we could rape – I didn't rape anybody – I didn't join them.[56]

No confirmatory official record of this incident has been found which, had it occurred as related, would have been a very serious outbreak of criminal indis-cipline unlikely not to be recorded. It would appear that the incident has become embellished by time and frequent re-telling. Nevertheless, the military author-ities did react firmly to white–black sexual liaisons and there are elements of the story that have the ring of authenticity.

The most serious form of insubordination was battlefield mutiny. There were many conditions in war theatres, one senior officer reported, which pushed troops to 'near-mutiny', but the ultimate act of refusing orders in battle seems to have been relatively rare.[57] One KAR battalion broke and ran during its first exposure to fire in the Burma campaign. Two battalions of the 11th East African Division refused to advance across the Chindwin river. According to Brig G. H. Cree, some of the soldiers said:

> No. You told us to go to the Chindwin and that would be our lot. After that we were going to go back. If we go to the Chindwin and cross the Chindwin we know quite well the next thing you will say is to go on to the Irriwaddy [*sic*]. And we will do whatever we're told to do, but we are not going any further.[58]

In the subsequent courts-martial the sentences handed out to the supposed ring-leaders were 'nominal'. Brig Cree mentions a number of similar incidents throughout the division 'usually taking the form of mass disobedience, i.e. refusal to go on parade'. He blamed the trouble partly on African resentment at the different treatment given to British troops over rations, access to alcohol in the NAAFI, leave and demobilisation. When Africans served alongside British units they could not help but compare their lot with that of white soldiers. 'In my view,' wrote Cree, 'we were lucky to have escaped with a few flare-ups instead of a more general revolt.'[59]

Many of the incidents of collective indiscipline and unrest were small and not serious – for example, an East African platoon during the Ethiopian campaign which refused to parade until a general had heard the men's grievances.[60] All too often, officers could not effectively identify the ringleaders and thus found it difficult to take disciplinary action. Grievances over poor food, lack of leave and excessive discipline were all compounded by inactivity and the slowness in repatriating African troops at the end of the war. The first demand after victory was to demobilise British troops who were required for reconstruction. African soldiers came a long way down the list of priorities and shipping to take them home from the Middle East and Asia was in short supply. The African military encampments in those two areas seethed with discontent and mutinous outbreaks were frequent there and on the transports carrying troops home. The unrest among High Commission Territory troops has already been mentioned. Most camps in India were in relatively isolated areas and soldiers became increasingly bored and more difficult to discipline.

Seemingly petty grievances could escalate into acts of collective defiance, as was the case with the 4th Auxiliary Group from Sierra Leone in the autumn of 1945 at Karvetnaga in India. The unrest, over the payment of hair-cutting allowances, occurred while most of the European officers and NCOs were away at the Bangalore Cricket fixtures. It would probably have fizzled out but for the arrival of a staff officer accompanied by armed and steel-helmeted troops who treated the affair as if it was a major mutiny.[61] When similar trouble occurred among soldiers of the 81st (West Africa) Division at Poona and Dhond, British troops were 'unobtrusively' moved into the area while Gen Sir Claude Auchinleck telegraphed to London expressing his fears at the possible effects on Indian public opinion if British troops had to fire on African soldiers.[62] When African troops were eventually repatriated, trouble occurred on board HMS *Ruys*, homeward bound to West Africa, when soldiers and NCOs removed their badges and manhandled British officers and NCOs – acts of insubordination described as 'very near mutiny'.[63] The slow process of postwar demobilisation left many men of the KAR angry and disgruntled. At Gilgil in Kenya in April 1946, 50 soldiers who had served in south-east Asia attacked a civil police station to release a comrade who had been arrested. In January 1947 at Gilgil, 150 askaris of the East African Army Ordinance Corps went on strike demanding to be instantly discharged; 5 KAR was sent to subdue them and in the resulting fighting six strikers were killed and 30 injured.[64]

South African troops

A measure of social control pervades all armies but perhaps more so in those where men are drawn from a society founded on acute racial inequalities. The Union Defence Force not only reflected all the social, economic and political injustices of South African society, but it also sought to uphold and perpetuate them. It is thus appropriate that Louis Grundlingh in the chapter of his thesis dealing with mutiny and upon which this section is heavily reliant, should first discuss the measures taken by the South African military authorities to closely regulate the activities of non-white soldiers.[65] The South African military sought to uphold *baasskap*, prevent fraternisation between Africans and other soldiers, prevent contact and especially sexual relations with white women, and prevent access to any influences such as films and magazines which might challenge or undermine policies of racial segregation and notions of black inferiority. Within South Africa civil law aided military law; in the less colour-conscious environment of the Middle East and southern Europe, where black South African troops served, it was much more difficult to police social behaviour.[66] However, given the power structures and the racial system of South Africa, military 'indiscipline' for African, Indian and Coloured soldiers of the Union Defence Force had a much wider meaning than it had for personnel in most other armies. Soldiers not only had to avoid breaching the petty restrictions of segregationist civil law but also follow a military disciplinary code aimed at rigidly maintaining racial discrimination.

Inevitably, black soldiers could easily fall foul of one set of laws or the other. Bold and awkward men, unprepared to be treated as inferiors, invited the label of 'troublesome' and thus rapid discharge from the army; the UDF had no place for blacks who engaged in 'subversive talk'. Pte Douglas Modolo was one such; he was discharged with a bad record, described by his commanding officer as an 'agitator, educated and exercises alleged qualifications to incite dissatisfaction ... exercises a bad influence'. Actually Modolo's army record showed only one very minor offence.[67] The conversation of two NCOs of the Cape Corps was reported by white soldiers to military intelligence to have included the following sentiments: 'I have tasted the freedom of Italy, Germany and France and now England. I am not going to stand for any colour bar in South Africa. We will stick together and cause a revolution.'[68]

Discrimination was at the heart of the SADF. In the Middle East, under dilution schemes 'Cape Corps Staff-Sergeants were forced to act as cooks and batmen to European privates', which along with racial disparities in rank and pay steadily fuelled discontent.[69] Harsh and indifferent treatment of African soldiers by white officers and NCOs often earned deep resentment and hatred. Recruits at the training depot at Welgedacht in South Africa wrote to their commanding officer in July 1942:

> We are ill-treated in this Depot by men who are supposed to be our seniors in rank ... Captain Fransi [*sic*] and his tall CSM often kick our ration of beer out of our hands. And when asking why do they do this answer is collected all these damn kaffers and march them inside. Final notice that next week we shall stone this Captain Fransi [*sic*] to death for it is gifted from above that his life and death is in black mans hand ... If are we not transferred rather he be transferred or if not what they must come away from our beer rations which in other words means there will be blood shed.[70]

Inside South Africa, but particularly without, many black soldiers proved troublesome to the military authorities. Martin and Orpen describe this 'rising tide of disciplinary problems' as due to 'lack of suitable officers and NCOs, failure to form Coloured and Native combatant units capable of developing their own pride and *esprit de corps*, and the insult to their loyalty and manhood implied by the refusal to arm Black volunteers'. This barely addresses the racism that touched every non-European soldier in the SADF.[71] Resentment was regularly expressed by black troops who purposely 'lost', stole and sold kit, or went on the rampage, as did men of the NEAS at Palmietkuil South in January 1943. A short time later 4 Battalion Cape Corps acted similarly at the same camp.[72] An illustration of the anxiety among whites at the riotous behaviour of non-European soldiers is provided by the outcry from the National Party in Parliament following a riot by 50 drunken Coloured soldiers on a train north from Cape Town in March 1943. In suppressing the disturbance the National Volunteer Reservists at Laingsburg fired on the men, killing one and wounding three.[73] Writing from the Middle East in late 1943, Col E. A. Sayer said that 'discipline is the one side of the work which causes me the most head-aches … and gives cause for much concern'.[74]

Acts of indiscipline were frequent and widespread among black soldiers, increasingly by 1942 as the SADF struggled with recruitment, the logistics of leave, food supplies, finding suitable officers, and imposing petty disciplinary restraints. The first official word of serious concern came in March 1943 when Col E. T. Stubbs, writing from the Middle East, reported to Gen Len Beyers:

> I need not … remind you of the increasing incidence of insubordination and crime amongst the non-European soldiers such as … the passive resistance and refusal to obey orders at both Booschpoort and Quaggapoort, the Wentworth incident of the 202 M.T. Coy., the mutinous behaviour of Native details it King's Park and the riots in Kimberley Barracks. These are just a few of the more recent incidents which are occurring with increasing intensity.

He concluded: 'Defence must prepare itself for a growing momentum of discontent ultimately resulting in a break-down of discipline by insubordination, mutiny and crime in N.E.A.S.'[75]

As black soldiers were labourers in uniform, strikes or desertion were obvious forms of protest. NMC Pioneers in the Middle East in May 1942 downed tools and refused to start on another tunnel until they were given leave. Eighty-five men were arrested and sent to Beirut. The official history said that the 'men found it difficult to adjust fully to army life', and that locally acquired drink contributed to the trouble. The Deputy Director, NEAS, who helped enquire into the incident, said years later that it was because the men had worked seven days a week without leave.[76] In September 1942 Cape Corps men in the Middle East refused to undertake artillery training, claiming that they had been enlisted as noncombatants, although the probable reason was their fear that such training would delay leave.[77] By the end of the war nearly four per cent of all black soldiers had deserted the army. A much greater worry for the military authorities was mutiny that developed from less obvious grievances and, in particular, any which seemed to challenge the racial *status quo*. These included some fairly mild incidents such as the disturbance at the depot at Valkfontein in June 1942, when 120 soldiers rebelled against abuse, inadequate food and harsh discipline; a clash with the police at Eshowe in November 1942; riots at a number of camps in early 1943; a stone-throwing incident at Standerton Remounts Depot in April 1943; and the mass break-out of men from the Quaggapoort camp in August 1943. Some riots developed from small incidents and racial slights. Recruits at

Welgedacht Depot in July 1941 reacted strongly to military police action in enforcing a queue. A rumour went up that a soldier accidentally stabbed by a guard had died and his friends called for revenge: 'Yes, you boer, you have injured that man but we will retaliate tonight'. In the ensuing riot, only quelled by police with teargas, several black and white soldiers were injured. Similar outbreaks of short-lived and non-lethal violent protest occurred at a number of camps and depots throughout South Africa during the war.[78]

Much more serious were the disturbances at the Germiston air force base in South Africa, in June 1942, and at the NMC camp at Garawi in Egypt in August 1943. The first, initially a dispute over entitlement to discharge and the methods of serving beer, escalated when the authorities' attempts to arrest six men were opposed by soldiers on parade who were armed with assegais. A white reserve brigade helped quell the mutiny and in the struggle three of the men resisting arrest were shot and killed. News of the incident discouraged recruiting; and the military authorities, reporting that white troops had fired only when confronted by armed Africans, decided that in future NMC troops should not carry assegais except in the course of duty.

As with many wartime mutinies, that at Garawi originated from accumulated grievances over the harshness of the white commander, a Maj Gibson, and his officers; lack of leave (it was widely known that Cape Corps troops received leave); and the conduct of the military police. One mutineer, David Sabiya, fortified with drink, was heard to say that 'he was going to kill all the Mboons today, meaning, "kill all the Dutchmen"', while another ring-leader, Joseph Dafet, reportedly said: 'There is going to be a lot of bloodshed in this place today'. On that morning, 17 August, trouble began in the guard tent. Officers were threatened with sticks and stones. With Dafet in the lead, soldiers shouting, 'go and get rifles' broke into the quartermaster's store. An attempt by a white officer to mediate was met with the retort by Elias Moshopbane: 'We don't want to see your white face here ... we are the enemy, let us get rifles and we will fight the lot of you'. In the end Dafet and two companions were arrested in Cairo and three soldiers were killed either by the mutineers or by troops suppressing the disturbance. At the subsequent court-martial six ringleaders were sentenced to be shot, and two were given life imprisonment and two others shorter terms. The death sentences were later commuted to life imprisonment. Despite the harsh treatment of the mutineers, Garawi remained a troublesome camp throughout the war.[79]

Conclusion

Dissent and mutiny in African colonial armies was not dissimilar to unrest in any other army. In the British Army soldiers' protests focused on a range of grievances similar to those given vent by African soldiers, and protest took similar form. However, a distinctive feature of colonial armies, and particularly the South African Defence Force, was that they were established on racial lines and discriminatory treatment pervaded every part of the service. Certainly European armies were shaped by class differences, with a distinctive officer class and other ranks drawn from the lower middle and working classes, although with wartime conscription these distinctions became more blurred. In contrast, in colonial armies the racial differences became more pronounced in the Second World War as more and more men from different areas were brought into the forces and as African soldiers served overseas and came in contact with other armies, including white soldiers. Racial differences and discriminatory treatment often lay at the heart of soldiers' grievances and protests in African colonial armies during the Second World War.

The wartime colonial and South African armies were overwhelmingly composed of civilians in uniform. Men plucked from the 'bush' or small towns, often involuntarily, were subject to a vast range of new experiences within a framework of unfamiliar order and restraint. In a relatively short time recruits were expected to adapt to this regimen and accept its coercions. Most mutinies were effectively strikes arising out of grievances that touch most men who have been removed from familiar surroundings and the comforts of home and placed in confined circumstances. Seemingly purposeless orders and activities, long hours, sometimes inadequate food, inactivity and boredom, sudden orders to move overseas and lack of leave, all added to the discontent of troops. These and all the petty injustices and inconveniences which are inevitable in the cumbersome machinery of racial discrimination combined to provide any number of recipes for discontent and collective insubordination. Given the conditions of service and the often limited consideration given to the interests of African troops, it is surprising that serious unrest did not occur more frequently.

Notes

[1] J. F. C. Harrison, *Scholarship Boy: A Personal History of the Mid-Twentieth Century* (London, 1995), ch. 9, pp. 107–14.

[2] TNA, CO968/147/4, 'Mauritus Regt: Employment in East Africa or Madagascar. Attitude of 1st Bn (Diego Suarez incident), 1943–45', Platt to WO, telegram, 23 December 1943.

[3] Ashley Jackson, *War and Empire in Mauritius and the Indian Ocean* (Basingstoke, 2001), ch. 5, provides a full account of the mutiny.

[4] TNA, CAB106/1580, 'Colonial military forces in the Second World War', by E. E. Sabben-Clare, nd. *c.* late 1945, paras 74 and 165; CO820/56/1 and CO820/56/2; WO32/15243, Select Committee on the Army and Air Force Acts, Note by the Departmental Committee, 6 May 1953.

[5] For a discussion of the difference between a strike and a mutiny see Timothy Parsons, *The 1964 Army Mutinies in the Making of Modern East Africa* (Westport CT, 2003), 'Introduction'.

[6] Michel Foucault, *Discipline and Punish: The Birth of the Prison* (Harmondsworth, Penguin edn, 1977), pp. 136 and 168, traces 'the body as object and target of power' through the organisation of European armies from the 17th century onwards.

[7] David Killingray, 'The "rod of Empire": The debate over corporal punishment in the British African colonial forces, 1888–1946', *Journal of African History*, 35, 2 (1994), pp. 201–16.

[8] See the House of Commons debates, 3 and 15 April 1930.

[9] TNA, WO203/4524.

[10] Jennifer Warner, 'Recruitment and service in the King's African Rifles in the Second World War', MLitt thesis, University of Bristol, 1985, p. 143.

[11] Wendell Patrick Holbrook, 'The impact of the Second World War on the Gold Coast, 1939–1945', PhD thesis, Princeton, 1978, pp. 208ff; David Killingray, 'Military and labour recruitment in the Gold Coast during the Second World War', *Journal of African History*, 23, 1 (1982), pp. 83–95.

[12] Parsons, *The 1964 Army Mutinies*, 'Introduction', provides a useful account of mutinies among armed forces, including colonial armies. Lawrence James, *Mutiny in the British Commonwealth Forces 1797–1956* (London, 1987), barely touches on mutinies among African troops during the Second World War.

[13] TNA, CAB106/1580, 'Colonial military forces in the Second World War', nd. *c.* late 1945.

[14] James, *Mutiny*, p. 13, offers a typology of mutinies.

[15] David Omissi, *The Sepoy and the Raj: The Indian Army, 1860–1940* (London, 1994), ch. 4; Cynthia M. Enloe, *Ethnic Soldiers: State Security in a Divided Society* (Harmondsworth, Penguin edn, 1980), pp. 33–38.

[16] TNA, FO2/155, Berkeley to Salisbury, 30 May 1898; and WO 32/8417. The mutinies by Sudanese troops were closely mirrored by two revolts among the *Force Publique* in the Congo Free State; see *La Force Publique de sa naissance à 1914* (Brussels, 1952); and F. A. Vandewalle, 'Mutineries au Congo Belge', *Zaïre*, 11, 5 (1957), pp. 487–514.

[17] M. W. Daly, *Imperial Sudan* (Cambridge, 1990), ch. 5.

[18] E.g. David Killingray, 'The mutiny of the West African Regiment in the Gold Coast, 1901', *International Journal of African Historical Studies*, 16, 3 (1983), pp. 441–54.

[19] C. H. Stigand, *Administration in Tropical Africa* (London 1914), p. 252.

[20] See Kenneth W. Grundy, *Soldiers Without Politics: Blacks in the South African Armed Forces* (Berkeley CA, 1983); Albert Grundlingh, *Fighting their Own War: South African Blacks in the First World War* (Johannesburg, 1987); L. W. F. Grundlingh, 'The participation of South African Blacks in the Second World War', PhD thesis, Rand Afrikaans University, 1986, ch. 2.

[21] Kenya had an all-white defence force from 1928 until it was disbanded ten years later; see C. J. D. Duder, 'An army of one's own: The politics of the Kenya Defence Force', *Canadian Journal of African Studies*, 25, 2 (1991), pp. 207–25.

[22] This view was put forward from a number of quarters, including by S. H. Barber, who eventually became public relations officer for all African troops in the Middle East; see his *Africans in Khaki* (London, 1948), p. 47.

[23] Max Hastings, *Retribution: The Battle for Japan, 1944–45* (New York, 2008), p. 83.

[24] BBC Africa Service. Joe Culverwell came to live in Britain after the war was over, teaching in Muswell Hill, London, and supporting the struggle of the Zimbabwe African National Union (ZANU) against the white regime in Rhodesia. After Zimbabwean independence he became a ZANU senator.

[25] TNA, CAB106/307, para 162.

[26] For example, see the several cases cited by Festus Cole, 'The role of the colonial army in Sierra Leone', paper presented at the International Symposium on Sierra Leone, Freetown, May 19–21, 1987, pp. 20ff; Luise White, *The Comforts of Home: Prostitution in Colonial Nairobi* (Chicago, 1990), p. 168.

[27] TNA, CO 820/52/34197, 1944–46, Colonial Office meeting, 12 July 1944.

[28] TNA, WO 32/11757, 'Disturbances in Asmara, 1946–47'. There had been similar but less serious incidents involving Sudanese and Eritreans at Massawa in February 1943 (11 Battalion SDF), and at Asmara in February 1945, and again in July 1946 (2 Battalion SDF).

[29] Most court-martial records appear not to have been deposited in the Public Record Office.

[30] TNA, WO32/10863, Court of Inquiry into mutiny of Somaliland Camel Corps, Burao, 10–12 June 1944.

[31] For example, TNA, WO32/10863. 'Court of Inquiry …', 1944.

[32] Thirty-five African soldiers were killed in the suppression of the mutiny at Thiaroye, which was over the question of back pay and demobilisation premiums. Thiaroye is an important landmark in Senegalese national consciousness and was commemorated in a film directed by Ousmane Sembène, *Le Camp de Thiaroye* (1988). See Myron Echenberg, 'Tragedy at Thiaroye: The Senegalese soldiers' uprising of 1944', in Robin Cohen, Jean Copans and Peter Gutkind, eds, *African Labor History* (Beverley Hills CA, 1978), pp. 109–28. On the *Force Publique* mutinies of February 1944 at Luluabourg (Katanga) and Jadotville, see John Higginson, *A Working Class in the Making: Belgian Colonial Labour Policy, Private Enterprise and the African Mineworkers* (Madison WI, 1989), ch. 8; Bruce Fetter, 'Luluabourg revolt at Elizabethville', *African Historical Studies*, 2.2 (1969); Mabiala Mantuba-Ngoma, 'Les soldats noirs de la Force Publique (1888–1945): contribution à l'histoire militaire du Zaïre', thesis, Université du Zaïre, Lubumbashi, 1980, pp. 169 ff.

[33] Quoted by Kevin K. Brown, 'The military and social change in Tanganyika: 1919–1964, PhD thesis, Michigan State University, 2001, p. 317.

[34] See Felix Cole, 'The Sierra Leone Army: A case study of the impact of the colonial heritage, 1901–1967', MA thesis, Fourah Bay College, University of Sierra Leone, 1987, pp. 187ff. The courts-martial can be followed in the *Daily Mail* (Freetown), 10, 13, 17, and 25 March 1939, and in the *Sierra Leone Weekly News*, 4, 11 March, 1 April and 5 May 1939. See also E. D. A. Turrey and A. Abrahams, *The Sierra Leone Army: A Century of History* (London, 1987), pp. 62–63, and Joseph A. Opala, *Sierra Leone Heroes* (Freetown, 1987), pp. 66–67.

[35] *Daily Mail* (Freetown), 25 March 1939.

[36] RHL, Oxford, Mss. Afr. S. 1734, Box VI, T. C. Watkins to David Killingray, November 1979.

[37] Oral accounts of the strike by pioneers, collected some 30 years after the event, almost inevitably have gained a mythical element. According to one account, Kenyan troops of 5 and 6 KAR refused to break

the strike, being unwilling to 'fire on their brothers'. Nyasaland soldiers were thus used and 'many [striking] soldiers were killed'. O. J. E. Shiroya, *Kenya and World War II* (Nairobi, 1985), pp. 35–36.

38 Michael Blundell, *So Rough a Wind* (London, 1964), pp. 50–51. See also Michael Blundell, *A Love Affair with the Sun: A Memoir of Seventy Years in Kenya* (Nairobi, 1994), pp. 48–49.

39 David Shirreff, *Bare Feet and Bandoliers: Wingate, Sandford, the Patriots and the Part they Played in the Liberation of Ethiopia* (London, 1995), pp. 309–10.

40 Waruhiu Itote, *'Mau Mau' General* (Nairobi, 1967). Later in the war Itote served as a mess steward in Burma.

41 W. R. Shirley, *A History of the Nigerian Police* (Lagos, 1950), pp. 66–68.

42 K. D. D. Henderson, *The Making of the Modern Sudan: The Life and Letters of Sir Douglas Newbold* (London, 1953), pp. 224–25.

43 Anthony Clayton and David Killingray, *Khaki and Blue: Military and Police in British Colonial Africa* (Athens OH, 1989), pp. 240–41. Also RHL, Mss. Africa s 1715, Box V, papers of Maj E. G. C. Haigh and J. B. Hobson, and Box XIX, G. K. Young. TNA, CAB106/1580, para 162, states that the men were not punished and were granted leave. CO968/11/7, minute by Rolleston to Calder, 20 March 1942: 'This is indeed a tragedy ... news will fly around East Africa and African morale both military and labour will be badly shaken.'

44 There were small mutinies in the Somaliland Camel Corps in November 1936 and March 1937 when men refused to use scrapers to remove dung from stables; a contributory factor was animosity towards NCOs. TNA, CO820/27, 1937.

45 Jama Mohamed, 'The 1944 Somaliland Camel Corps mutiny and popular politics', *History Workshop Journal*, 50 (2000), pp. 93–113.

46 TNA, WO32/10863, 'Future of Somaliland Camel Corps, East Africa', letter to OC, SCC, from 'Senior WOs and NCOs', 1 April 1944.

47 TNA, WO 32/10863, contains the proceedings of the Court of Enquiry, June 1944. Evidence of Sgt Musa Ismail.

48 TNA, CO968/150/4, 'Disbandment of Somaliland Camel Corps, 1944–45'.

49 TNA, WO32/01863, Platt comments on Court of Inquiry, June 1944.

50 TNA, DO35/1183/X1069/1/1, Part 2; also report by Maj Gray, 3 December 1945.

51 Ashley Jackson, *Botswana 1939–1945: An African Country at War* (Oxford, 1999), p. 232.

52 TNA, DO 35/1183/Y.1069/1/2, Part II. DO 35/1183/Y1069/1/1, files16–31, 'Disorders among Basuto Co. of APC – shooting in prison', 1946; and files 42–49, 'Reports on discipline'.

53 TNA, DO35/1184/Y/1/2, E. K. Featherstone, Resident Commissioner, Swaziland, to High Commissioner in Pretoria, 2 May 1945; also minute by H. B. Lawrence, 8 August 1945.

54 National Archives and Records Administration, Washington DC, R and A Reports, OSS–W–1710, 22 May 1945.

55 TNA, CO820/52/34197, CO report, September 1944.

56 BBC Africa Service. Interview with Marshall Kebby by Elizabeth Obadina, Lagos, 1989. This mutiny may also be that referred to in the *Newsletter* of the League of Coloured Peoples, June 1946, p. 60; other disturbances in India are also mentioned on p. 77. In the Liddell Hart Military Archive, Dimoline papers, 9/3, dd. early November 1945, there is brief correspondence on 'The employment of British nursing sisters in African hospitals' in India, with reference to 'incidents' and of British nurses being withdrawn from caring for African soldiers; Gen Dimoline opposed this, arguing that their care was much appreciated by the African rank-and-file, and that rare incidents should not result in hasty action.

57 RHL, Mss. Afr. s. 1715, Brig G. H. Cree, Box 3, file 57, pp. 25–26.

58 IWM, London, Department of Sound Recordings, Military Operations 1939–45, East Africa, Brig (then Maj) G. H. Cree, reel 3.

59 RHL, Mss. Afr. s. 1715, Cree, Box 3, file 57, p. 28.

60 Clayton and Killingray, *Khaki and Blue*, p. 240.

61 RHL, Mss. Afr. s. 1734, Box X, Capt R. R. Ryder, ff 52–56, 'Mutiny in India by Sierra Leone troops of 4 (WA) Auxiliary Group, Sierra Leone Regiment, 1945'; David Killingray interview with Ian Morris, Edinburgh, 28 September 1993. Mr Morris was a major with 1st Gambia Regiment at Karvet-naga in 1945 and witnessed the mutiny and the heavy-handed official response. Ninety-two men were tried by courts-martial and outcomes ranged from sentences of three years with hard labour to acquittals.

62 TNA. CO 820/56/36060, Auchinleck, C-in-C India, telegram to War Office, 2 October 1945.

63 NAG, Accra, BF4532, 'Disciplinary action: West African troops', secret, 1945.

64 TNA, WO 169/24336; WO 269/97, and WO269/106.

65 Grundlingh, 'Participation of South African Blacks', ch. 7.

66 The official historians of the wartime SADF resorted to patronising language in describing breaches

of the officially imposed racial codes in Italy: 'Unsophisticated NMC men were for the first time exposed to all the temptations of continental European life ... Their background was primitive and left them unable to cope with the emotional and moral stresses to which they were subjected in a Europe at war. Months were to pass before the problem was satisfactorily solved.' H. J. Martin and Neil D. Orpen, *South African Forces World War II. Vol. VI: The SADF in Italy and the Mediterranean 1942–5* (Cape Town, 1977), p. 99.

67 Grundlingh, 'Participation of South African Blacks', pp. 249–50. Some African soldiers were persistent troublemakers so that they were 'boarded home'. See the instance of an HCT soldier mentioned by Barber, *Africans in Khaki*, p. 63.

68 Quoted by Joel Bolnick, '*Sefala sa Letsamayananha*: The wartime experiences of Potlako Kitchener Leballo', Wits History Workshop papers, 6–10 February 1990, p. 21.

69 Martin and Orpen, *South African Forces World War II: Vol. VII*, p. 246.

70 Quoted in Grundlingh, 'Participation of South African Blacks', p. 254.

71 Martin and Orpen, *South African Forces. World War II: Vol. VII*, pp. 245–55.

72 *Ibid.*, p. 246.

73 Alan Paton, *Hofmeyr* (Cape Town, 1964), pp. 363–67.

74 Grundlingh, 'Participation of South African Blacks', p. 257.

75 *Ibid.*, p. 257.

76 N. Orpen and H. T. Martin, *Salute the Sappers: Part I* (Johannesburg, 1981), pp. 314–15; F. Rodseth, *Nbabazabantu: The Life of a Native Affairs Administrator* (Volda, 1984), p. 93.

77 Martin and Orpen, *South African Forces World War II. Vol. VII*, pp. 164–65.

78 Grundlingh, 'Participation of South African Blacks', pp. 258–68. See also Bolnick, '*Sefala sa Letsamayananha*', pp. 23–24, and the list of reported riots by the NMC within South Africa, November 1942–October 1943, p. 27, Appendix 2. It is not known what impact mutinies by white South African and British soldiers had on Africans; see Gerry R. Rubin, *Durban 1942: A British Troopship Revolt* (London, 1992), describing the occasion in January 1942 when 200 RAF personnel and a few soldiers walked off and refused to continue on the *City of Coventry*, bound for Singapore. The strikes by 50,000 RAF personnel in camps mainly in India but also in the Middle East and Malaya in November 1945–March 1946, influenced Indian Navy units to mutiny; see BBC 4, *Secret History: Mutiny in the RAF*, transmitted 8 August 1996, 9pm.

79 Grundlingh, 'Participation of South African Blacks', pp. 268–76.

5
War

'Hot war raged on all over the world.'[1]

'O ye Mammy, do not worry,
Though I may be far away,
If I lose my life on the battlefield
Where the bombs and the bullets are flying.'[2]

'Where have you been?' she asks him, trying to remove the KAR hat pin-folded on
one side from his head.
'Burma ... India ... Japan ... lands far away, soldier fighting for the king.'[3]

On a sunny morning in March 1944 a small detachment of West African and British soldiers of the 29th Casualty Clearing Station of the 6th West African Brigade stirred in their makeshift camp on the banks of the River Kaladan in Burma. As part of the 81st (West African) Division they had paddled their way down the river on flat open bamboo rafts, following the retreating Japanese forces. With nightfall they had tied up their rafts and slept between river and forest. With the light of morning a few Burmese from the village of Nyron came down to the river, attracted by the unusual sight of black men. Soldiers in various states of casual dress chatted, shaved and drank tea in preparation for the continued journey down the Kaladan. Isaac Fadoyebo, an 18-year-old Nigerian volunteer, stood drinking tea and talking to his countryman, the tall and imposing Sgt Duke, who was clad only in white vest and blue underpants. Suddenly

> gunshots rang out from the opposite bank ... we all ran for cover. A confused situation arose because we were badly positioned ... we could not do much to evade the gunshots in view of the fact that we were on the slope of the river. The heavy fire continued intermittently for more than one hour ... Each time the Japanese stopped firing, I made a number of abortive attempts to get away from the area. I did not know at the time that I had been wounded and I just kept on trying to move away. I was wondering as to what might have been responsible for my inability to lift myself off the ground and make a dash for shelter ... My right leg developed aches and pains. So was the left side of my abdomen immedi-

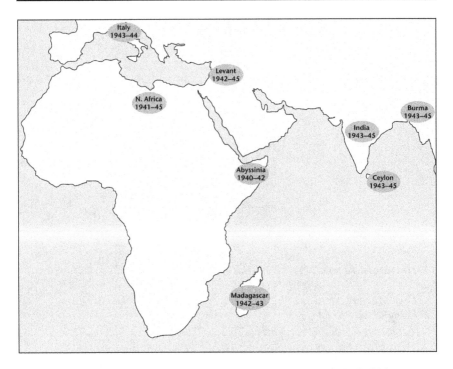

Map 3 *Areas of the world where African forces served 1940–1945*

ately below my ribs. I made an attempt to peep at my right leg and the left hand of my body and I saw a lot of blood. I then knew for sure that I had been hit by bullets in both parts of the body. I had a fractured femur very close to the knee and one bullet also pierced my stomach just below the ribs.[4]

Most members of the detachment were dead or, like Fadoyebo, badly wounded; a few had managed to escape relatively unscathed into the forest. Sgt Duke's body lay where he had stood 'with his tin mug clung to his hand', and the commanding officer, Maj Murphy, was mortally wounded. Fadoyebo's close friend Essien had also been hit and was lying close by:

> I noticed that Essien ... was in pains but I did not see any blood stain in his battle dress. I heard him saying, 'Take me O God! Take me O God!' all the time. After a short while, I observed that he was struggling for breath ... A few minutes later he stopped gasping and I then presumed that he was no more.

A Scots captain of the Royal Army Medical Corps, who was unwounded, came over to help Fadoyebo but as he did so the 'Japanese soldiers charged in with bayonets fixed'. They searched and stripped the dead and dying and ransacked the rafts, and when they realised that Fadoyebo could not stand up, left him and the other badly wounded men to die. Later in the day, Fadoyebo wrote, 'two friendly Indians came to me and showed signs of sympathy'. The Indians carried him away from the area and also brought some food. Fadoyebo was in great pain and a passing platoon of Gambian soldiers, attempting to break out from what was clearly Japanese-held territory, could do no more than find the wounded man a hiding place in the forest and leave him with another wounded soldier, David Kagbo from Sierra Leone. For the next nine months the two men, Fadoyebo constantly in pain, were fed and hidden from the Japanese by local people until rescued by a Gurkha patrol.

Fadoyebo's story is not only a remarkable tale of human endurance but also a rare account of the heat of battle written by an African soldier. Although thousands of African soldiers fought on the front line in the campaigns of the Second World War very few have described much of their personal experience in print or orally. The official war diaries of each African unit provide first hand reports of military operations. Written up by unit commanders when time allowed on flimsy paper with an indelible pencil, they now form part of the vast collection of War Office files kept in the National Archives at Kew, England. For the most part war diaries are bald accounts, composed under battle conditions and often hastily compiled and under-stated. Individual soldiers are occasionally mentioned but the diaries deal essentially with units rather than persons. Inevitably some war diaries did not survive the hostilities. During and immediately after the war various accounts were published describing the contribution made by African soldiers to the fighting. The emphasis again was on the role of units such as regiments and battalions; written with the fresh smell of war in the air these accounts did not minimise the mud, sweat, blood and terror of the battlefront. Where individual soldiers were mentioned it was to commend their heroism and bravery.[5] The semi-official regimental histories mainly detail the roll of battle honours; African troops have a central role but they are rarely allowed to speak and their actions are described from a Eurocentric viewpoint.[6]

The scholarly writing about African colonial soldiers since the late 1970s has focused largely on social and economic aspects of the military experience. Although a good deal of oral information has been collected from ex-servicemen in the former British colonies and South Africa, researchers have been little concerned to ask questions about the actual experience of battle. The material on the French *tirailleurs* is much richer.[7] And yet, a major agenda for many historians of modern conflict since the 1970s has been to tell the story of battle using the first-hand accounts of participants.[8] That few historians of Africa have bothered to do this is partly because historians' outlooks have been fashioned by the prevailing interest in social and economic history, but also because of the lack of personal accounts of battle from Africans. The vast majority of colonial soldiers were nonliterate, many were in noncombatant roles, and only one or two ex-soldiers have written and had published accounts of their military experiences. Interestingly when in 1989 the BBC Africa Service appealed to ex-soldiers for first-hand accounts of the war, very few respondents offered much information about their battlefield experience. Perhaps their perceptions of what was required had been in part shaped by the prevailing agenda of African historians and researchers.

The military campaigns

The purpose and practice of the British African Colonial Forces in peacetime was that they would be employed only within the African continent and not in wars against Europeans or in temperate regions. However, wartime crises forced a change in policy and in 1914–18, 1919–20, 1939–45, and in the late 1940s–early 1950s, African troops were used in imperial campaigns outside the continent.[9] South Africa generally eschewed putting non-Europeans into military uniform but did so in wartime, although mainly for them to serve as labourers. The total figure for all Africans from every colony – British, French, Belgian and Italian – as well as South Africa, who donned uniform during the Second World War, is rather difficult to compute (see Table 2). First of all, accurate figures are not always available; Italy claimed to have enlisted up to 250,000 men in one way and another, mainly from its newly acquired East African empire, but many were highly unreliable either as combatants or labourers. Secondly, men entered and left the armed forces at different times so there was some movement in and out of uniform throughout the war years. Often the figures given are the equivalent of snapshots showing military numbers at a given time. Thus in May 1945, when the British African forces were at their largest, there were *c.* 400,000 soldiers drawn from virtually every territory, but a total number larger than this served in the armed forces. South Africa recruited 123,000 non-Europeans for its defence force during the war years. The various French regimes probably enlisted 200,000 Africans for the war effort. Thus altogether something in the region of one million men, and a very small number of women, were put into military uniform of one kind or another by the different colonial powers in the war years 1939–45. This was the largest enlistment of manpower in the history of Africa. This African contribution to the war effort is often ignored in the scholarly history of the Second World War.

At the start of the war most colonial armies were small. The British forces in East and West Africa slowly began to be modernised after 1936 by Gen Sir George Giffard, then Inspector-General of the RWAFF, in order to meet a possible Italian threat. But to transform a lightly armed gendarmerie, lacking any transport of its own and with only low-calibre mobile artillery pieces, into a force that might withstand a modern army with tanks and air support, could not happen overnight. The Bren machine-gun was introduced into the Sudan Defence Force in 1938 – making the SDF the first force in the world to be equipped with this weapon – and armoured cars were constructed locally, using 30cwt Ford chassis with reinforced springs, and equipped with machine-guns.[10] Moving men was a major problem. Only in the last years of the 1930s did the KAR begin to have lorries to transport troops, and this still occurred only fitfully in the RWAFF well after war had broken out. Not one of the British colonies was in a real state to defend itself from a well-armed and determined enemy. The Anglo-Egyptian Sudan, situated astride the Nile valley, was to become a vital wartime supply-line to the Middle East. However, when Italy entered the war in mid-1940 the Sudan was defended by a few thousand troops, and there was not 'a single AA gun in the whole territory'. When the first Italian air raids took place Miles Lampson bemoaned 'our Sudanese nakedness'.[11] Kenya likewise had a long unguarded northern frontier, although arid territory served as an effective barrier. In West Africa, once France had surrendered, the British were faced with the prospect of long frontiers to be secured against a hostile Vichy regime that might allow its territory to be used for German naval and/or airbases.

Few Africans, whether the small number of regular soldiers or the new recruits, had seen or had much idea about the destructive power of modern weapons such as tanks, armoured cars, heavy artillery or military aircraft.[12] A Nigerian soldier wrote home from East Africa that

> I saw a wonderful thing called a "Tank". I saw a war motor. It was constructed like a tortoise, with wheels of rubber enclosed in chains. There are two men inside it and one machine-gun in front. When it starts moving it appears like a crocodile chasing a man.

At Wajir, in northern Kenya, a Gold Coast soldier described his first sight of armoured cars and some tanks going on patrol which 'appeared unlike the ordinary lorries with which we travel'. One soldier said 'Oh, these cars and tanks are very good for this war. If one company of this Battalion get about fifty of the cars and another company get about the same number of the tanks, I think we fit finish the war in East Africa for one week.'[13] Chinyanja-speaking troops from Nyasaland called tanks *kasinja* 'because they looked like a *Gule Wamkulu*. You could not see the people inside, you only saw the barrel of the gun'.[14]

Fighter and bomber aircraft were also a new experience. A Nigerian soldier recalled:

> On Monday the 28th November in the evening, about 6 o'clock, we were sitting down and we heard a noise like a 'dimm-dimm-dimm'. Together we lifted our eyes towards the sky; suddenly we noticed three Italian aeroplanes, and they were throwing bombs on our soldiers guarding a bridge in front of us about twelve miles away. We could see flames and fire like you would see a big bush fire.[15]

When war was declared in early September 1939, Britain's African colonial forces were placed on a war footing and came under War Office control. With these forces' small size and the paucity of military equipment this meant little more than measures to ensure that enemy aliens were apprehended and frontiers were effectively guarded. In East Africa the greatest anxiety was over Italian intentions. In 1937–38 London recognised that Italy was a grave threat and decided that African colonial defence should be coordinated with Imperial defence. It was agreed that in the event of conflict the War Office would assume responsibility for all African colonial forces. By December 1938 a West African expeditionary force for East Africa had been planned.[16]

The original plan utilising a West African expeditionary force was for troops to be transported by lorry across the continent, but this was abandoned in favour of moving them by sea. Anxious not to antagonise the Italians, the Cabinet did not authorise movement until May 1940; a further consideration of the War and Dominions office was that South Africa would commit troops to the defence of East Africa.[17] Shortly after the war began Winston Churchill, the First Lord of the Admiralty, urged that immediate steps be taken to see if 'African troops might be used in various parts of the Empire to relieve regulars for service in France'.[18] Both the Colonial and War Offices examined the question. Colonial Secretary Malcolm MacDonald argued that there were military and climatic objections to using Africans soldiers in France and political problems relating to their use in the Middle East as garrison troops. However, in April 1940 the War Cabinet agreed that African troops could be used outside the continent and MacDonald reluctantly accepted this 'new departure in British policy'.[19] Following this the Cabinet instructed that West African troops be moved to East Africa as soon as possible.

The collapse of France and Italy's entry into the war in mid-1940 brought the war into Africa. Italy's large East African army, which consisted of 80,000 European troops and many locally recruited soldiers of relatively unknown quality, possessed tanks, armoured cars, heavy artillery, and aircraft in numbers that far outweighed the puny defence forces of the Sudan and East Africa.[20] In North Africa, Italian forces posed a serious threat to Egypt and the strategic supply route through the Mediterranean. Vichy France had not only military aircraft in West and Equatorial Africa but also an army that considerably outnumbered and outgunned the RWAFF. The fear in London was that Vichy might ally itself to Berlin and allow Germany use of naval and air bases in West Africa. The first use of British West African troops, although not in any actual fighting, was in the abortive Free French attempt to seize the strategic port of Dakar from Vichy in September 1940.

The first campaigns of the war involving African troops were fought in Sudan and British Somaliland. The latter was thinly defended and no match for Italian military might, but Gen Archibald Wavell, then head of Middle East Command, determined to defend the colony. In the ensuing conflict the fighting mainly involved African troops with a stiffening of Europeans on both sides. The locally recruited and inadequate Somaliland Camel Corps was reinforced by Indian, KAR, newly-enlisted and untried Northern Rhodesian troops, and men of the Black Watch ferried over from Aden.[21] The KAR and Northern Rhodesians 'were at breaking point' and 'so was the imported Major-General's [Godwin-

146

Austen] nerve' (referring to Maj-Gen Reade Godwin-Austen). A company of the Black Watch was ambushed at night and in the chaotic retreat the African drivers outran their officer with the news 'Major killed, captain wounded, all finish, no good'.[22] With relatively small losses – 260 dead compared to more than 2,000 Italian troops – Godwin-Austen evacuated his force in mid-August 1940. Most men of the camel corps had rid themselves of their uniforms and disappeared, while Godwin-Austen showed his distrust of the local Somali police by disarming them under the threatening machine-guns of Indian troops.

Other than a few raids across the northern border of Kenya, which temporarily depressed the British, the Italians made little attempt at forward moves in East Africa. Despite their military strength the Italian forces were still largely preoccupied with consolidating control over recently conquered Ethiopia and dealing with local partisans. Wavell's victories in North Africa in early 1941 not only struck a blow at Italian morale but increased the isolation of Mussolini's East African empire. To counter the Fascist threat the British had built up a sizeable military force in Kenya composed of West and East African troops, and soldiers from South Africa, the Rhodesias, the Belgian Congo and Britain, and they had also begun developing the supply line up the Nile valley to Egypt. In February 1941 Gen Sir Alan Cunningham, commander of British forces in East Africa, ordered an attack from Kenya into Italian Somaliland; troops were also landed on the coasts of British Somaliland and Eritrea.[23] Much of the fighting was undertaken by West and East African and white South African troops. The advance was rapid; the river Juba was crossed and in less than a month the Italians had been routed in Somaliland. Much of the rest of the campaign, which involved some serious fighting to wrest Ethiopia from Italian control, involved mainly East and West African troops. Cunningham favoured using the white South African units partly because they were more mechanised but also for political reasons. Many senior officers thought African soldiers would not be reliable in battle conditions. This promotion of white troops over Africans was resented by the officers commanding East and West African troops. In the event the two white South African brigades did not perform very well in battle;[24] by and large the African troops did. After stiff fighting outside Harar by the Nigerian Regiment their brigade commander, Brig Gerard Smallwood, wrote to Cunningham:

> I think I may be permitted to take this opportunity to tell you how completely the Nigerian soldier has falsified all doubts as regards to his reactions to the conditions of these operations. It has been said that he could not go short of water; he has done so without a murmur. It has been said he could not fight well out of his native bush; at Marda Pass he fought his way up mountain sides which would be recognized as such even on the Frontier. It has been said that he would not stand up well to shelling and machine-gun fire in the open; at Babile, under such fire, men were trying to cut down enemy wire with their matchets. It has been said that he would be adversely affected by high altitudes and cold; at Bisidimo, after a freezing night on the hill, he advanced over the open plain at dawn with the same quiet, cheerful determination he always seems to carry about with him. He is magnificent.[25]

Sudan was a critical supply-line between East Africa and Egypt. However, Italy failed to deploy its much larger and more powerful forces effectively. As Daly argues: 'In the end, the Sudan was saved by Italian incompetence'.[26] Mobile units of the SDF harassed and routed Italians patrols on the long southern border. By the end of 1940, reinforcements of British and Indian troops, RAF bombers, and units drawn from a variety of British, French and Belgian colonial forces, enabled Gen Platt, the commanding officer in the Sudan, to launch a successful counter-offensive on Kassala, the only Sudanese town of substance to be held by the Italians.[27] Ethiopians enrolled in the Italian imperial army were of questionable loyalty and deserted in large numbers after these defeats in January 1941. At the same time British forces in Egypt successfully struck at the Italians in Libya and neutralised that military threat. From Kassala, Platt's forces entered Eritrea and joined in the advance on the Ethiopian capital of Addis Ababa which fell in April 1941. Nigerian soldiers' involvement in this successful campaign was marked by the Hausa poet Sa'adu Zungur:

> The Nigerians cleaved through to the Somali corner without halting.
> The Ethiopians drank freely in city, in encampment, and in village.
> Their enemy was knocked out. Ethiopia's troubles were over.[28]

But a grievance festered among some African troops – that white South Africans headed the triumphant march into Addis Ababa while African battalions were relegated to a secondary role.[29]

With the Italian surrender in May 1941, the main campaign in East Africa was over. In the autumn of that year West African troops were returned home to help secure the four colonies against any Vichy threat. By then official views regarding the value of African troops in military operations outside Africa had undergone considerable change. Lord Lloyd, who succeeded MacDonald as Colonial Secretary in May 1940, now strongly advocated using African troops in imperial campaigns. Japan's entry into the war in December 1941 further stretched British and Indian manpower resources and also focused defence strategy on the Indian Ocean. Increasingly the War and Colonial Offices accepted that African troops, whose military capacity had been proved in the East African campaign, should be made available for service outside the continent. In December 1941 the War Office asked that two East African brigade groups be sent to Ceylon so as to release British garrison troops.[30]

One little-known but highly significant campaign involving East, Central and South African troops was the assault on Vichy-held Madagascar in May 1942. The island had been blockaded by the British since July 1940, but by 1942 there was deep concern that the pro-German regime might provide the Japanese with submarine bases which would pose a serious threat to Allied shipping on the Cape route. In a two-stage campaign that began in May 1942 and ended with an armistice in early November, East African and South African troops fought their way down the island from Diégo Suarez in the north. They faced fierce opposition from French and French colonial troops (Senegalese *tirailleurs* and Malgache soldiers) who blocked roads to armoured columns.[31]

One major military need that Africa could provide was pioneers for Middle East Command. From late 1941 thousands of men were drawn from all parts of the continent to serve as uniformed guards, lorry drivers, dockworkers, miners, cooks, medical orderlies and general labourers in North Africa, the Middle East and Italy.[32] The vast majority of soldiers recruited in South Africa and the High

12 *Abyssinian Patriot leader, 1941*

Fascist Italy invaded the independent Empire of Abyssinia in October 1935. The small and poorly equipped Abyssinian army was unable to withstand the onslaught of a modern military machine that used tanks, artillery, airpower and poison gas. By May 1936 the Abyssinian forces had been routed and Emperor Haile Selassie had fled his country. However, many Abyssinian 'Patriots' continued a guerrilla war against the Italian invaders. As the threat of a European war with the Axis powers grew more likely, the British in East Africa established links with Patriot elements. When Italy entered the war in May 1940 Britain already had Abyssinian allies such as this man. Some 6,000 Patriots served alongside the British in the defeat of the Italians in the Horn of Africa, while others fought the Italians and each other on their own terms. Not all Patriots wanted the return of Selassie and continued hostility to his rule posed a serious dilemma for the British after he had been restored to Addis Ababa in May 1941.

(Source: Imperial War Museum, IND 7018)

149

Commission Territories were in pioneer units. The South African government had not intended non-Europeans to be involved in the war but when necessity dictated their use it was determined that they should be confined to noncombatant roles.[33] Thabe Nkadiment, recruited for the South African Non-European Army Services, was sent on a cookery course, but 'I did not do much work as they pushed me around a lot. Now and then somebody pointed something out to me but most times I did not understand and just let things drift along.' His brother Sekate Nkadiment recalled that 'I spent most of my time scrubbing floors and peeling vegetables'.[34] In North Africa noncombatants faced all the problems of being shelled and bombed but without the means to reply: 'drops of blood of tribesmen brave/On Libyan plains beneath Egyptian skies', wrote the Xhosa poet James Ranisi Jolobe of his fallen countrymen.[35] Conditions were also often harsh and extreme with hot summers and cold winters. Bent, in his account of the Bechuanaland Pioneers, wrote that in Italy the conditions of life for the greater part of the year were just miserable:

> sunny Italy was a myth, it rained at any time during the year; and the cold during half the year was intense. The company of great mountains through the merciless winter was nothing less than sinister. It was nearly as cold in the plains, quite as wet and much more muddy; once the rain came, it remained where it fell; feet would be damp all day and boots clogged with mud would be almost too heavy to drag along.[36]

Although pioneers were often given arms when in a combat zone their essential role was to serve as labourers in military uniform. Like the carriers of the First World War who were the arms and legs of the armies in Africa, the pioneers built the roads and railways, dug trenches, unloaded ships, drove trucks and guarded supplies and prisoners-of-war. Although African ex-servicemen often challenge this, the majority of soldiers recruited by the British and South Africans were actually employed in noncombatant roles. It was a role that took men into the front line and could be as arduous and dangerous as that of any combatant. For example, on a battlefield in Libya in 1941 Cpl Barry Gazi volunteered to carry a Red Cross flag to the enemy lines in an attempt to secure a truce so that the wounded could be removed more safely. 'I proceeded towards the enemy,' he said, 'under very heavy fire, shells were bursting around me and bullets were whining over my head. I cannot say what my feelings were at that moment.'[37] Pioneers from Bechuanaland in Italy in 1944 endured both the weather and the enemy:

Many of them whose work is to carry ammunition, food and clothes to the men in the line can only work under cover of darkness because of enemy shelling and mortar fire. This is a very arduous occupation for night after night with heavy loads on their shoulders they clamber up steep and dangerous slopes in rain and snow, deliver their loads and return (often carrying wounded men) to their little bivouac tents in the early hours of the morning.[38]

With the end of the Vichy threat in West Africa in late 1942 the military authorities began to consider using African troops 'for operations in Burma or eastwards'. Field-Marshal Sir Archibald Wavell, C-in-C India, preferred West Africans as 'they are used to jungle and to moving with porter transport which would be invaluable in certain parts of Burma and Malaya'. Given their military performance against the Italians, he thought that they 'should be able to compete with Japanese'.[39] The Chiefs of Staff Committee, meeting in late December 1942, agreed that West and East African troops should be ready for overseas service by June 1943.[40] The 81st (West Africa) Division was formed in March 1943 and the 82nd (West Africa) Division shortly afterwards. Each division consisted of 28,000 men organised into three brigades; both concentrated for training in Nigeria and then moved to Asia, the 81st in July and the 82nd in November 1943. Continued recruiting in West Africa provided additional drafts for the divisions. The first role for West African troops in Asia was as pioneers, cutting a jeep track to the banks of the Kaladan river – a route which became known as the 'West African Way'. In early February 1944 Gold Coast troops acted as a fighting formation in the Kaladan valley, and from then until the end of the Burma campaign in August 1945 West Africans were constantly employed as frontline troops against the Japanese.[41]

The first KAR troops arrived in Burma in mid-1944 to fight the 'Jampans', as Nyasa soldiers called the enemy. As part of the 11th Division they fought at great cost against the retreating Japanese in the Kabaw valley.[42] One soldier told Sabben-Clare that the Japanese were *majanja sana* – 'tricky fellows'.[43] The terrain made movement difficult and large quantities of supplies of food and ammunition had to be carried by head-porters along hilly forest tracks. At the start of the campaign many soldiers were afflicted by malaria, dysentery and scrub typhus, although improvements in tropical medicines made in Canada and the USA helped reduce disease rates steadily through the war. Generally the military authorities thought that West African soldiers performed well in combat roles if led by suitable British officers, although they were not always impressed with the control exercised to prevent excesses.[44] A captured Japanese diary stated:

> The enemy soldiers are not from Britain but are from AFRICA. Because of their beliefs they are not afraid to die; so even if their commanders have fallen they keep on advancing as if nothing had happened. It makes things rather difficult. They have an excellent physique and are very brave, so fighting against these soldiers is somewhat troublesome.[45]

However, it was believed by British officers – and they may have been right – that in battle the Japanese first attempted to kill white officers and so deprive African troops of their leaders. Thus it was common for European officers going into combat to blacken their faces in order to be indistinguishable from their African troops. At the end of the war in Burma, some West African troops were employed as garrisons in the Irrawaddy delta where they aided the civil power in riot control, patrols and dacoit hunting. The War Office planned to use West Africans as occupation troops in Burma, Malaya and Indochina but this was opposed by Lord Louis Mountbatten, who thought them unsuitable for such operations.[46] However, East African troops were used in garrison roles in Palestine in 1946 and soldiers from the High Commission Territories continued to be used as pioneers in the Middle East for several years after the war.[47]

The British Merchant Navy had for long employed African crews and many were recruited during wartime. James Adewale from Nigeria joined a British ship as a galley-boy at Dakar in 1943, and was paid off in Liverpool only to be 'recruited compulsorily and sent off to London'. Years later Adewale recalled:

It was made clear to me that the alternative to going to war was prison; I was put on a ship in London heading for Normandy loaded with war materials. On our way from Normandy we ran into enemy mines and our ship was blown up. Fortunately, I was one of the lucky survivors of the incident. Not that I knew what went on after the explosion: I only found myself later in an Edinburgh hospital.[48]

Adewale was on board another ship in Naples harbour when the war ended. He returned to Nigeria with 'exactly seven pounds in my pocket'. The result of his war, he said, was that 'I had come home with travel stories but without money'. Several thousand Africans, along with men from the colonies, served with the merchant fleet during the war and many lost their lives.[49]

Getting to war

As soon as they were trained, soldiers faced the long journey to the war front. A major problem throughout the war was having insufficient lorries or ships available to transport troops in the right place and at the right time. For example, in 1940 air, land and sea transport was discussed as means of getting West African reinforcements to East Africa. The economic and logistical problems of assembling sufficient trucks and drivers and then servicing an all-weather route that passed through the territories of other colonial powers were such that the sea route proved the quickest and most appropriate way to Kenya. Colonial armies lacked their own transport and in the first two years of the war this had be made good and drivers trained.

Many soldiers left the training centres by rail. An unnamed West African soldier wrote of his departure from Accra railway station on 30 May 1940,

> when thousands of spectators, both men and women, grown-ups and little children, flocked to see us leaving for East Africa. Much suffering and pain was in the tender hearts of some of the Spectators who thought perhaps they would not see the return of the happy band of warriors then going to fight and defend the cause of freedom.[50]

Pte Frank Sexwale, from South Africa and bound for the North African theatre, said: 'I cried a lot when the train left Durban. The realities of the situation dawned on me now. I was full of spirit when I joined but ... I found I was really trapped ... If we had choice I would not have gone.'[51] The vast majority of men enlisted from the traditional recruiting grounds of the interior or from central Africa had never seen the sea and certainly not large ships. Samson Muliango first boarded a ship at Mombasa: 'To a lot of us from Northern Rhodesia, it was the first time to see the Indian Ocean and to board a ship'.[52] For John Mandambwe, who had travelled by boat on Lake Nyasa, the remarkable thing about the Indian Ocean was that it was tidal and constantly moving.[53] Selogwe Pilane from Bechuanaland said: 'For me it was the first time I had seen a boat, even the first time I saw the sea. We were not really scared to be on the boat. Our only fear was how we would save ourselves if the boat sank, because none of us knew how to swim.'[54] A Nigerian soldier expressed his amazement at the size of the ships and also at the vastness and turbulence of the sea:

Since the day we left Lagos, we saw nothing but long stretches of water like the wide World, we saw no living creatures except ourselves on the steamship. Although the ships were such big ships, they were tossed about like a piece of calabash in the wind on the water. Sometimes the water was like big hills that wanted to fall on top of us. When we saw these big hills of water our senses were upset, but God protected us from all this except that we vomited.[55]

Seasickness severely hit Rabson Chombola, of the 1st Northern Rhodesian Regiment: 'It took us 14 days to get to Cylon [*sic*] before we reached Cylon I became frustrated and fell sea sick because I had never seen the sea before.'[56] James Okehie, in the Nigerian Signals Brigade of 82nd (WA) Division, starkly remembered his voyage to Asia by the bodies of water he crossed or passed. He wrote:

We left Ibadan by train for Ikoyi and harboured with 14 Batalion [*sic*]. We left with a convoy of ships at the Lagos Harbour after 2 weeks at Ikoyi; we joined the other West African troops at Gold Coast (Ghana) Gambia, Searaleon [Sierra Leone] and from thence to Gibralter [*sic*] we passed the Atlantic Ocean, Dead Sea, Red Sea, Arabian Sea, Mediteranian [*sic*] Sea, Suez Canal, Egypt, Gulf of Eden [Aden], landed at India after 3 months of safety voyage and lastly at Indian Ocean. We landed safely at KARACHI.'[57]

Fifty years after the event this sounds a dull voyage. Not all were so. Convoys were bombed, machine-gunned and menaced by submarines. The convoy on which Nathaniel Opara travelled made its way through the dangerous waters of the Mediterranean in September 1942: 'On arrival at Malta with 28 ships, enemy planes attacked us. They shot down about two of them, while the rest 10 went away after sinking one of our ships.' And then, he continues: 'We travelled for three months before we landed in India with great suffering in the ships because of the climate'.[58]

The sea caused deep apprehension if not fear for many soldiers. It was not only the unknown; the sea also separated men from home and family. When soldiers knew that they were due to go overseas the desertion rate increased, and the authorities took action to prevent this. For black South Africans the collective memory of the sinking of the troopship *Mendi* in the English Channel in 1917, with the loss of more than 600 men of the Native Labour Corps, acted as a deterrent to enlisting in the 1940s. The disaster had been kept alive by Mendi Day, 21 February, being observed by Africans in the Union as a day of remembrance for the dead.[59]

Similar disasters did occur at sea during the Second World War. In early May 1941 *Erinpura*, carrying two companies of Basuto soldiers from Egypt to Malta, was attacked in rough seas by Italian aircraft. A torpedo sank the ship within a few minutes with the loss of more than 600 men.[60] Ernest Molem Khomari from Basutoland remembered panic on board as soldiers rushed to get on deck, a struggle between the strong and the weak. 'When the sirens [sounded] ... we ran to the top of the deck ... when the ship was sinking ... people were rushing [about] some of them walking on top of the others.' Khomari fell into the sea. Although he could not swim he was able to get into a boat, but this capsized. In the water again he clung to debris, then reached a raft. It was dark and men in the sea 'were making prayers'. Eventually Khomari was picked up by a destroyer and taken to Benghazi.[61] Another major loss of life occurred in February 1944 when the SS *Khedive Ismail*, packed with more than 1,500 soldiers and *en route* from Mombasa to Colombo, was torpedoed in mid-ocean by a Japanese submarine. The ship sank rapidly with the loss of 1,134 lives, most of them members of 301 Field Regiment, East African Artillery.[62] These disasters were kept secret in order not to discourage continued recruiting. Alick Chintu, a signaller with the Nyasaland Field Regiment, remembered that *en route* to Colombo, although he was 'eating and sailing well on the Indian Ocean, much of his mind was in fear because of Topidos [*sic*] which were mostly planted in the Ocean by the enimies [*sic*]'.[63] Indeed, Japanese bombers later sank the ship on which he had travelled while it was in Colombo harbour.

Supply lines

Major supply lines stretching the length of Africa were created to feed the machine of war – first to East Africa and then to North Africa and the Middle East. All war fronts, in Africa and elsewhere, had supply lines which were often serviced by African troops. Lorries assembled in South Africa and destined for the South African forces in East Africa were driven north so as to save scarce shipping space. The first drivers were white but from September 1940 Indian, Coloured and black drivers were employed, organised in motor transport companies. Lorries were taken first to Broken Hill in Northern Rhodesia and then driven the 1,600-mile journey to Kenya.[64]

There was a crucial United States–British air supply route across the Atlantic to Takoradi in the Gold Coast and thence via Kano and Khartoum to the Middle East.[65] However, the major supply line in Africa was down the Nile valley through the Sudan, and was used to ferry war materials from East Africa to Egypt and the Middle East. This north–south route was more than 2,000 miles long, much of it consisting of rough dirt roads that were dusty in the dry season and liable to flooding in the wet months after October. Throughout 1942 large gangs of Sudanese labourers worked on long stretches of road through the southern Sudan to ensure that it stayed open. The route remained a strategic highway for the Allies until the Axis defeat in North Africa in mid-1943.

Before the war relatively few Africans possessed driving skills. Wartime training greatly increased the number, although tuition was often rushed. Early on in the war South African drivers were trained on a crude 'simulator' cab made of sticks and springs.[66] Musa Kihwelo, from northern Tanzania, was 'conscripted out of school to serve in the King's African Rifles' and 'attached to 72 Regiment Motor Transport as a driver fighting in the Italian Somaliland'. He said:

> I was taken to Moshi to be trained as a driver for only two weeks before I was sent to the war ... After leaving the depot we went to Nairobi where we were given Doch vehicles and then proceeded to Yata where we found the Gold Coast army. This was my first time to see black soldiers who could not speak Kiswahili ... Then at night we proceeded to Garisa River where South African Engineers helped us cross the river by using pantoons [*sic*]. We were not expert drivers, so we drove very slowly to the battle field where the soldiers disembarked. This is how I reached the front.[67]

The 18-year-old Gilbert Zulu, who enlisted in Northern Rhodesia, became a lorry driver. By 1941 he was working on part of the north–south road in Uganda: 'Our task was for transportation of carrying our fellow soldiers to everywhere they were needed or required, and again carrying war equipments, ammunition and food.'[68]

In North Africa most supplies were moved by lorry, but many battlefronts in the Levant and Italy could only be supplied by mules or porters negotiating mountain paths and rough country. Austin J. Dlamini, a Swazi pioneer, provided a graphic account of taking supplies at night to the Scots Guards on the Salerno front in 1943:

> All this ammunition and food had to be taken up the line immediately. Crump, crump, shelling continued. Grenades, mortar, ammunition of every description was off-loaded and a long solemn file of Swazi troops wound their tedious way ... Precipitous country extremely hampered their movements yet ... they grimly continued on their way to their various destinations ... Silently in single file up steep slopes, down deep ravines, this convoy wound its way. HALT! a challenge from a Scot's Guardsman broke the night stillness. The convoy went on. HALT! again a challenge rang on over the silent dark ravine. This time our own guard was challenging the Germans. Corpses on the pathway formed a horrid sight. We had taken the wrong path, we were right in German lines. Back again, and veering slightly right, continued on our way the heavy boxes of ammunition weighing down the now weary men ... On and on we went, it was getting lighter now. Enemy mortar fire was concentrated on our path. Whoomp, Whoomp, the explosions were deafening, the blaze of light dazzling, we closed our eyes, but still the light pierced through the greyness of dawn, everyone ran for cover, none knowing where, just plunged into darkness. What a terrifying few minutes. Gradually we reformed and made for our last post. Up and up we went, smoke curled up from various spots where the battle had just previously raged. A few Guardsmen lay dead ... their clothes smouldering from the missiles which caused their deaths ... Another challenge – HURRAH! At last we had made it. A quiet smoke and talk and down back ... carrying wounded and assisting others who refused to be carried. Down precipitous heights these Swazis laughingly continued, some with wounded on their backs, others carrying stretchers.[69]

In Burma the terrain also made it very difficult to employ motor vehicles. Most supplies had to be taken up to the front line by carriers or mules; airdrops were also made, particularly to advanced positions. Boats needed for the frequent river crossings had to be carried on the heads of the men of the auxiliary groups.

> [The] men carried the assault boats slung on one side in rope cradles hanging from transverse pieces of timber. Two men took post at the bows of the boat, one on each side of it, and two more similarly at the stern. The boat was then lifted up, the transverse timbers put on their heads, and it was then ready to be moved on. To carry it in any other way was impossible because of the narrowness of the track and dense bush on either side ... the winding nature of the mule track and its sharp ascents and equally sudden and steep descents soon made marching extremely difficult. Indeed it was so dark at times that nobody knew whether the path went up or down, to right or to left or straight on. It was bad enough for the ordinary soldier unencumbered with a load on his head but how the carriers managed it is beyond comprehension.[70]

The 82nd (WA) Division sign was crossed spears through a headpad, which symbolised 'through our carriers we fight'. For the second Arakan operation in June–

August 1944, the 81st (WA) Division was reorganised so that the entire force could operate on a head-carrying basis and dispense with vehicles altogether. Men 'carrying heavy loads on their heads' marched for 70 minutes and then had a 20-minute rest. Officers observed that a longer rest than that 'usually resulted in boredom, impatience to get going and, in the later stages of a march, stiffening up of the muscles of the feet'.[71] By the end of the war all African carriers in Burma were trained in the use of arms and carried them. Without their contribution the war against the Japanese in that area would have lasted much longer. As one official account says:

> The speed with which he [the Japanese] was bundled out of the ARAKAN is no small tribute to the prowess of the West African soldier who, alone amongst all the different nationalities from which the British Army in Burma was drawn, was capable of operating for months on end in the worst country in the world without vehicles and without mules and was alone able to carry all his warlike stores with him.[72]

The heat of battle

At the start of the war many European officials were uncertain how African troops would cope with the conditions of modern warfare. A widely held view was that they would react badly, becoming unmanageable if not panic-stricken, and thus should be used only in support tasks. This assumption was wrong: African troops performed under fire as well as if not at times better than other troops in most of the campaigns in which they were employed. Such earlier views should not surprise the modern reader. The then-current ideas about race and culture invested little trust in 'native' virtues or abilities. But then, official expectations at the start of the war about the response to aerial bombardment of British civilians, particularly the working classes in the large cities, were also seriously wrong.

Attempts by European officers to convey to African soldiers what modern warfare was like can have had little real effect. It was believed by white officials that good training and every effort to ensure a high level of morale and especially confidence in officers, offered the best preparation for the battlefield. African soldiers, particularly Muslims and pagans, but also Christians, went to war with amulets or charms that they had bought. Talismans were commonly worn by warriors in African warfare, and some believed that these helped to protect them in battle. 'Juju salesmen and traders in amulets were commonly found around army camps and also when contingents were due to go off to an active theatre.'[73]

Official propaganda disseminated via posters, speeches, radio and film vans attempted to inculcate civilians with a sense of the righteousness of the Allied cause. Newspapers issued to African troops, for example *Baraza* ('Gazette'), published for the KAR, strongly emphasised the moral dimensions of the war.[74] Even in South Africa, where non-Europeans constantly felt the barbs of racial discrimination, there were those who saw the war against Germany as a war for

156

freedom. As one Cape Coloured transport driver wrote in response to the question 'Why are we fighting?': 'War, poverty and death know no colour bar. It is for that reason that the non-Europeans have decided the fight is theirs too. In war at least it seems as if all men are truly brothers.'[75] However, Frank Sexwale, who served with the South African NMC, later regarded the conflict as 'a British war', 'a white man's war'.[76]

Brotherhood could, in certain circumstances indeed exist. L/C A. J. Hlope, a Zulu soldier from South Africa serving in the Middle East, found interacting with white British soldiers who accepted him as a human being to be a startling experience. In a letter written in 1943 which found its way into a Black British publication, he reported:

> What has shocked every black man from South Africa is the behaviour of your English Tommies. Their character is wonderful and to explain it can need many pages. They shake hands with us, they talk to us, they sit next to us in cinemas, they smoke cigarettes with us. Even when one goes to the British hospital he gets the same food with them, he lines into one line with you, he is given a bed in the ward same to other beds, and blankets, he is sent to the ward according to the nature of his sickness. They have offered us more kindness than God has done. It is the first time in life that we have seen people of that kind![77]

In Burma, Gen Hugh Stockwell, commander of the 82nd (West Africa) Division, was concerned about the morale of his troops. He sent his white officers a scathing memorandum condemning those who made indiscreet comments about the capabilities of African soldiers in battle. 'I myself consider that it takes a great deal of moral courage to set the African the example he deserves or give him the leadership which is so necessary.' Stockwell went on to admit that some units had performed badly, particularly during night attacks by the Japanese. The African, he stated, 'has not a fighting history, and as a rule therefore battle does not come naturally'.[78] Although some officers may have decried the battleworthiness of African troops, and Stockwell had to make do with the officers he could get, there were some who had a strong respect for the troops' valour in conflict. Many years after the war, a former officer cited the example of the bravery of a soldier of the Gold Coast Regiment. Wounded and left for dead when his unit was overrun by the Japanese, Pte Kewku Pong found a Bren gun and fought on until he fainted from loss of blood:

> He found himself on his own, in the dark of the night, quite badly wounded, with a considerable number of Japanese rampaging behind him and a very noisy battle going on behind him. No Britisher to tell him what to do, no African NCO, no other African; he ought to have been hopeless and helpless, and no one probably would have blamed him if he had discreetly gone to ground until all was quiet.[79]

It is difficult to sift through the various and conflicting views about white officers provided by African soldiers. There seems to have been relatively little resentment among nonliterate men from the traditional recruiting grounds that officers were white. Predictably and understandably this was not the case with many literate soldiers. But probably the most important issue was whether or not an officer was liked, respected and trusted by the men he commanded.

Bullying and insensitive officers were justifiably disliked and every sensible commanding officer had a number of junior officers that he wished removed from his command. Occasionally an African soldier 'snapped' and struck or tried to kill an officer. On the battlefield there are known cases of soldiers attempting to kill unpopular officers by throwing grenades at them. Such actions were not peculiar to African colonial regiments; they occur in every army and on every battlefield. However, in fighting there was a tendency for racial differences to become blurred. 'On the battlefield there was no distinction, but back at camp it was different,' said John Mumo from Kenya.[80] Waruhui Itote wrote that in Burma:

> Among the shells and bullets there had been no pride, no air of superiority from our European comrades-in-arms. We drank the same tea, used the same water and lavatories, and shared the same jokes. There were no racial insults, no references to 'niggers', 'baboons' and so on. The white heat of battle ... left only our common humanity.[81]

One way to boost soldiers' morale was to tell stories belittling the enemy. African soldiers experience fighting the Italians in East Africa may have misled them as to the Italian will to resist in Europe and certainly about the determination of the Germans. In south-east Asia, British morale plummeted after the fall of Singapore and the defeats in Burma. Belief in Japanese invincibility was widespread. African troops used in Burma from 1944 onwards were told that the Japanese were fierce fighters but it was also emphasised that the enemy was afraid of black troops. Kofi Genfi, who served in Burma with the GCR in 1943-45, recalled that the Japanese were an 'invisible enemy'.[82] John Nunneley tells of a captured wounded Japanese officer raging against 'blackamoores'.[83] Many years later Estos Hamis recalled:

> The Japanese were very much afraid of East African Division (black people). The Japanese do claim that the African do eat human flesh. When the E. A. soldiers killed an enemy (Japanese) they set fire and roast him. With this kind of treatment the Japanese believed that the Black people eat human flesh.[84]

According to Musa Kihwelo, who served in Burma with the KAR, men of 6 Battalion would terrify captured Japanese soldiers by killing one or two prisoners and then pretending to eat them.

> While they started to pretend to eat the 'meat' the other Japanese captives who survived would flee for their lives. This was intentional so that after they fled in terror they would spread the news that they were fighting against the cannibals who particularly enjoyed eating Japanese flesh.

Kihwelo adds that 'we knew that the trick was inhuman and not even a single European officer knew about it. But it helped to scare the Japanese'.[85] This is probably true; horrible things are done in wartime and there is sufficient complementary evidence to support at least some of Kihwelo's account.

In his lengthy account of his experiences in Burma, Isaac Fadoyebo wrote:

> Our Commanding Officer also told us that a Japanese soldier would normally prefer to die in the battlefield in the belief that his soul would go straight to 'Japanese heaven' a

158

heaven specially reserved for the souls of gallant Japanese troops who happened to be killed in action. What a belief! ... Although they were superior to us numerically speaking but in training and equipment we were definitely ahead of them. Some of their soldiers I came across had padded battledress on and their rifles were not as solid as ours.

Fadoyebo says the Japanese troops were resourceful in battle, 'a tiny set of men with big hearts'.[86] A European warrant officer who attempted to scare African troops was contemptuously dismissed by Fadoyebo as 'the most irresponsible [man] I ever came across during the military part of my life'. He was particularly careless, says Fadoyebo, and 'did a lot of damage to the morale of the boys. Each time we offended he would keep telling us that "in a few months time you will find yourselves in the jungle struggling to dodge the Japanese bullets". His utterances were such that we had not the slightest regard for him.'[87] According to Lt-Col R. N. Boyd it was important 'not to create too much of an image of a wonderful fighting soldier on the other [Japanese] side because, after all, what we wanted to inculcate in our chaps was that they were better than the Japs. And the angle we took was they were rather more animals than human beings.'[88] Mutili Musoma, from Machakos, Kenya, remembered that 'the Japanese was hard trained. He can't accept to surrender', and he went on to state that he had killed many Japanese with his broad-bladed *panga* when they refused to 'accept to be arrested'.[89]

Combat conditions in the forests and steep river valleys of Burma were exceedingly difficult. Kofi Genji of the Gold Coast Regiment remembered the 'jungle is hell' with its steep terrain, mosquitoes, malaria and heavy rain.[90] In an account in the *Ashanti Pioneer*, provided by 'G.C. 22790 Sjt. F.S. Arkhurst, Somewhere in the Kaladan Valley', African readers were informed of how 'our troops beat the jungle to reach the Japs':

December 28 [1943] was bright and cloudless when we hit the trail again. That morning we were to know how very tough the journey was going to be. The morning was quite tolerable, but as the day grew older we got a foretaste of the things to come. The hills now became higher and steeper, and rose and fell erratically. For hours we went uphill and downhill, until lungs seemed on the point of bursting and knees shook like aspen-leaves. We never thought there could be so many hills all in one stretch ... Next day our first big river ... We crossed and recrossed it all day long with such monotony ... On January 5 there was heavy rainfall throughout the night. Next day we moved out in drenching rain. The track has been washed slippery and the going was very difficult.[91]

In such conditions getting supplies of ammunition and food to troops in advanced positions was a slow and tedious process, as was the removal of the wounded, who had to be manhandled to dressing stations. A British officer described Sierra Leonean soldiers carrying 50 stretcher cases over the Pidaung range:

Bamboo ladders were built to get the stretchers up the rock face ... Nothing ... will ever compare with the perilous descent from the 2,300 foot escarpment ... The Europeans and the senior African NCOs went out with torches and guided the column in from the foot of the escarpment. By the light of bamboo flares the stretchers were passed hand over hand down the cliff faces, some Africans going on hands and knees to form a human bridge over the worst places.[92]

It was vital to maintain the morale of troops in forward positions. However, there were practical limits to what could be done although adequate supplies of food and prompt medical attention were obviously important ingredients. Soldiers had their own ways of boosting each other's morale. African soldiers often sang as they marched. Gerald Hanley describes East African infantry marching up to the front line in Burma, in pouring rain, singing loudly in Kiswahili:

They sang ... *Funga Safari* [which] means roughly, 'Let's go,' or 'We move.'

Let's move off;
By whose order?
By whose order?
The orders of the Captain, the orders of the Captain,
The orders of the K.A.R.[93]

Hanley records another KAR song from Nyasaland, '*Sole*'. The title is a Nyasa adaptation of the English word 'sorry', which can also mean 'trouble'.

Sole, Sole Sole,
We don't know where we are going,
But we are going away;
Sole, Sole, Sole.
Perhaps we are going to Kenya,
We are sorry we are leaving home,
But it is the war. Time of trouble.
Sole, Sole, Sole.
Young men are going to war.
We go to defend Kenya and Africa,
Because the enemy is near.
Sole, Sole, Sole,
Time of trouble.[94]

Adequate food supplies were not always forthcoming in frontline conditions. In small-scale peacetime operations African troops usually lived off the countryside. However, in large-scale operations of a modern war on foreign territory this was rarely possible. In 1941 soldiers of the Sudan Defence Force within Abyssinia, where vehicle- and even camel-borne supplies were insufficient, 'had to live off the countryside. At times it was most difficult to find any food, so even exhausted, dying camels were killed and eaten. We had no rations for four months.'[95] A detachment of Northern Rhodesian troops, stationed in the Lake Rudolf area and deployed to prevent cattle rustling, 'learnt to survive on goat's milk which we did not drink back home and chapati eaten with camel's milk. There was no choice.'[96]

On the front line in Burma, food was often in short supply even with airdrops. African troops had a different ration scale to Europeans but attempts were made to ensure troops had a high-nutrient diet including maize meal, rice, fresh meat, vegetables and groundnuts as well as sugar, tea, tinned milk and fruit.[97] Mustafa Bonomali, from Nyasaland, said that in Burma 'during operations we were given a ration just enough to keep us going but not to full satisfaction'.[98] Isaac Fadoyebo wrote that when troops were on the move 'meals became irregular and

13 *Parachute landing among a party of African soldiers bathing in the Pi chaung, Burma*

From 1943 to 1945 African troops from both West and East Africa fought in the Burma campaign against the Japanese. It was a war prosecuted in a tropical region of steep forested country intersected by rivers and streams (*chaungs*). To supply their forward lines the British used porters or carriers, the rivers, newly-constructed jeep tracks, and also airdrops by parachute. As can be seen in this photograph, airdrops were not always accurate and this one has missed the landing zone. In some cases Allied supplies fell into the hands of the Japanese. African and European soldiers used the river for bathing, although the more thinly wooded country at good camping places near to a river could leave troops vulnerable to enemy attack. Photographer unknown, date probably 1944.

(Source: Imperial War Museum IND 7018)

161

scarce; we ate if and when food was available'. Some way from the front line, he says, a Nigerian sergeant 'killed a big monkey with his rifle and we except the Sierra-Leonians had a good dinner with it. They refused to join us in the feast on the ground that monkey meat was forbidden in their culture.' Irregular meals led to fatigue and conditions worsened the closer the troops were to the front.

> With each passing day, our dry ration dwindled further. There was no cooking as such except boiling of water for early morning tea and occasionally in the evening we also boiled rice if we were able to lay our hands on some using corned beef for the stew. On a few occasions, we had to 'invade' Burmese farms situated on the banks of the river in search of anything that might be considered edible contrary to military discipline ... We usually picked up water melon and cucumber and the Burmese owners of the farm dared not resist us ... [Some] would take to flight as soon as they sighted us. I usually felt guilty after each 'operation' because the Burmese in that area were pathetic figures with few possessions beyond the clothes they wore and the farm crops.[99]

At other times 'a few grenades used to yield a rich harvest' of fish from the big pools along the rivers.

Ensuring an adequate supply of water was a major problem in many of the campaigns in which Africans served. In the North African desert the ration was one bottle of water a day, along with biscuits – 'harder than devil's shit', according to Paul Gobine of the Seychelles Pioneer Corps.[100] Despite the seasonal downpours in Burma's forests, drinking water was in short supply there also. Pools were often brackish and carriers suffered acutely. As one soldier recalled: 'At Burma Jungle, we suffered so much; one man had to use one water bottle for three weeks because the enemy had poisoned all streams and chaungs [tidal rivers]'.[101] On one occasion at a coastal position patrols of African soldiers were sent out to look for water.

> Most of them were back within the hour with reports that they had found water. When asked how they'd done it one of them went back to where the water had been found and came back with branch and said, 'You see these leaves? They are quite similar to the ones we get in such-and-such a district in Northern Rhodesia. And there's always water where these bushes are.'[102]

In the battle conditions of Burma efforts were made to ensure that African troops received salt tablets and necessary medicines. Malaria was a serious problem for European troops, but also for some Africans, and yellow mepacrine was used. Soldiers suffered from measles and scrub typhus. There were also cases of leprosy. A single compound Vitamin C tablet was also issued to counteract scurvy and beri beri.[103]

African troops were kitted out in khaki uniforms which Fadoyebo remembered as 'ugly and primitive looking blouse and semi-trousers'.[104] Under frontline conditions standards of dress and appearance became of less importance and most officers accepted that soldiers would look scruffy and unkempt. In Ethiopia, some West African troops grew beards.[105] Northern Rhodesian soldiers were involved in peacekeeping operations on the Uganda–Ethiopian border, where temperatures were so high 'you would find us half nude with guns hanging over our shoulders'.[106] Soldiers in Burma were issued with olive-green battledress for jungle operations. On the front line soldiers made do with what they had to hand; they slept in hammocks, cooked on wood fires, scavenged for extra food, and repaired their often ragged uniforms and broken boots as best they could.

Many soldiers have a very vivid recollection of the first time they came under fire. As part of the small force resisting the Italian advance into British Somaliland in August 1940, Lesa Kasansayika, of 1 Battalion Northern Rhodesia Regiment,

> felt death was imminent and that I will never go back home ... When the war became serious our defence broken our many colleague killed and some wounded then it was at midnight when our commander told us to pack up our belongings ... [we] set fire to our own vehicles we had at the Camp ... and route marching 25 miles to Berbera where we found War vessels ready for us to evacuate us across Red Sea.[107]

Another Northern Rhodesian soldier, Joseph Chinama Mulenga, was also in the fighting in British Somaliland. His company had prepared sand banks:

> Hardly an hour passed during lunch break at about 1200 hours, we were having rice ... when we heard rumblings. Fighter bombers had arrived. Before we could realise what was happening, the first bombs were dropped and exploded on top of the hill ... The whole mountain side was set ablaze in an inferno. There was confusion and heavy battle ensued.[108]

Few soldiers enlisted by the British had any idea what a modern battlefield would be like. A Seychellois army labourer in North Africa recalled that 'we were like cattle being led to the slaughter house'.[109] In the confused retreat in the face of the German advance into Egypt in 1941, many African soldiers were captured. The British offensive at El Alamein in October 1942 began with a vast artillery barrage at night. Charles Adams, of the Cape Corps Regiment, told how the guns went off 'like thunder; the flashes were as bright as daylight. For forty-five miles it was just guns. Thousands of guns.' After the barrage, said Frank Sexwale, 'then the noise of tanks and infantry'.[110] Samuel Accouche was a pioneer from the Seychelles serving in North Africa when he first came under fire:

> Under bombardment everybody throws themselves towards the dugouts. In the panic they fall over and are pushed to the sea ... Pity the soldiers who are not able to swim ... Myself I only escaped death by chance when we were at Mersa Matruh and we didn't know the power of bombs. A cistern was found very close to a small stone building covered with a slab of concrete which we used for cooking on. This cistern was about ten to twelve square feet. The walls were as thick as my thumb. It was empty. I was using it for shelter when I was on guard duty. I was convinced that a bomb would never pierce such a protection. One day when I was supposed to be on guard I found that my section was late with its work. Some one else had taken my place. It was on that day that the German planes turned up. They dropped their bombs and one fell thirteen and a half feet from the cistern. The shock lifted the cistern from the ground and threw in onto the place which we used for cooking and the debris pierced the cistern in such a way that it looked like a tea-strainer. If I had been on guard I would as usual have taken refuge in the cistern. What would have become of me? I would have been reduced to 'chatigni' 'requin'.[111]

Another soldier, belonging to the HCT troops but 'diluted' to serve with artillery in North Africa, wrote to his chief enclosing a photograph of the gun: 'With the aid of this gun the enemy can hardly succeed in shooting or capturing us … If the enemy gets lost and comes near us in his plane then it is his last day.' He went on to report that he and his comrades were 'calm and collected under all circumstances, burning only with the desire to get to grips with the enemy and so great is our ardour that we feel like tearing him with our teeth'.[112]

As soldiers went up the line towards the front the rumble of guns became steadily louder and then they saw the wounded and captured enemy troops. John Borketey, from the Gold Coast, said he had been 'very, very frightened because I was just a young soldier'.[113] Sgt P. G. Vandy from Sierra Leone was also in Burma in January 1944, advancing into the Kaladan valley. 'Within a few hours of attack, we began to see casualties on stretchers, and captured Japanese prisoners by African soldiers. Now the battle here began, everyday and everywhere you hear the sound of rifle firing.'[114] Musa Kihwelo's memory from Burma was of death and devastation: 'It was a horror for me to see many dead bodies being left for the animals and birds to eat. It was strange for me also to see the destruction of towns such as Mandalay … and even Rangoon itself.'[115] John Mumo, fighting with the 11th East African Division in Burma, vividly remembered when he was wounded in his right leg:

> I had just risen to give the men their orders when I was hit. It felt exactly as if a sharp knife had been drawn across my leg. I put a field dressing on the wound; then I went on fighting.[116]

The vast majority of African soldiers, in writing about their personal experience, have been singularly silent about any involvement in the close engagements that occurred in several of the campaigns. Interestingly, several men recount stories of colleagues but not of their own actions, although clearly they themselves were involved in such encounters. Nyasaland troops of 1/1 KAR, in Madagascar in 1942, fought at Andriba on the road to Tananarive with machetes and bayonets against the Senegalese Vichy forces.[117] It is clear from the official accounts of the war in Burma that close-quarter fighting took place. A. J. A. Kowa, who served with the Sierra Leone Battalion in Burma, described the repulse of a Japanese foraging party in which 48 out of 50 of the enemy were killed, while Musa Kiwhelo wrote of the KAR company – composed of men from southern Tanganyika and known as the *chui* ('leopard') company – which entered enemy lines and strangled Japanese soldiers.[118] Nigerian patrols fighting in the Kaladan in April 1944 returned to their own lines with the severed heads of Japanese soldiers. As one unnamed eyewitness said: 'I never saw men fight with more dash or ferocity. They came back and just dumped the heads. We were amazed.'[119] In Burma, as elsewhere, 'the enemy buried many mines which killed many of our soldiers'.[120] However, in the forest 'it was bad war … because of jungle the Japanese could fire from tops of trees'.[121] Another soldier remembered that 'many of men died in Burma at the hands of the Japanese because the Japanese would adeptly hide among the tree branches, jumping us from any direction, firing and then disappearing as they came'.[122] War brutalises, as Aziz Brimah remembered: 'You become a different person. You leave behind every civilian attitude, every gentle attitude.'[123]

The assault on Sicily involved troops from the High Commission Territories, some of whom were sent ashore to put up smoke barrages to conceal other operations. At Howe Beach, near Syracuse, a Bechuana smoke company landed in the morning, jumping into 5ft of water to wade for the beach, only to discover that they had wandered into German lines. Under attack from the air the pioneers ran for cover but after a few such incidents, the official account records, 'the men gradually got used to the bombing and "strafing" and did not run for cover as they did at first'. However, constant air attacks on Bechuana camps which caused many casualties did erode the morale of some units.[124] Austin J. Dlamini, with a Swazi anti-aircraft unit, took part in the landings at Salerno:

> Disembarking according to text book things were fine so far. We were assembled on the beach to realize only too well the order of the day was dispersal and moved to cover straight away. Once again an enemy plane came from no where, opened its machine guns on us and we fell on the ground, the feeling was that bullets were going through as little puffs of dust rose in multitudes through the ranks of men lying prone ... Just two weeks after our landing in the Salerno Bay, the hills at the Northern end of the Salerno Front were blasted as our gunners drove shells into the enemy machine gun nests. Dust rose from the targets and smoke caused by explosions which whirled down the hillsides as the dry scrub caught fire.[125]

The Seychelles Pioneer Corps also landed at Salerno – the men 'up to the chest in water, with our rifle, our haversack ... we hit the beach and start digging trenches, take cover', said Paul Gobine. He was also at Monte Cassino when ash from an eruption of Vesuvius settled on the ruined monastery, which his comrades saw as God's curse on them for the destructive war.[126]

Many African ex-soldiers who wrote brief war memoirs in response to the appeal on the Africa Service of the BBC in 1989, told of their realisation that 'war meant death or alive'. Rabson Chombola was only 14 days in the battle for Burma before 'my two right hand fingers were blown off by the Japanese gunners':

> I was brought back to India and admitted in India hospital ... When looked at my right hand two fingers missing and still alive and fit I told my commanding officer at transit Camp that I want to go back where I got injured to revenge ... When I heard the news that the War was over I looked at the scar of my two fingers blown off by the Japanese gunners I thought when I reach Africa ... I have a lame hand what will my wife and my parents say what had happened to me because now I will not be able to do manual work as I used to do before I was recruited into War.[127]

Usiwa Usiwa, from Nyasaland, served in East Africa and Burma. He remembers that 'every soldier was given a full dressing pack for wound treating' on the battlefield.[128] Many African medical orderlies were trained during the war and played an important role in the front line. Sylvester Lubala belonged to a medical unit of the East African Field Ambulance serving in Burma in 1944, where 'we worked both as stretcher bearers as well as nurses'.[129] On the Arakan and Kaladan fronts wounded men were evacuated by light aircraft. Isaac Fadoyebo, rescued from his long stay in the jungle but badly wounded, was airlifted out:

14 *1991 Swazi Smoke Company, 1944*

Most of the soldiers recruited from Swaziland were employed in various types of noncombatant labour. However, this did not preclude their being sent into battle zones. The men who formed 1991 Smoke Company had spent a year in Palestine before being sent to carry out dock work in the recently captured Libyan port of Tripoli. There they were reorganised as a smoke company and trained for the assault on Italy. Their task was to help put up smokescreens to cover the landings at Salerno in early September 1943. The official caption on this photograph, taken by Sgt Radford eight months later, on 13 March 1944, is 'Men of another smoke section run through the screen to their smoke point' – a fairly bland description of the realities to which they had been exposed at Salerno and later. Other soldiers from High Commission Territories served as porters supplying the advancing British and American front line in the initial stages of the attack on German forces in Italy.

(Source: Imperial War Museum NA 12870)

15 *White South African troops entering Addis Ababa, 6 April 1941*

The fighting against the Italians in the Abyssinian campaign involved soldiers of the KAR, RWAFF, SDF and Somaliland Camel Corps; local Patriot forces; and battalions from Britain, South Africa and India. A major prize was to capture Addis Ababa, the capital of Abyssinia. In early April 1941 two companies of 5 KAR in lorries raced ahead to the city. However, by command of a senior officer they were stopped on the outskirts. Entry to the city was to take the form of a more organised display of force led by white South African troops. This racial snub was deeply resented by African soldiers and their officers who had borne much of the fighting in Abyssinia. On the morning of 5 April a column set out for the city, the senior officers escorted by the Kenyan Armoured Car Regiment and followed by the South Africans, with the KAR behind them. The victors marched past ululating lines of Ethiopians – held back by armed Italian police and Black-shirts – to receive the formal surrender of the city.

(Source: Imperial War Museum K 297)

167

It was a bright afternoon; no clouds whatsoever. All of a sudden, we saw a tiny aircraft diving into the field and it quickly came to stop. The newly wounded soldiers, myself and David Kagbo were to fly out in that order. The plane was so small that it could not take more than one person at a time ... The new man whose head was heavily bandaged was the first to go. After an hour or so, the plane returned to pick me up. I went in as a stretcher case by lying on my back with the Pilot in the front. He lit a stick of cigarette and gave me one and we started our journey towards Cox Bazar Island [*sic*] situated on the Bay of Bengal. The light aircraft was tossed like a cork by one of the sea-storms or monsoon winds but not to a dangerous extent and finally we landed.[130]

Prisoners-of-war

The Italians captured a handful of African soldiers in the East African campaign. In the North African campaign of 1941–42 the rapid German and Italian advance captured some 35,000 Allied soldiers, including 2,000 Africans, mainly noncombatants from South and East Africa.[131] The African prisoners were put into compounds and their Axis captors used them as labour. Contrary to the Geneva Convention African prisoners were forced to unload munitions ships. During Allied air raids they were denied admission to shelters. Food was in short supply, the hours of work long and the treatment harsh. The Axis justification was that African troops were 'irregulars' and thus outside the terms of the Geneva Conventions. A few captives escaped, some to die in the desert, a few reaching Allied lines. Sgt Reuben Moloi of the South African Native Military Corps was captured at Tobruk in June 1942. After a few days he was placed in a makeshift camp at Mersa Matruh. With another prisoner he decided to escape and one night the two men wriggled through the wire and made their way into the desert where they parted. For several days Moloi, with little to eat or drink, guided himself by the stars until he wandered into the minefields that formed part of the defences of El-Alamein:

> The following night I again walked the night through and came to a fenced-in area like a minefield. I saw motor tracks across this field and then saw some sentries. I avoided those on duty and approached some who were sleeping. I went towards them to see if I could take some of their water. I then saw that they were wearing the steel helmets of our troops and I knew that I was among friends.[132]

Nzamo Nogaga, also captured at Tobruk, escaped with a companion from the Italian cages where he was held.

> After fifteen days my companion could not keep up and I suggested he should make for the coast. We separated and I never saw or heard of him again and am afraid that he perished. I carried on for twenty-eight days [helped by local people], when not far from El Alamein I was recaptured by the Italians ... My skin was peeling off and I was footsore.[133]

Nogaga spent the rest of the war as a prisoner. Taken to Rome he and other African prisoners were forced by the Italians to take part in propaganda films:

> We did not like these stunts as we were made to go naked all the time ... The treatment received in the various camps was mostly harsh ... By good luck I escaped the fate of many

of my fellow countrymen who were bombed in the harbours and docks of Tobruk ... In Italy we were not given subsistence diet. The Gifts and Comforts parcels and Red Cross gifts kept us alive. Personally the only dead meat I did not eat was dog's flesh. I ate horse, donkey, cat; anything to keep life in me. The reason I did not eat dog's meat was because no dogs came my way![134]

Following the 1943 Armistice, Nogaga along with other prisoners was taken by rail to Germany. There he experienced further ill-treatment and 'frost bite in the feet'. He was released by American troops from a camp near Munich in May 1945.

Both the Italians and the Germans used African prisoners-of-war for propaganda films. As far as is known, British African captives fared better in German hands than did French Africans, perhaps because many *tirailleurs* were combatants. The German propaganda film *Sieg im Westen* ('Victory in the West'), produced in 1941 to trumpet the German victories the year before, used French colonial captives, some of whom were killed in the making of the film.[135] However, an attempt by the Italians to film a demonstration of Italian physical superiority over African weakness went disastrously wrong. A fight was staged between Primo Carnera, the former world heavyweight boxing champion, and Kay Masaki, a South African of splendid physique but who had never been in a boxing ring in his life. The cameras began to roll and Carnera knocked down Masaki. However, Masaki picked himself up and with a terrific blow knocked out the Italian champion.[136]

African prisoners in North Africa pilfered food and goods to make their lives a little more bearable. L/C Job Masego of the South African 2nd Division was among prisoners forced to unload munitions in Tobruk harbour, and his thoughts turned to sabotage. From rubble about the camp he found cartridges and fuse wire and using the knowledge of explosives he had acquired as a miner he made a small explosive device in an empty milk tin.

I was sent to work at the docks and then conceived the idea of burning a boat. The first day I did not carry the tin and fuse. The second day I carried these things in my haversack but had no opportunity of doing damage as we did not work on the vessel. The third day we were taken by power-barge to a single-funnel steam boat. In the forenoon we were engaged in off-loading the boat. In the afternoon we were instructed to reload ... then petrol was brought, first in large drums and then in tins ... Koos came to me and I confirmed that I intended burning the boat and he said he would engage in conversation with the German guard ... I then placed the milk tin among the large petrol drums, covered it with straw. I led the fuse from the tin along the ribs of the boat to the hatch ... I then put a match to the fuse as I was closing the hatch which was on a hinge.

Back in the camp Masego 'saw smoke appearing ... [and] I then heard a succession of explosions. Later I saw a flame while explosions continued'.[137]

African prisoners in Axis hands were generally treated badly.[138] Some men captured in North Africa were soon released again by the advancing Allies. Others were shipped to Europe and experienced being bombed and torpedoed. Nelson Koza, a member of the NMC employed as a batman, was captured at Sidi Rezegh in November 1941. He was sent to 'Campo No. 22' near Rome from where he wrote letters to his wife and also to his officer, Maj Klein. One to Klein said:

I am so very much glad to have this time of dropping you this few lines letting you know that I am still well ... Please kindly also write me a letter to Chief Mamitwa and let him know I am still alife [*sic*].

Chief Mamitwa acted as the 'postbox' for Koza's letters to his wife Rosie, but these were slow to make their way from the turmoil of Italy via the International Committee of the Red Cross to South Africa. By 1944 Koza was in a German prisoner-of-war camp. 'Nelson wrote me a letter saying he is fit and well and that I have to ask you for his address, for there was no address on his letter,' Rosie wrote to Mrs Klein in mid-August 1944. However by then Nelson had died of 'tuberculosis of the lungs'. Of the 1,655 men of the NMC captured in North Africa, 381 died in captivity.[139]

South African prisoners of the Non-European Army Services were incarcerated in German POW camps at Babenhausen and at Chartres in France. They were half-starved and forced to labour on bombed buildings. In the winter of 1944–45 African prisoners-of-war formed part of a forced march from Saga in Poland westwards as the Germans retreated before the advancing Russians. Men who fell beside the road were beaten, shot or left to die.[140] At the end of the war liberated Africans were brought to Britain and placed in temporary camps, the South Africans in Sussex, the East Africans in Buckinghamshire and Staffordshire, to await repatriation. Conditions for the South Africans in the camp at Horsham, Sussex, were redolent more of a mining compound than of a recuperation centre, and this left bitter memories.[141] As well as African soldiers, African sailors and airmen also became prisoners-of-war. Of the latter, Flt-Lt Johnny Smythe from Sierra Leone, who joined the RAF in 1941, was the navigator in a bomber shot down over Ludwigshafen-am-Rhein in November 1943. He survived captivity in Stalag Luft I at Bad Vogelsang, the treatment that he received being better than that of his fellow white officers probably because the Germans thought that they might use him for propaganda purposes.[142]

In the case of the Burma campaign there are few records of African troops falling into Japanese hands and surviving for any length of time. The British authorities assumed that some of the West Africans reported missing in Burma 'may be made prisoners',[143] but all the evidence is that the Japanese either soon killed captured Africans out of hand or, as with Fadoyebo, left them to die of their wounds.[144] In February 1944 Pte Moriba Masseray of the Sierra Leone Regiment was captured by a Japanese advance party but he managed to escape under cover of darkness and rejoin his unit.[145] Similar good fortune favoured Pte Famara Manneh of 1 Battalion Gambia Regiment, who was captured and also got away to the British lines.[146] Predictably, African soldiers viewed the Japanese enemy harshly after being told of their brutality to captured Africans: 'We didn't spare them any longer. We shot them – we chopped their heads off,' said Aziz Brimah, formerly of the GCR. 'We didn't allow our officers to see. We just eliminate them.'[147] Later he added: 'This jungle war was not child's play – it was something very dangerous.'[148] The assessment of Bayly and Harper is that 'the British, Indian and African troops methodically and ruthlessly killed all Japanese, enraged by cases of atrocities against their own wounded'.[149] Field-Marshal Sir William Slim wrote that 'quarter was neither asked, nor given'.[150]

War casualties: the balance sheet

The global war that raged between 1939 and 1945 resulted in enormous casualties. Recent estimates suggest as many as 60 million deaths, the majority being civilians.[151] Africa's death toll formed a small part of this horrific figure. It involved few civilians and a relatively small number of military personnel. The fact that many Africans in uniform were employed in noncombatant roles, however resented it may have been at the time, certainly reduced the likelihood of men being killed or injured in battle. Nevertheless, however employed, soldiers fell sick and died of diseases or were injured in the many accidents that inevitably occur where heavy and dangerous equipment or volatile materials are handled in military situations. But death and physical injury are not the only debits of war. There is also the long shadow of psychiatric dysfunction and the pains of dislocated families and relationships that accompany war service. Thus it is impossible to compute the casualties of war; they are measured not just by the graves in distant military cemeteries or the maimed men in homes for the disabled but also by scarred minds and the indelible memories of sad separation and loss.

Africa's military casualties, representing something of the continent's contribution to the war of 1939–45, are not difficult to locate. They are in the names recorded on the war memorials around which groups of steadily depleting veterans stand in memory each 11 November. Others are in graves marked as 'an unknown soldier'. The official histories provide the bald figures but as always say nothing of the pain and anguish of wartime death and injury.

The wounded & maimed

During the war plans were made in most colonies to provide care and financial compensation for the seriously wounded and maimed, and also the widowed. Army welfare services were also developed from early 1942, although with limited staff, funds and facilities. By early 1943 the West African War Council had agreed to set up in Accra a hospital for the rehabilitation and training of disabled African soldiers, although 'admission should be a privilege and not a right'.[152] In the Gold Coast at the end of the war the government established limb-fitting workshops, staffed by Italians, for servicemen who had lost legs and arms. Provision was also made for blinded soldiers. At that time there were ten ex-servicemen blinded in both eyes, four in one eye, and 4,738 disabled to varying degrees and awarded pensions and gratuities.[153] Many of the welfare services were taken over by the various ex-servicemen's' bodies, such as the Gold Coast Legion, established under government auspices towards the end of the war.

War leaves scars on minds as well as bodies. Solomon Bandele 'came back from Burma in a straightjacket. This was not something he ever spoke about; it was the one taboo subject at home'. His wife spent ten years nursing him back to 'a semblance of normality', although at nights he would suddenly erupt into this terrified and unspeakably terrifying being who thought he back in the trenches; a being whose fury was so primeval, it required not just every member of the family but several neighbours to restrain him, to keep him from harming us and himself.[154]

Every colonial army had its score of broken veterans, the disabled, limbless, blinded, those 'knocked strange in the head' by the brutal misfortunes of war, its bullets, explosives and accidents. Some recovered, others struggled bravely and with family support to make the best of life with artificial limbs and a crutch; a few huddled away, never married and took comfort in drink.

Death & burial

In most sub-Saharan African societies death and burial are attended by rituals of great importance.[155] In times of crisis involving large numbers of deaths, for example during the influenza pandemic of 1918–19, the rituals accompanying death and burial often had to be ignored. This was frequently so during the Second World War. The bodies of soldiers killed in battle were sometimes not recovered and thus not formally buried. Deaths among soldiers due to accident or enemy action usually occurred away from home and often overseas which meant the body could not be repatriated for burial in accordance with local custom and practice. The dead were buried in local military cemeteries with appropriate rites for pagans, Muslims and Christians. George Shepperson, who served with Nyasa troops of the KAR, wrote a moving account of the Islamic burial of L/C Amidu, who was killed in 1944 by a badly driven lorry:

> All the mourners sank on their knees, the priests, holding tattered Korans at the head of the grave. One African had sprigs of laurel in his hands. Then the long ritual began. As one priest chanted from the Koran, earth was thrown into the grave by the other, then a few spots of holy water from the red oil-drums, then a spring of laurel by an African ... and so ... on.[156]

On the battlefield soldiers were buried individually. A white Southern Rhodesian serving in Somaliland graphically recorded the burial of the African dead:

> Poor Corporal Atang, self-abnegation and retiring modesty were part of you in life. Quietly getting on with your job you were when the bullet took you. How it would distress you to know that your grave is giving such trouble and keeping weary men from rest ... I step to the grave opposite Atang on his stretcher, an apprehensive finger marking [the] 'Shortened Form of Service for the Burial of the Dead' ... At last it's over. The shovels are busy again. They lower him gently. The bloodstained blanket is thrust aside ... Lastly there is Amadu, the Musselman [sic], who died clutching his beloved Bren gun. The Sergeant-major of 'D' Company and a group of co-religionists are there to honour the dead. Two descend into the grave, the body being passed to them from the stretcher, they lower it slowly to the bottom ... In a high resonant voice the chief mourner intones an old Arabic phrase, a prayer for the dead.[157]

Many of the bodies of East African soldiers killed in the East African campaign were later removed from temporary burial sites and re-interred at

Ngong War Cemetery just outside Nairobi. At the Abu Haggag railway station in North Africa, in June 1942, a German bombing raid killed more than 40 East African askaris, men of the AAPC recruited from Nyanza province. One survivor, Nuera Opiya, wrote home to his friend that there '40 people died in the same moment [and] ... many people were not counted but dead bodies were many as much as sand [*sic*]'. The victims, mostly Christians, were buried in a mass grave which was marked with a cross. An African minister conducted the committal prayers. More than 730 East Africans who died in the Burma campaign were buried in the official war cemetery at Rangoon. Throughout the war the colonial authorities were anxious to assure communities at home that the bodies of dead soldiers were being treated with due respect. A rare piece of limited research on this topic, on Kenya, has been undertaken by Owino. He writes that 'when government officials ... started meeting with community elders on the subject of death and burial, they found themselves immersed in a labyrinth of delicate African sensibilities and attitudes that were difficult to navigate'.[158] Official reports stated that the consensus was that community elders feared disturbing the spirits of the dead and thus the bodies of African soldiers should be left where buried. However, African soldiers who had been exposed to death appeared to have less fear of the dead. For some, dealing with the bodies of dead comrades became a familiar task. Victor Nunoo, of the Gold Coast Regiment, recalled that in Burma often the 'only way you can identify them is to pick their Army discs and their papers'.[159] It was not the custom for young men to do this, said John Mumo from Kenya; as a young unmarried man 'you were not supposed to touch a dead body. But when we went out to war we were compelled to do those things.'[160] Their concern was for honourable burial for their dead comrades together in a military cemetery without discrimination, with treatment similar to that given to white soldiers.

The First World War resulted in official rituals to remember military victims. The names or those of the units of those who had died in the Second World War were added to existing war memorials in towns such as Accra, Lagos, Nairobi, Dar es Salaam, and Maseru. The 11th hour of the 11 November, marking the Armistice in 1918, was the focus of an annual ritual of remembrance with civic dignitaries and military parades. Such ceremonies continue to this day, parades at the memorials attended by a steadily depleting and increasingly aged and, sadly to say, raggedly dressed and impoverished group of men who meet to remember dead comrades and their role in a war that took place faraway in the deep past of fading memory.

Notes

[1] BBC Africa Service, RSM Joseph Chinama Mulenga, formerly of the Northern Rhodesia Rifles.

[2] GCR soldiers' song in F. W. E. Fursdon, 'Draft conductor to Togoland: The West African goes home', *Army Quarterly*, 67, 1 (1948), p. 102.

[3] Ngũgĩ wa Thiong'o, *Petals of Blood* (London, 1977; 1986 edn), p. 231.

[4] Isaac Fadoyebo, *A Stroke of Unbelievable Luck*, edited and with an introduction by David Killingray (African Studies Program, University of Wisconsin-Madison, 1999), pp. 6–9. See also the meticulous study by John A. L. Hamilton, *War Bush: 81 (West African) Division in Burma* (London, 2001), p. 129.

[5] Wartime newspapers, especially those published for African troops (e.g. *Mandaleo*, *RWAFF News*),

included accounts of soldiers' bravery. Kenneth Gandar Dower wrote several official and unofficial accounts of the campaigns in East Africa and Madagascar; see his *Askaris at War in Abyssinia/Askari Vitani kwa Abyssinia* (Nairobi, 1943), an official publication in English and Swahili; and *Into Madagascar* (Harmondsworth, 1943), which includes material that appeared in the official *The King's African Rifles in Madagascar* (Nairobi, 1943). These books are well illustrated and provide accounts of African troops but soldiers are rarely allowed to speak for themselves. The exception is Dower's posthumously published *Abyssinian Patchwork: An Anthology* (London, 1949), which contains accounts by a number of African soldiers. The Burma campaign was written up almost immediately by anonymous semi-official hands; see *A Short History of the 1st (West African) Infantry Brigade in the Arakan 1944–45* (Calcutta, nd. *c.* 1946), and *Arakan Assignment: The Story of the 82nd West African Division* (New Delhi, nd. *c.* 1946); *History of the 3rd Battalion The Gold Coast Regiment, RWAFF, in the Arakan Campaign, October 1944 to May 1945* (Felixstowe, nd. *c.* 1945); *History of the 5th Battalion Gold Coast Regiment from 15th December 1943 to 13th February 1945* (nd. *c.* 1945); C. G. Bowen, *West African Way: The Story of the Burma Campaign, 1943–45* (Obuasi, nd. *c.* 1945).

6 See R. A. R. Bent, *Ten Thousand Men of Africa: The Story of the Bechuanaland Pioneers and Gunners* (London, 1952), is the most Afrocentric of such books although very few Africans have voices. See also Brian Gray, *Basuto Soldiers in Hitler's War* (Maseru, 1953); H. Moyse-Bartlett, *The King's African Rifles: A Study in the Military History of East and Central Africa* (Aldershot, 1956); A. Haywood and F. A. S. Clarke, *The History of the Royal West African Frontier Force* (Aldershot, 1964). Ian Gleeson's *The Unknown Force: Black, Indian and Coloured Soldiers throughout Two World Wars* (Rivonia, 1994), is replete with deeds of gallantry but nearly all the accounts are official and hardly any non-Europeans provide or are asked for their own experience of warfare. There are one or two books specifically on African military heroes, for example, E. Marling Salmon, *Beyond the Call of Duty: African Deeds of Bravery* (London, 1952); according to the preface, 'each hero's name and act of gallantry are true to record but dialogue and detail are reconstructed and partly fictitious'.

7 See Marc Michel, *L'appel à l'Afrique : Contributions et réactions à l'effort de guerre en A.O.F. 1914–1919* (Paris, 1982), ch. 15–18; Myron Echenberg, *Colonial Conscripts: The Tirailleurs Sénégalais in French West Africa, 1857–1960* (London, 1991), pp. 32–38 and 92–96; Nancy Lawler, *Soldiers of Misfortune: Ivorien Tirailleurs of World War II* (Athens OH, 1992).

8 The list is long and notable, including books by John Keegan, Lyn Macdonald, Martin Middlebrook, Ronald Fraser and Studs Terkel. There are many earlier novels about war but few concerning African soldiers; one such is Sidney Butterworth's novel set in Burma, *Three Rivers to Glory* (London, 1957), a reference I owe to George Shepperson.

9 David Killingray, 'The idea of a British Imperial African army', *Journal of African History*, 20, 3 (1979), pp. 421–36.

10 John Orlebar, *Tales of the Sudan Defence Force* (privately printed, 1981), pp. 48 and 62ff.

11 M. W. Daly, *Imperial Sudan* (Cambridge, 1990), p. 129.

12 Brig W. A. Dimoline, who had served with African troops since 1922 and commanded 26 Brigade KAR in Abyssinia, wrote: 'I was a little nervous as to how the African and particularly my own lot would react to shelling. They had never been shelled before and were "babies" as regards active warfare.' He was full of praise for their work in Abyssinia. Liddell Hart Military Archive, King's College London, Dimoline papers, 7/3 'The capture of Gondar', ts.

13 Dower, *Abyssinian Patchwork*, p. 61, and also the previous quotation.

14 Mario Kolk, *Can You Tell Me Why I Went to War? A Story of a Young King's African Rifle, Reverend Father John E. A. Mandambwe* (Zomba, 2008), p. 41. *Gulu Wamkulu*, the 'Grand Dance', involved a dancer concealed in a *kasinja* – an animal-shaped structure woven of bamboo.

15 Dower, *Abyssinian Patchwork*, pp. 61–62.

16 TNA. CO820/32/34220, secret memo to Malcolm MacDonald, 11 June 1938. CAB5/479, 'Control of African local military forces in war', September 1938; CAB5/510, 'Coordination of defence schemes in the African dependencies', secret memorandum, 27 July 1938; Haywood and Clarke, *History of the RWAFF*, p. 326.

17 TNA, WO193/16, Chief of Imperial General Staff, secret memorandum, November 1939. See also CAB65/5 14 (40)2, War Cabinet meeting, 15 January 1940; CAB66/3 WP(39)148, 'Review of military policy in Middle East: Report of Chiefs of Staff Committee', December 1939.

18 TNA, CAB65/1/53 (39)3, War Cabinet meeting, 19 October 1939.

19 TNA, CAB67/4 WP(G)(40)15, memorandum on 'Utilization of man-power resources of the colonial Empire', 22 January 1940; CAB65/5 23(40)3, 25 January 1940. Also WO193/121, 'Note on raising African forces', 26 June 1940; CAB65/6 93(40) 12, War Cabinet meeting, 15 April 1940. See further the paper produced for the Cabinet in 1945 by E. E. Sabben-Clare of the Colonial Office: CAB106/307, 'The colonial military forces in World War II'.

20 On the Italian conquest of Abyssinia and the subsequent war of 1940–41 see Alberto Sbacchi, *Ethiopia*

under Mussolini: Fascism and Colonial Experience (London, 1985), and Anthony Mockler, *Haile Selassie's War* (Oxford, 1984).

21 Great Britain, *The Abyssinian Campaign* (Ministry of Information, London, 1942), p. 18.

22 Mockler, *Haile Selassie's War*, ch. 20 'The Fall of British Somaliland', and p. 247 for the events recorded here.

23 The military campaigns of the war can be followed in detail in the various volumes of the *Official History of the Second World War*; for example, Maj-Gen I. S. O. Playfair, ed., *The Mediterranean and the Middle East. Vol. 1: The Early Successes against Italy* (London, 1954). The semi-official regimental histories also focus heavily on the wartime campaigns: Moyse-Bartlett, *King's African Rifles*; Haywood and Clarke, *Royal West African Frontier Force*. For general histories of the war see Peter Calvocoressi and Guy Wint, *Total War: Causes and Courses of the Second World War* (London, 1972); Gerhard L. Weinberg, *A World at Arms: A Global History of World War II* (Cambridge, 1994). For British military actions in Africa see Ashley Jackson, *The British Empire and the Second World War* (London, 2006).

24 This was Gen Alan Cunningham's view, quoted by Mockler, *Haile Selassie's War*, pp. 325 and 365.

25 Quoted by Mockler, *Haile Selassie's War*, pp. 367–68.

26 Daly, *Imperial Sudan*, p. 130.

27 For the Sudan's role in the war see Daly, *Imperial Sudan*, ch. 6; H. D. Jackson, *The Fighting Sudanese* (London, 1954); General Sir William Platt, *The Campaign Against Italian East Africa, 1940–41* (Khartoum, 1951); R. O. Collins, 'The Sudan Defence Force and the Italian Ethiopian campaign in the Second World War', unpublished paper presented at the conference on 'Africa and the Second World War', School of Oriental and African Studies, University of London, 1984.

28 Sa'adu Zungur, 'Welcome to the soldiers', in Dandatti Abdulkadir, *The Poetry, Life and Opinions of Sa'adu Zungur* (Zaria, 1974), p. 41, quoted by Michael Crowder, 'The Second World War: Prelude to decolonization in Africa', in Michael Crowder, ed., *The Cambridge History of Africa. Volume 8: From c. 1940 to c. 1975* (Cambridge, 1984), p. 17.

29 Ironically, in 1936, during the Italian invasion, Addis Ababa was first reached by colonial troops, but the Italian army forbade them to enter the Abyssinian capital, that privilege being reserved for metropolitan troops. See Massimo Zaccaria, '"*Arrivano gli ascari*": A visual record of the 5th Battalion's campaign in Libya, February–July 1912', p. 2 fn 5, unpublished paper presented at the AEGIS Conference, School of Oriental and African Studies, University of London, 2 July 2005.

30 TNA. WO32/3380, secret, December 1941. The Governor of Burma also suggested that East African troops could be employed in Burma. British Library, IOLR, L/WS/1/963, War Office to Under-Secretary of State Burma Office, 16 December 1941.

31 See Martin Thomas, *The French Empire at War 1939–45* (Manchester, 1991), pp. 139–49.

32 David Killingray, 'Labour mobilization in British colonial Africa for the war effort, 1939–46', in David Killingray and Richard Rathbone, eds, *Africa and the Second World War* (Basingstoke, 1986), pp. 68–96; and David Killingray, 'Labour exploitation for military campaigns in British colonial Africa, 1870–1945', *Journal of Contemporary History*, 24, 3 (1989), pp. 483–501; Ashley Jackson, 'Supplying war: The High Commission Territories' military-logistical contribution in the Second World War', *Journal of Military History*, 66 (2002), pp. 719–60, especially pp. 742–52.

33 Grundlingh, 'Participation of South African Blacks in the Second World War', pp. 18ff.

34 *Ibid.*, p. 177.

35 James Ranisi Jolobe, *Poems of an African* (Lovedale, 1946).

36 Bent, *Ten Thousand Men of Africa*, pp. 58–59.

37 Grundlingh, 'Participation of South African Blacks in the Second World War', p. 212.

38 ICS, Crowder papers, 16. S/133/2/1. *Newsletter* of Pioneers, February 1944.

39 TNA, WO106/4495, Wavell to War Office, 9 December 1942; WO193/91, Wavell to CIGS, personal, 19 December 1942, said he wanted West African troops 'for offensive action Autumn 1943'.

40 TNA, WO106/4499, 7 December 1942, and WO193/91, Chiefs of Staff Committee, 360th meeting, 30 December 1942. See also British Library, IOLR, L/WS/1/1328.

41 The military campaigns in south-east Asia are covered by the official war history: S. Woodburn Kirby, ed., *The War Against Japan: Vol. III and IV* (London, 1962 and 1965); also by Moyse-Bartlett, *King's African Rifles*, and Haywood and Clarke, *Royal West African Frontier Force*. The wider context of the campaign is splendidly explored by Christopher Bayly and Tim Harper, *Forgotten Armies: Britain's Asian Empire and the War with Japan* (London, 2004; Penguin edn, 2005).

42 Timothy H. Parsons, *The African Rank-and-File: Social Implications of Colonial Military Service in the King's African Rifles, 1902–1964* (London, 1999), pp. 29–35.

43 E. E. Sabben-Clare, 'African troops in Asia', *African Affairs*, 44 (1945), p. 157.

44 For example, TNA, WO32/10241, Swinton to Grigg, personal, 14 September 1943, quoting the opinion of General Nosworthy on the two divisions. Also WO106/4505, Giffard to CIGS, 18 February 1944. On excesses see WO203/309, 'Labour in Arakan', which records looting and the rape of women.

45 TNA, WO203/1966, 'History of 82nd (WA) Division', quoting George Kinnear, war correspondent of the *East African Standard*, 12 July 1944.
46 TNA, WO106/4819, Mountbatten to War Office, 22 September 1945.
47 TNA, FO371/52604, War Office to Under-Secretary of State Foreign Office, 26 March 1946.
48 BBC Africa Service, letter, James Adewale to Martin Plaut, 2 August 1989.
49 Laura Tabili, *'We Ask For British Justice': Workers and Racial Difference in Late Imperial Britain* (Ithaca NY, 1994), ch. 8.
50 Dower, *Abyssinian Patchwork*, p. 35.
51 Grundlingh, 'Participation of South African Blacks in the Second World War', p. 208.
52 BBC Africa Service, Samson B. D. Muliango to Martin Plaut, 11 July 1989.
53 Kolk, *Can You Tell Me Why I Went to War?*, p. 47.
54 Ashley Jackson, 'Watershed in a colonial backwater? The Bechuanaland Protectorate during the Second World War', DPhil thesis, Oxford, 1996, p. 78.
55 Dower, *Abyssinian Patchwork*, p. 33.
56 BBC Africa Service, Cpl Rabson Chombola to BBC Africa Service, nd. *c*. October 1989.
57 BBC Africa Service, James U. Okehie to Martin Plaut, 20 September 1989.
58 BBC Africa Service, Nathaniel Opara to Martin Plaut, 26 September 1989.
59 Albert Grundlingh, *Fighting Their Own War: South African Blacks and the First World War* (Johannesburg, 1987), pp. 93–96, 139–41; Norman Clothier, *Black Valour: The South African Native Labour Contingent, 1916–1918 and the Sinking of the 'Mendi'* (Pietermaritzburg, 1987).
60 TNA, DO35/141, 1944; Gray, *Basuto Soldiers*, pp. 26–30.
61 IWM, London, Department of Sound Archives, No. 118401, Ernest Molem Khomari. See also Christopher Somerville, *Our War: How the British Commonwealth Fought the Second World War* (London, 1998), pp. 191–92.
62 Brian James Crabb, *Passage to Destiny: The Sinking of the SS Khedive Ismail in the Sea War Against Japan* (Stamford, 1997).
63 BBC Africa Service, George P. Chintu (son of Alick Chintu) to Martin Plaut, 18 August 1989.
64 Gleeson, *The Unknown Force*, pp. 108–11.
65 Deborah W. Ray, 'The Takoradi route: Roosevelt's prewar venture beyond the Western hemisphere', *Journal of American History*, 62, 3 (1975), pp. 340–58; Anon., 'The Sudan's service in a global war: The story of a sector of the trans-African air ferry route', *Journal of the Royal African Society*, 43, 170 (1944), pp. 16–20.
66 See the photograph in Gleeson, *The Unknown Force*, p. 119.
67 BBC Africa Service, Musa Kihwelo to Martin Plaut, 15 June 1989 and 18 July 1989.
68 BBC Africa Service. Gilbert Malama Zulu, 1989.
69 BBC Africa Service, Austin J. Dlamini to Martin Plaut, 3 July 1989.
70 *Short History of the Ist (West African) Infantry Brigade*, p. 4.
71 *Ibid.*, p. 13.
72 *Ibid.*, p. 70.
73 Wendell P. Holbrook, 'War and tradition in the Gold Coast, 1939–1945', unpublished paper, pp. 22–24.
74 On civilian propaganda see Peter B. Clarke, *West Africans at War, 1914–18, 1939–45* (London, 1986); and Dower, *Abyssinian Patchwork*, pp. 39–40, for some views on the part of KAR soldiers.
75 Dower, *Abyssinian Patchwork*, p. 38
76 Somerville, *Our War*, p. 183.
77 The League of Coloured Peoples *News Letter*, 8, 46 (July 1943), p. 50.
78 TNA, WO203/4524.
79 Hamilton, *War Bush*, p. 226.
80 Christopher Somerville, *Our War*, p. 188.
81 Waruhui Itote, *'Mau Mau' General* (Nairobi, 1967), p. 27.
82 IWM, London, Department of Sound Archives, No. 18371, Nana Kofi Genfi.
83 John Nunneley, *Tales from the KAR* (London, 2000), p. 127.
84 BBC Africa Service, Estos Hamis to Martin Plaut, dd. Dodoma, 9 August 1989.
85 *Ibid.*, Musa K. Kihwelo to Martin Plaut, dd. Dar es Salaam, Tanzania, 18 July 1989.
86 Fadoyebo, *A Stroke of Unbelievable Luck*, ch. 4, p. 9.
87 *Ibid.*, ch. 4, p. 5.
88 IWM, London, Department of Sound Archives, Acc. No. 004418/08, reel 07, Lt-Col R. N. Boyd.
89 Somerville, *Our War*, p. 257.
90 *Ibid.*, p. 222.
91 *The Ashanti Pioneer*, 18 April 1944. I owe this reference to Yasuo Mizobe, 'African newspaper coverage of Japan (the Japanese Army) during World War II: The case of *The Gold Coast Observer* and *The*

Ashanti Pioneer, 1943–1945', unpublished paper, 2008.
[92] Hamilton, *War Bush*, p. 213.
[93] Hanley, *Monsoon Victory*, pp. 163–64. See also Anthony Clayton, *Communication for New Loyalties: African Soldiers' Songs* (Athens OH, 1979), p. 37.
[94] Hanley, *Monsoon Victory*, p. 164.
[95] Orlebar, *Tales of the Sudan Defence Force*, p. 74.
[96] BBC Africa Service, Joseph Chinama Mulenga, Lusaka, Zambia. nd. *c.* September 1989.
[97] Hanley, *Monsoon Victory*, pp. 106–7.
[98] BBC Africa Service, Mustafa Bonomali to Martin Plaut, dd. Salima, Malawi, 6 September 1989.
[99] Fadoyebo, *A Stroke of Unbelievable Luck*, ch. 4 pp. 9, 12.
[100] Somerville, *Our War*, p. 138.
[101] BBC Africa Service, Nathaniel Opara to Martin Plaut, 26 September 1989.
[102] IWM, Dept of Sound Archives, Acc. No. 004418/08, reel 07, Boyd; *A Short History of the 1st (West African Infantry Brigade*, p. 65.
[103] Hanley, *Monsoon Victory*, pp. 107, 254.
[104] Fadoyebo, *A Stroke of Unbelievable Luck*, ch. 4, p. 9.
[105] Dower, *Abyssinian Patchwork*, p. 63.
[106] BBC Africa Service, Joseph Chinama Mulenga, Lusaka, Zambia, nd. *c.* September 1989.
[107] BBC Africa Service, Pte Lesa Kasansayika, Ndola, Zambia, nd. *c.* November 1989.
[108] *Ibid.*, Joseph Chinama Mulenga, Lusaka, Zambia, nd. *c.* September 1989.
[109] Jean-Michel Dominique, 'The experience of the Mauritian and Seychelles Pioneer Corps in, and contribution to, the Egyptian and Western Desert campaigns, 1940–43', MA thesis, School of Oriental and African Studies, University of London, 1994, p. 18.
[110] Somerville, *Our War*, p. 168.
[111] Extract from a radio talk, 'The Seychelles and the Second World War', broadcast *L'Echo des Iles*, 15 January 1969, and published in Ministry of Education and Information, Republic of Seychelles, *Histoire des Seychelles* (Paris, 1983), pp. 175–76. *Chatini requin* is a Seychellois dish of sharkmeat with chutney.
[112] Quoted by Jackson, 'Supplying war', p. 746.
[113] Somerville, *Our War*, p. 230.
[114] BBC Africa Service, P. G. Vandy to Martin Plaut, dd. Daru, Sierra Leone, 8 August 1989.
[115] *Ibid.*, M. K. Kihwelo to Martin Plaut, dd. Dar es Salaam, Tanzania, 15 June 1989.
[116] Somerville, *Our War*, pp. 222–23.
[117] Dower, *KAR in Madagascar*, p. 24.
[118] BBC Africa Service, A. J. A. Kowa to Martin Plaut, dd. Yamandu, Sierra Leone, nd. *c.* September 1989 ; letter, Musa Kiwhelo to Martin Plaut, dd. Dar es Salaam, Tanzania, 18 July 1989.
[119] Quoted in Nigerian Army Education Corps and School, *History of the Nigerian Army 1863–1992* (Abuja, 1992), p. 88.
[120] BBC Africa Service, Nathaniel Opara to Martin Plaut, dd. Uba-Umuaha, Nigeria, 26 September 1989.
[121] *Ibid.*, Justin Master Phiri to Martin Plaut, Ndola, Zambia, nd. *c.* September 1989.
[122] Thomas Alfred Oluoch, quoted by Meshack Owino, '"For your tomorrow, we gave our today": A history of Kenya soldiers in the Second World War', PhD thesis, Rice University, 2004, p. 407.
[123] Somerville, *Our War*, p. 230.
[124] Bent, *Ten Thousand Men of Africa*, pp. 38–39.
[125] BBC Africa Service, Jachoniah Dlamini to Martin Plaut, dd. Big Bend, Swaziland, 3 July 1989.
[126] Somerville, *Our War*, pp. 205 and 236.
[127] BBC Africa Service, Rabson Chombola, dd. Ndola, Zambia, nd. *c.* September 1989
[128] *Ibid.*, Usiwa Usiwa to Martin Plaut, dd. Chichiri, Blantyre, Malawi, 25 July 1989.
[129] *Ibid.*, letter, Sylvester Lubala to Martin Plaut, dd. Mwanza, Tanzania, 27 June 1989.
[130] Fadoyebo, *A Stroke of Unbelievable Luck*, p. 52.
[131] See further David Killingray, 'Africans and African-Americans in enemy hands', in Kent Fedorowich and Robert Moore, eds, *Prisoners-of-War and Their Captors in World War II* (Leicester, 1996), pp. 181–204.
[132] F. Rodseth, *Ndabazabantu: The Life of a Native Affairs Administrator* (Volda, 1984), p.90; see also Gleeson, *The Unknown Force*, pp. 188–90.
[133] Nzamo Nogaga, 'An African soldier's experience as a prisoner-of-war', *South African Outlook*, 1 October 1945, p. 151.
[134] Nogaga, 'African soldier's experience', p. 151. For another account which is not wholly reliable, see Joel Bolnick, '*Sefela sa Letsamayanaha*: The wartime experiences of Potlako Kitchener Leballo', Wits History Workshop, 6–10 February 1990.
[135] David Irving, *The Trail of the Fox* (London, 1977), p. 72.

[136] *Springbok* (South African veterans' journal), 71 (March/April 1988), p. 1.

[137] *Cape Times*, 8 March 1976, p. 10, as told to Donald Woods by Job Masego; Maxwell, *Captives Coura-geous*, pp. 159–60; Grundlingh, 'Participation of South African Blacks', pp. 220–21.

[138] D. H. Barber, *Africans in Khaki* (London, 1948), p. 96, reports meeting 50 men of an East African company, captured at Tobruk and then taken to Italy and Germany, who claimed to have been well-treated.

[139] Jennifer Crwys-Williams, *A Country at War 1939–1945: The Mood of a Nation* (Rivonia, 1992), ch. 68, '"Very good batmen, sir": Private Nelson Koza, 1944', pp. 382–87. See also Guy Butler's poem, 'Cape Coloured batman', in *Stranger to Europe: Poems 1939–1949* (Cape Town, 1952).

[140] Grundlingh, 'Participation of South African Blacks', p. 218.

[141] *Ibid.*, pp. 222–23. Bildad Kaggia of the KAR was one of 12 East African soldiers sent to Britain to assist in repatriating East African prisoners-of-war; see *Roots of Freedom, 1921–1963: The Autobiography of Bildad Kaggia* (Nairobi, 1975), pp. 43–44.

[142] Roger Lambo, 'Achtung! The Black Prince: West Africans in the Royal Air Force, 1939–46', in David Killingray, ed. *Africans in Britain* (London, 1994), pp. 145–63; 'To hell and back', *West Africa* (London), 8–14 May 1995, pp. 704–5; *The Times* (London), 13 May 1995.

[143] TNA, CO 980/153, 'British Red Cross Society: West Africa', 1944.

[144] I owe this information to Dr Anthony Clayton: interview with Maj F. Bailey, 22 December 1980.

[145] E. D. A. Turay and A. Abrahams, *The Sierra Leone Army: A Century of History* (London, 1987), p. 76.

[146] TNA, WO 172/6699, 1 Gambia Regiment War diaries, March 1944.

[147] Somerville, *Our War*, p. 223.

[148] *Ibid., Our War*, p. 230.

[149] Bayly and Harper, *Forgotten Armies*, p. 388.

[150] William Slim, *Defeat into Victory* (London, 1955), p. 188.

[151] Weinberg, *A World at Arms*, p. 894.

[152] TNA, CO554/133/33819/1, WAWC (98) seventh meeting, Achimota, 28 January 1943.

[153] TNA, CO98/88. Legislative Council Minutes, reply to question, 29 March 1947.

[154] Biyi Bandele, 'First person', *The Guardian* (London), Family section, 30 June 2007, p. 3. Bandele's novel *Burma Boy* (London, 2007) is based on his father's wartime memories of the Burma campaign.

[155] There is an extensive literature on African mortuary and funerary practice. On a recent case, see David William Cohen and E. S. Atieno-Adhiambo, *Burying SM: The Politics of Knowledge and the Sociology of Power in Africa* (London, 1992). See also Rebekah Lee and Megan Vaughan, 'Death and dying in the history of Africa since 1800', *Journal of African History*, 49, 3 (2008), pp. 341–59.

[156] George Shepperson, 'The obsequies of Lance-Corporal Amidu', *Phylon: The Atlanta University Review of Race and Culture*, 12, 1 (1951), p. 62. In sending me a copy Shepperson wrote: 'This piece of "faction" is based on events at a K.A.R. holding battalion in Gilgil, Kenya, early in 1944. Most of it is fact. The few exceptions are names: "Amidu" was "Afiki", and only about two small episodes are fiction.'

[157] J. F. MacDonald, *The War History of Southern Rhodesia: Vol. 1* (Salisbury, 1947), pp. 110–11.

[158] Meshack Owino, '*Vifo na Mazishi*: The impact of war on Kenya African soldiers' beliefs and attitudes towards death and burials in colonial Kenya', in Beatrice Nicolini, ed., *Studies in Witchcraft, Magic, War and Peace in Africa* (Lampeter, 2006), pp. 151–70; Meshack Owino, '"For your tomorrow, we gave our today", pp. 394 and 450–54.

[159] Somerville, *Our War*, pp. 229–30.

[160] *Ibid., Our War*, p. 230.

6

Going Home & Demobilisation

I would like to urge our trustees to direct their minds not to a plan for getting rid of the demobilised soldier as quickly as possible, but to the laying of a new foundation for society – now.[1]

Recruiting and mobilising a large army from the African colonies for war was a process spread over several years. Demobilising such a large number of men once the war had finished took nearly two years and presented serious challenges to the military and civilian authorities in London and the colonies. In mid-1945 more than 300,000 African soldiers were serving in southern Europe, North Africa, the Middle East and Asia, as well as in Africa, and they had to be brought home, resettled and reabsorbed back into the civil life of the colonies. There were few precedents that offered practical lessons. The plans formulated in Britain for demobilising the home army were geared to the circumstances of a modern industrial state and the need to return rapidly to a peacetime economy.[2] Such a feeling of urgency did not apply to the officially perceived conditions and needs of colonial Africa in 1945–46. African demobilisation at the end of the First World War had a few helpful local illustrations to offer but not many; on that occasion the number of troops involved was much smaller and soldiers' origins, experiences and thus expectations were for the most part of a very different kind. The most appropriate body of experience was that of India, which at the end of the First World War had demobilised nearly three million men. By 1942 India had begun drawing up plans for the resettlement of soldiers when the war against the Axis powers was over.

The end of the war in Europe and the Mediterranean in mid-1945 was foreseen, whereas the Japanese surrender came unexpectedly following the dropping of the two atomic bombs in August that year. The main fighting may have ended, but major logistical problems remained for the victors. A large army of labour was needed for clearing up after a long war. Vast supply dumps of war material had to be secured and then disposed of, formerly enemy-held territory reoccupied and prisoners-of-war guarded. Moving men and material was a complex business involving co-ordination between various government departments – those of the Colonies, Dominions, War Transport, Admiralty, plus the War

Office and India Office – as well as the military commanders in the field and colonial administrations, which frequently resulted in competition rather than co-operation. Although considerable thought had been given by colonial governments to planning demobilisation and resettlement the process was tied in with military and imperial demands outside their control. They were consulted at times but more often than not had to fit in with plans made by imperial bodies. Thus the timetables for demobilisation and resettlement ended up being drawn out, often painfully so. Nevertheless the schemes themselves and the processes followed by most colonial administrations to return men to their homes can be regarded as fairly successful, although they fell far short of the goal of laying 'a new foundation for society' asked for by African soldiers such as Robert Kakembo.[3]

There were several major problems or challenges involved in demobilising African troops in former war theatres in three continents. The first and most important problem was largely an imperial question: the shortage of shipping. Ships had to be in the right place, and of the right type for transporting men. Priority was given to demobilising British troops, whose skills and labour were urgently needed to service British industry and for peacetime reconstruction. Africans came a good way down the priority list and their labour could be conveniently used in place of that of British troops *en route* for home. Thus the programme of demobilisation was closely tied into imperial economics. The second problem was how to occupy African troops and ward off boredom and frustration in the barren military camps of North Africa and India while they waited for transport to take them home. This was a burden that fell on the military authorities and which greatly exercised the patience of soldiers and the diplomatic and social skills of officers. And finally, for colonial administrations, there was the challenge of how ex-soldiers were to be resettled and reabsorbed back into the civil life of the colony. Clearly they would not be returning to their mainly rural homes unchanged; the important question was the degree to which the war years had changed them.

Resettlement and reabsorption required that as far as possible men should go back to their homes and resume their former work. At the same time colonial schemes included some provision for training and work for a certain number of men in order to utilise the skills they had acquired while in the army. Officials had some idea of literate soldiers' expectations but there was a general anxiety that they might be well beyond what could be offered by the meagre resources of war-strained colonial economies. Such anxieties were expressed by officials in Tanganyika as early as mid-1942:

> The numbers at present returning from Army life are only a trickle but they are increasing and when the war ends there will be an absolute avalanche. Such a state of affairs will make administration of Dar es Salaam Township, already difficult, quite impossible.[4]

The war disrupted colonial order, and the movement of men into the army exposed them to new forms of restriction but also to new freedoms and opportunities – for example, drinking alcohol. Officials in Uganda were concerned at soldiers drinking *waragi* ('Nubian gin'), introduced earlier in the century by Nubian troops and which flourished, illegally, on military encampments. Greater concern was expressed at returning troops who were excessive drinkers of *waragi*, who were often identified as political radicals.[5] A further concern was that returned ex-servicemen might constitute a destabilising influence in colonial politics, although the 'moral panic' which Furedi sees as consuming metropolitan and colonial administrators is exaggerated.[6] Certainly some officials voiced such fears, and this influenced planning at all levels, but in most colonies less sanguine views prevailed.

Resettlement schemes

Postwar colonial demobilisation was first discussed by a committee in London in 1942 and a circular despatch instructed each colony to formulate resettlement plans.[7] African colonial schemes drew on India's experience in 1918–20, with most schemes releasing men in stages, beginning with those who could most speedily be reabsorbed in their home areas.[8] Colonial authorities wished to prevent ex-soldiers congregating in the towns and forming bodies of unemployed or underemployed men who might become the focus of areas of discontent. In most colonies resettlement committees worked closely with labour officers. A West African team led by Lord Swinton, the Resident Minister, visited Nairobi in mid-1944 to discuss mutual schemes with their East African counterparts.[9] In South Africa demobilisation was also discussed early on in the war and resulted in the issue of a 'Soldiers' Charter' in April 1944 – a scheme that offered benefits to ex-servicemen according to rank, gender *and race*. White veterans were treated generously, non-Europeans very poorly.[10] In Southern Rhodesia, Joe Culverwell remembered on his return in 1945: 'I was disgusted when they gave us a compensation which was a quarter of what they gave to white soldiers.'[11]

Demobilisation posed potentially serious challenges for many colonies; the smaller the colony and its economy, the more serious the problem. Sir Marston Logan, Governor of the Seychelles, was greatly disturbed at the prospect of the demobilisation of local pioneers and the garrison being wound down:

> When the Pioneers are demobilized there will be some 1300 men thrown on to the local labour market and requiring to be re-absorbed in to the local economy. Moreover, the 500–600 people now employed on Military works on the islands will also lose their employment ... The Pioneers, having been in receipt of British rates of pay and British standards of food, will inevitably be discontented with the prospect of a return to much lower standard of living in which the economy of this Colony is obliged to acquiesce. The present family allowances and allotments will of course be cut off.

Logan went on to state that the pioneers represented one-third of the total workforce aged 20–40 and when their average savings of 1,000 Seychelles rupees had been 'dissipated' in three to six months then trouble would result.[12] In Nyasaland in 1945 it was estimated that on demobilisation the colony would have to accommodate 4,000 army drivers and veterans who had built up wartime skills in medical, clerical and educational roles.[13] There were other immediate views of the consequences of demobilisation. One woman, writing from Kenya in 1944, feared mass discontent when African soldiers returned home. Army life, she argued, had put into 'shocking relief' the normal living conditions of Africans, and army service had made them familiar with 'the comfort of clean body and laundered clothes'.[14] Another writer was more concerned with East Africans soldiers' mentalities, that war had 'detribalized African minds' and that ex-servicemen would be less inclined on their return to submit to chiefly authority.[15]

The military were to be responsible for demobilisation and conducting drafts of men to the home areas, while labour departments were charged with finding work for certain ex-servicemen.[16] The Army and colonial administrations faced a shortage of men suitable to act as draft conductors and resettlement officers. Most schemes had a network of centres in districts to work in cooperation with field administrators. It was expected that the vast majority of men would go back to their rural homes and resume work as farmers. In certain schemes ex-soldiers were given assistance with tools and agricultural advice but this tended to be small-scale and limited in scope and value. Nevertheless, most soldiers went back to farming. In the Northern Territories of the Gold Coast in 1946, resettlement officer Michael Gass recalled that:

> there were few problems and those stemmed mainly from delays in the payment of gratuities. A very high proportion [of ex-soldiers] went straight home and were quietly reabsorbed into village life, using their savings to get married (or to acquire an additional wife) and to buying a bicycle or some other luxury. Comparatively few sought paid employment, at least in the first year.[17]

Not all soldiers went back to their former rural lives without protest. Resettlement in white-settler-dominated Kenya, where there was a growing pressure on land in the African reserves, raised problems barely encountered in the West African colonies. The Kenya resettlement plan reflected the ideas of officials and white settlers, that the vast majority of African soldiers would not only return to their rural homes but would also resume life as subsistence farmers.[18] The returning Tanganyika askaris who said that 'before the war I cut sisal and I think I will return home and cut sisal again',[19] comforted white settlers intent on blocking African advancement and colonial officials with fixed ideas on African labour, but this was not a hope or expectation held by many returning soldiers. Such attitudes on the parts of settlers and officials disregarded both the skills and the ambitions for economic and social improvement acquired by many soldiers during their war service, and also the increased population pressure on land in the rural areas that had occurred during the war years.[20]

The greatest headache for colonial administrations was the demand for paid civilian employment by newly released soldiers who had learned a trade in the army. The low level of economic development in the postwar colonies meant there were not enough jobs to meet demand. In all colonies, and in South Africa, the men most difficult to satisfy were those who had been recruited from among the literate and often urban sections of the population. They returned home with high expectations of economic opportunity and social advancement, often to be cruelly disillusioned.[21] Frank Sexwale's view of South Africa was that the country he returned home to in 1945 was worse than when he left; conditions for non-Europeans had not improved.[22] A crude estimate is that fewer than ten per cent of all those employed in colonies were in receipt of money wages, the government being the largest single employer; it was highly unlikely that this percentage would increase substantially in a short time so as to absorb ex-servicemen. There were few secondary industries or potential openings for the electricians, carpenters, engineers and other artisans trained by the army and released onto the market, most of whom expected to receive work and an income commensurate with their new skills and the experience gained within the ranks. Government, in London and the colonial capitals, had thought this might happen – indeed in the Gold Coast the authorities knew about soldiers' expectations because military intelligence tapped their letters home[23] – but they were still ill-prepared to meet the demands. More might have been done, but it is difficult to see how, with the resources and understanding then to hand, colonial regimes could have met soldiers' demands. Colonial government lacked the infrastructure and the necessary skilled personnel for planning economic change or for controlling inflation, that inevitable concomitant of global war, which further reduced soldiers' hard-won savings and fuelled their unease.

Booklets were prepared for literate soldiers with advice on what they were likely to expect on their return home. *Release and Resettlement of African Other Ranks* – an ironic title given that all African soldiers but one were 'other ranks' – was distributed at the ratio of one to every five literate West African soldiers. The booklet appealed in paternalistic terms to the industry and self-reliance, sobriety and good sense of the men and stressed the need for their continued obedience to authority. Men awaiting demobilisation were urged to 'take every opportunity of practising your trade and of learning about the world'. Soldiers were warned that in future 'whether you do well or ill will rest largely in your hands and on whether you can work hard and honestly. Work will not come to you if you sit down, you must go and find it.' The booklet also set out the scale of gratuities that soldiers could expect and advised them to obey traditional authorities: 'Obey your Native Authority, give honour to age, and be willing to teach others all that you have learned without shouting about what you have done. Do not waste your money to make a show in order to impress people; impress them by your wisdom and self-control.'[24] As always, there were crooks and tricksters about ready to relieve gullible ex-servicemen of their money, or to make false claims in order to extort cash from overstretched officials.

Some returning soldiers hoped to set up in business as lorry drivers or traders. They faced severe and unequal competition from Indian traders in East Africa and Lebanese merchants in the West African colonies, and they also found it difficult to get credit from European-owned banks. Bland and expansive promises made by army officers in wartime proved largely empty in peacetime. Military officials who toured Kenya in early 1946, visiting discharged soldiers to measure their reactions on their return to civilian life, reported their reactions:

In Burma [we were] told that we had fought well, and that on our return our DCs would meet all the requirements. Where are all the surplus Army vehicles going to? In the army we were told that we would be able to purchase old Army lorries freely. We see them being sold to Indians in great quantities.

You Europeans seem to be in two groups – those in the military, who promise us many things, and those in civil life who now say the opposite.

In the army we gave answers to questionnaire stating what work or what training we would like on discharge. What action is being taken on this?

You say 'where is the money to come from' but there was plenty of money for war – why is it not forthcoming for peace?[25]

In most colonies the authorities attempted to ensure that all soldiers, including nonliterate men, understood long before they reached home that there would not be jobs available for all ex-servicemen. Nigeria, for example, had to cope with 100,000 ex-servicemen, many with newly acquired technical skills, in an economy where the total wage-labour force numbered only 300,000. Clearly there was not going to be waged work for all who wanted it, as was made clear in the *Annual Report of the Nigeria Department of Labour* for 1945.[26] Official attempts to alert soldiers to this do not seem to have reduced their expectations that they should be properly rewarded for their wartime service. Large numbers were to be sadly and bitterly disappointed that the long years spent away from home enduring boredom, hard work and danger seemed to be disregarded. It rankled most with those men, either volunteers or conscripts, who had some level of literacy, acquired in schools or during their time in the army. Literacy and trade skills had often been gained or developed in one of the specialist corps of the army. By 1945–46 in all parts of British colonial Africa there were men who had learned skills as electricians, carpenters, mechanics, drivers, builders, clerks, hospital orderlies. The majority of these had come not from the traditional military recruiting grounds but from cities and towns and from areas such as southern Nigeria and the Gold Coast Colony where mission schools had long been active in providing primary education.

Soldiers who were literate or possessed marketable skills tended to be alert to personal progress in civil society. They were far less likely to be content to return to their pre-war work and economic condition than were, for example, the peasant farmers who came from the old recruiting areas and constituted the largest number of wartime recruits. Army life had also accustomed all soldiers to receiving good food, medical care, clothing and boots, as well as regular pay. This comprehensive package of welfare services would cease with demobilisation. All the evidence indicates that soldiers who were literate or had trade skills felt most keenly the loss of such provision. It was a tragedy that postwar colonial economies were simply too weak and ill-developed to be able to absorb and put to good use all of these skills that had been rapidly acquired and developed in the brief war years. At no single time in colonial Africa had such a high level of human investment potential been available. The failure of the colonies to find employment for ex-servicemen not only dissipated a fund of goodwill but failed to capitalise on skills useful for postwar development.

The long wait

The demobilisation of African soldiers was a long drawn-out process. The last soldiers returned home in early 1947, very many months after the war had ended in Europe and in Asia. Demobilising the millions of men in the British armed forces was clearly going to take some time, and soldiers knew this. However, information and explanation was not always passed down the chain of command and even when it was it was not always accepted as satisfactory by men whose only thought was to get back home. Many men became deeply resentful and a constant current of rumours fuelled discontent; truculent troops were slow to obey commands and in certain instances this led to open mutiny among British and African units. African soldiers in the military encampments in India, North Africa and the Middle East had many reasons for dissatisfaction. Demobilisation was desperately slow and the camps provided a boring routine. Soldiers believed that they had joined to fight a war and now that the war was over they were entitled to go home. When they heard of white soldiers leaving for Britain this further compounded suspicions of racial discrimination already felt over differences in pay and conditions. To their great anger soldiers who had fought in Italy in 'diluted' units were returned to labour units and put to work in North Africa and the Levant. Most military camps were isolated from towns in order to minimise conflict between soldiers and civilians and local leave was restricted for the same reason. It is not surprising that African soldiers became angry and that military camps heaved with bitter talk.

The military authorities were faced with the problem of how to occupy African soldiers' time while they waited for demobilisation orders. Officers as well as men were dissatisfied and found it difficult to raise and maintain soldiers' morale. In south-east Asia there was some discussion about using African troops for garrison duties in Burma, the territories of the future Malaysia, and Java. This was rejected on political grounds; African troops were not thought to be sufficiently reliable in areas that might prove politically volatile. However, KAR troops in India's Bihar province were kept in a state of readiness due to the security situation, and in Palestine they served as garrison troops and occasionally exchanged shots with white Jewish opponents of the British presence. Demobilisation meant there was also a manpower shortage and all too often use was made of any available troops irrespective of political considerations. But for most African soldiers in the Middle East region their main employment was as labourers clearing up the debris of war. In the Indian encampments there were relatively few labour tasks other than those required for general camp maintenance. So, how were restless soldiers to be kept occupied in the long and dreary wait to go home? Michael Blundell captures one picture:

> I was promoted, after the surrender of Japan, to an organization designed to keep all the *askaris* and British troops happy during the demobilization process which took place over some 18 months. I had an amazing organization, an education unit headed by a Lieut-Colonel and a Major from England, radio teams, newspaper editors and journalists, comedians, troupes of actors, dance halls, artists, many of them individualists, some weird and most odd ...[27]

Race continued to determine allocation and British troops received the prime share of these goods and services.

Other than labour tasks the military authorities resorted to 'planned recreation', expanding the sporting and educational facilities in the camps and also, where possible, arranging local conducted tours of towns and places of interest. However, resources were limited for all of these activities. Only a small number of soldiers enjoyed any local leave or visits and most were confined to the proximity of the camps. Educational provision for soldiers was late in being organised. Wartime military education, such as it was, was strictly geared to military ends – it aimed to give men the requisite skills to carry out military duties. This mainly involved instruction in basic English with a limited number of classes in literacy and numeracy. For the most part provision was piecemeal and haphazard. For example, by mid-1945 there were fewer than 250 teachers of all kinds employed by West African Command in all theatres, although some technical instruction was carried out within specialist corps such as the engineers and signallers. And many more literate men had enlisted in the West African regiments than in any other African colonial force. In early 1945 the Duke of Devonshire, under-secretary of state at the Colonial Office, visited Asia and the Middle East and reported on welfare provision for African troops. The story that he brought back was one of general neglect. The African C-in-C's conference in March 1945 demanded that further educational staff be appointed but this came at a time when Europeans who could fill such posts were beginning to be demobilised.[28]

In late 1944 and early 1945 Lt-Col George Wigg (later Lord Wigg) toured East and West Africa and reported on army educational provision. He recommended that this should be focussed on each corps, that English instruction should be expanded, that greater use be made of material from the Army Bureau of Current Affairs, and that new vocational schools be established.[29] Wigg's report followed closely after the memorandum on *Mass Education in African Society*, and although there is no close connection between the two, Wigg certainly thought that the army should contribute to mass education. In London, the mass education subcommittee, deliberating on east and central Africa, urged that governments should 'cash-in on the returning askari as the greatest asset that mass-education could have in the [native] reserves that provokes the urgency of the task in hand'.[30] By late 1944, army educational corps had been set on firmer bases for the RWAFF and the KAR.[31] However, by the time that more serious attention was being given to educating African soldiers the military forces were being run down and there was the consequent shortage of staff.

The long journey home

Several African units were sent home in 1945, with some 25,000 men – more than 25 per cent of Kenyans in uniform – discharged by the end of the year.[32] It was argued, for example with reference to troops from the HCT, that the best policy was first to send home a number of older men, who would provide a stabilising influence on both civilians and returning younger men. The vast majority of Africans were demobilised throughout 1946 and into the first months of the next year. One or two soldiers remember their 'demob' dates with great precision. L/C Mussa K. Kihwelo, of the EAASC, wrote about his journey from Burma home to Tanganyika:

> On 5/5/46 I left Rangoon and arrived in Mombasa, Kenya, on 18/5/46. I was overjoyed to set step on my continent although I had not reached my country to see my relatives … On 21/5/46 I arrived in Nairobi and received my discharge on the following day. I left Nairobi on 23/5/46 and arrived home, Tanganyika, four days later. It is difficult to explain how happy I was to see my relatives after being away from them for a long time.[33]

The journey from India – travelling to the port, boarding the ship and crossing the sea, disembarking and then waiting for transport home – was another long period, although at last soldiers were going home. Joseph Maliselo, who served with the Northern Rhodesian Regiment, said: 'After the war it took us about three months to reach home i.e. one month in India, three weeks in Nairobi, Kenya, and about one month in Lusaka before we received our discharge letters.'[34] Many of the soldiers in Italy were sent first to camps in the Middle East until transport was ready to ship them back to southern Africa. Despite the many years that have passed Jachoniah Dlamini recollects well the farewell by Italians to African soldiers at the start of their long journey home to Swaziland:

> We returned home in January, 1946, having embarked from Ancona and sailing to Egypt, where we off loaded all the equipment that we had used during the war. We then sailed to Durban, with a stop at Mombasa for water and fuel. From Durban we travelled to Swaziland, via the train and bus. We spent more than nine months in and around Ancona, when we were leaving to return to Swaziland, the town people all came to say farewell. That is they were shouting *hambani kahle* which is siSwati for goodbye. The trip home took a little over four months.[35]

After troopships arrived in ports such as Mombasa, Durban, Lagos or Takoradi, for most men embarkation was followed by a further tiring journey by rail and road to their homes. As Chama Kadansa explains:

> The war came to an end in 1945 while I was in Burma in the town of Rangoon. On our coming back after the war, we boarded ships which brought us to Mombasa in Kenya … From Mombasa, we got on lorries to Nairobi, passing through Iringa, Dodoma, Arusha, and Kisumu to Lusaka. We travelled day and night except during meal times. From Lusaka we were taken back to our home districts by war trucks. While in Lusaka, the Governor … entertained us with local beer, each of us being given just a tumbleful [*sic*] of it. A cow was also slaughtered to provide meat for the victorious soldiers. A sum of £5 was given to each of us in appreciation for our contribution.[36]

As troopships docked people curious to see the returning warriors stood on the quayside. Occasionally there were relatives waiting but few families had any idea when or whether their men would come back from war. Sometimes the soldiers were given an official welcome. Isaac Fadoyebo describes his arrival in Lagos:

> As we were being ushered into waiting vehicles one could hear a band set blaring out 'For they are jolly good fellows …'. Curious spectators possibly dock officials engaged themselves in a stampede to catch a glimpse of us – world war veterans. From the questions people asked us they seemed to feel that those who were courageous enough to go into the battlefield for any reason whatsoever deserved respect and everywhere we went they gazed at us with amazement.[37]

The authorities in each colony were extremely anxious that ex-soldiers should return as soon as possible to their homes. There were social, economic and political reasons for this. As mentioned, they did not want bands of men with money congregating in the towns where they might act as a politically destabilising presence. It was important for soldiers to be seen in their home communities and that their savings and skills should contribute to the development of those areas.

187

The Gold Coast resettlement plan offers an example typical of the schemes implemented in other British colonies and also in South Africa. The Demobilization Centre at Takoradi, the main port of embarkation, was designed to accommodate between 5,000 and 7,000 men for a period of 6–18 days. From there they were to be sent by road and rail to smaller dispersal centres which could each hold 200–400 men for 12–48 hours. Groups of soldiers, accompanied by a draft-conducting officer (usually an NCO), would then be moved to staging camps which provided overnight shelter for 100–200 men. As far as possible soldiers were delivered near to their home villages. It was also important to ensure that men did not spend all of their money or withdraw all that had been accumulated in the post office savings bank.

Home at last

Many of the soldiers returning home had not seen their families for several years. Home leave had been rare and letters to and from families occasional; some families had not heard from a husband, brother or son at all. Silence and long absence sometimes led families to believe soldiers had died. When Alick Chintu of the KAR came home to his village in Malawi in 1946 'his parents and friends were very happy to see him back home, as most of them thought he was dead'.[38] This was a not uncommon belief and a cause of considerable bewilderment to families. Mustafa Bonomali, who had served with the KAR in East Africa and Burma for most of the war, found his homecoming required proof not unlike that experienced by Martin Guerre:

> At home we were warmly welcomed. Our parents and relatives could not believe seeing us alive such that they asked us to put off our clothes so that they could see if our bodies were not marked anywhere. They swore that if another war broke again they could never let us go.[39]

Nikolaus Abdon enlisted in 1939 and did not return home to Tanganyika until well after the war was over.

> After leaving my family all of my family members lost hopes of seeing me again therefore celebrated my death ceremony as up to when I came back in 1947 I found my mother in the dress which indicated traditionally that she lost one of her children. It was unbelievable joy when they heard that I was alive – just because most of my village mates were never seen again.[40]

People often thought that if soldiers had gone away together to war then they would return together if they had survived. When soldiers did not they were thought to be dead. A modern military system might take soldiers from one village or area but in the course of a long war they might find themselves placed in different units and employed in different localities. And demobilisation was implemented in stages. In a village on the slopes of Kilimanjaro, in northern Tanganyika, 'home people were frightened as the other soldiers came back without my father. They thought he was dead. When he came home [later] everybody, relatives and others were so much happy to see him again alive.'[41] Rightson Kangwa's family 'was very happy to see me back home without a scratch', although 'in the same village I came from there was great grief because of their family [member] did not return home [and they] went crying to the District Commissioner to make enquiries'.[42] Isaac Fadoyebo, limping from his war wound, left Lagos by truck for the last stage of the journey to his home village in southern Nigeria:

> In those days Emure-Ile was not the main road as it is today. One had to get down at a junction on the major road and do the rest of the journey by foot. The truck managed to stop at the then Emure-Ile junction and I came down with my luggage including a push bicycle which I bought in Lagos when I discovered I could still manage to ride despite my disability. I looked round and saw a road-mender which had just closed and was going towards the road camp. I hired him to assist me in carrying my luggage to Emure-Ile for a fee of four pence. He had no idea as to my history ... and so one can imagine his fright when he saw me surrounded by nearly everybody when we got to my place ... The distance between the junction and Emure-Ile was less than a kilometre and as soon as I was sighted the whole village rocked. Some people could not believe their eyes while others were frightened away to avoid seeing a dead person ... It never crossed my mind that I would create such a scene on getting home. I was hugged by my parents and other relations after they had splashed sand on me. The belief of our people was that anybody who reappeared alive after his death had been mourned, should have his body sprayed with dust – a sort of ritual.[43]

Many returned soldiers were the focus of popular attention. As Jachoniah Dlamini recalls: 'When I went to my village to see my family, everyone came to see if it was me, alive and home from the war. Everyone wanted to know what I had experienced. My father slaughtered an oxen [sic] to feast upon in celebration of my safe return.'[44] Sgt James Igwe, from Nigeria, wrote to his former officer, Capt M. V. Crapp, describing his homecoming:

> In fact it was a red letter day in my village, I was welcomed with drums, symbols [sic], and Chief Okokwo's double barrel roared several times as a signal of honour in our custom and tradition. Fifteen he goats were killed for me. Other villagers were invited for dinner.[45]

Invariably conditions at home had changed considerably since men went away to war. Returning Swazi troops, trucked up from Durban, were met by the Resident Commissioner and a representative of the King of Swaziland. The King's representative

> told us we might find that things had changed while we were gone, in some cases, we would find children in our household who we did not know and in some cases we would find no one at all at home, but that we should not take these matters into our own hands but rather we should report these matters to the proper authorities.[46]

Estos Hamis was welcomed home as a hero but after the plentiful provisions of the army, particularly three regular and substantial meals a day, the one thing he found in the village which shocked him was famine. 'There was no food, people had nothing to eat. No money, and the availability of food was so scarce hence very expensive. Anyway as he came back with some money, then his family didn't suffer the same as before.'[47] There is a poignant edge to the memories that remained with RSM Joseph Mulenga about his return to his Northern Rhodesian village home:

It was common to see those who had lost their wives to others in the villages, including their children, who they had left behind to roam about ... This caused so much emotional and mental suffering. None of us who saw these things could escape remorseful feelings ... A few old boys could not readjust to old adaptations.

Mulenga also discovered that the distant war in which he had fought had influenced the social and economic structure of his village or town.

During the war years African urban centres grew in population and size. Mining areas such as the Copperbelt of Northern Rhodesia attracted African labour from villages within the colony and also from neighbouring colonies. When Joseph Mulenga reached home he found great changes:

Others found their former villages non-existent because of so many other reasons. Either death had taken its toll of the aged or there were just no young people to carry on with life. With no support, idle dependants also died and most dwellings remained empty for a long time. Active young people left villages for towns to get jobs. Some of our comrades, remained desolate and embittered for a long period of time before something meaningful could be found. Others rose above their fellow men, running their own businesses and other ventures through initiative.[48]

Returning home was often a difficult time for ex-servicemen. Army life, exposure to new ideas and the experience of warfare had changed soldiers' perspectives and expectations. Wives had also changed, grown older, grown distant. Families had suffered from the long years of separation. And disillusionment over monetary entitlements, housing and employment prospects made the business of resuming domestic life difficult. In Cape Town May Santon, a Coloured soldier's wife, said it was a very bad time 'when the men came home'.

There was lots of unhappiness, murder was done; knew a friend, he just got so mad he killed his wife. Things like that happened. Girls with children from other men, and so on, but it was a bad bad time in 1944, '45, it was bad years, there wasn't any good mostly.

Pressed on the bad postwar years, she replied that 'there was no work for the men, there were no houses for them and ... there was no money saved ... There was nothing the war did for us Coloured.'[49]

Although soldiers were welcomed back from the war they could not expect to be treated as heroes or special cases for very long. In some areas returning soldiers were met with hostility. Let Rus Osakwe, a private in the RWAFF from northern Nigeria, speak of what he saw:

Back home the lot of us ex-soldiers were received with hostility and much suspicion. Many people said we were returning from India with bad diseases. Others said we had graduated in crimes. And truly some of the returning ex-soldiers justified these cynicisms by going out to steal, extort, rape and terrorise the impoverished [they were] outcasts undeserving of any sympathy or regards. The lot of us became a bunch of laughing stock.[50]

Soldiers' savings

It is not possible to assess accurately the amount of money that soldiers brought back with them at the end of the war. Deferred savings, usually one-third of pay but sometimes more than that, plus encouragement to save through post office savings schemes and money sent home for safekeeping by relatives, meant that careful and fortunate soldiers might return home with a tidy sum of money. That was the ideal. In fact most soldiers were disappointed at the small amount of money they had as the result of their absence and hard work. A Coloured soldier in Cape Town viewed the handout from the Defence Force with some anger: 'Bugger all they gave me. Eighteen pounds, that was just for clothing. Bugger all. Eighteen pounds they gave me here at the Athlone barracks.'[51]

In Nigeria it was estimated that gratuities ranged from £30 for an RSM to about £24 for a private soldier;[52] a Bechuana private soldier with five years' service could expect to have £64 in his post office savings bank along with any other money that he had saved.[53] Some soldiers came back with only a few pounds; others had enough to buy a bicycle, sewing machine or clothing to bring home to the village as an indication of their new wealth and also money put aside for cattle or brides. Nana Kofi Genfi, from Kumasi, who joined the GCR in 1938 and ended the war as a sergeant, returned home with £50 in back pay, which was considerably more than the average saved by other Gold Coast soldiers.[54] Wartime inflation reduced the value of savings and presented those soldiers who had been familiar with a money economy with a very different picture from that which they had formerly known. Obviously the impact of inflation varied from place to place. In towns and wherever imported manufactured trade goods and foods were marketed, prices had increased by 50 per cent or more during the war years. The long tentacles of international inflation reached even to remote areas and were reflected in higher prices for livestock and higher bride prices. Returning soldiers put more money into circulation and thus also contributed further to the inflationary spiral as they competed for goods.[55]

The low level of monetary reward for war service is a constant refrain from old soldiers in all parts of former British colonial Africa. Many feel that they did not receive what they had been promised. Usiwa Usiwa, a lance-corporal with 2 Battalion KAR who had served in Somaliland, wrote that after the war ended a choice was given to some soldiers:

> You had to choose between going home and continuing to be a soldier. I chose to go home and went. Britain gave me about £50 as a reward. And that was all. Honestly, I did not feel that the war played a role making the history of my country. I FEEL USED AND FORGOTTEN.[56]

Another ex-soldier of the KAR, Batison Geresomo of Malawi, said:

> It was in 1945 we were discharged after conquer all the rulers of the world. We were taken in lorries, transfer for home. It took us about a month to reach home because we could stop at a place to rest and so on till we reached home. When we reached home, we were

welcome to our respective District Commissioners. We were told to go home after giving us about £85.00.[57]

The memory of Pondaponda Tembo, also of the KAR, was that 'after I was discharged there was no terminal benefit given to me. We were just left like that …'[58] Another soldier who had served with the Nigerian Regiment of the RWAFF said that all he received was his savings, about £83, 'and till this day I got no further contact with Britain'.[59] More than 40 years after the war had ended Pule Motlhabane, a former soldier with the Bechuanaland forces, spoke bitterly of money that he thought he should have received:

> I can't remember how much I had in my savings but it was very small and we didn't get anything else. I was always expecting some more money because it had been promised. It was easy for me to go back to my old life after having had so many experiences while I was away from home. Those who didn't go to war respected us, and I personally felt very proud within myself because I had participated.[60]

James Adewale's savings amounted to a mere £7 and he said that he 'found it difficult to re-enter the main-stream of life' in Nigeria. 'It was then,' he wrote, 'that I started thinking of those who put me into the war in the first place … War and its aftermaths has left a bitter taste in my mouth.'[61] Certain resettlement schemes made provision for ex-soldiers to receive tools and implements to help them as farmers. Literate men were offered training courses but as these did not always automatically lead to work men were reluctant to sign up. Most colonies sold off surplus army vehicles at favourable terms to help ex-servicemen get into the transport business; sometimes this worked, but the cost of maintenance and finding spare parts was always an initial problem. Nevertheless, one of Swaziland's main bus operators began his commercial career with an old army lorry in which he fitted seats. In South Africa, as in British colonies, ex-servicemen complained that money owed to them had been withheld. They probably had more reason for distrusting the words of white authority than most people north of the Limpopo. The South African authorities offered some men bicycles as part of their gratuity but this offer was not always well received. As L. Monyamane retorted in 1980: 'What did I get? I got a bicycle – do you think a bicycle is worth the life of a person?' Another soldier, Henry Thai, complained in an undated letter: 'They forced me to accept a bicycle. I do not want it. I want a wardrobe, a table, 4 chairs and a stove.'[62]

Small savings and gratuities were soon spent. Justice Banda's money only lasted a month and 'this made many ex-servicemen to maintain their families very hard. The welfare of ex-servicemen was jeopardies [sic], through lack of financial suport [sic]. This resulted in the break up of homes through poor living conditions.'[63] Ex-servicemen might be popular, providing drinks and the odd cash handout along with wartime stories, but as with the Prodigal Son, as soon as the money began to disappear so too did the friends. 'Travel stories without money' offered little attraction. Soldiers' hopes that they would be returning to money sent home and entrusted to relatives were often dashed. Arriving home in mid-1946 after his years away fighting in the RWAFF, Etim Attah looked forward to enjoying the fruits of his labour:

I came back home very happy. Unfortunately my hope of coming back home to settle comfortably was dashed, because the little savings I had been sending home had been squandered by my ungrateful brothers, who thought that I would never come back alive from the army.[64]

Postwar employment

The vast majority of returning soldiers were nonliterate and returned straight to their homes in the rural areas. Some were averse to returning to peasant production, but without modern skills and literacy the only wage labour available in nearby towns was as messengers, gardeners, cleaners or watchmen, and there were not enough of these jobs to meet demand. To the consternation of the colonial authorities a few men went to larger towns in search of employment, and ineffective repatriation schemes failed to reverse this drift. Many literate soldiers had high expectations of what they would be able to do after the war, as is evident from their surviving letters; they hoped for wage employment using the skills acquired or honed in the army. Many were dismayed to find that jobs were not available. 'There is one thing, of a serious ailment on my part', wrote Sgt James Igwe, on his return to Nigeria: 'This is: I have been demobilised without a job, and I am depressed by the agony of both joblessness and wastage which is rather too killing on my side'.[65]

Government trade and vocational training courses were available for a selected and thus limited number of African ex-servicemen. These offered training in carpentry, brickmaking, building, pig and poultry husbandry, blacksmithing and fitting, tailoring and shoemaking. The uptake was patchy in most colonies, but a small number of men did emerge from such courses with new skills that enabled them to find regular wage labour. Finding employment for unskilled ex-servicemen was more challenging for colonial governments. Kenya's Central Employment Bureau was able to place more than 7,700 ex-servicemen in jobs, while the Gold Coast Resettlement Advice Centres dealt with more than 76,000 enquiries from demobilised soldiers, not all for work, between May 1945 and March 1948.[66]

Nonliterate soldiers, often peasant farmers, also had hopes for more cattle, access to land, perhaps a house with a corrugated-iron roof, or the chance of schooling for their children. Phaladi Sesinyi, interviewed in Botswana by Ashley Jackson in April 1995, recalled his ambitions:

> After the war finished I expected to go back home and continue my day to day work as a man ploughing for the children, buying livestock and clothes for the children, and I managed to do that. I was more interested than before in sending them to school. We set a good example to the men who didn't go to war, and we were regretting that we didn't have any education, so we couldn't advise anyone who was not on the right track because we didn't have any certificates, so we couldn't be role models.[67]

An ex-soldier's wife, Taboka Borotho, also interviewed by Jackson, recollected that:

> Some soldiers invested their money building houses and some wasted it buying drinks. My husband invested it in cattle. This was mainly because my husband's father would tell

193

his son what to do. When the men came home they enjoyed having money and spent it so when it was finished some looked after their cattle, some stayed at home, and some went to work in the South African mines.[68]

Soldiers' wartime letters contain frequent comments regarding the work that might be available for them at the end of the war. Would they be able to get their former jobs back? Would their war service be recognised? Would they be able to use their new knowledge? Would training courses be available? And what wages could they expect to earn? A survey conducted among 222 Nigerian soldiers in 1945 asked them 'What are you going to do after the war?' or 'What would you like to do?' More than 90 per cent of literate and more than 60 per cent of nonliterate men replied that they wished to be employed by the government. All ranks recognised the value of education and there was widespread demand for schools and new educational opportunities, as well as concerns over medical facilities, housing, the price of goods, exemption from taxation and levels of gratuities. In addition it was reported that 'many soldiers who have seen the advance of industrialization in India ask if new industries cannot be set up by the Government in West Africa'.[69]

However, many West African soldiers, invariably those who were literate, did not believe the government was going to do anything for them. They did not accept that the government had the capacity to provide them with work when they returned home. Gerald Plange, the African editor of the Gold Coast *Daily Echo*, published in Accra, visited troops in Burma in 1945. From New Delhi he reported on what he had seen and heard to the head of the Public Relations Office at the Gold Coast Department of Information:

> It was somewhat disconcerting, however, to find that these assurances [government promises of work] were received with considerable scepticism and many of the men stated quite frankly – even in the presence of officers – that they did not believe that government would do anything for them ... Some of the troops based their belief on what they regarded as the government's past record, but others, with greater penetration, wanted to know how, with the best intentions government could find work for them all. They wanted to know how the thousands of tradesmen in the army could be given jobs which would utilize their technical training when even in the army many men had been trained but had been kept waiting for months without being drafted to a unit where they could put their knowledge to practical use.[70]

In fact, in the Gold Coast the vast majority of ex-soldiers with skills were able to find work, a few with the government but most in the private sector. Those most disappointed were the fairly large number of men with low levels of skills – for example, with only basic English and a level of literacy insufficient for clerical work, or possessing only a limited knowledge of vehicle mechanics or electrical work. Government and private employers had very few openings for these men or indeed for the slowly increasing number of young men who had been given similar levels of skills by the educational systems that had expanded fairly rapidly during the war years. A knowledge of mechanical matters gained in the army enabled a few soldiers to set up motor repair works using rudimentary tools.[71] Justice Banda's experience in failing to find work in Nyasaland was not untypical. He was, he wrote, not happy with colonial Government. Because we were promised when the war was over we would be given jobs. But alas, when we came back home at our discharge centre we were only told that the Government had not enough jobs to offer us, all you could do find your own means [*sic*].[72]

When ex-soldiers refused to accept jobs they were offered, demanded higher pay than other workers or complained excessively, they soon exhausted public sympathy and patience. In the Gold Coast the press accused ex-servicemen of being 'infected' with a 'Burma complex' and a 'superiority complex' and point-edly suggested that they should be 'self-reliant' and accept the work that was offered to them.[73]

Black and Coloured South African soldiers also were only too keenly aware that after the war they would be competing for jobs in a labour market where the interests of whites were protected by both customary practices and a battery of racially discriminatory employment laws. In 1942 an unnamed South African corporal wrote to Margaret Ballinger, a white member of parliament who repre-sented 'native' interests, about postwar employment for blacks and Coloureds:

You are aware that there are many well-educated Africans in the Springbok Army. After the war does it mean that they will all get the one and half penny jobs? This question has rather worried many of us. We feel we should be treated by employers on the same basis as Euro-pean soldiers. Can't you persuade the chief bodies of employment to reserve decent posts for African soldiers? It seems to us that by the time we return to civil life, we shall have to start from the bottom.[74]

Two years later a skilled soldier wrote to the director of the NEAS:

I am anxious to go on poultry farming as soon as I leave the army. There are only two things I can do. Also building but there is so much colour prejudice in the building trade that I am very reluctant to go back to the trade especially in the Transvaal ... I could build for Africans but the big controller would crash me in the circumstances [*sic*]. Poultry farming seems the only alternative.[75]

The rapid expansion of manufacturing industry in wartime South Africa helped to erode many of the white job reservation agreements and gave black and Coloured people new opportunities to access skilled work. There was also a great increase in movement of people from rural areas to the towns, including thousands of Africans. However, by the end of the war these economic and social changes and the increasing assertiveness of black labour unions alarmed many whites. On the one hand industry wanted cheaper labour; on the other hand white populism demanded more rigorous influx control over African migration and settlement in towns and a reassertion of job reservation.[76] African ex-soldiers often found themselves at the bottom of the pile and unable to find work to fit the skills they had learned in the army. For example, C. Cukatha was only one of many ex-soldiers who wrote to the director of NEAS in 1946:

I served as a soldier for 3 years and 11 months and when I was discharged I could not get a job and I was not able to go back to my pre-enlistment work. So in despair I came and worked here on the mine ... What I want to know, Sir, is whether or not I have still got some claim on the Government to help me to obtain a suitable job.'[77]

Soldiers often carried with them a slip of paper signed by their former commanding officer stating that they had performed well as soldiers. A few men obtained letters of recommendation from Europeans with whom they had served, which they carried with them as they hawked for work. However, some who had committed only a minor military offence might find that their discharge papers, which were demanded by potential employers, damned their cause. Any black mark gained in uniform shadowed a man in civilian life. A typical situation, says Grundlingh, is that of N. F. Kawushe, a former South African soldier, who wrote to the director of NEAS in March 1946:

> It is the slur on my character more than anything else that is worrying me. I served in the UDF for 33 months in which time I committed one record [breaking out of barracks] for 20 minutes ... Mine was a heartrending affair to a man who was prepared to see this war through ... It is now over 19 months since I was discharged from the army, I have been asking and pleading and I am pleading again today that my case be please looked into. This word indifferent is a punishment in itself what have I done to deserve it? It is a deliberate blacklist because it is well known that no European will employ anybody with that word on his discharge certificate.[78]

Ex-soldier W. Mncwabe had hoped that his years in the army would have helped him get a non-manual job, but as he wrote in 1948: 'I am here at Crown mines doing underground work and is very hard to me. I shall be very glad if I can get a job as a orderly in the military hospital or guarding as I used to do it before.'[79] Had he turned to the newspapers, he might have seen an advertisement headed 'They are earning more MONEY!, the 'Lyceum College, P.O. Box 5482, Johannesburg', complete with a photograph of 'Mr. A. Musbi', in his military uniform, offering commercial courses that promised a range of qualifications.[80]

In Tanganyika postwar employment was available for only a few African ex-servicemen, complained the ex-KAR soldier Sifael Massawe. 'Britain never did anything to the Army men especially Africans, but Europeans and few Africans who were well educated, got employed by the ... Overseas Food Corporation in Kongwa and Nachingwea Districts. Others were employed in to Government offices.' Unfortunately, wrote his son-in-law, 'Mr. Massawe didn't get anything.'[81] A certain number of ex-servicemen were employed as policemen either by the government or by native authorities, as Chama Kadansa remembered: 'Farms and police or messenger jobs were again promised, no such farms were actually given. However, police jobs were given in towns and at Bomas to those who wanted them.'[82]

As gratuities and savings ran out and the chance of finding work diminished by the day, ex-soldiers became increasingly angry and desperate. In the Gold Coast the press commented on the rise in incidence of suicides among ex-servicemen. Anwell Siame, who had served with the Northern Rhodesian Regiment as a medical orderly, could find no paid work and said 'I wanted to hang myself simply because I had no chance of going back to school, no where to get money to support my family and since I had no education qualifications I had no were [sic] to find employment, so I joined the world of starvation.'[83] A slight step up from 'the world of starvation' was the precarious business of selling food from a market stall or beside the road. Nairobi had a 'Burma market' which was 'situated on a piece of waste land, where a number of Africans, mostly ex-soldiers, had set up stalls ... [This] filthy place ... had no sanitation at all, and all water had to be fetched in a bucket from a quarter of a mile away.'[84]

Perhaps there are more stories of distress than success. The former breeds complaints while the latter does not. Skilled, unskilled, literate and nonliterate ex-servicemen did find jobs or managed to carve out a living for themselves by dint of hard work or good fortune. Certainly Nikolaus Abdon, from Bukoba in Tanganyika, used the money he had from the army and looking back years later he wrote that 'we dressed well, built housed [sic] – I got married same year when I came back i.e. 1947 and with my co-ex-soldiers we started a group of music band'.[85] James Mpagi from Uganda, who had joined the KAR straight from school in 1940, also fell on his feet, helped by his literacy and service in the East African Army Education Corps and work with a mobile propaganda unit. He said that 'Britain treated me very well indeed. I was given training, after which I was given a job, and a very good job indeed which led me to be the District officer i/c of Community Development.'[86] E. R. A. Gyem, an ex-signaller in the Gold Coast Regiment, informed his former officer that eight of his comrades, 'the following old boys', had found jobs: three with Posts and Telegraphs, one as a town council clerk, another with water supply in Kumasi, and one with a native authority, while Juma Sante had 'set his tailoring shop up in Nkawkaw', and Moses K. Essel 'had rejoined the Army and is in 2GCR'.[87] Throughout British colonial Africa in the late 1940s and early 1950s there were men working for government and for private concerns, or who were self-employed, using a variety of skills learned in wartime which had enabled them to compete successfully in the labour market. But for every ex-serviceman in a job – and waged work was often the most sought-after employment – there were perhaps two who had not found it so easy.

The sick & wounded

Those men who found it most difficult to find work were those who were unwell, wounded or maimed due to military service. A few soldiers never recovered from the psychological effects of war and provision for their needs was slender. Physical wounds were relatively easy to identify; mental scars were not, so that some ex-soldiers severely damaged by their war experiences received neither pensions nor gratuities. Soldiers blinded during the war rarely found employment and in northern Nigeria the number of blind beggars alerted the authorities to the urgent need for rehabilitation services.[88] In South Africa sick and unemployed ex-servicemen were even rounded up by the police and sent to work as cheap labour on white-owned farms – a condition little better than forced labour, as Looseboy Moneri complained to the authorities:

> Today they do'nt [sic] want me here, when I come from the war. I have wounded from War, I can not work any more ... I require to advice me where shall I stay ... They wants [sic] to arrest me without any fault ... Now I ask what is my freedom ... because here Wolmaransstad they do not want native soldiers.[89]

The condition of discharged sick and impoverished South African soldiers was summed up by Joseph Ngoetjana in an undated letter that he wrote to the military authorities:

> The most saddening thing is this: Our demobilised men are experiencing a great difficulty in connection with finance – strolling along the streets, and stating that our Native Commissioners disregard their position. Wait, wait, wait for a indefinite time for their gratuity ... Do you see that our men will soon indulge into wrong practices, e.g. theft, murder and the like, only through the distressing financial position.[90]

Some soldiers who were maimed feared that they might not be able to work as farmers. Rabson Chombola lost two fingers in Burma and he told his commanding officer that he was 'not going to my home village because of this lame'.

> My commanding officer told me do not worry because of this lame you can see some of your colleagues have lost their arms some their legs and some have died do not worry of this lame when you get home you will be rewarded by the Government. The Government is going to give you a place to make a farm and built you a good house to live in etc. But after all these promises became a night dream which never came true.[91]

A small number of veterans bore mental and physical scars of war that made it very difficult for them to settle to any form of regular employment. Disability pensions granted to maimed soldiers helped in the short term but their real value was steadily eroded by postwar inflation. Veterans suffering from wartime illnesses and fortunate enough to work had to go where they were directed. This was the predicament of David Alao, formerly of the Nigerian Regiment, writing from Ibadan in mid-1946:

> Owing to my sickness, I could not get a job till now, but I received a message from the Labour Office recently and I was informed that there will be a job for me under the Forestry Department if I can agree to go to any part of Nigeria. This is more or less like the Army. At any rate, I must be ready to do so or I shall be without a job.[92]

Pensions?

A continuing complaint of many ex-servicemen, to be heard from all parts of former British colonial Africa, is that they did not receive the pensions promised by the British authorities. It is among the first plea that modern researchers are likely to encounter when they visit groups of former soldiers, some of whom live in ex-servicemen villages. Pensions were only awarded to men seriously maimed in the war. Pensions specific to war service did not exist in the British Army, neither did they for African colonial troops. The idea of pensions for all soldiers is probably rooted in the war itself, perhaps fuelled by recruiters' false promises or by rumour, and compounded by returning soldiers' grievances at the erosion of their savings by wartime inflation. Mama Moshi, who enlisted in the Gold Coast Regiment in January 1943, recalled that because of inflation 'by that time [1946] the money is not much ... I go there for three years and the money they give me is £52 ... all the money saved from Burma in three years'.[93] In late 1945 a recently returned sergeant argued that 'we soldiers have got used to a higher standard of living and we cannot be expected to be content with the wages Europeans pay us in Nyasaland'.[94]

Wounded and disabled soldiers did receive pensions and awards. In West Africa it was agreed in May 1941 that payments should be up to 30 shillings a month. Officials in both the War Office and Colonial Office thought a figure half that sum would be reasonable but this was strongly opposed by Sir Alan Burns, Governor of the Gold Coast:

> To discharge a totally disabled soldier with a pension of less than half the amount required to keep him alive in most parts of the Colony proper is a proposition which this Government cannot possibly accept ... The Government's view on the subject is so strongly held that it is prepared to pay half the cost of all disablement pensions provided the rates originally proposed ... which are approximately double the rates now proposed, are adopted.[95]

Burns won his point with the support of Brigadier Bishop who also condemned London's suggestion as 'ungenerous, unjust and quite indefensible on any grounds whatsoever'. Under the Gold Coast War Pensions Ordinance 1943, disablement awards were graded by rank at a maximum of one shilling per day with awards of between £4 and £50 for next-of-kin. Disability awards were increased by up to 50 per cent in 1945 in line with inflation. In the next two to three years the War Pensions Board looked at various claims. For example, in the Gold Coast in 1945–46, the Board examined 2,930 cases and reviewed 785, and granted 1,199 pensions, 978 gratuities and 510 compensation awards. By early 1947 a total of 4,738 ex-servicemen, disabled in varying degrees, were receiving awards.[96] It was not always easy to pay disability pensions as ex-servicemen moved about. After independence failing bureaucratic systems and inflationary pressures made it difficult for new states to meet all pension obligations.

Conclusion

The demobilisation of large numbers of African soldiers caused the Imperial authorities and the colonial administrations a great deal of concern. There was considerable uncertainty as to what might happen when thousands of men with new experiences, skills and hopes returned home. It was not known whether ex-servicemen would willingly go back to their former rural pursuits or whether they would become a destabilising influence with respect to the colonial order. Consequently, resettlement plans were prepared well in advance of the end of the war, public relations departments paved a propaganda path and military censors attempted to glean information on what returning soldiers thought, hoped and planned. Demobilisation, and thus resettlement and reabsorption, were implemented in stages spread over nearly 18 months, carefully executed in order to return soldiers to their home areas with their monetary savings intact, and designed to minimise any potential economic or political problems. Employment schemes were introduced and in all the colonies a certain number of soldiers were provided with paid work or training opportunities. That all men who asked for work or training did not get it should occasion no surprise. Colonial economies were not *dirigiste* and despite the great increase in government control during the war they were hardly equipped to act as employment agents. Fears that discontented ex-soldiers might be a cause of unrest were largely unfounded. Given the vast number of men who went away to war and who then returned home with a variety of new ideas and experiences, and a potential to be troublesome, their resettlement and reabsorption can be credited as a success. For the British colonial authorities, that this was accomplished with relatively little disorder was a cause of surprise and relief.

Notes

[1] Robert H. Kakembo, *An African Soldier Speaks* (London, 1947), p. 6.

[2] Rex Pope, 'British demobilization after the Second World War', *Journal of Contemporary History*, 30, 1 (1985), pp. 65–81.

[3] This is not the view of all those who have examined demobilisation plans; for example, Isola Olomola, 'The demobilization of Nigerian troops 1946–50: Problems and consequences', *Odu*, New Series 13 (1976), pp. 40–59, argues that the authorities failed to plan adequately for ex-servicemen. See also G. O. Olusanya, 'The resettlement of Nigeria's ex-soldiers after World War II: A guide for the present', unpublished paper presented to the Tenth Annual Congress of the Historical Society of Nigeria, December 1969.

[4] Andrew Burton, '*Wahuni* (the undesirables): African urbanisation, crime and colonial order in Dar es Salaam, 1919–1961', PhD thesis, London, 2000, p. 215, and *African Underclass: Urbanisation, Crime and Colonial Order in Dar es Salaam* (Oxford, 2005), pp. 87 and 107–9.

[5] Justin Willis, *Potent Brews: A Social History of Alcohol in East Africa 1850–1999* (Oxford, 2002), pp. 173–74.

[6] Frank Furedi, *The New Ideology of Imperialism: Renewing the Moral Imperative* (London, 1994), ch. 2. See also Furedi, 'The demobilized African soldier and the blow to white prestige', in David Killingray and David Omissi, eds, *Guardians of Empire* (Manchester, 1999), pp. 179–97. There was the danger that educated ex-servicemen, rather than being 'cultural missionaries', might turn into troublemakers; see Werner Glinga, '*Tirailleurs sénégalais*: A protagonist of African colonial society', in P. F. de Moraes Farias and Karen Barber, eds, *Self-Assertion and Brokerage: Early Cultural Nationalism in West Africa* (Birmingham, 1990), pp. 149–71.

[7] Various schemes are discussed in: Wendell P. Holbrook, 'The impact of the Second World War on the Gold Coast, 1939–1945', PhD thesis, Princeton, 1978, ch. 5; David Killingray, 'The colonial army in the Gold Coast: Official policy and local response 1890–1947', PhD thesis, London, 1982, pp. 384–404; Ashley Jackson, *Botswana 1939–1945: An African Country at War* (Oxford, 1999), ch. 11; Timothy H. Parsons, *The African Rank-and-File: Social Implications of Colonial Military Service in the King's African Rifles, 1902–1964* (Oxford, 1999), pp. 231–54; Joanna Lewis, *Empire State-Building: War and Welfare in Kenya 1925–52* (Oxford, 2000), pp. 198–243; Gardner Thompson, *Governing Uganda: British Colonial Rule and its Legacy* (Kampala, 2003), pp. 268–87.

[8] For example, the Kenya Government's *Report of the Sub-Committee on Post-War Employment of Africans, 1944*, discussed by R. Fane, 'The return of the soldier: East Africa', *Journal of the Royal African Society*, 42 (1944), pp. 56–60.

[9] Swinton papers, Churchill College, Cambridge, II 270/5/6, Swinton to Stanley, secret, 1 July 1944.

[10] L. W. F. Grundlingh, 'The participation of South African Blacks in the Second World War', DLitt et Phil thesis, Rand Afrikaans University, 1986, ch. 8; Jacklyn Cock, 'Demobilisation and democracy: The relevance of the 1944 "Soldiers Charter" to Southern Africa today', paper presented at University of the Witwatersrand History Workshop Democracy: Popular Precedents, Practice, Culture', 13–15 July 1994, pp. 1–6. For the demobilisation of white South Africans see Neil Roos, *Ordinary Springboks: White Servicemen and Social Justice in South Africa, 1939–1961* (Aldershot, 2005), ch. 7.

[11] Quoted by J. K. Seirlis, 'Undoing the United Front? Coloured soldiers in Rhodesia 1939–1980', *African Studies*, 63, 1 (2004), p. 82.

[12] TNA, CO968/106/1 No. 10, Logan to Gen Kenneth Anderson, HQ EAC, Nairobi, 8 June 1945.

[13] Memorandum: 'Post-war training and employment for African ex-servicemen in Nyasaland' [nd. *c.* 1945], quoted by Timothy J. Lovering, 'Military service, nationalism and race: The experience of Malawians in the Second World War', in R. Ahuja *et al.*, eds, *The World in World Wars: Experience, Perceptions and Perspectives from the South* (Leiden, forthcoming).

[14] Fane, 'The return of the soldier: East Africa', p. 58.

[15] A. J. Knott, 'East Africa and the returning askari', *Quarterly Review*, 285, (1947), pp. 98–111.

[16] This role is described in F. W. E. Fursdon, 'Draft conductor to Togoland: The West African goes home', *Army Quarterly* 57, 1 (1948), pp. 101–10.

[17] RHL, Oxford, MSS. Afr. s. 1734, Box VI, letter, Sir Michael Gass to David Killingray, 4 February 1980.

[18] See David L. Easterbrook, 'Kenyan askari in World War II and their demobilization with special reference to Machakos district', in Bismarck Myrick, *et al.*, eds, *Three Aspects of Crisis in Colonial Kenya* (Foreign and Comparative Studies/Eastern Africa XXI, Syracuse University NY, 1975), pp. 27–60.

[19] Quoted by Kevin K. Brown, 'The military and social change in Tanganyika, 1919–1964', PhD thesis, Michigan State University, 2001, p. 393.

[20] See O. J. E. Shiroya, *Kenya and World War II* (Nairobi, 1985), ch. 4.

[21] These economic and social ambitions and expectations are richly set out in the more than 600 letters written by soldiers from the Gold Coast which were intercepted by the military censor and are in the National Archives Ghana, Accra, BF 692 Sf11. Although I read through these letters in 1979 unfortunately it was not then possible to photocopy them.

[22] IWM, London, Department of Sound Archives, No. 18406, Frank Sexwale.

[23] TNA, CO968/142/14516/41, West African War Council (193), 29 May 1944, memorandum by Swinton.

[24] Extracts from the booklet are included in PRO. CO98/87, 'Demobilization and Resettlement of Gold Coast Africans in the Armed Forces'.

[25] Quoted in Shiroya, *Kenya and World War II*, p. 75.

[26] 'Strong representation were made through the Secretary of State, to the War Office in early October [1945] to impress on the minds of serving Nigerian troops the correct state of affairs in order to eliminate from their minds any false impression that there was sufficient employment for all.' *Annual Report of the Nigeria Department of Labour 1945*, p. 22, quoted by Anne Phillips, *The Enigma of Colonialism: British Policy in West Africa* (London, 1989), p. 146.

[27] Michael Blundell, *A Love Affair with the Sun: A Memoir of Seventy Years in Kenya* (Nairobi, 1994), p. 82.

[28] TNA, CO820/55/34542A/41, report of the Duke of Devonshire's visit to West African troops, 24 February –14 March 1945; WO203/2021, Commander-in-Chiefs' conference: East and West African Forces', HQ ALFSEA, 1 March 1945.

[29] George Wigg, *Lord Wigg* (London, 1972), pp. 108–12.

[30] RHL, Mss Brit. Emp. S.322, Creech Jones papers, Box 34/1 ff20, Advisory Committee on Education in the Colonies: Mass Education Sub-Committee, subsequently published as *Mass Education in African Society*, Col 186 (1944).

[31] John Shuckburgh, 'Civil colonial history of the war', unpub. ts, vol. 4, pp. 42–45.

[32] Hal Brands, 'Wartime recruiting practices, martial identity and post-World War II demobilization in colonial Kenya', *Journal of African History*, 46, 1 (2005), p. 107.

[33] BBC Africa Service, Mussa Kihwelo to Martin Plaut, dd Dar es Salaam, Tanzania, 15 June 1989.

[34] *Ibid.*, Joseph Maliselo to Martin Plaut, dd. Ndola, Zambia, 4 October 1989.

[35] *Ibid.*, Jachoniah Dlamini to Martin Plaut, dd. Mbabane, Swaziland, 19 July 1989.

[36] *Ibid.*, Chama Mutemi Kadansa to Martin Plaut, dd. Ndola, Zambia, 17 July 1989.

[37] Isaac Fadoyebo, *A Stroke of Unbelievable Luck* (Madison WI, 1999), p. 58.

[38] BBC Africa Service, George P. Chintu, son of Alick Chintu, to Martin Plaut, dd. Lilongwe, Malawi, 18 August 1989.

[39] *Ibid.*, Mustafa Bonomali to Martin Plaut, dd. Salima, Malawi, 6 September 1989.

[40] *Ibid.*, Nikolaus Mugisha Abdon to Martin Plaut, dd. Bukoba, Tanzania, 20 June 1989.

[41] *Ibid.*, Ngaraito Makiti to Martin Plaut, describing his father Estos Hamis coming home after the war, dd. Dodoma, Tanzania, 9 August 1989.

[42] *Ibid.*, Rightson Kangwa to Martin Plaut, dd. Ndola, Zambia, nd. c. July 1989.

[43] Fadoyebo, *A Stroke of Unbelievable Luck*, p. 60.

[44] BBC Africa Service, Jachoniah Dlamini to Martin Plaut, dd. Mbabane, Swaziland, 19 July 1989.

[45] RHL, Mss. Afr. s. 1734, Box II, Igwe to Crapp, 15 September 1945.

[46] BBC Africa Service. Jachoniah Dlamini to Martin Plaut, dd. Mbabane, Swaziland, 19 July 1989.

[47] *Ibid.*, Estos Hamis to Martin Plaut, describing the return home of his father, Ngaraito Makiti, to the Kilimanjaro area after the war, dd. Dodoma, Tanzania, 9 August 1989.

[48] *Ibid.*, Joseph Chinama Mulenga to Martin Plaut, dd. Lusaka, Zambia, 6 June 1989.

[49] Karen Daniel, 'Life in Claremont: An interview with May Santon', *African Studies*, 60, 1 (2001), pp. 53–54.

[50] BBC Africa Service, Rus Osakwe to Martin Plaut, dd. Kano, Northern Nigeria, 1 August 1989.

[51] Kevin Greenbank, '"You chaps mustn't worry when you come back": Cape Town soldiers and aspects

of the experience of war and demobilisation 1929–1953', MA thesis, Cape Town, 1995. Interview with 'R. F.', pp. 13–14.

[52] Nigerian Army Education Corps and School, *History of the Nigerian Army*, p. 98.

[53] Jackson, 'Watershed in a colonial backwater', p. 346.

[54] IWM, London, Department of Sound Archives No. 18371, Nana Kofi Genfi.

[55] For attempts to compute returning soldiers' savings see Killingray, 'Colonial army in the Gold Coast', pp. 388–90; Grundlingh, 'Participation of South African Blacks', pp. 340–44; Jackson, 'Watershed in a colonial backwater?', pp. 346–48.

[56] BBC Africa Service, Usiwa Usiwa to Martin Plaut, dd. Chichiri, Blantyre, Malawi, 25 July 1989.

[57] *Ibid.*, Batison Geresomo to Martin Plaut, dd. Ntchisi, Malawi, 9 October 1989.

[58] *Ibid.*, Pondaponda Tembo to Martin Plaut, dd. Ntchisi, Malawi, 26 July 1989.

[59] *Ibid.*, Rus Osakwe to Martin Plaut, dd. Kano, Nigeria, 1 August 1989.

[60] Jackson, 'Watershed in a colonial backwater?', p. 343.

[61] BBC Africa Service, James Adewale to Martin Plaut, dd. Akure, Nigeria, 2 August 1989.

[62] Grundlingh, 'The participation of South African Blacks', p. 363.

[63] BBC Africa Service, Justice C. Banda to Martin Plaut, dd. Blantyre, Malawi, *c.* 19 June 1989.

[64] *Ibid.*, Etim Akpan Attah to Martin Plaut, dd. Iboko-Offot, Nigeria, 12 June 1989.

[65] RHL, Mss Afr. s. 1734, Box II, James Igwe to Capt M. V. Crapp, 15 September 1945.

[66] Killingray, 'The colonial army in the Gold Coast', pp. 396–404; Meshack, "For your tomorrow, we gave our today", ch. 10.

[67] Jackson, 'Watershed in a colonial backwater?', p. 343.

[68] *Ibid.*, p. 343.

[69] TNA, CO554/140/33779, 'Summary of problems arising out of resettlement of ex-soldiers of 82 Division', secret, GHQ West Africa, 1 September 1945.

[70] National Archives of Ghana, Accra, BF5062, Gerald Plange to A. Campbell, dd. New Delhi, 28 June 1945. Campbell reported that he regarded Plange as 'level headed and sensible'.

[71] See David Edgerton, *The Shock of the Old: Technology and Global History since 1900* (London, 2006), pp. 83–84, for a later description of Ghana which is applicable.

[72] BBC Africa Service, Justice C. Banda to Martin Plaut, dd. Blantyre, Malawi, nd. *c.* 19 June 1989.

[73] *Ashanti Pioneer*, 15 October 1946, p. 2; *Spectator Daily*, 12 August 1946; and *Daily Echo*, 8 October 1946.

[74] Grundlingh, 'The participation of South African Blacks', p. 370.

[75] Quoted *ibid.*, p. 348.

[76] See most usefully William Beinart, *Twentieth-Century South Africa* (Oxford, 1994), ch. 5.

[77] Quoted Grundlingh, 'Participation of South African Blacks', p. 348.

[78] *Ibid.*, p. 365.

[79] *Ibid.*, p. 365.

[80] *The Bantu World*, 4 May 1946, p. 10.

[81] BBC Africa Service, Julius Mosha to Martin Plaut, writing about his father-in-law's wartime experiences, dd. Dar es Salaam, *c.* November 1989. The Tanganyika Groundnut Scheme at Kongwa employed a few 'African drivers and craftsmen ... delighted to return to service life'; John Iliffe, *A Modern History of Tanganyika* (Cambridge, 1979), p. 441.

[82] BBC Africa Service, Chama Mutemi Kadansa to Martin Plaut, dd. Ndola, Zambia, 17 August 1989.

[83] *Ibid.*, Anwell Siame to Martin Plaut, dd. Kasama, Zambia, nd. *c.* September 1989. Mr Siame became the provincial general secretary of the Commonwealth Ex-Servicemen's League in Zambia.

[84] Muga Gicaru, *Land of Sunshine: Scenes of Life in Kenya before Mau Mau* (London, 1958), p. 145.

[85] BBC Africa Service, Nikolaus Mugisha Abdon to Martin Plaut, dd. Bukoba, Tanzania, 20 June 1989.

[86] *Ibid.*, James Mpagi to Martin Plaut, dd. Kampala, Uganda, 14 August 1989.

[87] RHL, Mss Afr. s. 1734, Box IV (168), E. R. A. Gyem to J. A. L. Hamilton, dd. Effiduasi, Ashanti, 6 December 1946.

[88] John Iliffe, *The African Poor: A History* (Cambridge, 1987), pp. 208–9.

[89] Grundlingh, 'The participation of South African Blacks', p. 360.

[90] *Ibid.*, p. 361.

[91] BBC Africa Service, Rabson Chombola to Martin Plaut, dd. Ndola, Zambia, nd. *c.* November 1989.

[92] RHL, Mss. Afr. s. 1734, Box II, David Aloa to Capt M. V. Crapp, 17 May 1946.

[93] Interview: Mama Moshi by David Killingray, Accra, April 1979.

[94] Quoted by Lovering, 'Military service, nationalism and race'.

[95] TNA, CO820/47/34393/A, Pensions, 1941–42.

[96] TNA, CO820/54/34393/4, 1944–45, CO98/88, Legislative Council Minutes, reply 29 March 1947.

7
Ex-servicemen & Politics

'What improvements may we expect to find in the Divisions and in our villages when we return?'[1]

It is widely acknowledged that the Second World War constituted a watershed in the recent history of sub-Saharan Africa and that it marked either the end of the beginning or the beginning of the end of European colonialism in Africa. By 1945 the Western European colonial states had suffered defeat or siege and declined in political and economic power. In a pyrrhic victory, they were over-shadowed by the two superpowers, the United States and the Soviet Union. By the end of the war the political balance in Africa had also changed. The colonial powers were still in charge – indeed, it was widely believed that their rule would continue for a very long time – but the seeds of change had been sown, increas-ingly during the war but also in the years preceding 1939. Within 15 years of the war's end a large part of Africa was either independent or well on the road towards that goal.

Official perspectives

During and immediately after the war, officials and observers understandably commented on the likely effects that exposure to modern warfare and overseas travel would have on the several hundred thousand African soldiers who had been enlisted.[2] A few, mainly in the colonies, feared that on returning home the soldiers were likely to constitute a destabilising influence and could be a threat to future colonial rule.[3] Lord Hailey, writing in 1941, said: 'It is, of course, too early to judge of the full reactions of the present war on the African outlook, though they cannot fail to be far-reaching.'[4] In 1945, and based on his own first-hand observations, he reported that although 'war experiences had a very marked effect on the troops themselves … their return had had less immediate effect on the structure of African society than many colonial authorities had anticipated'.[5] The South African government's refusal to arm black troops was partly influ-enced by white public opinion but it also reflected fears about what messages this might give large numbers of Africans especially when they were removed from the narrow racial agendas of the Union. The novelist Joyce Cary, in a small book written in 1944, commented: 'This war, far more than the last, must change Africa,' and then went on to add that African soldiers 'may stand aside from revolutionary movements, [but] they are making comparisons between wages, conditions and hopes'.[6] The anthropologist Meyer Fortes remarked in 1945 on the 'revolutionary' influence of the war, which might well 'prove to have been the outstanding instrument of social progress in West Africa for fifty years'.[7]

It has often been said that the military experiences of Africans during the Second World War shattered white prestige. Ndabaningi Sithole, the Zimbabwean nationalist leader, wrote in the late 1950s of the war puncturing the myth of white supremacy:

> Thousands of African soldiers went abroad on active service. The English street girls of London, the French street girls of Paris and the Italian street girls of Naples did not help to preserve the white myth. African soldiers ... found themselves at the front-line war with one purpose in view – to kill every white soldier enemy they could get hold of ... African soldiers saw white soldiers wounded, dying, and dead. Bullets had the same effect on black and white. This had a very powerful psychological impact on the African. He saw what he used to call his betters suffer defeat ... and once more he was impressed by the fact that it was not the fact of being black or white that mattered. After suffering side by side with his white fellow soldiers the African never again regarded them in the same light. After spending four years hunting the white enemy soldiers the African never regarded them again as gods.[8]

More forcefully, Michael Crowder argued that as a result of the war 'the myth of colonial invincibility was destroyed, and the self-confidence of the colonial powers and administrators who sustained the myth dissipated. The colonial emperor had no clothes.'[9] This conclusion would have surprised many colonial officials in the late 1940s. The colonial emperor was then still well clothed and officials were overwhelmingly confident that despite the war speeding the pace of economic and political change, it would be many decades, generations possibly, before colonial territories were able to rule themselves. We now know that the pace of change was much more rapid than thought possible even by nationalists. The question of white prestige still needs to be addressed. The idea of Europeans maintaining their 'prestige' before African subjects is a European construct and, as Bruce Berman argues, fails to reckon with the 'complex, but often shrouded, underworld of collaboration, negotiation and conflict at local levels that ultimately tied the colonial state to African societies and significantly constrained its power', although some whites thought that a pale skin-colour endowed them with prestige; no doubt there were Africans who also believed this.[10] However, the history of 20th-century colonial Africa does not reveal many instances where Africans thought or acted as if white men were 'supermen'. Images do not of themselves uphold systems of rule; it is economics and the effective exercise of political and coercive power which sustains regimes. And in the pre-1939 years, there were many Africans all over the continent who had challenged colonial government and felt the strength of that power, but also gained some idea of the weight and the limitations of their own collective power. The economic and social changes ushered in by the Second World War helped African nationalists to gain a new political focus, that they could lay claim to territorial 'nation' states. But the corollary of this was the steadily growing realisation in the metropoles of the major colonial powers that there were increasingly diminishing economic and political gains to be had from holding on to formal African empires.

Once the war was over, soldiers waited to go home. Demobilisation took time and in camps all over India and the Middle East men chafed at enforced idleness, boredom and the slowness of repatriation. European soldiers, required as labour for reconstruction, were given priority over African and other troops, but even among these there was unrest and considerable dissent. In African army camps during 1945–46, many men became increasingly angry at long delays which indicated potential trouble for colonial authorities. The real anxiety was about the future attitudes and expectations of educated Africans who might become a focus for unrest in the towns. A small booklet written in 1944 by a serving soldier, Robert Kakembo, and eventually entitled *An African Soldier Speaks*, made some modest and seemingly unthreatening suggestions about the need for changes to the colonial order. The Colonial Office, fearful of reaction in East Africa, banned it from general publication and East African Command produced a limited edition of 400 copies with 'Confidential. Not for Publication or Circulation' stamped on the front cover, for distribution to district officers, with a warning that these were the ideas that might be expected from educated ex-servicemen.[11]

Three years after the war ended, an ex-servicemen's protest in the Gold Coast was dispersed with violence by the police, and this marked a radical turning point in the history of the colony. The official enquiry reported that

> a large number of African soldiers returning from service with the Forces, where they had lived under different and better conditions, made for a general communicable state of unrest. Such Africans by reason of their contacts with other peoples including Europeans had developed a political and national consciousness. The fact that they were disappointed at conditions on their return, either from specious promises made before demobilization or a general expectancy of a golden age for heroes, made them the natural point for any general movement against authority.[12]

The following year the Coussey Committee on constitutional reform in the Gold Coast, chaired by an African judge, reported that of 'the new forces at work, perhaps the most important was the attitude of mind of the ex-Service men who now returned from the battlefields of the world'. They returned, said the report,

> with a knowledge of other nations, possessing no higher standards of cultural, social and intellectual development, who nevertheless are now ordering their own affairs. Moreover, having fought in the defence of freedom, they considered it their right that they should have some share in the government of their land. These ideas quickly spread throughout the whole country.[13]

Two years later Arthur Creech Jones, who had recently served as Secretary of State for the Colonies, wrote that 'the experience which came to tens of thousands of colonial soldiers in the war years released influences and stimulated ideas which were incalculable. They became more racially aware; new political notions dawned and spread among people who had previously been conscious only of kinship and tribal associations'.[14]

205

Historians' perspectives

Given the weight of these contemporary events and judgements it is not surprising that the African history and political analysis written during and immediately after the period of independence should give a prime place to ex-servicemen as agents in the African nationalist 'struggle for freedom'. Thomas Hodgkin, in his stimulating book on nationalism in colonial Africa written in the mid-1950s, stated that 'the experience of African servicemen in the various theatres of war' was 'too familiar to require detailed repetition here', while George Shepperson argued that the war 'accelerated the nationalist tendency in Nyasaland' while 'lowering ... the European's prestige'.[15] George Bennett, in a political history of Kenya published in 1963, spoke of African soldiers overseas becoming 'aware of the aspirations of the nationalist movements in Asia'.[16] A few years later Ali Mazrui summed up the generally accepted view: 'In short, African military experience abroad in the 1940s contributed to the birth of African nationalism at home.'[17] Schleh, in a study of Ugandan and Ghanaian ex-servicemen, stressed their postwar political activity, although in the same year G. O. Olusanya wrote of the 'political unimportance of ex-servicemen' in Nigeria.[18] The idea that ex-servicemen played a significant role in nationalist politics is presented either directly or implicitly by Coleman, Davidson, Langley, Mazrui and Tidy, and in the research done by Shiroya in East Africa.[19]

The persuasiveness and the persistence of this idea is readily understandable. They are views which continue to have currency. For example, Crawford Young recently wrote of 'the volatile vector of disgruntled ex-servicemen at war's end', the conflict marking 'a rupture in expectations'.[20] However, Michael Crowder offered a word of caution at various times in the 1980s, arguing that insufficient research had been undertaken to allow a proper assessment of the role of former soldiers in nationalist politics.[21] In the final volume of the *Cambridge History of Africa*, David Williams stated, from his limited experience of serving with West African troops in Ethiopia, that it was unlikely that soldiers returned home 'as new men with new ideas'. Yet, he says, 'a wider experience and perspective had been gained, and if this seemed rather undramatic at the individual level, collectively it contributed to a critical evaluation of the post-war colonial situation'.[22]

One or two scholars, using archival sources and also oral evidence, have continued to promote the idea of ex-servicemen as significant nationalist activists. Adrienne Manns (later Israel) collected oral evidence from Ghanaian ex-soldiers involved in the events preceding the riots in February 1948, and she concluded that the Ex-Servicemen's Union played a prominent role in nationalist politics.[23] The role of Ghanaian ex-servicemen as political martyrs and heroes in the post-war nationalist struggle had by then long been a central part of the mythology of Ghana's modern history.[24] A few years ago Frank Füredi, using material drawn mainly from the British National Archives, argued that a 'moral panic' seized many European officials as they contemplated the impact of thousands of demobilised African soldiers returning home and then questioning the colonial order. However, when wider evidence is used it is difficult to see how such conclusions can be sustained. There is little supporting evidence for this in parallel Dominion Office papers or in the official archives in Kenya, Malawi, Ghana and Botswana.[25]

Such ideas about the place, role and influence of ex-servicemen have not gone unchallenged. Today the weight of informed scholarship would now agree with Richard Rathbone's argument, made a good many years ago with respect to Ghana, that the contribution of ex-soldiers to nationalist politics was no greater than that made by any other occupational or interest group.[26] This conclusion has been supported by other research on Ghana by Headrick and by Killingray, on South Africa by Grundlingh and, in the last few years, by the detailed studies on the African rank-and-file carried out by Parsons, Brown, and Meshack in East Africa, Jackson in Botswana, Simelane in Swaziland, and Lovering in Malawi.[27] Clearly more research needs to be done, and there are the resources to do such work, but the overwhelming consensus now is that ex-servicemen made a much less significant contribution to nationalist politics than once was thought.

Wartime political experiences

It is obvious that military service, especially overseas, helped to broaden the perspectives of African soldiers; it may also be, as suggested by David Williams above, that such service helped them to view critically the colonial society to which they returned. Men who had known little beyond the narrow confines of a village were thrust into a world of new experiences. It has been argued that for some men that experience led to a new political consciousness, an awareness of the colonial order and a desire to see it changed. Undoubtedly this was so for a small number of soldiers, particularly those who had some formal education, although there is little evidence of overt nationalist activity by ex-soldiers *en masse* on their return home. What experiences specifically are supposed to have given soldiers this new awareness? Some of this is myth, but as with all such ideas there is just enough truth to warrant closer investigation. The majority of wartime recruits (and this is more true for those from certain territories than others, such as the High Commission Territories) came from conservative peasant backgrounds where there was a strong tradition of loyalty to indigenous authority. Army life did challenge these authorities' bounds for some men, but most soldiers returned from the war with an unchanged and conservative frame of mind and went back to their rural home areas.[28] Soldiers of the KAR marched to a song, *Tufunge Safari*, which looked forward to the end of war and return to a rural world:

> When we have beaten the enemy we shall come home,
> And the children will be waiting and clapping their hands,
> We shall start digging our gardens,
> And we shall look after our cattle for ever.[29]

'My hopes were not too high,' one soldier told Timothy Parsons. 'The war gave me many skills – I wanted a plot of land [and] the chance to use them.'[30]

One myth is that African soldiers serving overseas came into extensive contact with US African-American troops and from them learned various political ideas.

The idea that black Americans and Africans would actually have anything in common has been fuelled by the rhetoric of pan-African sentiment. There are a number of recorded instances when African soldiers and civilians who spoke English met black American troops, mainly in North Africa, southern Europe and India. For example, both Warihiu Itote and Bildad Kaggia describe conversations with African-Americans who encouraged them to demand fair treatment from their officers.[31] In most cases these would have been little more than chance meetings, with contact unlikely to have been sustained for any length of time. It is also important to look at the subsequent political history of both men to see why they might have recorded such detail. As far as possible the British colonial and military authorities took decisive steps to keep African troops away from black American soldiers. London gained Washington's assent to black Americans not being stationed in any British colony in Africa, while African-American troops in Liberia would not be allowed to pass through British territory.[32] There were, wrote Lord Swinton, the Resident Minister in West Africa, 'strong objections on political and general grounds to the employment of such troops in West Africa' where relations between white US soldiers and local troops had at times been tense. American soldiers of either race had much higher levels of pay than African troops and this, argued African colonial governments, encouraged prostitution and inevitable rivalry with African soldiers. The East African authorities talked of 'unfortunate incidents resulting from the temporary stationing of American coloured troops in Nairobi', and the Colonial Office referred to a similar uneasy situation in Trinidad.[33] By February 1944 the West Africa War Council could report that the 'proposal to use American coloured troops in British West Africa could be regarded as dead'.[34]

Another myth is that the political awareness of African soldiers was honed by contact with Asian nationalists. Again, this is hardly borne out by what actually happened to African troops in India. The British and Indian authorities planned encampments for African troops away from centres of population. This was done more to reduce the likelihood of communal unrest, particularly over women, than from any fear that African soldiers might be politically 'infected' by Indian nationalists.[35] African soldiers were not generally permitted to roam free from the camps and when small parties of selected NCOs visited cities such as Bombay and Calcutta they were invariably accompanied by a British officer. Thus relatively few Africans serving in Asia had any sustained close personal contact with local civilians. Service in North Africa, the Middle East, India and Ceylon gave African soldiers a first taste of large cities and the sight of acute poverty. It is clear from soldiers' letters as well as from official reports that African soldiers were surprised and often disgusted by the poverty and squalor they saw in cities such as Cairo, Bombay and Calcutta.[36] As one Ghanaian ex-serviceman recalled, Indians were 'lazy people ... always begging, but kind people'.[37] Many African soldiers from East Africa and Natal, areas with substantial populations of Indian background, now viewed Indians with contempt as poor, vulnerable and despised – a marked change from the received image of members of the Indian merchant class back home. In India, African soldiers also encountered racial antagonism from shopkeepers who refused to serve them. Such experiences helped to reinforce racially based antagonism towards Asians. Letters from soldiers began to appear in the Swahili press condemning Asian men who married or lived with African women, and a number of *askaris* demanded that Indians should be repatriated to India and all Asian immigration into Kenya stopped.[38]

However, the idea that African soldiers were influenced by Asian political activists continues to circulate, is repeated in scholarly texts and is certainly widely believed in Africa itself. This is not to deny all influence, but the idea of men from the West African bush sitting in the bars of Bombay and discussing with Congress activists how to overthrow colonial rule is highly unlikely. A few of Adrienne Mann's informants claimed to have met and talked with Indian and Burmese 'intellectuals'; one ex-soldier, Medu Fulani, recalls meeting Burmese near Rangoon, although he said he did not understand the ideas that they talked about.[39] Another ex-serviceman claims to have heard Gandhi speak in Madras. Two Nigerian soldiers wrote home to say that they had met Gandhi: 'Ganhihiji [*sic*] treated the West Africans with respect, asked them how they liked India, and if they had any questions.'[40] Through the 1920s–40s Gandhi and the Indian nationalist struggle inspired many West Africans, so it is not surprising that a few literate soldiers should mention his name. Clearly care needs to be taken in accepting at face value claims by ageing African ex-servicemen of contacts with and influence from Asian political activists 40 or more years earlier. In Ghana in particular, the idea that ex-servicemen were in the forefront of the 'nationalist struggle' is so pervasive that it often seems difficult for former soldiers not to claim some involvement.

The vast majority of soldiers drawn from the traditional recruiting grounds of colonial Africa had little knowledge or understanding of modern politics, although this did not mean that their grievances did not assume political significance.[41] Lack of knowledge of English and nonliteracy acted as major barriers to the transmission of new ideas, as the military authorities were only too aware. Only a very small number of men gained a basic knowledge of English and even fewer acquired basic reading skills. In some military units, such as those recruited from Bechuanaland, chiefs were enlisted as NCOs and continued to exercise traditional authority over the rank-and-file. Rasebolai Kgamane, who was next in seniority and close to Tshekedi Khama, was the only regimental sergeant-major in the Bechuanaland forces.[42] Another *Kgosi* was Kgari of the Bakwena, who served as a sergeant-major during the war.[43] The soldiers most likely to be influenced politically by wartime experiences were those who enlisted from the non-traditional recruiting areas, men who had some years of primary schooling and had acquired basic literacy and numeracy, tradesmen, and those from towns who had gained some familiarity with modern systems. The best-educated soldiers were those most likely to be promoted, to become senior NCOs and warrant officers, to improve their technical skills and serve as army instructors and teachers. On demobilisation they were more likely to find employment in government service and commercial firms and thus less likely to be involved in overt political activity.

Despite all that has been said there were plenty of wartime experiences of soldiers – especially overseas – that might serve as political catalysts. Racial discrimination of various kinds clearly rankled with many soldiers; it was amplified when men from different colonies served alongside each other. This was encountered by West Africans serving overseas, on passage via South Africa and particularly in white settler Kenya.[44] A frequent comment by West African soldiers was that Kenya 'is not a good country for the black man'.[45] Reuben Tackie, editor of the mimeographed *Kintampo Camp Weekly*, produced at an army base in central Gold Coast, complained:

> In the RWAFF, troops are not known as 'troops' or as 'soldiers': they are known as 'Africans'. 'I saw Africans,' 'there are too many Africans here' are phrases which one hears too often even in a force comprising almost entirely of Africans. Is this discrimination necessary?[46]

Levels of pay, rations and conditions of service were a source of obvious grievance. West African soldiers received higher pay than did East African, and white soldiers were paid more than Africans. There was also overt racial discrimination which although part of daily colonial life in settler East, Central and South Africa, was at least largely absent from the West African colonies, and white officers and NCOs who displayed discriminatory views were strongly resented by the rank-and-file of and largely unwelcome in West African units. Similar problems were encountered in India. After the war, Sabben-Clare at the Colonial Office recorded that 'the general run of Indian Army officers did not take kindly to other "native troops" in their preserves'.[47] Racially discriminatory proscriptions pervaded the military; Africans were prevented from watching certain films, given restricted access to towns and areas of towns, and confined to camp when white soldiers were not, and there was some resentment at the way news reports and official films failed to give sufficient credit to the role of black troops in battle. L/C John Ejirika complained to a British officer:

> The film 'Burma Victory' was seen even more than twice. Only Indian, American and English troops were seen there. No record of African hard fighting in Burma even in Kaladan Valley where we lost so many African troops. It was clearly stated that Indian troops won the battle in Kaladan in which I have to say is black lies.[48]

The military authorities in India attempted to monitor the attitudes and aspirations of African troops; similar intelligence reports were also gathered on Indian and British units. The vast majority of reports on West Africans refer to soldiers' concerns over welfare issues, although there are occasional brief references to quasi-political activities. For example, in September 1944 two 'societies' existed within the 81st Division although, concluded the report, both appear to be 'simple "tea party" committees'.[49] A year later it was reported that a number of Africans sympathised with strikes in Nigeria and were annoyed at the suppression of certain Nigerian newspapers. Several 'associations and brotherhoods' of a 'semi-political nature' also came to light within the 82nd Division, and although deemed 'apparently not subversive' they were banned by divisional headquarters.[50] At the 82nd Division commanders' conference in May 1945, one senior officer reported that 'literate Africans were keenly interested in post-war planning developments in West Africa'.[51] At the end of that year Capt J. James, senior resident in Nigeria, and Col S. Hall of GHQ, West Africa, visited India 'to collect first-hand information concerning the general outlook of West African troops in India and SEAC and their views on post-war development'.[52]

The most significant influences in helping to shape Africans' views of Europeans came from two directions: contact with whites outside Africa, and more formally from the programmes of education initiated by the military authorities. African soldiers' views of Europeans were often based on experiences of racial discrimination in the colonies, especially in settler colonies. Encountering white men who were not conditioned by colonial mentalities enabled African soldiers to engage with and view whites differently. Sylvia Leith-Ross, a perceptive commentator on Nigeria, recalled in her memoirs that

> from conversations with observant Africans who had been in contact with our troops or sailors, for the first time in their lives these Africans had met a number of Europeans *less educated than themselves* ... You could not help feeling that this discovery was perhaps the final insidious blow which shattered the crumbling edifice of white superiority.[53]

A similar example is cited by the filmmaker Ousmane Sembène, who served in the French colonial army in 1944–46:

> In the army we saw those who considered themselves our masters naked, in tears, some cowardly or ignorant. When a white soldier asked me to write a letter for him, it was a revelation – I thought all Europeans knew how to write. The army demystified the coloniser; the veil fell.[54]

The various army education instructors made small-scale attempts to channel literate soldiers' aspirations by using discussion materials supplied through the Army Bureau of Current Affairs (ABCA). Earlier 'official' discussion groups, recalled Moses Danquah of the Gold Coast Regiment, were usually organised by chaplains and interested officers but tended to avoid political issues.[55] Obviously political ideas had a currency among a small number of soldiers. The books and magazines sent to African troops were vetted but it was not possible to place soldiers within a mental *cordon sanitaire*. For example, in the African sergeants' messes in the Middle East all kinds of literature circulated. By late 1945 political issues could not be avoided and there were discussions on economic development, colonialism and the political future of Africa. Certain of these discussion groups were led by non-regular British officers and NCOs, wartime conscripts with leftish and radical ideas, who even encouraged Africans to discuss agendas which the colonial authorities would not have allowed. At the same time a few African soldiers casually encountered European soldiers who were willing to talk about economic and political change in Africa. It may well be that radically minded British officers and NCOs played a more important role in stirring a sense of African political consciousness than the Asian and African-American influences claimed by an earlier literature.[56]

Inevitably, given the large number of soldiers enlisted from British colonial Africa, there were one or two men who wrote letters critical of the colonial order which were received by veteran nationalists or occasionally appeared in the African press. For example, a Gold Coast soldier wrote a parody of Psalm 23 which appeared in September 1944 in the *African Morning Post*, published in Accra; part of it said:

> The European merchant is my shepherd,
> And I am in want;

He maketh me to lie down in cocoa farms;
He leadeth me beside the waters of great need;
He restoreth my doubt in the pool parts ...

The general managers and profiteers frighten me.
Thou preparest a reduction in my salary
In the presence of my creditors.
Thou anointest my income with taxes;
My expense runs over my income
Surely unemployment and poverty will follow me
All the days of my poor existence,
And I will dwell in a rented house for ever![57]

Another Gold Coast soldier, Emil K. A. Sackey, of 835 Company West African Army Service Corps, stationed in India, wrote to the veteran Ghanaian nationalist Kobina Sekyi in September 1945. Referring to the West African trade unionist Isaac Wallace-Johnson, who had been imprisoned at the start of the war for his nationalist activities, he said:

> We have finished the war physically, but it is not over. We have to struggle for liberty; at home the suppression is great ... We are discovering the truth of Wallace-Johnson's writings: and I would to God that He gives us more Wallace-Johnsons when we come back home. We have made up our minds to help build the country, free from all oppression.[58]

Sekyi, writing in October 1945 to Kwame Nkrumah in London, said that the Aborigines' Rights Protection Society, a conservative and moribund nationalist organisation, was thinking of 'setting up a new press which proposition emanated from some of our boys in khaki engaged overseas'.[59] Herbert Macaulay, the elderly doyen of Nigerian nationalists, also received letters from soldiers serving overseas. One in September 1945 from Pte Theo Ayoola, written from Poona, India, declared: 'We all overseas soldiers are coming back home with new ideas ... We have been told what we fought for ... That is "freedom". We want freedom nothing but freedom.'[60]

How much weight should be given to this small number of letters? They may be but a handful although it is significant that they are extant and show that a small number of literate soldiers were interested in economic and political developments in postwar West Africa. Conversely, there were also soldiers who wrote sympathetically of British colonial rule. Moses Danquah, to whom reference has already been made, contributed an article to the *West African Review*, the house journal of the Elder Dempster Shipping Company, in which he criticised the high-handed British prewar colonial policy which excluded Burmese from economic activities; however, he went on to argue that 'politically, Burmans had no justified cause for discontent ... [which] the British had made magnanimous, if dilatory, gestures to satisfy'.[61] The next month, January 1946, another Gold Coast soldier wrote to the *Review*: 'We have fought against fascism, the enemy of mankind so that all people, white or black, civilised or uncivilised, free or in bondage, may have the right to enjoy the privileges and bounties of nature.'[62]

Cpl Samson Yeboah, a clerk at GHQ Accra, argued in an article entitled 'Self Government Now?', published in the official newspaper *RWAFF News* in January 1945, that the Gold Coast was not 'ripe' for self-rule because the colony lacked educated manpower and a sense of national unity.[63] Balanced against these predictable indications of political awareness by a few literate soldiers must be placed the very large number of private letters, written by soldiers or by regimental scribes to family members and chiefs, which detail personal grievances, aspirations and fears. These letters are for the most part unselfconscious and concerned with wives and family matters, payments home, and future education and employment opportunities. Some of these issues could be, and were, translated into political demands immediately after the war, but overt political questions are rarely mentioned.[64]

The general conclusion that can be drawn from this available evidence is that African soldiers were little concerned with political issues but much more interested in family issues and economic and social grievances. For a small group of demobilised servicemen such grievances were heightened by inflation, postwar shortages and failure to find employment. Any political awareness on the part of soldiers must also be placed in the context of the development of broader territorial politics. In West Africa the 1930s, the war years and the immediate postwar years were periods of increased protest at the policies of colonial governments, over cocoa prices, conscription, prices of imported goods and unemployment. This provided fertile ground for anti-colonial political organisations such as the Zikists in southern Nigeria and the United Gold Coast Convention, founded in 1947, and inevitably some ex-soldiers found in these nationalist movements an expression of their own particular discontents. Demobilised soldiers helped form the Ogoni Central Union in 1945, a social and cultural organisation aiming to represent all Ogoni in the Niger Delta area, and bodies like this could form nascent political organisations ready to respond to particular issues affecting specific peoples and interest groups.[65] They also gave ex-soldiers experience of organising a local lobby – experience that could later be used for political purposes. Some men joined the army in wartime with political ideas already awakened, and for them military service undoubtedly provided opportunity for further reflection and discussion. But throughout British colonial Africa the vast majority of skilled and literate soldiers found employment after the war and were not in any way involved directly in patriotic nationalist politics. For the rank-and-file Westcott's conclusion for Tanganyika seems to be accurate for much of Africa: that military service developed the muscles of men more than their minds.[66]

Territorial identity & patriotism

Did military service help to encourage a sense of African and territorial or 'national' identity? Service in a military force gave men an increased awareness of belonging to one territory; this probably helped override certain particular and ethnic differences although, for some, it may well have helped to emphasise differences in origin, language and culture, especially between soldiers who were literate and those who were nonliterate. It seems unlikely that service alongside troops from other African territories helped to develop a strong pan-African feeling. To argue thus is to minimise existing deep ties of ethnic and cultural affinity, and to project an ideal of brotherhood which is belied by the actual relationships between soldiers of different backgrounds within the same regiment and from the same colony. It can be argued that military service had the opposite effects – that by close association with other soldiers men became more conscious of their cultural and ethnic differences. For example, in the Gold Coast there was marked antipathy between northerners and Asantes and also between various ethnic groups within the north such as the Dagomba and Konkomba.[67] Certainly, while on service overseas men from a particular regiment tended to ally against soldiers from another regiment or colony, for example in bar brawls or contests over women. There was considerable hostility between West African troops stationed in East Africa and men recruited from the three East African territories. Men of the Gold Coast Regiment were known as *machorogozi* or *ngorogiosi*, both appellations derived from the regimental title.[68] Chinyanja-speaking soldiers from Nyasaland in the KAR complained of prejudice from East Africans. Uniforms, encampments and the regimental spirit helped to provide this thin veneer of solidarity, which probably did not go very deep and was ignored in conflicts within the regiment, when ethnic identity overrode much else.

The British idea of regimental loyalty was in part imposed on colonial units. For example, the regiments of the RWAFF each bore a territorial name – such as 'Gold Coast Regiment' or 'Northern Nigeria Regiment' – and on each soldier's uniform was a shoulder-flash bearing the name of the colony. This helped forge a sense of both regimental and territorial identity, and for a handful of soldiers perhaps even an idea of nascent patriotism. Soldiers from Nyasaland had a strong sense of 'Nyasa' identity, argues Lovering, and a parallel view is supported by Brown for Tanganyikan *askari*.[69] Twenty years after the end of the war Waruhui Itote, later the Mau Mau 'General China', described 'the first time I ever thought of myself as a Kenyan'. It was in 1943 'in the Kalewa trenches on the Burma Front', during long discussions with a British soldier who challenged Itote: 'I don't understand you Africans who are out here fighting. What do you think you are fighting for?' A bit later the British soldier said: 'At least if I die in this war … I know it will be for my country. But if you're killed here, what will your country have gained?' Itote wrote: 'What he'd told me never left my mind.'[70] Wartime service provided many young men with a range of new experiences and opportunities. For a relatively small number, such as Itote, it helped promote new ways of thinking, which fostered old and new grievances and encouraged them to begin to question the colonial order.

Ex-servicemen & African politics

Despite all that has been said, some ex-servicemen did play an active part in African politics and that role now needs to be assessed. The focus of most literature has been on anti-colonial nationalist politics. Territorial politics and the demands of new political parties to succeed the colonial rulers are obviously important parts of Africa's postwar history, but they are not the whole story. There was also politics at the local, grassroots level, with young men, including returned soldiers, challenging the rule of indigenous chiefs or demanding a greater say in the 'native administration'.[71] Some soldiers had little respect for the native administration, and often none for the Native Authority Police.[72] At the third *kgotla* at Serowe in Bechuanaland, at the height of the Seretse Khama crisis in mid-1949, at least 8,000 men attended from all over the reserve, 'many of them wearing their greatcoats and uniforms from World War II'.[73] This aspect of local politics, which often aimed to influence the structures created by the colonial state, has attracted far less attention from scholars. During the decades of the 1950s–60s, as new African states were created, academic attention was given to writing a 'nationalist' history that inevitably focused on the role and activities of territorial parties. These parties held the high ground, produced newspapers, generated documentation and were seen as the future rulers of independent territorial states, successors to the European rulers. The reverse was the case for local or chieftaincy politics. Scholars' attention was largely on the 'national' picture and little attention was given to micropolitical activity which was more difficult to research and academically less attractive. The two colonies in which ex-servicemen made most impact on national politics were the Gold Coast and Kenya, so more attention will be given to them. At the same time we will look selectively at the role of veterans in local political affairs.

West Africa

In the Gold Coast, an ex-servicemen's union had been established after the First World War, led by and mainly catering for men from the southern Colony and Ashanti. During the mid-1930s the union's leadership played an active role in the protests against the Italian invasion of Ethiopia.[74] Towards the end of the Second World War a new Gold Coast Legion was formed. Modelled on the British Legion, and recognised by the Government 'as the sole agency for serving the needs and representing the interest and views of ex-servicemen', the organisation was formally inaugurated in February 1945. By mid-1948 it was reported to have more than 36,000 African members.[75] In 1946 Robert Ben Smith, a veteran of both wars and a former chief clerk of the Gold Coast Regiment, was appointed by the Governor to a seat on the Legislative Council to watch over the interests of ex-servicemen. The legion was apolitical and through its branches was concerned with a welfare programme for former soldiers and their dependants.

As an official body the legion failed to meet the grievances of a number of ex-servicemen. They re-formed an Ex-Servicemen's Union in 1946, led by B. E. A. Tamakloe, who had served in the First World War and been the secretary of the pre-war union.[76] According to the Watson Commission, by early 1948 the union claimed 6,650 members organised in a number of branches. Some veterans talked in radical terms: 'There is an army of us here who helped defeat the Germans, and we show the British our strength on our land, with all the people behind us.'[77] Such heated rhetoric is always present in times of tension and needs to be carefully balanced against the other views expressed by ex-soldiers at the time. A short-lived union newspaper, *Ex-Service*, was published in 1947. The union was critical of Government failures to provide adequately for the needs of ex-servicemen, and as such it attempted to function as a trade union. It was not a political organisation but mainly concerned to articulate soldiers' grievances and to find work for its members. A petition to the Governor in February 1948 listed seven specific grievances: the release of 12 ex-servicemen serving prison sentences, increased pensions for disabled soldiers, additional rehabilitation funds, more rapid Africanisation of the RWAFF, exemption of ex-servicemen from levies, greater effort by Government to find work for former soldiers, and prompter payment of war-service gratuities. The legion was denounced for its non-cooperation, and particularly Robert Ben Smith who 'is not a true representative of the ex-servicemen of this country, owing to the fact that he knows nothing of the conditions of life of the ex-servicemen. He has no contact, influence, no understanding of the ex-servicemen of this country.'[78]

These specific grievances of ex-servicemen need to be placed in the broader context of postwar discontent in the Gold Coast. Government had failed to control inflation, curb the high price of goods imported by foreign companies, or reduce the high level of unemployment which was most severely felt in the burgeoning towns of the south. In addition, official policies on cutting out infected cocoa trees, in an attempt to control swollen-shoot virus in the cocoa-growing districts, alienated thousands of farmers. Disgruntled ex-servicemen swelled the ranks of the unemployed and underemployed in the southern towns, and at an ex-servicemen's rally addressed by the Governor in Accra in June 1947, 'their behaviour was a clear indication to all who watched the proceedings that trouble was ahead'.[79] At the same time the local military commander, Maj-Gen William Dimoline, warned the authorities 'that it is essential that real political development should keep pace with the material and social development which is planned, both in order to satisfy the widening political horizons of the new class including the returned soldiers'.[80] In this growing situation of economic and social unrest, the Ex-Servicemen's Union played a minor but crucial role which was to change the political face of what was once complacently described as a 'model colony'.

The United Gold Coast Convention (UGCC), founded as a national movement in August 1947, viewed ex-servicemen as useful 'raw material' in the political struggle. Tamakloe declared that the union supported the UGCC, and the two organisations shared common protest platforms. On Saturday 28 February 1948, the union organised a march to present their petition to the Governor at Christiansborg Castle. The straggling column of some 2,000 abandoned the officially authorised route and in the ensuing confrontation with the police two ex-servicemen were killed and another was mortally wounded.[81] Gold Coast nationalism gained its first three martyrs: Sgt Cornelius Adjetey, Cpl Attipoe and Pte Odartey Lamptey,[82] and riots broke out in Accra and in other towns. Government promptly arrested the six principal leaders of the UGCC, including the convention's secretary, Kwame Nkrumah. The result was 'the sudden, violent transformation of the political scene' in the Gold Coast.[83]

The agenda of the Ex-Servicemen's Union was not overtly political. The leaders of the union expected the UGCC to stand with them and in return the convention saw militant and relatively well-organised ex-soldiers as useful allies in the bid to pressure the colonial government for constitutional and economic change. As Adrienne Manns argues:

> Overall, the ex-servicemen became both a real and a symbolic reservoir of support for the escalated political demands of the nationalist leaders. Though not necessarily transformed

into militant nationalists, they did emerge as a group more likely than other young men, to expect greater post-war concessions and rewards from the British administration and to turn against British rule if their expectations remained unmet.[84]

Manns also says that 'veterans were no better represented than other interest groups, such as businessmen and teachers ... Veterans were prominent not so much because of their numbers, but because of their militancy, their experience with discipline and organised violence, their willingness to act as a group, and their easily identifiable grievances against the government.'[85] As a result of the shootings of February 1948 and their political aftermath, many ex-servicemen have claimed that they played a prominent role in the nationalist struggle. This has been reinforced by a nationalist historiography according the ex-servicemen a primary role which has fed back to veterans, leading them to assume what Steven Knapp has called a 'collective authority'.[86]

Among well-educated African ex-soldiers, disillusionment with their lot in the postwar world did not necessarily lead to overt political action. But it did help to sour race relations. B. B. Amoo, who came to Liverpool just after the war to study agriculture, was reported as stating:

> I was in the British Army and fought the Italians at Addis Ababa. I determined to come to this land we call our Motherland. I found people who despised us. We have been taught the good side of the English, but you have been taught the bad side of the coloured man. I have not had the chance of being among decent folk.[87]

Ex-soldiers, including members of the union, which was beset by rivalries, played an active role in the politics of the UGCC and also in Nkrumah's more radical Convention People's Party (CPP), formed in June 1949.[88] At political demonstrations in the period up to the elections of 1951, the ex-servicemen's presence was often obvious although invariably their aim was to promote their own sectional grievances over back pay and jobs and not a party-political agenda. For example, ex-servicemen were involved in the Positive Action protests of January 1950 but, as Owusu says, ex-soldiers, like 'the majority of people ... were interested in then, and in the future, amelioration of economic hardship. That was the limit of their political interest.' Paul Edua, the leader of the Ex-Servicemen's Union in the southern Gold Coast town of Swedru, claimed –with some justification, argues Owusu – that the success of the Positive Action campaign in Accra and elsewhere was due to the activities of the former soldiers. The union demonstration in Swedru, involving some 400 men in their old khaki uniforms, aimed to 'frighten people to go Positive Action, refuse to buy from Europeans' and to 'force the D.C. [district commissioner] to take serious notice of their economic demands'. The ex-servicemen met secretly and then the column set out towards the town, 'accompanied by war songs and cries', en route singing "*Soldier ei yei ya ko aba oo yei* ... [We are the soldiers who have returned from active service overseas ...]"]'.[89]

In the south of the Gold Coast and also in Ashanti, individual ex-servicemen did become political activists but there is little firm evidence to support the idea that ex-soldiers formed a coherent group within the nationalist movement. Soldiers' interests remained solidly sectional. This 'myth of the ex-servicemen' in Gold Coast politics has been corrected by Richard Rathbone, who claims that 'from a careful analysis of the antecedents of activists, and in particular branch notables, it seems clear that ex-servicemen were represented in no more than their overall national proportions'.[90] Most ex-servicemen in the south of the Gold Coast, the more economically advanced region of the colony, were bystanders to politics. In the economically poorer Northern Territories, the traditional recruiting ground for the army, ex-servicemen appear to have had little economic or political impact. In a study of the region, Ladouceur concluded that army experience 'did not have any significant effects on the North. The demobilized soldiers became neither agents of rural modernization nor supporters of radical political movements and political unrest.'[91]

More than 110,000 Nigerians enlisted in the war and more than 30,000 served overseas in East and North Africa, and in Asia. Coleman, in an important early book on Nigerian nationalism, argued that 'it is therefore not surprising to find ex-servicemen among the more militant leaders of the nationalist movement during the post-war period'.[92] Olusanya contests this. Certainly, he said, war experience 'made the Nigerian soldiers more politically conscious than ever before', but the assumption 'that the ex-soldiers played a significant role in the politics of Nigeria breaks down when subjected to critical analysis'.[93] There was good reason for ex-soldiers to be discontented. Two years after the war, well over one-third of veterans were still unemployed. 'The brave new world they had fought for,' wrote Mokwugo Okoye, secretary-general of the Zikist movement and also an ex-soldier, 'had easily faded into a rotten world of unemployment and frustration.'[94] Several factors reduced the possible effectiveness of ex-servicemen in Nigerian politics.

First of all, as in several other colonies, the ex-servicemen's organisations were localised and poorly funded – often being little more than personal fiefdoms. A Supreme Council of Ex-Servicemen had been launched in Lagos in 1948, but this only represented soldiers in the south of the country. There was also the National Federation of Ex-Servicemen's Association of Nigeria and the Cameroons and the Lagos Ex-Servicemen. There were, complained the *West African Pilot*, a multiplicity of ex-servicemen's organisations which acted in isolation from each other and lacked unity.[95] Nigeria was a large country with relatively poor communications, so there were serious logistical problems to creating a territory-wide organisation. A second major reason for the organisations' ineffectiveness was poor leadership. Ex-soldiers who were educated or had good management skills were among the first to find jobs. Too often the leaders of ex-servicemen's organisations were men with little competence to do so. They fell victim to personality clashes and rivalries over ethnicity and politics.

The greatest weakness 'making for the political impotence of ex-soldiers', says Olusanya, was the deep divisions within the nationalist movement.[96] A few ex-soldiers became minor political leaders in the National Council of Nigeria and the Cameroons, and also in the Zikist movement,[97] but these were largely regional and ethnic groupings which had little claim to influence other than in parts of the south, and certainly not in northern Nigeria, from where the overwhelming majority of soldiers came. Compared to the Francophone states, where several leading politicians had served in the army – such as President Léopold Senghor of Senegal and M. Yace, President of the National Assembly of Côte d'Ivoire – few Nigerian ex-servicemen, other than J. M. Johnson, Federal

Minister of Labour in 1960–63, held office higher than backbenchers in the federal and regional legislatures.[98] Some ex-servicemen were active in politics – indeed Heelas Chukwuma Ogokwe, who tried to murder Chief Secretary Hugh Foot in February 1950, was a war veteran and ardent Zikist.[99] But the seizure of the town of Umuahia in 1951 by ex-soldiers was a local reaction to demands to pay tax when many men were unemployed. The trouble was quickly quelled and some of the ringleaders imprisoned.[100]

The small ethnic and regional unions, leagues and parties in Nigeria offered a sphere of possible political activity for returned servicemen. For example, ex-servicemen took a prominent role in the Tiv Progressive Union, one of the bodies representing the acephalous Tiv of Nigeria's Middle Belt area. After 1945 ex-servicemen were prominent in the campaign to secure a Tiv paramount chief, a *Tor Tiv*. Partly due to their efforts a former soldier, Makeri Zakpe, who was chief of police and prisons in the native administration, was selected and installed as the first *Tor Tiv* in April 1947, although this move was not universally popular. Ex-servicemen were also directly involved in protests and the subsequent revolt against the imposed Yoruba chief at Makurdi in late 1947. When party politics arrived on the scene in the mid-1950s, ex-servicemen were again active in the United Middle Belt Congress (UMBC) opposing the Northern Peoples' Congress. As one veteran told an interviewer in 1990:

> We did not tolerate any nonsense in our land and we provided fire for everything in Tivland. Right from 1946 onwards, ex-soldiers were in the forefront or provided the stimulus for every major event in Tivland. The first *Tor Tiv* and the first indigenous chief of Makurdi were both ex-servicemen. It was because ex-servicemen came to the rescue of the UMBC that they were able to sustain NPC aggression during the 1960s riots.[101]

This may have been a former soldier exaggerating the role of his fellows, but undoubtedly a number of ex-servicemen did play a sustained active role in the 'tribal' politics of the Tiv, although perhaps to no greater extent than other groups and interests.

Little is known about the impact of returning soldiers on the political institutions of rural society. Chiefs in Sierra Leone expressed fears that ex-servicemen would cause trouble and use their wider experience and gratuities to challenge indigenous authority. The Governor, Sir Hubert Stevenson, assured chiefs that the 'Burma boys', as ex-soldiers were called, would not cause trouble. Nevertheless, ex-soldiers did intervene in the politics of native administration and become agitators in many of the chiefdoms, particularly the south-east. For example, in the Kissi chiefdom Kai-Tungu ruled with a firm hand, but many ex-soldiers refused to accept his authority. 'Between 1948–50', says Lavalie in a brief paper, 'intrigues and demonstrations led by ex-servicemen were prevelant in many Chiefdoms in the Provinces'.[102] Some former soldiers engaged in illicit diamond mining, using skills in jungle warfare acquired in Burma to protect their operations.[103]

The Sierra Leone Ex-Servicemen's Association was formed in late 1947 but was only formally recognised by the Government in 1954. It functioned as a voluntary organisation, 'a purely Benevolent Society with the primary objects of seeking and safeguarding the general welfare, social, literary, moral and economic of the Ex-Servicemen'.[104] The association took no part in politics and it appears that the Sierra Leone People's Party saw little value in attempting to mobilise the support of the ex-servicemen's organisation.

East Africa

The East African colonies, and particularly Kenya, were dominated by a small number of white settlers. In Kenya European farmers controlled the White Highlands which had been alienated mainly from Kikuyu peasants. High agricultural prices in wartime brought prosperity to many white farmers and also to some Africans who squatted on their farms. Many aspects of urban life were changed by the war which also brought large numbers of European and African troops to the major towns of Nairobi and Mombasa.[105] In 1940, with the serious Italian threat to East Africa, a total ban was placed on all African political activity in Kenya and certain leaders were detained, including those of the Kikuyu Central Association (KCA), which campaigned over the lost lands. Nevertheless, according to James Beauttah, soldiers serving with the KAR, men like Isaac Githanju, 'actively recruited for the KCA in the armed forces'.[106] Kenya's constitution was far behind those of the Gold Coast and Nigeria, with the first African to join the Kenya Legislative Council being nominated only in 1944; unlike the case in West Africa, rigid racial segregation was imposed in Kenya by law. But in 1944 the ban on African political activity was lifted, and in October the first territorial political party was formed: the Kenya African Union (KAU). Thus the Kenya to which soldiers returned at the end of the war had undergone significant socio-economic and political changes, and many veterans expected that these would benefit them.[107]

War service had conferred privileges on and widened the social and economic horizons of soldiers. These new ambitions were expressed by two *askaris* in November 1944:

> There are hundreds of Askari who joined this War … These Africans are expecting liberty for which they have been fighting. This new life, of course, cannot be obtained without money, and money that is being received by one who is being employed. Their fighting will be of no use if, after the war, a man will be released to go to his village and sit idle without employment. This is contrary to what he is fighting for.[108]

James Beauttah, who had been a politician in the central provinces since the 1920s, recalled that

> the returning soldiers brought back a completely different attitude towards the European. They had seen the white man do work that in Kenya only blacks did. They had seen white men killed and wounded, crying like babies with shell shock; they had seen stupid white men get better jobs than Africans just because they were white; they had fought alongside white soldiers and had learned that dirty white men stink just as badly as dirty black men. They returned with a confidence and desire to change the system in Kenya.[109]

Many of the soldiers returning home to Kenya after the war had learned a number of lessons and honed some expectations while they had been away: they were less likely to accept racial discrimination, they demanded a more equitable distribution of land, and they had learned that it might be possible to challenge colonial authority, and also that violence could be used against white men. It is hardly surprising that officials saw the actions of some soldiers as truculent.[110] Gakaaru wa Wangau, from Nyeri, had been expelled from the prestigious Alliance High School in 1940 and soon after enlisted in the KAR. During his service in East and North Africa he met 'many Africans from the then British colonies' and realised that 'although black people were shedding blood for the British cause, the British persisted in treating them as slaves'.[111] He joined the KAU.

The colonial authorities and many white settlers viewed the demobilisation of thousands of troops, whose hopes and expectations were unlikely to be realised, as a potentially destabilising influence. Kango Muchai, a driver with the KAR who had served in East Africa, Madagascar and Asia, later recalled that while in the army

> we Africans were told over and over again that we were fighting for our country and democracy, and that when the war was over we would be rewarded for the sacrifices we were making ... For my part I was only trying to be given a small piece of land somewhere and to be treated a little more decently by the Kenya Government and white settlers ... These hopes and dreams of mine were quickly crushed on my return home. The army talk was false propaganda intended only to get Africans like me to risk our lives for Britain and the white settlers of Kenya. The life I returned to was exactly the same as the one I left four years earlier: no land, no job, no representation and no dignity.[112]

The bitterly disillusioned Muchai joined the Kikuyu Central Association in 1949 and took an active part in anti-colonial politics. So did John Gatu, who had been a wireless operator in the KAR. When he left the army he went to London and took a course in journalism. Returning to Kenya, Gatu became assistant to Henry Muoria, editor of *Mumenyereri*, 'The Giguyu National Bi-Weekly', 'because he was the editor of the most important nationalist paper'.[113] Editing such newspapers in postwar Kenya meant walking a very narrow line determined by sedition laws. Girdhari Lal Vidyarthi, the Kenyan Indian editor of the *Colonial Times*, 'was fined KSh2,000 in 1945 for writing a critical editorial entitled "Burma Week", in which he condemned discrimination against the returning African soldiers, who were left helpless in the "native reserves" while their white counterparts were granted many acres of land in the so-called White Highlands as well as development loans'. In the next two years Vidyarthi was sentenced to prison and also fined for criticising in print the treatment given to African veterans.[114]

Many East African soldiers learned new ideas while on overseas service, and on their return some were determined to resist the harsh racist formulae of the white-settler-dominated state. There must have been many men who angrily shared the sentiments expressed in the letter of one *askari* caught by the censor: 'Long hair has stolen my country away.'[115] And it was not only white oppressive attitudes and policies that angered African soldiers. Asian traders in East Africa were resented also, especially as competitors to veterans starting up as retailers; black soldiers' contact with impoverished people in India only helped to sharpen that disdain.[116] But such anger alone does not turn demobilised soldiers into political activists.

Shiroya suggests that some soldiers acquired pan-African ideas during military service.[117] Maybe a few did, but they cannot have been more than an insignificant minority. One such was an army signaller in India who, calling himself 'The Dreamer', advocated an 'African Continental Union':

> When will Tanganyika alone bring Africa freedom? ... I have now been two years and seven months in India ... In many offices ... you will see that the P.C. is an Indian and the D.C. a European. In many workshops they are mixed up; you do not see only Europeans in charge as they are in Africa. I asked them ... is this because of education, or for what reason? They told me: No, not at all; these things have come about because of the unity of the association of The All-India Union ... Truly Indians have unity. It is not the union of a game alone, like drunkards or children, but a union with the power to lift up the whole of India ... I mourn for my own Africa. When shall we Africans be free like this?[118]

In the three British East African colonies, ex-servicemen were relatively little represented in nationalist politics at the territorial level. Iliffe says of Tanganyika in this period that 'generally the soldiers' political contribution was surprisingly small',[119] while Schleh, writing about Uganda, says that there was no mobilisation of ex-servicemen into nationalist politics, perhaps because the parties barely existed in the immediate postwar years.[120] In the most recent research on this subject, Timothy Parsons states that 'former *askaris* were noticeably absent from the East African nationalist movements'. He concludes by stating:

> The political influence of East African veterans has been largely overstated ... Ex-servicemen bitterly resented their treatment but lacked the means to express their grievances through political protests ... the relative wealth and practical experience of prosperous ex-askaris also made them respected men in their home communities ... Thus, veterans were much more likely to be agents of economic and social change, rather than instigators of political unrest.[121]

Army service, far from creating radicals critical of the colonial order, often proved a conservative influence. Soldiers learned order and discipline and notions of industrial time, and the kind of skills that increased their labour value to white employers and the colonial regime. As a result many ex-servicemen found work, including minor posts in the colonial bureaucracy as clerks, policemen and chiefs. In the mid-1950s an organiser for the Tanganyika African National Union was reported as saying: 'It is impossible to tell an ex-askari from any other person. They went into the army as illiterates and they remained "empty-headed", forgetting everything but how to give a snappy salute and say "Ndio, Bwana" ['Yes, Master']'.[122]

Soldiers enlisted from and returning to the rural areas were more likely to be involved in local rather than territorial politics, indeed valued members of their communities.[123] For example, among the Kamba, long regarded by the British as the premier martial race in Kenya, many of the chiefs and local political leaders during the late 1940s–50s were ex-servicemen. They were also among the wealthiest in the community and thus likely to be of conservative disposition. In Buganda, Spartas Mukasa was a leader of the Bataka Party which was a Ganda pressure group. Similarly, other veterans belonged to groups promoting Bunyoro and other ethnic interests.[124] Former soldiers also played an active part in the politics of indigenous authority; for example, on the Madi Council in northern

Uganda, reorganised in 1946, 'members were chosen from all classes, particular care being taken to see that the educated class and ex-askari were represented'.[125]

The officially recognised ex-servicemen's organisations in East Africa and Nyasaland were the African sections of the British Legion. Governments exercised effective control over these bodies. Several other veterans' groups were established, often with an ethnic or local focus. For example, in Kenya there was the Nyeri District Ex-Soldiers' African Friendly Association, locally known as *Ndesefa*,[126] and also the Kikuyu Ex-Servicemen's Education Union. Both were small and poorly led and did not survive for very long. Ex-servicemen's groups often had a specific political agenda – to oppose the *kipande* (the pass required to be carried by Africans) and government agricultural policies, or to demand African representation in the legislative council or the expulsion of Asians.[127] Some veterans formed self-improvement organisations such as *Ikundo ya Mbaa Lili* ('the Knot of the Band of the Lili'). Open to all Kamba ex-servicemen, it raised money for educational purposes. 'Politics' meant different things to different groups of ex-soldiers. To the National Ex-Servicemen's Union of Kenya, active in Nyanza Province in the 1950s, it meant pressuring Britain over the 'unkept promises' to soldiers. The Kenya Ex-Servicemen's League had a similar agenda. The leadership of both these bodies was weak and unreliable.[128] Robert Kakembo, to whose booklet reference has been made, was a founder member of the Kawmawo ('Survivors') Group of ex-servicemen in Buganda which was concerned with postwar development issues. In effect it was little more than a Ganda pressure group but one which the colonial government watched with concern; it tried to co-opt Kakembo from the group with the offer of a government post.[129]

In Kenya it was more difficult for Kikuyu than for Kamba ex-soldiers to return to civil life in the rural areas. Few Kikuyu servicemen were chiefs or headmen, or served on local 'native councils' – all such positions were taken by better-educated men who had not gone off to the war. Many ex-soldiers found it difficult to get trading licences and to return to agriculture. White alienation of Kikuyu land and population growth put intolerable pressures on farmlands. Work was difficult to find and when their small savings were used up restless Kikuyu ex-servicemen joined the growing ranks of the urban unemployed. In the burgeoning slums of dispossessed Nairobi, unemployed and alienated ex-servicemen served as leaders of the Kikuyu *Anake wa 40*, the 'Forty Group' of petty traders, thugs, thieves and prostitutes, whose authority was enforced by the use of oaths, prefiguring the methods of the violent, rural anti-white settler Mau Mau movement of the late 1940s and 1950s.[130] Some of the Forty Group also saw themselves as nationalist leaders and held the KAU in contempt, seeing it as slow and too conservative. The political desperadoes of the Nairobi slums had close links with Kikuyu squatters on white-owned farms and also with radical elements in the KAU. This prepared the ground for the violent confrontation between Mau Mau and the white settler state and African conservatism in the 1950s.[131]

Only a handful of ex-soldiers joined the KAU in Kenya. As Brands argues, this was because the aims of such political organisations 'tended to clash with the aims of the formers askaris'.[132] Some veterans, but again only a few, were active as trade-union leaders. During the Mau Mau emergency of the early 1950s, many of these men were swept up in the government net and accused of involvement in violence. For example, Paul Ngei, a Kamba from Machakos, served overseas with the KAR and became an education instructor. When he returned home he founded the outspoken newspaper *Uhuru wa Afrika* and become branch secretary of the Kenya African Union in his home town. Arrested during the Mau Mau emergency he was charged with managing Mau Mau and imprisoned for seven years. Convicted along with him was Bildad Kaggia, a Kikuyu, whose military service had taken him to Britain. On his return to Kenya in 1945 he became a militant trade-union leader and a leader of the KAU.[133]

Within the Mau Mau movement itself there were some ex-soldiers, although few field commanders had combat service that might have been of use in the forest war. Stanley Mathinga and Waruhui Itote were exceptions, having served overseas – Itote with 3/6 Tanganyika Battalion. Others active in Mau Mau were Karigo Muchai, who had been in the East African Army Service Corps; Dedan Mugo Kumani, whose job had been that of a hygiene instructor; and Dedan Kimathi, who had been a latrine orderly for a few months.[134] But, as Parsons argues, for every radical ex-serviceman in nationalist politics there was also one active moderate – for example, politically aware men such as Justus Kandet ole Tipis, Musa Amalemba and Jonathan Nzioka (the latter two former army education instructors) who served on the Legislative Council.[135]

The formation of a territorial nationalist party in Tanganyika lagged some years behind that of Kenya. Nevertheless, ex-soldiers from the First World War were involved in protest politics – notably Kleist Sykes, who helped found the Tanganyika African Association (TAA) in 1929.[136] The TAA grew in size during the latter years of the Second World War, and contacts were established with radicals such as George Padmore in London. Among the new members of the TAA in the late 1940s and early 1950s were ex-soldiers who had fought together in Burma, educated townsmen such as Dossa Aziz, James Mkande and Kleist Sykes' sons Abdulwahid and Ally Sykes. One recent account describes these men making a pact at Imphal on Christmas Eve 1945, to found a political party when they returned home to Tanganyika after the war. 'Ally Sykes remembered that Abdulwahid wrote the name of the proposed party in his diary': the Tanganyika African National Union. Ally Sykes, in a recent interview with Brennan, 'categorically denied that Indian nationalists influenced Tanganyika veterans at all'.[137] In 1951 the TAA was lagging and the presidency had passed to Thomas Plantan, a former soldier with little education.[138] When Julius Nyerere became president of the TAA in 1953 (with Ally Sykes as secretary), the movement revived and within 15 months it had broadened its structure and appeal to become the Tanganyika African National Union (TANU), a nationalist party pledged to fight for self-government. The first TANU membership card was copied by Ally Sykes from his British Legion card.[139] TANU was led by Nyerere and Ally Sykes became the party's first treasurer.

Southern & Central Africa

The most significant political fact in the British territories of Central and Southern Africa, and South Africa itself, in the immediate postwar years was political and economic dominance by whites. Most military recruits came from the rural areas and were nonliterate men, and returned to the rural areas after their period of service. The impact of the war was considerable, not least for soldiers who had come from societies where racial lines were tightly drawn but who had had occasional encounters with white people on equal terms. Robert Nxumalo, a sergeant in the Native Military Corps, recalled years later that 'in Egypt we found there was no colour bar. We were stationed in the desert. I'll never forget the first time I had a drink with a white officer!'[140] South Africa's economy had been altered by wartime industrialisation and urban growth. Of necessity some racially discriminatory laws and practices had been allowed to lapse – for example the pass laws and regulation of African movement to the towns – although by 1945 there was growing white political pressure to re-impose and tighten such restrictions.[141] And African and non-European political parties, the major one being the African National Congress (ANC), were relatively weak and presented little effective opposition to the entrenched and powerful white regime. So politically the South Africa to which black and Coloured soldiers returned in 1945–46 remained much the same as the one they had left. According to Z. K. Matthews, the veteran African nationalist:

> The colour bar was as rigid as ever; the pass laws and the poll tax laws were enforced just as stringently. There was no sudden rise in wages and the fact that a man had been on active service did not carry much weight with employers, military pensions were meagre and did not afford economic security. All these things engendered a mood of insecurity.[142]

The new ideas gained in wartime by African servicemen had relatively little impact on South African political activity. Ex-servicemen were too few in number, mainly nonliterate, and dispersed mainly in rural areas. Louis Grundlingh argues that 'most ex-servicemen were indistinguishable from their contemporaries who did not participate in the war [which] ... cautions one not to exaggerate the Second World War as a catalyst'. Changes in the lifestyle of some African soldiers were not due to their military training and experiences, but much more to 'larger processes of industrialisation and urbanisation unleashed by the War'. Ex-servicemen had no impact as a group but only as individuals, partly because their 'pre-War experience, education and status ... were more important in moulding them politically than their military experience'.[143] A good example of this is the Coloured communist James La Guma, who had been active in the South African Communist Party and in trade unions since the 1920s, and who joined the Indian–Malay Corps when he was aged 40. On being demobilised in 1947, La Guma continued his political activities.[144]

Predictably, a few soldiers wrote letters home and to the African press about 'equal rights for all civilized men', enquired about joining the ANC, or later recalled their hopes and ambitions for a future South Africa. Robert Nxumalo, who was to become the assistant editor of the popular magazine *Drum*, recalled that 'during the war I often heard how it was going to be different after we got home. I even heard white South Africans say that when they got home they were going to see that this colour-bar foolishness was done away with.'[145] In the long list of names of Southern African politicians there are very few who can claim military service or that the experience of war shaped their political lives.

However, two names do stand out: Patrick Leballo, who had been an army driver in East and North Africa, and was then active in the ANC in Orlando in the early 1950s (although his own account of his life must be treated with great caution);[146] and Herman Toivo ja Toivo, who served with the South African army until 1945, co-founded the Namibian nationalist South West African People's Organisation while he was working in Cape Town, and was imprisoned on Robben Island in 1968.

As elsewhere in Africa, political protest did not have to be made through organised political parties. There were other means and platforms in the form of labour unions and veterans' organisations. As Peter Alexander has argued, in looking at the role of ex-soldiers in the building strike of 1947, 'the impact of radicalized ex-servicemen on labour movement politics merits further attention'.[147] For example, at the height of the apartheid system the vice-president of the South African Ex-Servicemen's League, addressing the annual Cape Corps service in Cape Town's City Hall, denounced government policy: 'We fought against Nazi Germany's treatment of the Jews. Surely, therefore, on a day like this, in a place like this, we have a right to speak out when we feel that, in our society in our own country, we experience oppression and discrimination?'[148] Coloured ex-servicemen returning to the Cape Province at the end of the war found that many of the jobs they had formerly done had been taken by Africans.[149] In 1946 Coloured ex-soldiers with their families became illegal squatters in Orlando West, Johannesburg. Led by Samuel Kono, they established a site they called Tobruk, after the battle in North Africa in which many Africans had fought – 'a name with a stark symbolism of resistance in South Africa, particularly among ex-servicemen'.[150]

However, the most sustained and effective political protest by ex-servicemen in South Africa came not from non-Europeans but from whites. The officially created British Empire Service League, founded in 1921, was a white organisation; Coloured ex-servicemen could join the separate South African Coloured Ex-Servicemen's League. Many white ex-soldiers were radical but also racist and played a prominent role in the military actions of the Rand Rebellion in 1922.[151] Twenty years later the left in South Africa embraced a non-racial policy. Left-wing soldiers serving in East Africa, including members of the South African Communist Party, formed the Springbok Legion in 1941.[152] This was a kind of soldiers' trade union, a non-discriminatory organisation with a mixed-race membership which aimed to 'carry over into peace-time the co-operation which existed between the races during the war'.[153] Through its official organ, *Fighting Talk*, and public meetings, the legion strongly opposed the Afrikaner-dominated National Party's programme of apartheid. Of the Tobruk squatter camp, *Fighting Talk* said: 'A grateful country repays its debts with an illegal right to stretch a few sacks over slender poles. An African's home is his castle.'[154] In the run-up to the general election of May 1948, the legion lost ground. Demobilisation had proceeded fairly smoothly and the left-wing leadership of the legion quarrelled with other ex-servicemen's organisations over the policy to be adopted towards the election. According to Fridjhon, out of the Springbok Legion 'a more radical leadership emerged willing to use the shell of the war veterans' organization for precisely located political ends'.[155] The War Veterans' Action Committee, formed in May 1951, distanced itself from the legion and eventually became a larger and more significant ex-servicemen's organisation, the War Veterans' Torch Commando, which in 1951–52 actively opposed government plans to remove eligible Coloured voters from the franchise. At the height of its power in late 1952, the Torch Commando had a large membership and had joined a United Front with the United Party and the Labour Party to oppose the government.[156] However, claims by certain leaders of the commando that a day of protest 'would bring the country to a virtual standstill' alienated political allies and provided ready ammunition for the government. The front collapsed with the National Party victory in the elections of 1953. Despite its radical voice the Torch Commando had a rather ambiguous attitude to Coloured ex-servicemen.

In Southern Rhodesia between mid-1940 and August 1945 only 2,100 indigenous men were enlisted into the Rhodesian African Rifles. When they returned from the war they had expectations of new opportunities of work and wages, but were met with unequal rewards meted out by a rigid racially discriminatory order. When ex-servicemen protested they risked harsh punishment – one man being beaten by European policemen because he 'complained that as someone who had risked his life in the last war for freedom of white men in Rhodesia, he desired a little courtesy'.[157] Few in number and lacking institutional cohesion, ex-servicemen in Southern Rhodesia contributed little to African labour militancy in the general strike of 1948 or to subsequent nationalist activity in the country.[158] The realities of white racial intolerance in the two Rhodesias were forcibly emphasised by Stewart Gore-Brown in a debate on racial discrimination in the Northern Rhodesia legislature; addressing the Governor, he reminded him of the African contribution to the war effort: 'I would ask whether those men back from Burma who marched past you, Sir, the other day, I would ask whether they are stinking kaffirs?'[159]

If African ex-servicemen had little influence on the great political changes that occurred in South Africa after 1945, it is not surprising that the relatively small number of former soldiers in the neighbouring High Commission Territories also had a negligible political impact. These were societies where indigenous rulers still wielded considerable power and influence. Indeed, in Bechuanaland men had enlisted in the army along with headmen who became NCOs. Some Swazi ex-soldiers were absorbed into traditional courts where they served as presidents or assistants. These courts helped to perpetuate and strengthen the traditional political system and at the same time to resist incursions by modern institutions. Vonya Ndwandwe, who after war service became president of the National Court at Manzini, said:

> I became *Ndabazabantu* (court president) here because of my loyalty to my king and nation. This is the loyalty I demonstrated by going to the war and holding myself there as a Swazi ... If these courts were not there the white man would change us to his ways and we would lose our identity. That should not be allowed to happen.[160]

Such veterans were often hostile to the small political groups which challenged the authority of indigenous institutions. In their eyes, if there was a struggle for autonomy then it was to 'give power to our king not to educated crooks'.[161] The few Swazi ex-soldiers who challenged indigenous institutions had to confront chiefs who were in charge and 'always ready to kick out such people from their areas of jurisdiction'.[162] The small political groups in post-war Swaziland were isolated because 'if you were not in favour of the King it means you are against the Nation'.[163]

According to Charles Arden-Clarke, the Resident Commissioner in Basutoland, by late 1943 Basuto troops in North Africa 'have heard of the Atlantic Charter and the Beveridge Report and want to know to what extent the principles underlying their statements ... are to be applied in their own countries'.[164] However, in the HCTs no territorial political organisations existed that might serve as platforms for such ambitions. Such political activity by ex-servicemen as occurred was confined to protests within indigenous political structures. For example, some non-Tswana soldiers in Bechuanaland became involved in the ongoing struggle against the dominance of the Bangwato polity and in demanding greater autonomy from Tshekedi Khama.[165] The absence of men at the war, as Mokopakgosi suggests for Kweneng in Bechuanaland, removed potential political leaders from local polities and effectively strengthened the position of indigenous rulers.[166] Indeed, chiefs and headmen, and not only in the HCTs, often sent politically troublesome men to the army in order to halt their activities.

The consensus of research on the HCTs is that ex-servicemen had a negligible political impact on politics. Kinyaga-Mulindwa, based on his 'initial investigations', suggests that 'after their return from the war ex-servicemen did not play a significant or even a passive role in the pre-independence politics' of Bechuanaland.[167] More recently this is supported by Jackson, who says that 'war service did not see the radical transformation of Africans into Westernized, politically active citizens, though of course in some cases war service did provide a fund of knowledge and a receptivity to new perspectives that could later be worked upon by politicians'.[168] Shackleton also agrees, although without supporting evidence, that veterans 'shared a bond with members of their own communities but never organised as a group to fight for their veteran benefits or employment opportunities for ex-servicemen'.[169] That is as may be. But it did not prevent individual ex-servicemen from firmly expressing their political grievances and ambitions. Keoboka Kgamane, reluctantly appointed by the DC at Serowe as the 'Senior Tribal Representative', came to London as a member of a six-man Bangwato delegation in April 1952. At a meeting with the reactionary-minded Commonwealth Secretary, Lord Salisbury, Keaboka reportedly told him:

> In 1941 he had been a soldier and had gone to Italy. There the troops had been issued with currency inscribed with the language of Mr. Churchill's Atlantic Charter declaration about the four freedoms. Those freedoms were now being denied to the Bangwato although they had fought loyally in the war. The Bangwato needed protection from Rhodesia and the Union, but the banishment of Seretse meant that the government favoured the Union.[170]

Conclusion

The more than 450,000 soldiers recruited by the British from the African colonies returned home at the end of the war, most of them to the rural areas from which they had been recruited. Contrary to many popular assumptions their influence and impact on territorial and nationalist politics was slight. The vast majority of African soldiers were reabsorbed back into rural life. A small number did take an active part in trade unions and political parties, helped by the skills and knowledge obtained during war service. The ambitions of returning soldiers did not to any large degree involve political action. Rather, they were concerned initially with personal and domestic matters, the welfare of the family, agricultural betterment, improvement in the home village, and with using their gratuity either to buy consumer goods to improve their immediate lives or to establish a business. As John Hargreaves has written: 'Most of the groups and individuals whose horizons had been widened by wartime mobilization remained primarily concerned to defend or advance their own economic interests or cultural values; political consciousness was not born in nationalist costume'.[171]

Notes

[1] *Nigeria Annual Reports for the Northern, Western and Eastern Provinces, 1944*, quoted by Michael Crowder, 'The 1939–45 war and West Africa', in J. F. A. Ajayi and Michael Crowder, eds, *History of West Africa: Vol. 2* (London, 2nd edn, 1987), p. 684.

[2] For example, see the memorandum sent in May 1942 to provincial administrators and heads of departments by Sir Charles Dundas, governor of Uganda (1940–44) which spoke of the likely new expectations on the part of Africans, both those serving in the army overseas and those remaining at home, for 'new method and treatment' in accord with ideas of 'liberty and equality' for which the administration, after the war, must attempt to adapt to 'a new order'. Quoted by Anthony Kirk-Greene, *On Crown Service: A History of HM Colonial and Overseas Civil Service* (London, 1999), p. 217.

[3] Frederick Douglass, the African-American abolitionist leader, had declared in Philadelphia in July 1863: 'Once let the black man get upon his person the brass letters US, let him get an eagle on his button and a musket on his shoulder and bullets in his pockets, and there is no power on earth or under the earth which can deny that he has earned the right to citizenship.'

[4] Lord Hailey, *Native Administration and Political Development in British Tropical Africa. Report by Lord Hailey ... 1940–42*, confidential, 1941, p. 10, reprinted with an introduction by A. H. M. Kirk-Greene, 1979. Fifteen years later Hailey briefly mentioned the significance of wartime military service although he did not invest this with undue importance over other events; see Lord Hailey, *An African Survey Revised 1956* (London, 1957), p. 253.

[5] Lord Hailey, 'Post-war changes in Africa', *Journal of the Royal Society of Arts*, 103, 4955 (July 1955), p. 580.

[6] Joyce Cary, *The Case for African Freedom and Other Writings* (revised and enlarged edn, London, 1944), p. 152.

[7] Meyer Fortes, 'The impact of the war on British West Africa', *International Affairs*, 21 (April 1945), p. 206. Unfortunately neither Fortes nor any other anthropologists at the time collected evidence from ex-soldiers about their experience of the war and their peacetime ambitions.

[8] Ndabaningi Sithole, *African Nationalism* (Cape Town, 1959; 2nd edn, London, 1968), pp. 162–63; also pp. 47–49. Ali Mazrui has written: 'To witness a white man scared to death under fire was itself a revelation to many Africans, who had previously seen white men only in their arrogant commanding position as a colonial elite'; see his 'Africa entrapped: Between the Protestant ethic and the legacy of Westphalia', in H. Bull and A. Watson, eds, *The Expansion of International Society* (Oxford, 1984), p. 297.

[9] Michael Crowder, 'Introduction', in Crowder, ed., *The Cambridge History of Africa. Vol. 8: From c. 1940 to c. 1975* (Cambridge, 1984), p. 21; see also John Hatch, *A History of Postwar Africa* (London, 1965), p. 54; Roland Oliver and Anthony Atmore, *Africa Since 1800* (Cambridge, 3rd edn, 1981), pp. 208–9; Phyllis M. Martin and Patrick O'Meara, eds, *Africa* (Bloomington IN, 2nd edn, 1986), p. 142.

[10] Bruce J. Berman, 'Ethnicity, patronage and the African state: The politics of uncivil nationalism', *African Affairs* 97 (1998), p. 314, fn. 26.

[11] After the war the booklet was published in Britain with a preface by George C. Turner, of Makerere College, as R. H. Kakembo, *An African Soldier Speaks* (Edinburgh, 1946). Various officials at the Colonial Office in mid-1945 unsuccessfully argued that Kakembo's manuscript should be published; see TNA, CO822/118/46776.

[12] Colonial Office, *Report of the Commission of Enquiry into Disturbances in the Gold Coast 1948* (Watson Commission) (Colonial No. 231) (HMSO, 1948), para. 20 A (i).

[13] Colonial Office, *Gold Coast: Report to His Excellency the Governor by the Committee on Constitutional Reform 1949* (Colonial No. 248) (HMSO, 1949), para. 25.

[14] Arthur Creech Jones, 'British colonial policy with particular reference to Africa', *International Affairs* 27, 2 (1951), pp. 176–83.

[15] Thomas Hodgkin, *Nationalism in Colonial Africa* (London, 1956), p. 142; George A. Shepperson, 'External factors in the development of African nationalism, with particular reference to British Central Africa', *Phylon: The Atlantic University Review of Race and Culture* 22, 3 (1961), p. 219.

[16] George Bennett, *Kenya: A Political History* (London, 1963), p. 112.

[17] Ali A. Mazrui, *Towards a Pax Africana: A Study of Ideology and Ambition* (London, 1967), p. 162.

[18] Eugene I. A. Schleh, 'Post-service careers of African World War Two veterans: British East and West Africa with particular reference to Ghana and Uganda', PhD thesis, Yale University, 1968; and 'The post-war careers of ex-servicemen in Ghana and Uganda', *Journal of Modern African Studies*, 6, 2 (1968), pp. 203–20; G. O. Olusanya, 'The role of ex-servicemen in Nigerian politics', *Journal of Modern African Studies* 6, 2 (1968), pp. 221–32.

[19] James S. Coleman, *Nigeria: Background to Nationalism* (Berkeley 1958), asserts without offering any evidence: 'It is therefore not surprising to find ex-servicemen among the more militant leaders of the nationalist movement during the post-war period', p. 254. See also Basil Davidson, *Africa in Modern History: The Search for a New Society* (London, 1978), pp. 199 and 203; J. Ayodele Langley, *Pan-Africanism and Nationalism in West Africa 1900–1945* (Oxford 1963), pp. 344–46; Ali Mazrui and Michael Tidy, *Nationalism and New States in Africa* (London 1984), pp. 11, 14–21; Ali A. Mazrui, ed., *UNESCO General History of Africa. VIII: Africa since 1935* (London, 1999),' Introduction' by Mazrui, pp. 1–14; Okete J. E. Shiroya, 'The impact of World War II on Kenya: The role of ex-servicemen in Kenyan nationalism', PhD thesis, Michigan State University, 1968; and *Kenya and World War II* (Nairobi 1985), pp. 154–55.

[20] Crawford Young, *The African Colonial State in Comparative Perspective* (New Haven CT, 1994), pp. 184–85.

[21] Michael Crowder, 'The Second World War: Prelude to decolonisation in Africa', in Crowder, ed., *The Cambridge History of Africa*, p. 32.

[22] David Williams, 'English-speaking West Africa', in Crowder, ed., *Cambridge History of Africa. Vol. 8*, p. 337.

[23] Adrienne Manns, 'The role of ex-servicemen in Ghana's independence movement', PhD thesis, Johns Hopkins University, 1984. See also Adrienne M. Israel, 'Measuring the war experience: Ghanaian soldiers in World War II', *Journal of Modern African Studies*, 25 (1987), pp. 159–68; and 'Ex-servicemen at the crossroads: Protest and politics in post-war Ghana', *Journal of Modern African Studies*, 30, 2 (1992), pp. 359–68.

[24] A. Adu Boahen, *Ghana: Evolution and Change in the Nineteenth and Twentieth Centuries* (London, 1975), pp. 153–54. For a school text see F. K. Buah, *A History of Ghana* (London 1980), p. 149.

[25] Frank Füredi, *The New Ideology of Imperialism* (London, 1994), ch. 2.

[26] Richard Rathbone, 'Businessmen in politics: Party struggles in Ghana, 1949–57', *Journal of Development Studies*, 9, 3 (1973), p. 390–402.

[27] Rita Headrick, 'African soldiers in World War II', *Armed Forces and Society* 4, 3 (1978), pp. 501–26; David Killingray, 'Soldiers, ex-servicemen, and politics in the Gold Coast, 1939–50', *Journal of Modern African Studies*, 21, 3 (1983), pp. 523–34. On Ghana, Wendell P. Holbrook adopts a position which is in neither camp: see 'Oral history and the nascent historiography for Africa and World War II: A focus on Ghana', *International Journal of Oral History* 3 (1982), pp. 148–66. See also L. W. F. Grundlingh, 'The participation of South African Blacks in the Second World War', unpublished DLitt et Phil thesis, Rand Afrikaans University, 1986, ch. 9; Timothy Parsons, 'East African soldiers in Britain's colonial army: A social history, 1902–1964', PhD thesis, Johns Hopkins University, 1996, ch. VI; and Parsons' subsequent book, *The African Rank-and-File: Social Implications of Colonial Military Service in the King's African Rifles* (Oxford, 1999), p. 209. See also Ashley Jackson, *Botswana 1939–1945: An African Country at War* (Oxford, 1999), ch. 11; Hamilton Sipho Simelane, 'Veterans, politics and poverty: The case of Swazi veterans in the Second World War', *South African Historical Journal* 38 (1998), pp. 144–70; Kevin K. Brown, 'The military and social change in colonial Tanganyika', PhD thesis, Michigan State University, 2001, pp. 316–47 and 415–19; Timothy John Lovering, 'Authority and identity: Malawian soldiers in Britain's colonial army, 1891–1964', PhD thesis, Stirling University, 2002, and 'Military service, nationalism and race: The experience of Malawians in the Second World War', in R. Ahuja *et al.*, eds, *The World in World Wars: Experience, Perceptions and Perspectives from the South* (Leiden, forthcoming). Cf. Myron Echenberg, *Colonial Conscripts: The Tirailleurs Sénégalais in French West Africa, 1957–1960* (London 1991), ch. 9.

[28] Simelane, 'Veterans, politics and poverty', pp. 147–50.

[29] Anthony Clayton, *Communication for New Loyalties: African Soldiers' Songs* (Athens OH, 1978), p. 37.

[30] Parsons, *The African Rank-and-File*, p. 231.

[31] Warihiu Itote, *'Mau Mau' General* (Nairobi, 1967), p. 11; Bildad Kaggia, *Roots of Freedom, 1921–1963* (Nairobi, 1975), pp. 26–27.

[32] TNA, CO968/72/13011/27, 1943. Also Ulysses Lee, *United States Army in World War II: Employment of Negro Troops* (Washington DC, 1966), ch. 15.

[33] Annette Palmer, 'Black American soldiers in Trinidad 1942–44: Wartime politics in a colonial society', *Journal of Imperial and Commonwealth History* 14, 3 (1986), pp. 203–18.

[34] TNA, CO968/92/2, 'Employment of African personnel alongside American coloured troops, 1943–44.'

[35] TNA, CO820/55/34458C, Tadman to Rolleston, most secret, 5 February 1945; TNA, WO203/2268, 'Morale: South East Asia Command', secret, 1944–46. See also Ralph Thomas, 'Indian malcontents and West African soldiers: Some thoughts on the Indian problem', *West African Review*, November 1944, p. 55. Also TNA, CO554/33779, 'Summary of problems arising out of resettlement of ex-soldiers of 82nd Division', secret, GHQ West Africa, 1 September 1945.

[36] For example, TNA, WO172/6590, War Diaries, HQ 81st Division 'G' Branch, secret, intelligence report, 23 November 1944.

[37] Interview, David Killingray with Kwame Asante, Accra, April 1979.

[38] James Brennan, *'Taifa': Africa, India and the Making of Nation and Race in Urban Tanzania*, (forthcoming), ch. 7, 'Civilization, racial-continental thought, and African nationalist projects, 1940–61'; Meshack Owino, '"For your tomorrow, we gave our today": A history of Kenyan soldiers in the Second World War', PhD thesis, Rice University, 2004, pp. 503–8.

[39] Manns, 'Role of ex-servicemen', p. 92.

[40] Clarke, *West Africans at War*, p. 53, quoting *Daily Times*, 7 March 1946.

[41] For example, Jomo Kenyatta in *Kenya: The Land of Conflict* (Manchester, 1945), written while he was in Britain, refers to a report in the *Times* of East African soldiers serving in Burma and comments that Britain is readier to exploit their services than reward them and that the banning of the Kikuyu Central Association (KCA) and wartime conscription of labour for white settler farms is likely to lead to 'bloody insurrection'.

[42] His commanding officer (influenced by ideas of aristocratic hierarchy?) reported: 'RSM Rasebolai had not only all the real dignity of an African of good breeding, but he had the modesty of demeanour and above all, that rarest of all things in an African, a capacity for understanding the white man'; quoted by Bent, *Ten Thousand Men*, p. 9. See also Susan Williams, *Colour Bar: The Triumph of Tshekedi Khama and his Nation* (London, 2006), p. 243.

[43] Michael Fairlie, *No Time Like the Past* (Edinburgh, 1992), pp. 138–39.

[44] Kakembo, *An African Soldier Speaks*, pp. 12–18 on 'Relationships'; Israel, 'Measuring the war experience', pp. 159–68.

[45] Margaret Wrong, 'British policy in Africa', *Christian Newsletter*, Oxford, 1942, col. vi.

[46] *Kintampo Camp Weekly*, 15 March 1946, quoted by Israel, 'Measuring the war experience', p. 159.

[47] TNA, CO537/1894, 'Colonial defence', note by E. E. Sabben-Clare, 11 February 1946.

[48] Letter in possession of Eric Lanning, Surrey: NA44150 L/C John Ejirika to Eric Lanning, dd. Jhansi, India, 21 December 1945.

[49] TNA, WO172/6590, War Diaries, HQ 81st Division, G Branch, secret, intelligence report, 25 September 1944.

[50] TNA, WO203/2268, 'Morale: SEAC', secret, 1944–46.

[51] TNA, WO172/9561, War Diaries, 82nd Division, secret, divisional conference, HQ, 1–18 May 1945. See also David Pratten, *The Man-Leopard Murders: History and Society in Colonial Nigeria* (Edinburgh, 2007), p. 173.

[52] TNA, WO172/9562, War Diaries, 82nd Division, 'Note to all RWAFF units', 1 October 1945.

[53] Sylvia Leith-Ross, *Stepping Stones: Memoirs of Colonial Nigeria 1907–1960* (London, 1983), pp. 116–17.

[54] Quoted in *The Guardian*, Review section, 14 May 2005, p. 22.

[55] Moses Danquah, 'Chaplain was a jungle wallah', *Ghana World Magazine*, 1 (Jan–Feb 1959), pp. 33–39.

[56] For an example of a communist British NCO in India discussing politics with Indians, see Clive Branson, *British Soldier in India: The Letters of Clive Branson* (New York, 1945), p. 31.

[57] *African Morning Post* (Accra, Gold Coast), 2 September 1944; it was also reproduced in *WASU*, the journal of the West African Students' Union in London.

[58] Quoted by J. Ayodele Langley, *Pan Africanism and Nationalism in West Africa 1900–1945* (Oxford 1973), p. 345. See p. 346 for another letter, from Tpr Kojo Taiwah to Sekyi, 12 December 1945.

[59] National Archives of Ghana, Cape Coast, Acc. No. 77/1964, ARPS correspondence, 1936–45, Sekyi to Nkrumah, 1 October 1945.

[60] Quoted in Davidson, *Africa in Modern History*, p. 199.

[61] Moses Danquah, 'Tragedy of Burma: British failure in Burma before the war', *West African Review*, December 1945, p. 33.

[62] *West African Review*, January 1946, p. 30.

[63] *RWAFF News*, 31, 24 January 1945, p. 2.

[64] National Archives of Ghana, Accra, BF3692, SF11, contains some 600 letters from soldiers retained by the censors. Institute of Commonwealth Studies, University of London, Michael Crowder papers, boxes MC17 and 18, include more than 200 letters from Tswana servicemen in North Africa addressed to Tshekedi Khama.

[65] Godwin Loolo, *A History of Ogoni* (Port Harcourt, 1981), p. 20.

[66] N. J. Westcott, 'The impact of the Second World War on Tanganyika, 1939–1949', PhD thesis, Cambridge, 1982, pp. 294–98.

[67] See Enid Schildkrout, 'The ideology of regionalism in Ghana', in William A. Shack and Elliott P. Skinner, eds, *Strangers in African Societies* (Berkeley, 1979), pp. 183–207. On northern divisions see David Tait, *The Konkomba of Northern Ghana* (London 1961), pp. 9–10.

[68] Luise White, *The Comforts of Home: Prostitution in Colonial Nairobi* (Chicago, 1990), ch. 7, and specifically pp. 167–72.

[69] Shepperson, 'External factors in the development of African nationalism', p. 220; Lovering, 'Military service, nationalism and race'; Kevin K. Brown, 'The military and social change in Tanganyika, 1919–1964', PhD thesis, Michigan State University, 2001, p. 270.

[70] Itote, *'Mau Mau' General*, pp. 9–10.

[71] In Kenya ex-servicemen demanded that war veterans be allocated places on local native councils and tribunals, something that the authorities rejected. However, in 1947, when elections were held for the Machakos district native council, six ex-servicemen were elected, 'all young and all traders'. See David L. Easterbrook, 'Kenyan askari in World War II and their demobilization with special reference to Machakos district', in Bismarck Myrick, *et al.*, eds, *Three Aspects of Crisis in Colonial Kenya* (Foreign and Comparative Studies/Eastern Africa XXI, Syracuse University NY, 1975), pp. 47–48.

[72] Brown, 'The military and social change in Tanganyika', pp. 333–39; Hal Brands, 'Wartime recruiting practices, martial identity and post-World War II demobilization in colonial Kenya', *Journal of African History*, 46, 1 (2005), p. 116.

[73] Diana Wylie, *A Little God: The Twilight of Patriarchy in a Southern African Chiefdom* (Hanover NH, 1990), p. 184.

[74] Killingray, 'The colonial army in the Gold Coast', pp. 404–8.

[75] *West Africa*, 21 August 1948, p. 840.

[76] Shortly after the riots of February 1948, sparked off by the police firing on a demonstration of ex-servicemen, Tamakloe broke with the union and formed a rival Ex-Servicemen's Association which appears to have remained largely moribund.

[77] Interview quoted by Richard Jeffries, *Class, Power and Ideology in Ghana: The Railwaymen of Sekondi* (Cambridge, 1978), p. 45.

[78] TNA, CO964/6, petition of Ex-servicemen's Union to Governor Creasy, 28 February 1948. Printed in *Report of the Commission of Enquiry into Disturbances in the Gold Coast 1948* (the Watson Commission), Appendix 15.

[79] Henry B. Cole, 'The grievances behind the Gold Coast riots: Position of the ex-servicemen', *African World*, April 1948, p. 12.

[80] TNA, WO 269/141, Major-Gen Dimoline to under-secretary of state, War Office, top secret, 18 June 1947.

[81] Dennis Austin, *Politics in Ghana 1945–1960* (London, 1964), pp. 73ff., deals with the incident and the subsequent riots. See also the official *Report of the Commission of Enquiry*, ch. 2.

[82] See the photograph of the three men in *The Military Veteran* (Veterans Association of Ghana, 1986), pp. 13–14. Sgt Adjetey was a veteran of both world wars; he was promoted and decorated in 1944 while serving in Burma. See the entry in L. H. Ofusu-Appiah, ed., *The Encyclopaedia Africana Dictionary of African Biography. Vol. 1: Ethiopia–Ghana* (New York, 1977), pp. 187–88.

[83] Austin, *Politics in Ghana*, p. 11.

[84] Manns, 'The role of ex-servicemen', pp. 96–97. Eugene Schleh, 'Post-service careers of African World War II veterans: British East and West Africa with particular reference to Ghana and Uganda', PhD thesis, Yale University, 1968, concludes that Gold Coast ex-servicemen formed a cohesive interest group and that their grievances were translated into organised political activity within the nationalist movement.

[85] Manns, 'The role of ex-servicemen', p. 138.

[86] Steven Knapp, 'Collective memory and the actual past', *Representations* 26 (1989), pp. 123–49.

[87] *The Manchester Guardian*, 30 October 1948.

[88] Nkrumah in his *Autobiography* (London, 1957), p. 105, described the launching of the CPP 'on behalf of the C.Y.O. [Committee on Youth Organisation], in the name of the chiefs, the people, the rank and file of the Convention, the Labour Movement, our valiant ex-servicemen … Sergeant Adjetey and his comrades who died at the crossroads of Christiansborg during the 1948 riot …' Details of government monitoring of the activities of the Ex-Servicemen's Union are in TNA, CO537/4728 and CO537/4732, 'Political intelligence reports: Gold Coast 1949'; CO537/7233, 'Political intelligence reports, West Africa: Gold Coast', 1951.

[89] Maxwell Owusu, *Uses and Abuses of PoliticalPower: A Case Study of Continuity and Change in the Politics of Ghana* (Chicago, 1970), pp. 179–81.

[90] Rathbone, 'Businessmen in politics', p. 392.

[91] Paul Ladouceur, *Chiefs and Politicians: The Politics of Regionalism in Northern Ghana* (London, 1979), p. 68.

[92] James S. Coleman, *Nigeria: Background to Nationalism* (Berkeley, 1958), p. 254.

[93] G. O. Olusanya, *The Second World War and Politics in Nigeria 1939–1953* (Lagos, 1973), pp. 96–97; and 'The role of ex-servicemen in Nigerian politics', *Journal of Modern African Studies* 6, 2 (1968), p. 221.

[94] Mokwugo Okoye, *Storms on the Niger: A Story of Nigeria's Struggle* (Enugu, nd, 1981), p. 134. See Pratten, *The Man-Leopard Murders*, pp. 185–89 and 258–59, on wartime inflation in south-eastern Nigeria, especially of bride prices that affected returning servicemen. Also Ayodeji Olukoju, 'The cost of living in Lagos 1914–45', in David M. Anderson and Richard Rathbone, eds, *Africa's Urban Past* (Oxford 2000), pp. 134–40.

[95] *West African Pilot*, 24 March 1949.

[96] Olusanya, *Second World War and Politics*, p. 101.

[97] PRO, CO437/4727, 'Nigeria: Political summary', December 1948, indicates the part played by ex-servicemen in the Zikist movement and various affiliated trade unions and churches.

[98] N. J. Miners, *The Nigerian Army 1956–1966* (London, 1971), pp. 14–15. Dr John Karefa-Smart, Minister of External Affairs for Sierra Leone, 1960–64, was president of the Sierra Leone Ex-Servicemen's Association; he had studied medicine in Canada and served as an officer in the Royal Canadian Army Medical Corps, 1943–45.

[99] TNA, CO583/302/13, Macpherson to Secretary of State, 25 February 1950.

[100] Olunsanya, *Second World War and Politics*, p. 99.

[101] Akaatenger John Aond'akaa, 'Military recruitment and its impact on the Tiv, 1914–1970: the case of Gboko', BA project, University of Jos, 1991, p. 52.

[102] Alpha M. Lavalie, 'The role of Sierra Leonean ex-servicemen in the politics of decolonisation, 1945–1961', unpublished paper, 1989, pp. 4–5; Martin Kilson, *Political Change in a West African State: A Study of the Modernization Process in Sierra Leone* (Cambridge MA, 1966). p. 180.

[103] Peter Greenhalgh, *West African Diamonds 1919–83* (Manchester, 1985), p. 172.

[104] Statement by the Secretary-General, reported in *Daily Mail* (Freetown), 7 February 1948, p. 1.

[105] Kakembo, *An African Soldier Speaks*, p. 18.

[106] John Spencer, *James Beauttah Freedom Fighter* (Nairobi, 1983), p. 39.

[107] Parsons, *The African Rank-and-File*, pp. 231–54.

[108] Cpl David Mubwanga and Cpl Daudi Mnubi, of the EALMS, to 'Askari Mzee' (editor of *Askari*), 14 November 1944, quoted by Parsons, *The African Rank-and-File*, p. 231.

[109] Spencer, *James Beauttah Freedom Fighter*, p. 56.

[110] Gardner Thompson, *Governing Uganda: British Colonial Rule and its Legacy* (Kampala, 2003), p. 271.

[111] Christina Pugliese, *Author, Publisher and Gikuyu Nationalist: The Life and Writings of Gakaaru wa Wanaju* (Bayreuth, 1995), p. x.

[112] Kango Muchai, *The Hard Core: The Story of Kango Muchai* (New York, 1966), p. 14.

[113] Bodil Folke Frederiksen, '"The present battle is the brain battle": Writing and publishing a Kikuyu newspaper in the pre-Mau Mau period in Kenya', in Karen Barber, ed., *Africa's Hidden Histories: Everyday Literacy and Making the Self* (Bloomington IN, 2006), pp. 297 and 312 fn 33.

[114] Bethwell A. Ogot, 'Mau Mau and nationhood: The untold story', in E. S. Atieno Odhiambo and John Lonsdale, eds, *Mau Mau and Nationhood* (Oxford, 2003), pp. 25–26.

[115] Michael Blundell, *A Love Affair With the Sun: A Memoir of Seventy Years in Kenya* (Nairobi, 1994), p. 86.

[116] Carl G. Rosberg and John Nottingham, *The Myth of 'Mau Mau': Nationalism in Kenya* (Stanford, 1966), pp. 236–37.

[117] Shiroya, *Kenya and World War II*, p. 60.

[118] John Iliffe, *A Modern History of Tanganyika* (Cambridge, 1979), p. 376.

[119] *Ibid.*, p. 377.

[120] Eugene P. A. Schleh, 'The post-war careers of ex-servicemen in Ghana and Uganda', *Journal of Modern African Studies*, 6, 2 (1968), p. 218. Amii Omara-Otunnu, *Politics and the Military in Uganda 1890–1985* (London, 1987), p. 39, states that 'in Uganda … the ex-servicemen concerned themselves with their own social and economic betterment rather than realising any radical political ideals. On the wider political scene, they played virtually no role in raising the political consciousness of the people nor did they agitate vociferously for political causes.'

[121] Parsons, *The African Rank-and-File*, p. 260. Thompson, *Governing Uganda*, p. 269, comes to a similar conclusion for Uganda.

[122] Quoted by J. Gus Liebenow, *Colonial Rule and Political Development in Tanzania: The Case of the Makonde* (Nairobi, 1971), p. 162.

[123] The *Uganda Annual Report for 1948* stated: 'The majority of the ex-*askaris* have quietly slipped back into the village life of the rural peasant without apparently having derived from their travels or experiences any desire for anything different.'

[124] David E. Apter, *The Political Kingdom in Uganda: A Study in Bureaucratic Nationalism* (Princeton, 2nd edn, 1967), pp. 254–55. See the recent assessment by Thompson, *Governing Uganda*, pp. 280–83.

[125] Quoted by Schleh, 'The post-war careers of ex-servicemen', p. 209.

[126] James Beauttah referred to this organisation as being 'strong', but that is doubtful. Ex-servicemen of the *Ndesefa* put money into a dried-vegetable factory outside Nyeri and, according to Beauttah, although the company was successful the government refused to allow Africans to take over the factory; it was closed and many ex-servicemen lost their investments. See Spencer, *James Beauttah Freedom Fighter*, p. 58.

[127] See Roseberg and Nottingham, *Myth of "Mau Mau"*, p. 237; Parsons, 'East African soldiers in Britain's colonial army', pp. 276–77.

[128] Parsons, *The African Rank-and-File*, pp. 247–49.

[129] Schleh, 'Post-war careers of ex-servicemen', pp. 212ff.

[130] Frank Füredi, 'The African crowd in Nairobi: Popular movements and élite politics', *Journal of African History* 14, 2 (1973), pp. 282–83.

[131] Recent books on the Mau Mau movement include David W. Throup, *Economic and Social Origins of Mau Mau* (London, 1987); Tabitha Kanogo, *Squatters and the Roots of Mau Mau* (London, 1987); and Frank Füredi, *The Mau Mau War in Perspective* (London, 1989).

[132] Brands, 'Wartime recruiting practices', p. 122.

[133] Kaggia, *Roots of Freedom*, chs 7–9.

[134] Waruhui Itote , *'Mau Mau' General* (Nairobi, 1967); Muchai, *The Hard Core*; Tabitha Kanogo, *Dedan Kimathi: Makers of Kenya's History, No. 3* (Nairobi, 1992).

[135] Parsons, *The African Rank-and-File*, p. 256.

[136] Daisy Sykes Buruku, 'The townsman: Kleist Sykes', in John Iliffe, ed., *Modern Tanzanians: A Volume of Biographies* (Dar es Salaam, 1973), pp. 97ff.

[137] Mohamed Said, *The Life and Times of Abdulwahid Sykes (1924–1968): The Untold Story of the Muslim Struggle against British Colonialism in Tanganyika* (London, 1998), pp. 57–58; Judith Listowel, *The Making of Tanganyika* (London, 2nd edn, 1968), pp. 121–22, locates the event to Kalieni Camp, outside Bombay. See also Brennan, *'Taifa'*, ch. 7 (forthcoming).

[138] Iliffe, *Modern History of Tanganyika*, pp. 507–8; Mohamed Said, 'Founder of a political movement: Abdulwahid K. Sykes', *Africa Events* (September, 1988); Brennan, *'Taifa'*, ch. 7, (forthcoming).

[139] Listowel, *Making of Tanganyika*, p. 226.

[140] Robert St John, *Through Malan's Africa* (Garden City NY, 1954), p. 224.

[141] Leonard Thompson, *A History of South Africa* (New Haven CT, 1990), pp. 178–86.

[142] Z. K. Matthews, *Freedom for My People: The Autobiography of Z. K. Matthews. Southern Africa 1901–1968* (Cape Town, 2nd edn, 1968), p. 145.

[143] Louis Grundlingh, 'Aspects of the impact of the Second World War on the lives of Black South African and British colonial soldiers', *Transafrican Journal of History*, 21 (1992), pp. 22 and 32. See also Grundlingh, 'The participation of South African Blacks', pp. 401ff.

[144] H. J. Simons and R. E. Simons, *Class and Colour in South Africa 1850–1950* (Harmondsworth, 1969), pp. 427–503, and 532.

[145] St Johns, *Through Malan's Africa*, p. 226.

[146] Joel Bolnick, *'Sefela sa Letsamayanaha*: The wartime experience of Potlako Kitchener Leballo', Wits History Workshop, 6–10 February 1990; Gail M. Gerhart, *Black Power in South Africa: The Evolution of an Ideology* (Berkeley, 1978), pp. 138ff.

[147] Alexander, *Workers, War and the Origins of Apartheid*, pp. 108 and 200 fn 125.

[148] Quoted by W. Grundy, *Soldiers Without Politics: Blacks in the South African Armed Forces* (Berkeley, 1983), p. 88.

[149] Ian Goldin, *Making Race: The Politics and Economics of Coloured Identity in South Africa* (Harlow,

1987), pp. 70–71.

[150] A. W. Stadler, '"Birds in the cornfield": Squatter movements in Johannesburg, 1944–1947', *Journal of Southern African Studies* 6, 1 (1979), p. 100; Baruch Hirson, *Yours For the Union: Class and Community Struggles in South Africa, 1930–1947* (London, 1989), pp. 157–58.

[151] See Jeremy Krikler, *White Rising: The 1922 Insurrection and Racial Killing in South Africa* (Manchester, 2005).

[152] Neil Roos, *Ordinary Springboks: White Servicemen and Social Justice in South Africa, 1939–1961* (Aldershot, 2005), is a detailed history of this neglected organisation.

[153] Ellen Hellman and Leah Abraham (eds.), *Handbook on Race Relations in South Africa* (Cape Town, 1949), p. 662.

[154] *Fighting Talk*, March 1947, pp. 22–23; J. O'Meara and A. Rodolph, *Springbok Legion: The History and Policy* (Johannesburg, 1944). The membership of the Legion is contested: Simons and Simons, *Class and Colour*, p. 540, claimed 40,000 members, whereas Gwendolen Carter, *The Politics of Inequality: South Africa since 1948* (London, rev. edn, 1962), p. 311, argued that there were only 3,000.

[155] Michael Fridjhon, 'The Torch Commando and the politics of white opposition: South Africa 1951–1953', African Studies Seminar paper, University of Witwatersrand, 1977, p. 177.

[156] Carter makes the rather exaggerated claim, in *Politics of Inequality*, ch. 12, that the Torch Commando by late 1952 had nearly a quarter of a million members.

[157] Lawrence Vambe, *From Rhodesia to Zimbabwe* (London, 1976), pp. 127–28.

[158] David Johnson, *World War II and the Scramble for Labour in Colonial Zimbabwe* (Harare, 2000), p. 27.

[159] Quoted in Christina Lamb, *The Africa House: The True Story of an English Gentleman and his African Dream* (New York, 1999; Penguin edn, 2000), p. 248.

[160] Quoted by Simelane, 'Veterans, politics and poverty', p. 149.

[161] Zambodze Mavundla, interviewed 1996 and quoted in *ibid.*, p. 150.

[162] Kampene Semelane, interviewed 1996 and quoted in *ibid.*, p. 151.

[163] Mpikayipheli Dlamini, interview 1996 and quoted in *ibid.*, p. 153.

[164] Quoted by Ashley Jackson, 'Watershed in a colonial backwater?', 1996, p. 299.

[165] *Ibid.*, pp. 267–71 and 351–52.

[166] Brian Makopakgosi III, 'The impact of the Second World War: The case of Kweneng in the then Bechuanaland Protectorate, 1939–1950,' in David Killingray and Richard Rathbone, eds, *Africa and the Second World War* (London, 1986), p. 174.

[167] D. Kiyaga-Mulindwa, 'The Bechuanaland Protectorate and the Second World War', *Journal of Imperial and Commonwealth History* 12 (1984), p. 567.

[168] Jackson, 'Watershed in a colonial backwater?', p. 330.

[169] Deborah A. Shackleton, 'Imperial military policy and the Bechuanaland Pioneers and Gunners during the Second World War', PhD dissertation, Indiana University, 1997, p. 323.

[170] TNA, DO35/4143, 'Record of meeting, 21 April 1952', quoted by Williams, *Colour Bar*, pp. 228–29.

[171] John D. Hargreaves, *Decolonization in Africa* (London, 2nd edn, 1996), p. 74.

8

The Social Impact of War Service

'Truly Chief we have enlarged our ideas.'[1]

'When we go back to our villages and towns we don't want to go back to the past. We want to go back to the future.' [2]

The war years saw the largest mobilisation and movement of men within and out of Africa in modern history. Altogether more than one million men left their homes, which were mainly in rural areas, to serve in the military forces of the colonial powers. In British Africa and South Africa the total number of men enlisted was in the region of 600,000. Although wartime recruitment was eventually extended beyond the traditional recruiting grounds the majority of soldiers continued to be drawn from those areas. The social and economic impact of this large and sustained process of enlistment and lengthy service, often overseas, was for many men profound. Men recruited from remote rural areas had no visual image of the new artefacts and scenes they would encounter. For the most part they came from a world without books or illustrations, having had few reference points to prepare them for what they were going to see. For example one recruit, having recently encountered the railway, believed that ocean-going vessels ran on tracks under the sea. And yet adaptation was relatively speedy and new sights, sounds and experiences were readily absorbed. Adapting to change, even profound change, has been an ingredient of human experience throughout history. There were many similarities between wartime military service and the processes of migrant labour to the mines of central and South Africa. Both military service and migrant labour involved men leaving rural areas for a lengthy absence from wives and children, with all the strains that this imposed on family relationships and rural production. Migrant labourers in southern Africa often lived in predominately male compounds or barracks, a regulated environment involving various measures of social control; there were new languages and skills to be acquired; and migrants were exposed to modern technology and to urban culture. A good deal has been written about the social history of migrant labour, less on the social impact of soldiers in wartime, the subject addressed by this chapter.

The social history of the war years, whether concerned with specific groups such as the military or with African society as a whole, must be placed squarely on the continuum of economic and social change occurring in 20th-century colonial Africa. Africans across the continent (in certain parts more than others) had engaged with Western ideas and processes; they had been migrants and towns had grown; new transport systems had developed, schools and literacy were extended, and new religious ideas arrived along with modern ideas about health and politics. War is often an accelerator of social change and this was no exception for Africa during the years 1940–45. The social impact of military service in wartime can be looked at from two different viewpoints: the effect on the individual soldier and his family, and the broader effects on African societies.

The soldiers' experience

The army enlisted men with a purpose: to fashion and train a disciplined force for war. This involved taking a man from his home and putting him through a course of training which in the process socially conditioned him to a new, albeit temporary, way of life. The impact this had on African soldiers is little recorded. Few men wrote of their experiences; indeed most were nonliterate and thus incapable of conveying in print what they had undergone. Thus the historian is faced with a challenge in trying to recapture the experience of men who went off to war long ago. This requires an imaginative interrogation of the available documentation and a perceptive use of oral information, much of which has been provided by elderly men.

The first encounter with the military system with its new ways and discipline is often vividly remembered by many former recruits. Amadu Moshi, a railway worker in the Gold Coast, looked back with anger: 'We were told: you don't join army, you don't work. A white man came and gave orders.'[3] Agolley Kusasi, from the northern Gold Coast, looked back on his entry to the army as marked by betrayal: 'The chief told me to go and do something [in Bawku] and I was put in the army.'[4] Many men remember the rigours of discipline and unfamiliar notions of industrial time that now began to regulate their lives and actions. To those who had some experience of modern urban life and industrial work this would not have seemed strange. However, to those from rural areas this was indeed a novel and at first a confusing world to enter.

Part of the discipline was learning new hierarchies of rank. The initial contact was most probably not with a European officer but with African NCOs who had the job of inducting men into the ranks, often in a language which was not the recruits' vernacular. An African NCO's word was law and perhaps only eventually did a new recruit come into contact with a white NCO or officer. Isaac Fadoyebo, a Yoruba from southern Nigeria, resented the authority and style of northerners who were NCOs:

> Military training was supervised by indigenous non-commissioned officers who were rough in mind and in some cases callous to the extreme. We were not allowed to have access to the white commissioned officers. The highest rank we could deal with direct was Warrant Officer I popularly known as Regimental Sergeant Major – RSM. They would shout at us as if we were not human beings and generally developed hatred for those of us who had a bit of education.[5]

Military hierarchy in colonial armies was largely about race, whereas in European armies it invariably involved social class with officers mainly drawn from the upper and middle classes and the other-ranks from the lower classes. In all the British African colonial armies there were separate facilities for Europeans and Africans. Barrack accommodation, messes and lavatories were racially segregated, as was noted with some anger by Bildad Kaggia and Isaac Fadoyebo.[6] As one British observer wrote: 'In the army itself, there was strict segregation, and the British NCOs messed separately from the African NCOs ... the British sergeant was "senior" to the African sergeant.'[7] Within a short time of arriving in a military camp this segregation must have been obvious to most recruits, although it is questionable whether it was ever really resented other than by a small number of mainly literate Africans. Indeed, suspicions among the regular African soldiers about the first African officer to be appointed in the Gold Coast Regiment indicate that men had been conditioned to think of officers as exclusively white. Throughout the war there are accounts by African soldiers and white NCOs and officers of close contact between white and black, officers and men. Military action involving mutual dependence of men and officers overrode barriers of race and class that were impenetrable in peacetime; there is much evidence of close working relationships between African soldiers and their white officers especially on the battlefield. Isaac Fadoyebo wrote of the reliance between European and African soldiers serving in Burma, cemented by the rigours of living together while engaged in jungle warfare:

> Officers and men of all ranks often exhibited [an] inclination to come together intimately and sometimes shared food and other things. Each soldier would appear to be his brother's keeper and the difference in rank would hardly be noticed.[8]

But there are also a few accounts, from both African and European sources, of unpopular European officers being killed by African soldiers in such a way to make it appear as an accidental or battle death.[9] Whatever the relations between Europeans and Africans created by the circumstances of war, there can have been few white men drawn from South Africa or the settler colonies of East or Central Africa who thought that the temporary breaches to the colour bar in wartime signalled any need for a change in social and official policies on race once peace had been restored. In contrast, to many literate African soldiers the loosened racial relationships of war indicated that postwar colonial society should and must be different.

A uniform marked a man out as a soldier. A uniform was a strange and rough garment especially for men accustomed to being clad only in light and loose clothing, and did not necessarily provide patterns for future clothing. Boots were also unfamiliar and like the uniform often ill-fitting, and took some time to get used to. Isaac Fadoyebo recalls that new recruits often received inappropriate clothing from army stores:

> The outfit for drilling was a pair of khaki shorts and a thick long sleeved woollen jersey or cardigan. The pants were neither long nor short; they went down below the knee and stopped half-way between the knee and the ankle. In other words they were neither shorts nor trousers. We did not like the mode of dressing ... Imagine wearing a woollen pullover without underwear and staying in the sun marching for hours in a tropical country during

the dry season; it could be unbearably warm. We had to appear in the same cardigan daily for a whole week including Saturdays. We were issued with two pairs of pants and one jersey. One could clean a pair of pants during the week and put on the other but as for the jersey a recruit had to wear it for six days running before it could be washed. Again one could imagine the amount of perspiration that it might have absorbed during the course of drilling in the sun for hours on [a] daily basis. The cardigans were made of pure wool … we washed ours ordinarily and with the result that they shrank. Mine was reduced in size to the extent that it could hardly cover the upper part of my stomach.[10]

Even ill-fitting boots could be highly prized and wearing them certainly gave soldiers a desire to own shoes. Cladding half a million soldiers in uniform and providing them with boots helped introduce a social change in clothing styles and accelerate new consumer demands, although soldiers are generally eager to get out of uniform. Perhaps one day a social historian will see this reflected in the figures, if they exist, for the importation and manufacture of shoes and clothing in postwar Africa. Soldiers' uniforms and belongings were carried in kitbags bearing each man's military number and regimental insignia. Military identification was by rank, number and name – sometimes a name given by the army rather than the man's family name. Thus soldiers might be officially identified by their place of origin or where they had been recruited – as with Isa Fort Lamy, who came from the French colony of Chad, and Abdulahi Gombe, from the area of that name in northern Nigeria. Lists of casualties, published in the official gazettes of each colony, were presented in this way: 'NA/108691 Pte Maiwade Zaria', or 'NA/44754 Pte. Alabi Oshogbo'.[11] Non-numerate soldiers were expected to learn their identity number even if they lacked the facility to use numbers.

Communal sleeping arrangements in barracks were also new to most recruits. Soldiers rapidly had to adjust to the loss of privacy and abandon any modesty before strangers. Beds and blankets may not have been so novel but the idea that bedding had to be folded and inspected would have been new for most men. The army wanted order so boots had to be polished and uniforms and clothing washed and pressed – tasks that few men were used to doing, as this was normally regarded as 'women's work'. A similar order applied to communal eating. Men who had long been familiar with eating with their fingers, perhaps in a squatting position, were introduced to new foodstuffs and new ways of eating. However, the novelty of this must not be exaggerated. Men conscripted in North America and Europe in the same period, for example from rural areas or urban slums, also found the army to be a startlingly new regimen unlike any they had experienced before. For the African soldier newly arrived from a rural home the military encampment offered bread, canned meat, metal plates, tea to be drunk from a tin mug and perhaps beer from a bottle, plus brought the requirement to learn all the chores involved in preparing and clearing up a meal served to several hundred men. New experiences of food – for example, the taste of bread and tea – were first acquired in the army, and ex-servicemen created a postwar demand for new foodstuffs from stores and manufacturers. The spread of bread-baking in both Nigeria and the Gold Coast is closely linked to the requisite skills being learned in the army and that ex-soldiers had acquired the taste and thus demanded the product.[12]

It is only in the last 20 years that scholars have begun to study the use and the spread of tobacco and alcohol in Africa. The military authorities were agnostic on the former and very cautious about the latter. Cigarettes were relatively cheap and available to soldiers, readily on sale in army stores and sold singly or in packets of five, so that many men acquired the habit of smoking in the army.[13] It seems that few soldiers smoked pipes, although the evidence of wartime photographs indicates that some literate soldiers did use them. Smokers invariably used matches. Smoking might be addictive but it was unlikely to make soldiers unfit for duty. Military service introduced soldiers to and gave many a taste for industrially manufactured cigarettes and beer. Alcohol was closely regulated by the military authorities and frowned on by most Christian missionaries. However, whereas British officers and NCOs were given a monthly beer ration this was not given to African NCOs, a discriminatory practice which naturally was resented. Several years after the end of the war, the *Accra Evening News*, the paper of Nkrumah's Convention People's Party, linked wartime military service with the consumption of alcohol and tobacco and the rise of hooliganism:

> Our Nanomen [chiefs] ... are responsible for making youth hooligans ... Nanomen convinced the cream of this Nation to enlist in the Army to fight for world freedom which did not directly effect the Gold Coast ... Boys who did not and dared not drink or smoke for fear of their parents or elders, on their discharge from the Army became first class drinkers and smokers.[14]

The wartime military was seen as a great training ground for ideas about hygiene and sanitation. The extent to which the lessons learned in the army – for example, the need to use clean water and the reason for burying refuse – were transferred to postwar civilian life is a matter of conjecture; little firm evidence is available. Nevertheless, the habits of four or five years' service probably did inform the subsequent practice and behaviour of many men, although it is debatable whether this was then passed on to wives and children. In all probability the most influential purveyors of modern hygienic ideas were soldiers' wives when they lived in the lines in the pre- and postwar years. At the start of the war in 1939 soldiers' wives were sent to their home villages and new recruits were not officially allowed to have women in the barracks. Running water, taps, lavatories and toilet paper became part of the everyday life of African soldiers.[15] So did regular haircuts and shaving. Soldiers were expected to be neat and clean in appearance and were not permitted to have beards.[16] However, of necessity these rules were dropped in battlefield conditions when circumstances resulted in men becoming scruffy, unshaven and ill-kempt. This can be seen from many of the official photographs of Africans serving in the North African and Burma campaigns where water, often in short supply, was restricted to use for drinking and some basic washing. Uniforms became worn and patched; soldiers who had been tailors or shoemakers in civilian life earned additional money by repairing the boots and clothes of their comrades, while some, less commercially minded, helped them to use a needle and thread.

In civilian life many soldiers would rarely have encountered modern medicine. On entry to the army every man was subjected to a rudimentary medical examination. Its rigour varied with the supply of recruits and the need to fill quotas. But certainly the army had a strong interest in keeping soldiers fit and well. Regular medical inspections were carried out, invariably involving inoculation and some dental care. When large intakes of recruits resulted in lowered medical standards, determined efforts were made to ensure that those in that category were carefully nourished in order to turn them into effective soldiers, a process that might take three or more months. Oral medicines and injections became an accepted part of the soldier's life. The extent to which indigenous or 'folk' medicine was used by soldiers is unknown. It is probably safe to assume that it was regularly resorted to for many minor ailments, as indeed was the case for millions of people in Western societies. For medical officers the largest concern, and the main role for curative medicine, was combating malaria and venereal disease. In the case of the latter it was more effective to prevent any outbreak of VD by issuing free contraceptives to soldiers and instructing them how to use them. The purpose was a military one: to keep soldiers fit for service. In civilian life after the war these conditions were absent; former soldiers might have known about malaria-prevention ideas and contraception but the army was no longer there with its command structures to enforce tedious rules, or with its free welfare services. Attempts to change sexual attitudes and behaviour, as is well known from contemporary campaigns to promote family planning and reduce the risk of HIV/AIDS in Africa, are confronted by entrenched social and cultural norms with men in particular resistant to new ways of thinking and acting.

One early economic consequence of the creation of African armies was the increase in the use and circulation of modern coinage. Payment in coin and its use in markets extended the modern money frontier which for the colonial authorities was both a source of profit and made tax collection easier.[17] Colonial armies, as with much other government service and employment in the modern sector of the economy, offered regular weekly wages in coin. In peacetime the wage-earning sector of the colonial economy was small, often little more than 5–10 per cent of the total working population. In wartime this increased as governments extended their activities, not least in recruiting and paying soldiers with money, a proportion of which was then remitted to wives and families as dependants' allowances. Many men who before the war knew little of money and its uses became familiar with a modern money economy as a result of war service. A soldier from Sierra Leone sent on service to East Africa and then to India or the Middle East would at various times have become familiar with a number of currencies, both coin and script, each with different rates of exchange. Soldiers were also very aware of differences in pay given in different colonial armies. Sometimes innocent and naïve soldiers were defrauded by unscrupulous money dealers and merchants in India and North Africa, but there is some evidence to show that most Africans became adept at manipulating different currencies and markets in order to protect their own financial interests. In wartime the soldier was a consumer and also, through the system of compulsory deferred payments, a saver. The intention of the latter was that the soldier should not leave the army empty-handed. The tragedy for many soldiers on demobilisation at the end of the war was that their expectations as potential consumers were reduced by a shortage of basic goods and their savings by inflation. Of that problem most men became all too well aware on their return to their home colony. As Robert Kakembo put it in his non-radical pamphlet published in 1946, African soldiers have learnt the value of money and they have been taught to love necessary luxuries – things like cinema, wireless broadcasts, newspapers. The wearing of boots has to them become a necessity, hats and good uniform are becoming a daily wear in their lives. Toilet soap, hair cream, razor blades, cigarettes are becoming indispensable in a soldier's life, and many other little things.[18]

A soldier's life involved a large amount of time waiting about for things to happen. The military authorities could arrange activities – the usual rounds of drill, training and inspection – for some of the time, but they could never fill all the time in the day. The idea of 'modern' leisure was new to many Africans, although when opportunity offered men had always sat around in familiar or spontaneous groups to chat, gamble and drink. In the army formal 'time-off' work, the day out, the outing, and so on, those organised periods of recreation, were new to many soldiers. Leisure took a variety of forms. For much of the time soldiers made their own individual and communal entertainment, with singing and dancing generally encouraged by the authorities. Songs might be impro- vised; for West Africans favourites included a Burma song which included the lines: 'I went to the jungle one Saturday night/And there I met many many Japanese,' and a more nostalgic one entitled 'Home Again'.[19] Gambling, ever popular with many soldiers, was officially forbidden for fear that it might lead to antagonism and bitterness between men. Official sporting events were arranged by officers by pitching teams from one battalion against another. In overseas postings where men were in unfamiliar surroundings, often in isolated camps, officially arranged leisure activities took on a new importance in the attempt to keep men from brooding in idleness and as part of a necessary re-creation of morale. At the official level there were educational classes, the provision of reading material, games, choirs and bands, organised visits to towns, rest centres in major cities specifically for African soldiers, and a range of religious activities such as services and prayer meetings. Leisure time and activity were certainly given a new meaning for thousands of men as a result of their wartime service.

Recreation for soldiers involving sporting activities was closely linked to phys- ical fitness and health, both vitally necessary for effective fighting and labouring men, and perhaps equally to social control. It is difficult to know to what extent such activity influenced soldiers' later lives. Did men come home from the war and continue with sports, or continue to take an interest in sports, as many had done while on military service? Relatively little research has been done on the history of football – one of the sporting activities prominently promoted by the army – in Africa. This involved not only players but also many more spectators, as is clearly shown by the reports on matches in the official newspapers issued by the military and the African press. For example, a Nigerian soldier serving in India, C. A. Obashori, wrote to the *West African Pilot* in April 1945 on why he preferred football.[20] The same issue of the newspaper contained a photograph of the 'Association Soccer Champions in SEAC' [South East Asia Command], a West African team which had played 18 games in a row without a single defeat, 'and recently beat an English team 3.1'. A month later the *Pilot* reported that an RWAFF football team had won a match against a team from a Chinese battalion.[21] Was this translated into the creation of and support for teams in sub- Saharan African colonies after the war? Boxing was also encouraged by the army, with inter-battalion competitions – an activity which was supported by large numbers of spectators.[22]

Soldiers' families

Recruitment, whether undertaken voluntarily or by conscription, removed men, and mainly younger men, from rural areas and thus agricultural production. In Southern Africa and areas of Central Africa military service also took men out of the migrant-labour system. The result was to remove producers and providers of income and place the burden, especially of rural production, on women, the young and the elderly. Keomantswe Mothogaba of Serowe, in Bechuanaland, recalled the war as a time of hunger and of great hardship in terms of workloads. One ex-serviceman interviewed by Gaele Sobott appeared to have little understanding of the burdens placed on women. He said: 'a woman/wife is a thing of the home, for children and for feeding the husband. Sorghum is eaten by those children, ploughing is done with cattle that belong to the husband.'[23] When conscription for the military occurred in areas where forced labour was imposed for agricultural production, then the burden was heavy for those left in the countryside. It is not surprising that agricultural output often fell, and even more so when rains failed – as they did in various parts of East Africa in the early 1940s – so that rural communities faced acute suffering. The absence of men on military service placed on women the additional task of caring for children and relating to kin. Many children grew up without knowing a father, a feature common throughout much of the belligerent world in the 1940s. The social consequences of this common deprivation were manifold, but while it has been reasonably well researched for Western countries it remains little explored for Africa. Indigenous social structures and the nature of the extended household probably meant that in Africa, the impact of a father's absence was less profound than in France, Germany or Britain, where the nuclear family structure was more common. Of greater significance, perhaps, is the fact that many of those recruited in Africa were younger men, aged 18–30, and that they continued the process of growing up and reaching maturity in the army, where they learned a new sense of independence which meant they were not willing to accept the constraints of indigenous and family authority after they were demobilised. Complaints from older men and families about the changed attitudes of ex-servicemen were common all over Africa in the years immediately following the war.

If the war and the absence of men placed burdens on soldiers' wives and parents, it also offered some women new opportunities and responsibilities, and a new independence. Some women used this freedom robustly. Relations within families and kin groups were changed, with soldiers' wives now exercising roles not previously performed, relating to their attitudes towards parents, control of children, the use of land and property, and how family money – including remittances – was spent. In many families and kin groups this resulted in tensions and conflicts. Where a soldier had named a male relative as the recipient of his remittances, such as a father, uncle or brother, then power over his wife and family might be placed in the hands of another man. On the other hand, the wife of a soldier who received regular payments from her husband's army income might find herself in a position to act with an independence not previously enjoyed when her husband was at home. If the woman was widowed and received a pension or lump sum from the army she might become a more attractive marriage partner. Equally, women often saw the attractions of marriage to a soldier or ex-serviceman with money or a regular income.[24] In western Kenya some widows sought to marry their daughters to ex-servicemen, popularly known as 'KAR men', who were believed to possess money and who as sons-in-law, in order to defend their idea of masculinity, would have to support the widowed wife's mother.[25] Belisi Shego, who was widowed early in the war, said

> no widowed mother could ever refuse marrying her daughter to a KAR man; they had a lot of money, and many women went with them and within two days the dowry was paid, they were married, and the men returned to the KAR the following day.[26]

African soldiers' earnings pushed up bride price over a large part of East, Central and Southern Africa. Absence from home and wife opened rifts in family relationships. Soldiers returned home to hear rumours and gossip about a wife's infidelity. Kenda Mutongi argues that too little attention has been given to this aspect of ex-servicemen's lives. 'Thus the ex-military men's re-adaptation to the private spheres of their households presented them with what too often proved to be overwhelming challenges; they often became violent, sometimes so violent that their cases were brought to trial.'[27] Kwame Agyapon, a shoemaker who enlisted in 1941 and served with the GCR in India, left three wives in Asante. He 'found it difficult to be without women when overseas', while his senior wife was 'fond of sexual indulgence'. When he returned home he discovered that his senior wife had 'got a child by another man'. Because he desired her still he forgave her, accepted a pacification fee from her lover and resumed sexual relations with her. However, when he proved to be impotent his senior wife presented him with 'a bill amounting to £113-6-8', being her 'claim for the subsistence for the five years he had been away'.[28] Some men who had gained new ideas were dissatisfied with a wife who lacked the knowledge or the understanding to match their husbands' new expectations. Predictably, soldiers abandoned their wives and the number of divorces increased. For certain unmarried ex-servicemen, 'marrying well' was important. James Kinziri, who had served in the KAR, said that 'an educated man felt proud when his wife was a *mustarabu* ['civilised' in Swahili, from 'to be an Arab']', and if a wife kept a clean house 'it reflected well on the man. People respected him; they said that so and so is keeping a modern house.'[29]

New technologies

Modern technology undoubtedly came as a great surprise to many men who joined the army direct from remote rural areas. However, the impact must not be exaggerated as the exposure to new ideas and technologies was usually gradual, not startlingly sudden, and took place in the company of a mixed group of men some of whom were already familiar with many of the ways of the modern world. Even men from villages far from a modern town were more than likely to have heard from others who had been migrant labourers stories about modern ways. Few areas of Africa were beyond the tentacles of modern commerce, which brought even to remote villages the products of the industrial world, such as manufactured crockery and utensils, knives and machetes – a variety of light-weight goods which could be easily transported and which found a ready market on the gradually extending frontier of the modern money economy. The penetration of Africa by Western manufactured goods had been going on for centuries but had expanded following colonial occupation, as new roads and railways were built and new market structures developed, enabling imported goods to reach new areas of the continent more easily.

Soldiers to whom exposure to new technologies was not a new experience could serve as guides and mentors. Soldiers from the 'bush' were not plunged immediately into a large town. Most African towns were small and featured social configurations not far removed from those found in village life. Large cities were different, but for the vast majority of soldiers these were only encountered at a later date. By that time urban centres were not so strange, and the bustle of people, roads and motor traffic, and items such as kerbstones, drains, street-lights, high buildings, walls and fences, and all the accompanying sounds and smells afforded a new world which could be viewed with interest as much as it also needed to be understood.

The majority of soldiers received their training in places far from their homes. A good many men were sent out of the colony of enlistment to a neighbouring colony for part of their training; for example Gold Coast troops underwent jungle-warfare training in Nigeria, while soldiers enlisted in Nyasaland were invariably sent to Tanganyika or Kenya. This movement, as also the final move to the war theatre, involved travel by train and ship. Oral evidence from African soldiers provides little comment about travel by train but there are numerous vivid recollections of the sea and transport by ship to North Africa, via the Cape route, and across the Indian Ocean. Another memorable experience for a small number of soldiers was travelling in an aeroplane. Although the first sight of an aircraft excited alarm or wonder, continued exposure to the world of modern technology tended to blunt surprise at the new.

Different cultures

In various parts of Africa where they were stationed, and also in the Mediter-ranean and Asian theatres, African soldiers met troops from other parts of the continent and of the world, and mixed with local people and tasted something of their cultures. As far as possible the military authorities tried to regulate contact between soldiers and local communities, but this was not always prac-tical. It mattered less in sub-Saharan Africa where the authorities considered people to be more similar, than in areas where races and cultures were deemed to be markedly different. The major fears were the strong likelihood of tensions created by soldiers' demands for women, the possibility of religious disputes, and most importantly the possibility that if African soldiers had close and partic-ularly sexual relations with women of a lighter skin colour, concepts of white racial dominance would be breached, with dire consequences for the colonial order at the end of the war.

Placing military camps in remote areas helped put some distance between African soldiers and local populations. Visits by soldiers to the larger cities such as Cairo, Bombay or Calcutta were usually in small selected groups conducted by an officer. There is no clear picture. Sometimes an officer might take one or two African soldiers to a concert or play. For example George Shepperson, serving as an officer with the KAR, recalls taking Nyasa *askari* to tea at the home of a Goan gentleman in Bombay in 1944, where they were entertained with gramophone recordings of songs by Paul Robeson.[30] The available evidence indicates that most Africans who visited cities were literate men. Occasionally a battalion or regimental team might play a game of football against a team from a European or Indian unit. Groups of African soldiers were also taken to meet Indian troops; for instance, in 1944 men from the RWAFF spent a few days with the 6th Rajput Rifles near Delhi. The African and Indian soldiers ate together and watched boxing matches.[31] There is no way of knowing how many soldiers actually took part in these crosscultural encounters or what impact they had. All soldiers who went overseas became in some ways accidental tourists. Some undoubtedly returned home enriched in mind and with their social and political awareness deepened. Others, and it may be the majority, were exposed to a range of new sights and experiences but these had little significant influence on how the soldiers thought or on their subsequent lives. We should not think African soldiers' experiences to be markedly different from those of soldiers from any other part of the world. Foreigners were foreign, their cultures and mores strange and their food unpalatable, and thus foreigners were not the subject of great curiosity. However, women were women everywhere, when men were sexually frustrated. Perhaps for many men memories of overseas military service were of long periods of dull and tedious inactivity punctuated by rare moments of excitement.

New skills & ideas

To what extent did wartime experiences and military instruction and education equip soldiers to perform different roles and to develop new expectations for civilian life? War service broadened men's horizons, heightened the ambitions of many, and equipped some who were then able to assume new roles as civilians. Army education – the more formal approach to learning not directly related to military performance – was only developed late in the war and largely in response to demands from anxious senior officers about large numbers of idle men in encampments in North Africa and India. Army education differed markedly from education in most formal schools in British colonial Africa. The majority of primary schools and the very few secondary schools were in the hands of Christian missionaries. By contrast, army education was secular and adult, and offered much that was technical and practical. Many of the European teachers were also secular-minded, with a world-view very different from that of most Africans employed as army teachers, who were themselves invariably products of mission schools. Ironically, white conscripts, both officers and NCOs, serving as teachers may have been one of the more radicalising influences on African soldiers' in the latter stages of the war.

Practical training in the army, in mechanical and electrical skills, offered many soldiers new opportunities for wage employment and thus social mobility after the war. For example, at the end of the war there were many soldiers who had learned to drive lorries and how to maintain and repair them. Men who before the war had never handled a spanner or screwdriver or seen welding returned home with new skills which they expected to be able to use. The war contributed greatly to the motor revolution in Africa. Many army lorry drivers had ambitions that on demobilisation they would establish transport services; Nigerian soldiers at Chittagong in India, for example, were reported in 1946 to be planning the 'Calabar Transport Service' with the slogan 'Always at Your Service'.[32] And some ex-servicemen did indeed go into the transport business after the war. Barely documented are those former soldiers who established small repair yards and garages, or who returned to rural areas but were known to their neighbours to have the skills to repair bicycles, clean carburettors and shape scrap metal into useful implements.[33] For example, in Onitsha, the major town of eastern Nigeria, returning soldiers used their war earnings to set up small businesses and trades as mechanics, furnituremakers, shoemakers, blacksmiths and ironmongers, while 'others used their money to establish printing presses or to become traders'.[34]

The educational opportunities provided by army service, which were considerably wider than what was offered in the formal classes organised by the Army Education Corps, contributed trained men to help service the 'second colonial occupation of Africa' in the postwar years. Pte D. Thamane, a medical orderly from the High Commission Territories, wrote of using his new skills after the war:

> About work it was good for me and I like it because I will help myself tomorrow or after the war apply for the general hospital and get it if I know the work. I will like that the captain to teach me a lot for that work of being orderly.[35]

Isaac Fadoyebo, also a medical orderly but returning home to a 60 per cent disability allowance as a result of war wounds, became a clerk in the civil service. Although many literate men had difficulty finding wage employment immediately after the war, the colonial economies did slowly expand in the late 1940s to provide new labour opportunities in both the public and the private sectors.

In terms of education one of the most important new skills to be acquired by African soldiers was learning a new language, particularly English, but also Swahili or Hausa. The ability to speak the vernacular lingua franca of large parts of East and West Africa had an immediate value; but much more valuable was English, which offered the possibility of economic and social advancement in civil life. John Mandambwe learned to speak both English and Swahili, useful skills which probably helped his promotion to staff-sergeant and also in his postwar life in Nyasaland.[36] Darrell Bates reports an African soldier learning English as stating:

> We all want to learn English. It is the key ... the key to the future. When we go back to our villages and towns we don't want to go back to the past. We want to go back to the future. But we must have the key to it ready in our hands. Otherwise the opportunity will slip away.

And when Bates asked if Swahili was not another sort of key, the African replied 'but it is only a little key'.[37] A Muganda soldier saw his wartime service in the army as an education in itself: it had taken him to countries overseas and he had learned four languages, experiences wider than those gained by young men who had attended a civilian school. Such experience was probably similar for a fair number of African soldiers in the years 1939–46.

The army required literate and numerate men. Margaret Wrong, reporting on her journey in West Africa in 1944–45, argued that 'the war has increased the desire for literacy'.

> Many men who entered the forces illiterate have learned to read, as have many of their womenfolk who want to read, and write in order to keep in touch with their men. For West African troops English is the language used in the Army. Accompanied by an African education officer, I visited the Army Trade and Clerks' Schools housed in Elmina Castle and the smaller castle that overlooks it. Battlements, guardrooms, courtyards and dungeons were adapted to uses undreamed of by the Portuguese who built them in the fifteenth century or their Dutch successors whose emblems are woven into the fine ironwork. In these schools Africans were receiving six months' instruction before going overseas. Civics were included in the course. In one classroom on the battlements an African was explaining the importance of paying a water tax in order to have a public water supply. My African guide and I lunched in the mess with the European officers.[38]

Many soldiers learned functional English in the army which gave them the ability to move into areas of paid employment, especially in urban centres, which before the war had not been possible. In one transit camp in India soldiers could attend classes where English, arithmetic, bookkeeping, banking and commercial subjects were taught – all subjects which could be turned to use in civilian life. That particular transit camp had a cinema and there were supplies of books and magazines. The Indian press reported 'all-African debates with an African chairman', one topic for West Africans being 'a political issue': 'Should the Four Colonies (Nigeria, Gold Coast, Sierra Leone and Gambia) be centrally administered?'[39] Edward Twining, the Director of Labour in Mauritius, believed service overseas for men of the locally raised Pioneer Corps would lead to Anglicisation. In 1941 he wrote:

> It will take an appreciable number of young men into a robustly British environment and should get them away from their slave complex and from the French language and cultural associations which tend to maintain this distressing psychological outlook. We will have our problems when they return no doubt but that is another matter.[40]

However, it would be wrong to think that soldiers, however dull their life in camps, eagerly queued in large numbers to volunteer for classes in order to learn to speak and read English. English lessons attracted relatively few men; the majority were those who already had some primary or secondary schooling and saw that the army provided an opportunity for self-improvement. Nevertheless, the army gave thousands of soldiers their first real exposure to ideas about literacy and numeracy. Each soldier had an army and a unit number, rifles were numbered, and firing practice involved straightforward concepts regarding number and position. Some nonliterate soldiers had letters to their families written for them by battalion 'scribes' or literate friends, while those who could read had access to a range of books, magazines and newspapers, including those specifically published and distributed for the use of soldiers. It was common for literate men to read newspapers to their nonliterate compatriots who could also look at the photographs in picture magazines. Newspapers helped open a wider world to men who before the war rarely saw print or understood what it actually meant. Literate soldiers returning home to southeast Nigeria from India had an oblique influence on the development of Onitsha market literature. They 'brought with them copies of Indian pamphlets containing, among other things, guides to examinations, model letters, love stories and good-luck and love talisman', and these, along with booklets that contained cover pictures of film stars and actresses, influenced the format of the Onitsha pamphlets.[41]

In their travels many soldiers encountered the gramophone, the radio, wristwatches, cameras and moving film. Western-style music and its African derivatives were increasingly available. On troopships music was sometimes broadcast to the troops. Radio broadcasting greatly increased during the war with specific programmes directed at African soldiers. A small number of men became signallers and thus increased their knowledge of and familiarity with electrical gadgetry, as well as radio and telephone. In 1944–45 messages from soldiers serving in India and Burma were recorded on gramophone discs to be played to families at home in West Africa. The army had always encouraged military bands and in wartime this enabled some men to form dance-bands and to acquire or utilise skills on a range of instruments. Concert-party troupes such as the Gold Coast Two Bobs entertained troops to 45-minute shows, one being a propaganda play entitled *The Downfall of Adolph Hitler*. Several actors in the troupes – such as Bob Coles, Bob Vans and I. K. Ntama – enlisted in the GCR and went to Burma; army service gave them 'new options and creative outlets'. Bob Vans's acting career began during his army service in Burma, where he was tasked with entertaining the troops. 'After the war, Vans and I. K. Ntama, founded the Burma Jokers, which later became the Ghana Trio.'[42] The *West African Pilot* reported in 1945 that at Lagos several soldiers returning from India carried guitars.[43] The cinema was popular with African troops although films were carefully vetted before screening to avoid any scenes depicting scantily clad white women or close relations between black men and white women. Official war films were fairly safe, although one Gold Coast soldier commented to a reporter after seeing *The True Glory* that there was 'Too much killing – very sad.'[44]

The army photographed soldiers as a means of certifying identity. Official photographs were also taken of soldiers in training and in battlefield situations.[45] Photographs of soldiers taken for propaganda purposes showed the transformative effect of army service: no longer sullen savages but a cheerful, smiling healthy group of soldiers.[46] Many men soon became aware of the possibilities of photography and a few soldiers acquired cameras, although these could not be taken into the front line. There were photographic studios in most African and Asian towns and these plied their trade with soldiers, taking exposures of individuals and groups carefully arranged against a backcloth. The personal photograph became a prized possession – something to be sent home to families and sweethearts. Instead of being merely the subject of a photograph, Africans now ordered and paid for images of themselves – a photograph that they commanded

16 *African soldiers having their photograph taken*

One new experience for many soldiers from rural Africa was to see illustrated magazines. The printed page might mystify and challenge nonliterate men, but photographic images did provide some insight into new dimensions of the modern world. It was not uncommon for soldiers to decorate the walls of their barracks with pictures torn from illustrated magazines. Large numbers of soldiers first encountered photographs during army service; images were taken of individuals, of units, and of military training. In this picture two West African soldiers are photographed in what may well be an Egyptian or Levantine street. Large numbers of soldiers sent copies of such photographs home to parents and other relatives, introducing a wider number of people to the idea of photography. This particular picture was taken by an unnamed official photographer; the date is unknown.

(Source: Author's collection)

250

and possessed. As a result of the war, within the African colonies there was a greater circulation of and exposure of people to news especially about the course of the war. The payment of remittances brought women together and news was exchanged orally; mobile vans of government information departments showed films and transmitted radio broadcasts in rural districts; newspaper pictures and photographs of men serving overseas revealed something of a world not seen before.

The army required soldiers to identify their religious beliefs. This had a practical purpose – for example, so as to avoid feeding Muslims pork. Muslim mallams and Christian padres were appointed to the RWAFF and KAR, the system becoming more effectively organised by the latter part of the war. Mallams and padres helped with social control, dealing with the psychological problems of soldiers and with difficulties arising from anxieties about distant families. A missionary in Adamawa sent a monthly newsletter to all the soldiers from his district, and in Burma Mallam Habila Aleyideino served as the contact man, bringing them news of home and mosque.[47] Although there are frequent reports, from both officials and soldiers, of church services, prayer meetings, gatherings to sing hymns and Bible classes, next to nothing is known about the religious experiences of African soldiers in wartime. Researchers simply have not asked the questions, perhaps lacking the ability to discuss religious belief or more likely shying away from a province deemed personal and 'private'. There is a good deal of evidence to suggest that Europeans respected and did not mock an African's religious beliefs. When Amos Lymo from Moshi, a telegraphist in the KAR serving in Burma, came under fire he leapt into a trench with a European who turned to him and said: 'You Amos can pray; you better pray now.'[48]

Despite the idea in the minds of many Africans that Christianity was closely identified with modernity, adherence to indigenous religious beliefs remained strong. This was also the case with soldiers recruited from areas that were predominantly Muslim; the ideologies of the ancestors and spirits retained a very strong hold over many men's minds. Military service may have exposed men to new ideas but in all probability it did not substantially change their spiritual perceptions of the world. The pervasive power of ideas held since childhood and the influence of the indigenous social and spiritual order in the villages to which many men returned exercised a far-reaching control. A soldier returning to a rural home, after the initial hiatus, could slip back into old ways and patterns of living. Rural life, in any case, was intimately constrained by the immediate material needs of making a living, of food supply, questions of land, crops and cattle, anxieties about rain, and the need to raise cash for taxes and school fees. Indigenous belief systems provided an accommodating intellectual framework for rural dwellers which operated powerfully even on the thought processes of young men who had been away for some time as migrant labourers or soldiers.

Conclusion

To translate the social impact of war service involving several hundred thousand men from many different African societies is a well-nigh impossible task. The empirical evidence is slight. There is a danger of exaggerating the social influences brought by the war on Africa, but also of underestimating those influences. Certain unequivocal and uncontroversial statements can be made: many thousands of soldiers returned home with new skills – an ability to speak another language, with functional literacy and numeracy; the ability to drive a motor vehicle, handle a telephone, use a range of tools; and knowledge of hygiene practices enforced by the military. A few ex-servicemen became progressive farmers, encouraged by the ideas and practices that they had seen in Egypt or India, and with help from demobilisation schemes. A good many men were anxious to apply their new knowledge to improving their own lives and opportunities, and also desired that their children should attend school and receive the benefits and advantages of formal education. However, personal hopes often failed to be realised in a postwar world where life was constrained by lack of money and opportunity, by inflation, and by social pressures. For some men military experience marked a change in lifestyle. Silebatso Masimega, interviewed by Ashley Jackson in Botswana, said:

> Before [the war] men were living like pigs, but they became civilized ... Illiterate Batswana were living in filthy conditions. Now when they were in the Army, they were able to wash, shave, brush teeth, eat well. And when they came back there was a change in their personality – they were clean until they grew old. Their homes were clean. They showed an example, by making a latrine inside their quarters, and many people copied them, and sent their children to school. They showed people to live in healthy conditions and most people copied from the families of returned men.[49]

There may be some force in this claim, but caution is required. In 1941–45 some 11,000 Batswana entered military service – nearly 20 per cent of Bechuanaland's adult male population. Were even half of those men to have had the influence claimed the impact on health and sanitation would surely have been more openly documented in the society at large.

Soldiers came back from the war having acquired a whole range of ideas about the modern world. However, these new ideas and notions should not be interpreted in a whiggish sort of way. Just because they were 'modern', the products of an industrial world, that did not mean that Africans returning to their homes necessarily desired them or wished to embrace them. There were practical material objects to be taken home – a bicycle or a sewing machine, and the odd luxury item. Human beings are invariably pragmatic about past experiences, picking only what will be useful for the next part of the journey. Many of the practices and ideas encountered in the army in all likelihood simply did not register with soldiers as worth retaining. Of course, ideas were there which might be recalled and reactivated when required, but for the most part African rural life probably offered little opportunity, encouragement or scope for such thinking and activity.

Colonial officials feared that the war and overseas service by so many Africans might seriously undermine white prestige, that blessed status which, so it was believed, enabled a small number of Europeans to rule so many relatively docile Africans. These anxieties were more strongly expressed in the white settler colonies of East Africa, particularly Kenya, and in South Africa. It was feared that 'undisciplined' Africans back from the war would be unwilling to return to the land, while their view of white people would have been seriously compromised by their contacts with 'undesirable' people and ways of life in the Middle East.[50] However, it is also necessary to look critically at the idea of 'white prestige'. This was an idea formed in the minds of Europeans, a mental construct or myth, and like many recent myths based on certain assumptions about white superiority supported by selective observations. Europeans talked of threats to 'white prestige', and maybe a few Africans did act in ways that confirmed belief in such threats, but the history of Africa does not lend support to it. Not long before this time Africans had fought against white control, and after control was established there were revolts and other forms of opposition to the imposition of alien white rule. In the 1930s Africa had seen a new spate of organised and sustained protest by African peasants and workers against European planters, mining companies, foreign trading concerns and their allies the colonial governments. 'White prestige', if it existed other than in the minds of Europeans, was certainly being steadily challenged. The war years provided Africans with further circumstances and experiences that helped to further encourage that process.

So, how did African soldiers at the end of the war view Europeans? For some African soldiers the term 'white' embraced more than just Europeans. Skin colour has always been a crude means of identification. Europeans were not always clearly identifiable. 'European' might mean a person who wore Western clothing or had a lighter-coloured skin, and this could mean calling some North Africans and Indians 'white'. Thus African soldiers who said that they had had sexual relations with 'white' women in Ceylon and in Egypt most likely were referring to Ceylonese and Egyptian women. Many Africans had fought alongside and also against white soldiers and seen white allies and enemies alike exposed to the traumas of war. In 1941, at the end of the East African campaign, thousands of Italian prisoners-of-war had been herded into barbed-wire cages to be guarded by African troops, a powerful expression of white defeat and black triumph which, argues Bates, cannot but have changed the attitudes of East African askaris in particular. Likewise, seeing the squalor and poverty of India and Burma influenced the way in which many Africans regarded Asians in East Africa.[51] Phaladi Sesinyi from Bechuanaland recalled that in the Mediterranean theatre:

> We used to see white people asking for food and we knew that they were poor. So we used to give them food and cigarette, and we were shocked because we know white people as rich people. But we didn't take much notice because we were at war.[52]

However, it seems reasonably safe to assert that most soldiers, who came from the traditional recruiting areas, went home to parts of Africa where white people were rarely encountered. Indirect rule ensured that day-to-day administration was in the hands of indigenous authorities; the collection of taxes, rural policing, courts, prisons, and the requisitioning of labour were all managed, mismanaged and abused by Africans. The few Europeans heard of or encountered were most likely to be Christian missionaries running schools or dispensaries, institutions which did not necessarily intrude into indigenous life and yet which might also offer help. Of course, some of the ex-servicemen going back to a rural home carried grievances about the war and these could be directed against white authority in its various forms. That is to be expected. The point worth emphasising is that the vast majority of soldiers came from rural areas, returned home to those areas, and readjusted to rural life reasonably well given the circumstances of several years' absence. Authority was challenged in rural areas, but it was the authority of the elders and chiefs, and rarely direct white colonial rule.

A similar case can be put forward for many of the soldiers who on demobilisation returned to or remained in or near to urban areas. However, there were some who presented a rather different picture. These were men who had acquired skills in the army and their expectations of civilian opportunities were high. Postwar unemployment, inflation, and rivalry in the labour market from men equally skilled who had not gone to war, reduced their chances and increased their discontent. These were the ex-servicemen who could be said to challenge 'white prestige'. Their close experience of a variety of white men during army service probably did something to change their social attitudes to white people in general, while the frustrations of postwar civilian life invariably focused on white colonial authority. Unlike the rural areas where chiefly rule predominated, invariably in the urban and peri-urban areas colonial authority *was* the source of power that had to be challenged. It might be more satisfactory to see this as less a challenge to 'white prestige' than a continuing process of protest that now began to be expressed more firmly through trade unions and formally organised modern political parties.

Notes

[1] CSM Kgolo, writing to Chief Tshekedi Khama towards the end of the war, quoted by Ashley Jackson, 'Watershed in a Colonial Backwater? The Bechuanaland Protectorate during the Second World War', D. Phil, Oxford, 1996, p. 95.

[2] Quoted by Darrell Bates, *A Fly-Switch from the Sudan* (London 1961), p. 104.

[3] Quoted by Wendell P. Holbrook, 'Oral history and the nascent historiography for West Africa and the Second World War', *International Journal of Oral History* 3, 3 (1983), p. 166.

[4] Interview by David Killingray, Accra, 5 May 1979.

[5] Isaac Fadoyebo, *A Stroke of Unbelievable Luck* (University of Wisconsin-Madison, 1999), p. 26.

[6] Bildad Kaggia, *Roots of Freedom, 1921–1963* (Nairobi, 1975), p. 32; Fadoyebo, *A Stroke of Unbelievable Luck*, p. 27.

[7] D. H. Barber, *Africans in Khaki* (London 1948), p. 92.

[8] Fadoyebo, *A Stroke of Unbelievable Luck*, p. 61 and also ch. 4.

[9] Information from Prof George Shepperson on an incident in Burma where a grenade was tossed into the dugout of an unpopular officer, with fatal results – the practice known in the Vietnam War as 'fragging'.

[10] Fadoyebo, *A Stroke of Unbelievable Luck*, p. 26–27.

[11] The names in this paragraph are taken from the *Nigeria Gazette*, 29, 31 (15 June 1944), pp. 311–12.

[12] P. Kilby, *African Enterprise: The Nigerian Bread Industry* (Stanford CA, 1965), chs 1 and 2. African-owned bakeries developed in many towns, e.g. Kumasi in the Gold Coast.

[13] See for example Fadoyebo, *A Stroke of Unbelievable Luck*, p. 40.

[14] *Accra Evening News*, 26 August 1950, quoted by Alistair Chisholm, '"We have the right to live as men!" Youth and politics in Accra, *c.* 1930–1950', paper presented to African History Seminar, School of Oriental and African Studies, University of London, 12 November 1997.

[15] African colonial armies were integrated into the structures of the British army during the war; lists of commissariat supplies to be dropped to frontline troops in Burma during 1944–45 provide an indication of what had become the accepted norm for African soldiers.

[16] Fadoyebo, *A Stroke of Unbelievable Luck*, p. 26.

[17] David Killingray, 'The colonial army in the Gold Coast: Official policy and local response, 1890–1947', PhD thesis, London, 1982, p. 216.

[18] R. H. Kakembo, *An African Soldier Speaks* (Edinburgh, 1946), p. 27.

[19] Report in *Victory*, 23 July 1945, pp. 9–10.

[20] *West African Pilot*, 25 April 1945, p. 4.

[21] *Ibid.*, 10 May 1945, p. 4.

[22] Again there are many reports in the press, e.g. *Nigerian Daily Times* (Lagos), 20 May 1946, 'Gold Coast beat Nigerians in inter-brigade boxing', with reports of the skill of Sgt R. A. Codgoe, 'veteran welter-weight of Accra', and Sgt J. N. Oku, 'known for over 10 years as "Harry Corbett" of the Gold Coast ring'.

[23] Gaele Sobott, 'Experiences of Batswana women during the Second World War', *Pula: Botswana Journal of African Studies* 13, 1/2 (1999), pp. 96 and 100.

[24] See the letters to the *West African Pilot* women's column, 'Milady's Bower': e.g. 'She prefers an ex-soldier to a news vendor', 22 March 1946.

[25] Kenda Mutongi, '"Worries of the heart": Widowed mothers, daughters and masculinities in Maragoli, Western Kenya, 1940–60', *Journal of African History*, 40 (1999), pp. 68–69, 74–75, 76–80 and 85.

[26] Mutongi, '"Worries of the heart"', p. 76.

[27] *Ibid.*, p. 80.

[28] T. C. McCaskie, *Asante Identities: Modernity in an African Village 1850–1950* (Edinburgh, 2000), p. 167.

[29] Mutongi, '"Worries of the heart"', p. 73. In their film *The Wedding Camels* (1980), the MacDougalls include a Turkana man, Lorang, who had served in the KAR. 'On the basis of this experience [he] … wonders aloud with his friends whether the white man's way of marrying off his daughter is not more sensible than their own'. Paul Henley, 'Fly in the soup', *London Review of Books*, 21 June 2001, p. 37.

[30] Prof George Shepperson, speaking at the centenary conference on Paul Robeson, School of Oriental and African Studies, University of London, 17 April 1998.

[31] See photograph and report in *Statesmen* (Delhi), 30 November 1944, and *Civil and Military Gazette* (Lahore), from an undated cutting, *c.* November 1944.

[32] *Nigerian Daily Times* (Lagos), 11 May 1946.

[33] Cf. the example of car maintenance in Ghana in David Edgerton, *The Shock of the Old: Technology and Global History since 1900* (London, 2006; paperback edn, 2008), pp. 83–85.

[34] E. N. Obiechina, ed., *Onitsha Market Literature* (London, 1972), p. 5.

[35] TNA, DO35/1183/Y.1069/1/1, 1945.

[36] Mario Kolk, *Can You Tell me Why I Went to War? A Story of a Young King's African Rifle, Reverend Father John E. A. Mandambwe* (Zomba, 2008), pp. 44 and 47.

[37] Bates, *A Fly-Switch from the Sudan*, p. 104.

[38] Margaret Wrong, *West African Journey* (London, 1946), pp. 59–60.

[39] See reports in *Statesman* (Calcutta), 9 January 1945; and *Statesmen* (Delhi), 12 January 1945.

[40] TNA, CO 167/920/8, 31 December 1941, quoted by Ashley Jackson, '"A remote island in the Indian Ocean": Mauritius and the Second World War', unpublished paper, 1998.

[41] Obiechina, *Onitsha Market Literature*, pp. 5–6.

[42] Catherine M. Cole, *Ghana's Concert Party Theatre* (Bloomington IN, 2001), pp. 87–8, 136 and 167 fn 9. See also John E. Collins, 'Ghanaian highlife', *African Arts* 10, 1 (1976), pp. 62–68, and *West African Pop Roots* (Philadelphia, 1992).

[43] *West African Pilot*, 24 April 1945, p. 1.

[44] *Times of India* supplement, report on 'West African troops in Bombay celebrate victory', 23 September 1945.

[45] Many of these photographs were published in official books, newspapers and magazines (e.g. *Victory*) and also made available to African newspapers. One of the best collections is in the Imperial War Museum, London.

[46] For example, see the two photographs in Alec Dickson, 'Army education in Africa', *Overseas Education* 17, 1 (1945), p. 230.

[47] Margaret Nissen, *An African Church is Born: The Story of Adamawa and Central Province in Nigeria* (Dashen, 1984), p. 184.

[48] An interview recorded by Bengt Sundkler, Moshi, 1961; see Bengt Sundkler and Christopher Steed, *A History of the Church in Africa* (Cambridge, 2000), p. 618.

[49] Ashley Jackson, 'Watershed in a colonial backwater?', pp. 349–50.

[50] Frank Füredi, 'The demobilised African soldier and the blow to white prestige', in David Killingray and David Omissi, eds, *Guardians of Empire* (Manchester, 1999), pp. 179ff.

[51] Bates, *A Fly-switch from the Sudan*, p. 107.

[52] Quoted by Jackson, 'Watershed in a colonial backwater?', p. 98.

Postscript

The Second World War had a profound impact on colonial Africa, signs of which were obvious to some but by no means all observers at the end of the war. By 1945 the major European colonial powers had declined in global power and status and were now overshadowed by two new superpowers, the United States and the Soviet Union. In fact, the war had been won by Soviet manpower and American financial and industrial power. France and Belgium, although among the 'victors', had suffered defeat and foreign occupation in 1940–45. Italy had rapidly lost the empire that it had gained mainly in the 20th century by conquest. Although among the Allied 'Big Four' powers, Britain had also suffered a decisive defeat at Singapore in 1942, and the wartime 'Quit India' campaign pointed up the acute difficulties of retaining control over the subcontinent.

Although India's future within the Empire was almost certainly a lost cause, Europeans acquainted with Africa, along with most literate Africans, expected colonial rule in the continent to endure for many years to come. The Colonial Office continued to recruit men and women for a lifetime of service in Africa. Colonial control was firmly entrenched and faced few serious indigenous challenges. African political parties were small and poorly funded and led by urban conservative elites, with limited influence mainly restricted to the towns. Trade-union membership had grown during the war years and continuing measures were being taken to prevent unions from engaging in politics. Like previous governments, the new Labour government in Britain, despite its own deep trade-union roots, was unwilling to see this kind of political linkage develop in the colonies. Africa's exports of mineral and agricultural resources were seen as vital to Britain's postwar economic recovery and as a means of propping up a weak sterling system against the power of the American dollar.[1] Postwar plans were also in hand to encourage further European emigration to the white settler colonies of Kenya and Southern Rhodesia as well as to South Africa.

Despite this confidence of continued alien control over Africa colonies, the war had subtly and profoundly brought change to the continent. Towns had grown in size, wartime shortages compounded by inflation hit real incomes and generated discontent, felt most keenly and increasingly expressed by people in the expanding urban centres. Although the tentacles of state control had spread

256

wider after 1940 in order to gather men and material for the war effort, the state apparatus did not include provision for postwar employment, housing, urban improvement and welfare services, particularly education. Early on in the war it was officially recognised that the interwar orthodoxy of indirect rule through indigenous chiefs constituted an unsatisfactory future means of colonial governance. African men born in the early decades of the 20th century and educated in mission schools were invariably hostile to indigenous rulers, and wartime population movement and urban growth had also made indirect rule seem a shaky foundation for African constitutional advancement. The British response was to turn away from supporting traditional rulers and from 1947 onwards to attempts to build local government with the support of literate and formally educated Africans – 'modern' men and women. This change came about only gradually and there were many areas of Africa where it still had to be implemented in the mid-1950s.

Attitudes in Britain towards Empire also changed during the war years. The interwar idea of trusteeship was increasingly supplanted by notions of 'partnership' with colonial rulers and African subjects co-operating in future economic and political development. Overseas territories were no longer to be places to be exploited but to be developed to the advantage of indigenous peoples as well as Britain. However, no colonial power thought of relinquishing control over African territory, and the right to colonial rule was not questioned. What was under serious discussion was how colonial rule was organised and conducted. In the new bipolar world order the possession of Empire promised economic resources and also global status and prestige. Racial paternalism remained but with the recognition in Britain's non-settler colonies that Africans had a more prominent role to play in the economic and social development of their own territories, albeit with continued European guidance and at a pace chosen by London. In 1950 racially discriminatory policies were common around the world: such systems formed the bedrock of most colonial rule, at their harshest in white settler colonies; the system of race segregation in South Africa after 1948 was given a new legal shape by *apartheid*; the United States was founded on racial difference and African-Americans suffered the indignities of widely practised institutional racism; and in Britain successive governments argued that anti-discriminatory legislation was impracticable.

The wartime ideas of a welfare state also influenced Africa. The Colonial Development and Welfare Acts of 1940 and 1945 invested capital in African economic development, due recognition being given to the idea that welfare was closely linked to economic progress. The war had shown to a much larger number of people that Africa was on the move economically, and that increased demands for consumer goods required larger and regular investment in education, health and welfare, along with more efficient transport infrastructures. Africa's incorporation into an expanding and modernising world market, although one that Britain could control for her own ends, required the investment of human resources and capital.

Many officials in London increasingly recognised that constitutional reform was necessary in certain African colonies, although this did not imply any rapid move towards territorial independence. By 1946 the Gold Coast had a new constitution and a legislative council with an elected African majority. In sharp contrast, in Kenya, on the other side of the continent, only a single African had been appointed by the governor in 1944 to the otherwise all-white legislature. Britain ended the war economically exhausted, but at the same time the colonial service continued to recruit larger numbers of officials and technicians for employment in what Lonsdale has called the 'second colonial occupation of Africa'. Thus as African nationalist political ambitions stirred, London pursued policies to exploit Africa's resources to help meet Britain's postwar sterling crisis. At the same time increasing numbers of white settlers emigrated to Kenya and Southern Rhodesia. All of this was evidence of Britain's intention to stay in Africa for a very long time.[2]

The nationalist aspirations that emerged after 1945, most actively in West Africa, were different from the conservative 'nationalist' ideas of two decades earlier. Italy's invasion of Abyssinia in 1935, and Britain's feeble response, along with unrest sparked by policies to meet the years of economic depression, served to galvanise West African political activity but also led to a stronger sense of identity with Africa by the millions of people in the African diaspora in the Americas. The urban-based 'patriot' parties of the educated elites, with their narrow political agendas, were already being challenged in the late 1930s by radical 'young men' who argued for an end to colonial rule. The ideas contained in the Atlantic Charter of 1941 inspired many African political thinkers across the continent and helped to change the political landscape of much of post-war Africa, particularly in West Africa.

The major upheaval came in the Gold Coast. In August 1947 a liberal lawyer, Joseph Danquah, helped to form a new political party, the United Gold Coast Convention (UGCC), which demanded 'self-government in the shortest possible time'. The leaders invited Kwame Nkrumah, then a student in London, to return home to become the general secretary of the party. It was a volatile moment in the history of the Gold Coast. Postwar inflation, a shortage of goods, lack of paid work and antagonism towards European-owned companies and banks excited African hostility to colonial rule. In Accra in late February 1948 the police fired on an ex-servicemen's demonstration intent on presenting griev- ances on their living conditions to the governor. Two veterans were killed. Riots followed and spread to other towns, with angry crowds attacking Europeans and looting shops. Twenty-nine people died in the riots. The Governor, fearing a communist plot – Cold War fears raged across Africa – declared a state of emer- gency and arrested the leaders of the UGCC, including Nkrumah. London appointed a commission of enquiry and also set about speeding up constitu- tional change in the Gold Coast.

Already Nkrumah's left-wing views and political ambitions proved very different from the bourgeois ideas of those who had appointed him. His vision was for a territory-wide mass party supported by ordinary people – by cocoa farmers, peasants, mineworkers and townsmen, which included 'verandah boys', the often disillusioned and underemployed younger men with but a few years of formal schooling. Nkrumah moved away from the UGCC and in August 1949 created his own populist party, the Convention People's Party (CPP). Even though Nkrumah was again imprisoned, the CPP won the 1951 elections and while still in prison Nkrumah was invited by the colonial governor to become 'leader of government business'. The nationalist success in the Gold Coast provided example and encouragement for new political parties in other colonies in West Africa and elsewhere across the continent.

In the postwar world Africa assumed greater strategic significance for the colonial powers and also for the United States. Whatever constitutional changes came for African colonies, it was vital that they should not become attached to the Soviet bloc. Africa's mineral resources were significant for the West, and British defence strategies incorporated the continent in its Cold War policies. Policymakers in London maintained Suez as a strategic military base, with Kenya as a short-lived further base linked by a notional line of defence from Lagos across the continent to Mombasa on the Indian Ocean. The Suez Canal, astride the route to Asia and the vital oil supplies of the Persian Gulf area, was guarded by British troops until 1954. An attempt by Britain to reassert control over the canal in 1956 failed disastrously and emphasised not only the country's imperial decline but also London's economic dependence on the United States. Another notion played with by some politicians, following the independence of India, was the formation of a large African Imperial Army that would take the place of the Indian Army. Perhaps fortunately for Africa this was no more than an idea. Nevertheless, military labour continued to be recruited in the High Commission Territories and the Indian Ocean islands and employed in the Middle East until the early 1950s. Ironically, just as the Mau Mau emergency was being declared in Kenya in 1952, crowds lined the streets of Nairobi to watch men of the King's African Rifles march off to fight in an anti-communist colonial war in Malaya.

After the war most African colonial forces reverted to their peacetime roles. One marked difference was that local battalions were now increasingly equipped and trained to aid the civil power. Most colonial forces were slowly enlarged in size and provided with an armoured car or two. Well beyond the dates of independence, beginning with Ghana in 1957, the officer corps remained overwhelmingly European. Africanisation was a slow process, the majority of new officers being drawn from among educated men which, in the case of the future Ghana and Nigeria, meant appointing men from the south of the country. Thus many African armies continued to gain their rank-and-file from the traditional recruiting grounds while the officer corps came from a different ethnic group or groups. The result was that at independence African military hierarchies were divided ethnically and geographically, power and authority being in the hands of those who could use it to their own ethnic or institutional advantage. In the run-up to and after independence African armies tended to grow in size, sovereign status requiring larger forces with more modern equipment. The primary role of armies in independent Africa differed little from that of colonial forces: they were mainly employed in securing frontiers and for maintaining internal law and order. This latter role often pitched the army into the position of serving as the agent for an authoritarian African government. This was a dangerous position for African regimes to be in; the army they relied on to keep them in power could also turn their guns against the regime. The first African military coup occurred in 1958 in the Sudan, the next in 1963 in Togo, and thereafter coups and counter-coups became a common feature of African politics.

But what of the veterans of the Second World War, the men with whom this book has been concerned? Some veterans re-enlisted immediately after the war.

The vast majority of men did not. But old loyalties and allegiances die hard and on special occasions, for example the 11th November Armistice Day parade at war memorials, small groups of men would gather to remember their former comrades. A few ex-servicemen, members of local legions, continued to live in veterans' villages. Their numbers, as with those who assemble on Armistice Day, steadily dwindle; as African economies failed so their standards of living declined, their clothes became more ragged, and age has taken an increasing toll on their health. Scholars who have talked to ex-servicemen and carefully recorded their memories of an increasingly distant war when they fought for Britain, have also listened to their stories of official neglect and of unpaid benefits. 'Lest we forget,' the phrase of Rudyard Kipling often inscribed on war memorials, is an apt one for the forgotten men of the African colonial forces. In an email that I received in September 2008, Staff-Sergeant John Howlett, a British soldier with contacts in Ghana, wrote:

> The veterans (1000 left from WWII) ... are in a sorry state having not received a penny from the government since Sep 07 and the Veterans Association are unable to pay for their vehicles (i.e. fuel and insurance) and medical fees for their members. The state lottery used to give then a sufficient handout but this has stopped since Sep 07. I raise money where I can but it is difficult to help them all and so I sponsor Cpl O— because of his extraordinary character, courage and strength to stand up for his colleagues when most want to ignore them.

However, against this rather depressing note is the strong sense of pride that many African ex-servicemen still hold as they look back on their wartime service and experiences.

Notes

[1] As with the unsuccessful and exploitative Groundnut Scheme in Tanganyika, 1946–50.
[2] See further Frederick Cooper, *Africa since 1940: The Past of the Present* (Cambridge, 2002), chs 1–4; James S. Coleman, *Nigeria: Background to Nationalism* (Berkeley CA, 1958); John Hargreaves, *Decolonisation in Africa* (Harlow, 2nd edn, 1998); John Darwin, *Britain and Decolonisation: The Retreat from Empire in the Post-War World* (Basingstoke, 1988); Gifford Prosser and Wm Roger Louis, eds, *The Transfer of Power in Africa: Decolonization 1940–1960* (New Haven CT, 1982).

Bibliography

PRIMARY SOURCES

The National Archives, Kew, Surrey

CAB 5
CAB 65
CAB 66
CAB 67
CAB 106

CO 98
CO537
CO 554
CO 583
CO 820
CO 822
CO 964
CO 968

DO 35

FO 2
FO 371

WO 32
WO 106
WO 169
WO 172
WO 193
WO 203
WO 269

House of Lords Record Office

Sorenson Papers, SOR65/A
University of Cambridge
Swinton papers, Churchill College

Institute of Commonwealth Studies, University of London

Michael Crowder Papers (MCP)

BBC Africa Service

Interviews and letters from African ex-servicemen

British Library

India Office Library and Records

Rhodes House Library, Oxford (RHL)

Mss. Afr. s. 1734, Box VI
Mss. Afr. s 1715, Box V
Mss. Afr. s. 1715, Box III, Brig G. H. Cree
Mss. Afr. s. 1734, Box X, Capt R. R. Ryder
Mss. Afr. s. 1734, Box VI, letter, Sir Michael Gass to David Killingray

National Archives of Ghana

Accra; Cape Coast; and Tamale

Liddell Hart Archive, King's College London

Dimoline papers 7/1–9/12
Stockwell papers 5/3

National Archives and Records Administration, Washington DC

R and A Reports, OSS-W-1710, 22 May 1945

ORAL SOURCES

British Broadcasting Corporation

Imperial War Museum, London, Department of Sound Records

PP/MCR/68, Brig Ian Bruce, 'They put us in boots' (ts)

India Office Records and Library (IORL), British Library, London

Interviews

By Dr Anthony Clayton:
Maj F. Bailey, 22 December 1980
By David Killingray:
Kwame Asante, Accra, April 1979
Prof B. L. Jacobs
Eric Lanning, Surrey
Ian Morris, Edinburgh, 28 September 1993
E. E. Sabben-Clare, Oxford, 1980
Prof George Shepperson

OFFICIAL

Colonial Office, *Report of the Commission of Enquiry into Disturbances in the Gold Coast 1948* (Watson Commission) (Colonial No. 231) (HMSO 1948)
Colonial Office, *Gold Coast: Report to His Excellency the Governor by the Committee on Constitutional Reform 1949* (Colonial No. 248) (HMSO 1949)
Uganda, Annual Report for the year 1948 (London: Colonial Office, 1949).
Parliamentary Debates, House of Commons

NEWSPAPERS ETC

African Morning Post (Accra, Gold Coast)
African Outlook
The Ashanti Pioneer (Kumasi)
Cape Times (Cape Town)
Daily Mail (Freetown)
Fighting Talk (Johannesburg)
Gold Coast Independent
The Keys (journal of the League of Coloured Peoples, London)
Kintampo Camp Weekly
Mandaleo
The Military Veteran (Veterans Association of Ghana, Accra, 1986)
Newsletter (of the League of Coloured Peoples, London)
Nigerian Daily Times (Lagos)
RWAFF News (Cairo and Bombay)
The Sierra Leone Weekly News (Freetown)
Springbok (South African veterans' journal)
Star (Johannesburg)
Statesman (Calcutta)
The Times (London)
Times of India
Victory
WASU (journal of the West African Students Union, London)
West Africa (London)
West African Pilot
West African Review (London)

UNPUBLISHED

Seminar papers, etc

Bromber, Katrin, 'Do not destroy our honour: Wartime propaganda directed at East African soldiers in Ceylon (1943–44)'. Available online at: <www.sasnet.lu.se/EASApapers/22Katrin Bromber.pdf> accessed 20 September 2009.

Chisholm, Alistair, '"We have the right to live as men!": Youth and politics in Accra, *c.* 1930–1950', African History Seminar, School of Oriental and African Studies, University of London, 12 November 1997.

Cock, Jacklyn, 'Demobilisation and democracy: The relevance of the 1944 "Soldiers' Charter" to Southern Africa today', University of the Witwatersrand, history workshop on Democracy: Popular Precedents, Practice, Culture, 13–15 July 1994.

Cole, Festus, 'The role of the colonial army in Sierra Leone', International Symposium on Sierra Leone, Freetown, May 19–21, 1987.

Collins, R. O., 'The SDF and the Italian–Ethiopian campaign in the Second World War', Conference on Africa and the Second World War, School of Oriental and African Studies, University of London, May 1984.

Fridjhon, Michael, 'The Torch Commando and the politics of white opposition: South Africa 1951–1953', African Studies Seminar, University of Witwatersrand, 1977.

Hirson, Baruch, 'Not Pro-Boer, and not Anti-War – just indifferent: South African blacks in the Second World War', Conference on Africa and the Second World War, School of Oriental and African Studies, University of London, May 1984.

Holbrook, Wendell P., 'War and tradition in the Gold Coast, 1939–1945', nd.

Jackson, Ashley, '"A remote island in the Indian Ocean": Mauritius and the Second World War', 1998.

Lavalie, Alpha M, 'The role of Sierra Leonean ex-servicemen in the politics of decolonisation, 1945–1961', School of Oriental and African Studies, University of London, 1989.

McLaughlin, Peter, 'Collaborators, mercenaries or patriots? The "problem" of African troops in Southern Rhodesia during the First and Second World Wars', African History Seminar, School of Oriental and African Studies, University of London, 6 February 1980.

Mizobe, Yasuo, 'African newspaper coverage of Japan (the Japanese Army) during World War II: The case of *The Gold Coast Observer* and *The Ashanti Pioneer*, 1943–1945', Re-Evaluating Africa and World War II workshop, Rutgers University, 27–29 March 2008.

Mutiso, S. K., 'Indigenous knowledge in drought and famine forecasting in Machakos District, Kenya', Conference of the African Studies Association of the UK, Stirling, 8–10 September 1992.

Ntabeni, Mary, 'Labour mobilization for the war effort in Swaziland, 1940-1942', unpublished paper.

Olusanya, G. O., 'The resettlement of Nigeria's ex-soldiers after World War II: A guide for the present', Tenth Annual Congress of the Historical Society of Nigeria, December 1969.

Shackleton, Deborah A., 'Recipe for "failure": Integration of Botswana soldiers within British units during the Second World War', 37th conference of the African Studies Association of the United States, Orlando FL, November 1995.

Shuckburgh, John, 'Colonial civil history of the war', unpublished ms, 1949 (copies in National Archives, Kew; Rhodes House Library, Oxford; Institute of Commonwealth Studies, University of London).

Zaccaria, Massimo, '"Arrivano gli ascari": A visual record of the 5th Battalion's campaign in Libya, February–July 1912', AEGIS Conference, School of Oriental and African Studies, University of London, 2 July 2005.

Theses

Aond'akaa, Akaatenger John, 'Military recruitment and its impact on the Tiv, 1914–1970: The case of Gboko', BA project, University of Jos, 1991.

Brown, Kevin K., 'The military and social change in colonial Tanganyika, 1919–1964', PhD, Michigan State University, 2001.

Burton, Andrew, '*Wahuni* (the undesirables): African urbanisation, crime and colonial order in Dar es Salaam, 1919–1961', PhD, University of London, 2000.

Clarke, Sabine, 'Specialists or generalists? Scientists, the Colonial Office and the development of the British colonies 1940–1960', PhD, University of London, 2005.

Cole, Festus, 'The Sierra Leone Army: A case study of the impact of the colonial heritage, 1901–1967', MA, Fourah Bay College, University of Sierra Leone, 1987.

Dominique, Jean-Michel, 'The experience of the Mauritian and Seychelles Pioneer Corps in, and contribution to, the Egyptian and Western Desert campaigns, 1940–43', MA, School of Oriental and African Studies, University of London, 1994.

Greenbank, Kevin, '"You chaps mustn't worry when you come back": Cape Town soldiers and aspects of the experience of war and demobilisation 1929–1953', MA, University of Cape Town, 1995.

Grundlingh, L. W. F., 'The participation of South African Blacks in the Second World War', PhD, Rand Afrikaans University, 1986.

Holbrook, Wendell P., 'The impact of the Second World War on the Gold Coast, 1939–1945', PhD, Princeton University, 1978.

Jackson, Ashley, 'Watershed in a colonial backwater? The Bechuanaland Protectorate during the Second World War', DPhil, University of Oxford, 1996.

Killingray, David, 'The colonial army in the Gold Coast: Official policy and local response, 1890–1947', PhD, University of London, 1982.

Lovering, Timothy John, 'Authority and identity: Malawian soldiers in Britain's colonial army, 1891–1964', PhD, University of Stirling, 2002.

Manns, Adrienne, 'The role of ex-servicemen in Ghana's independence movement', PhD, Johns Hopkins University, 1984.

Mantuba-Ngoma, Mabiala, 'Les soldats noirs de la Force Publique (1888–1945): Contribution à l'histoire militaire du Zaïre', Université du Zaïre, Lubumbashi, 1980.

Ntabeni, Mary N., 'War and society in colonial Lesotho 1939–1945', PhD, Queen's University, Kingston ONT, 1997.

Owino, Meshack, '"For your tomorrow, we gave our today": A history of Kenyan soldiers in the Second World War', PhD, Rice University, 2004.

Parsons, Timothy, 'East African soldiers in Britain's colonial army: A social history, 1902–1964', PhD, Johns Hopkins University, 1996.

Rozier, John Paul, 'The effect of war on British rule and politics in the Sudan 1939–45', DPhil, University of Oxford, 1984.

Shackleton, Deborah A., 'Imperial military policy and the Bechuanaland Pioneers and Gunners during the Second World War', PhD, Indiana University, 1997.

Schleh, Eugene, 'Post-service careers of African World War II veterans: British East and West Africa with particular reference to Ghana and Uganda', PhD, Yale University, 1968.

Shiroya, Okete J. E., 'The impact of World War II on Kenya: The role of ex-servicemen in Kenyan nationalism', PhD, Michigan State University, 1968.

Warner, Jennifer, 'Recruitment and service in the King's African Rifles in the Second World War', MLitt, University of Bristol, 1985.

Westcott, N. J., 'The impact of the Second World War on Tanganyika, 1939–1949', PhD, University of Cambridge, 1982.

Films and broadcast

Sembène, Ousmane, *Le camp de Thiaroye* (Senegal, 1988).
BBC, 'Mutiny in the RAF' in series *Secret History*, BBC 4 television, transmitted 8 August 1996.

SECONDARY SOURCES

Abdulkadir, Dandatti, *The Poetry, Life and Opinions of Sa'adu Zungur* (Zaria, 1974).
Adekson, J. Bayo, 'Ethnicity and army recruitment in colonial plural societies', *Ethnic and Racial Studies*, 2, 2 (1979), pp. 151–65.
Akurang-Parry, Kwabena O., 'Africa and the World War II', in Toyin Falola, ed., *Africa. Vol.4: The End of Colonial Rule. Nationalism and Decolonization* (Durham NC, 2002).
Alexander, Peter, *Workers, War and the Origins of Apartheid: Labour and Politics in South Africa, 1939–48* (London, 2000).
Anderson, David, *Empire of the Hanged: The Dirty War in Kenya and the End of Empire* (London, 2005).
Anderson, David M., and David Killingray, 'Consent, coercion and colonial control: Policing the Empire, 1830–1940', in David M. Anderson and David Killingray, eds, *Policing the Empire: Government, Authority and Control, 1830–1940* (Manchester, 1991), pp. 1–15.
Anderson, T. Farnworth, 'The diet of the African soldier', *East African Medical Journal*, 20, 7 (1943), pp. 207–13.
Ankrah, Roy, *My Life Story* (Accra, 1952).
Anon., 'Troops from the Gold Coast', *Pathé Gazette*, 20 January 1941.
Anon., *A Spear of Freedom* (Nairobi, 1942).
Anon., 'The Sudan's service in a global war: The story of a sector of the trans-African air ferry route', *Journal of the Royal African Society*, 43, 170 (1944), pp. 16–20.
Anon., *A Short History of the 1st (West African) Infantry Brigade in the Arakan 1944–45* (Calcutta, nd. *c.* 1946).
Anon., *Arakan Assignment: The Story of the 82nd West African Division* (New Delhi, nd. *c.* 1946).
Anon., *History of the 3rd Battalion the Gold Coast Regiment, RWAFF, in the Arakan Campaign, October 1944 to May 1945* (Felixstowe, nd.).
Anon., *History of the 5th Battalion Gold Coast Regiment from 15th December 1943 to 13th February 1945* (nd or place).
Anon., *The King's African Rifles in Madagascar* (Nairobi, 1943).
Apter, David E. *The Political Kingdom in Uganda: A Study in Bureaucratic Nationalism* (Princeton, 2nd edn, 1967).
Armour, Charles, 'The BBC and the development of broadcasting in the British Colonial Empire', *African Affairs*, 83 (1984), pp. 359–402.
Asante, S. K. B., *Pan-African Protest: West Africa and the Italo-Ethiopian Crisis 1934–1941* (London, 1977).
Ashton, S. R. and S. E. Stockwell, eds, *British Documents on the End of Empire. Series A, Vol. 1: Imperial Policy and Colonial Practice 1925–1945* (London, 1996).
Atkins, Keletso E., *The Moon is Dead! Give us our Money! The Cultural Origins of an African Work Ethic, Natal, South Africa 1843–1900* (London, 1993).
Austin, Dennis, *Politics in Ghana 1945–1960* (London, 1964).

Ayendele, A. E., *The Educated Elite in the Nigerian Society* (Ibadan, 1974).

Azikiwe, Nnamdi, *My Odyssey: An Autobiography* (London, 1970).

Bandele, Biyi, 'First person', *The Guardian* (London), Family section, 30 June 2007, p. 3.

Bandele, Biyi, *Burma Boy* (London, 2007).

Barber, S. H., *Africans in Khaki* (London, 1948).

Bassett, R. H., 'The chaplain with the West African forces', *Journal of Royal Chaplains' Department*, 49 (July 1950), pp. 21–24.

Bates, Darrell, *A Fly-Switch from the Sudan* (London, 1961).

Bayly, Christopher, and Tim Harper, *Forgotten Armies: Britain's Asian Empire and the War with Japan* (London, 2004; Penguin edn, 2005).

Bediako, K. A., *A Husband for Esi Ellua* (Accra, 1967).

Belgian Congo, Force Publique, *La Force Publique de sa naissance à 1914* (Brussels, 1952).

Bennett, George, *Kenya: A Political History* (Oxford, 1963).

Bent, R. A. R., *Ten Thousand Men of Africa: The Story of the Bechuanaland Pioneers and Gunners 1941–46* (London, 1952).

Beinart, William, *Twentieth-Century South Africa* (Oxford, 1994).

Berman, Bruce J., 'Ethnicity, patronage and the African state: The politics of uncivil nationalism', *African Affairs*, 97 (1998), pp. 305–41.

Blundell, Michael, *So Rough a Wind* (London, 1964).

Blundell, Michael, *A Love Affair with the Sun: A Memoir of Seventy Years in Kenya* (Nairobi, 1994).

Boahen, A. Adu., *Ghana: Evolution and Change in the Nineteenth and Twentieth Centuries* (London, 1975).

Boahen, A. Adu, *African Perspectives on Colonialism* (Baltimore MD, 1987).

Bolnick, Joel, '*Sefala sa Letsamayanaha*: The wartime experiences of Potlako Kitchener Leballo', in *Wits History Workshop Papers*, 6–10 February 1990 (Johannesburg).

Bowen, C. G., *West African Way: The Story of the Burma Campaign, 1943–45* (Obuasi, nd. *c*. 1945).

Brands, Hal, 'Wartime recruiting practices, martial identity and post-World War II demobilization in colonial Kenya', *Journal of African History* 46, 1 (2005), pp. 103–25.

Branson, Clive, *British Soldier in India: The Letters of Clive Branson* (New York, 1945).

Brendon, Piers, *The Decline and Fall of the British Empire 1781–1997* (London, 2007; paperback edn, 2008).

Brennan, James, '"Taifa": Africa, India and the making of nation and race in urban Tanzania', chapter 7, (manuscript).

Buah, F. K., *A History of Ghana* (London, 1980).

Bull, H., and A. Watson, eds, *The Expansion of International Society* (Oxford, 1984).

Burton, Andrew, *African Underclass: Urbanisation, Crime and Colonial Order in Dar es Salaam* (Oxford, 2005).

Buruku, Daisy Sykes, 'The townsman: Kleist Sykes', in John Iliffe, ed., *Modern Tanzanians: A Volume of Biographies* (Dar es Salaam, 1973), pp. 95–114.

Butler, Guy, *Stranger to Europe: Poems 1939–1949* (Cape Town, 1952).

Butterworth, Sidney, *Three Rivers to Glory* (London, 1957).

Cain, P. J., and A. G. Hopkins, *British Imperialism: Crisis and Deconstruction 1914–1990* (1993).

Callwell, C. E., *Small Wars: Their Principle and Practice* (London, 1896).

Calvocoressi, Peter, and Guy Wint, *Total War: Causes and Courses of the Second World War* (London, 1972).

Cardinall, A. W., *The Natives of the Northern Territories of the Gold Coast* (London, 1921).

Cardo, Michael, '"Fighting a worse imperialism": White South African loyalism and the

Army Education Services (AES) during the Second World War', *South African Historical Journal*, 46 (2004), pp. 141–74.

Carter, Gwendolen, *The Politics of Inequality: South Africa since 1948* (London, revised edn, 1962).

Cary, Joyce, *The Case for African Freedom and Other Writings* (revised and enlarged edn, London, 1944).

Cell, John W., 'Colonial rule', in Judith M. Brown and Wm Roger Louis, eds, *The Oxford History of the British Empire. Vol. VI: The Twentieth Century* (Oxford, 1999), p. 232.

Chipman, John, *French Power in Africa* (Oxford, 1989).

Clarke, F. A. S., 'Recollections: 1940–41', *West African Review* (September 1950), pp. 1057–60.

Clarke, Peter, *West Africans at War 1914–18, 1939–45: Colonial Propaganda and its Cultural Aftermath* (London, 1986).

Clayton, Anthony, *Communication for New Loyalties: African Soldiers' Songs* (Athens OH, 1979).

Clayton, Anthony, *The British Empire as a Superpower 1919–39* (Basingstoke, 1986).

Clayton, Anthony, Anthony Clayton, 'Sport and African soldiers: The military diffusion of western sport throughout Sub-Saharan Africa', in W. J. Baker and J. A. Mangan, eds., *Sport in Africa: Essays in Social History* (London 1987), pp. 114–37.

Clayton, Anthony, *France, Soldiers and Africa* (London, 1988).

Clayton, Anthony, and David Killingray, *Khaki and Blue: Military and Police in British Colonial Africa* (Athens OH, 1989).

Clothier, Norman, *Black Valour: The South African Native Labour Contingent, 1916–1918 and the Sinking of the Mendi* (Pietermaritzburg, 1987).

Cohen, David William, and E. S. Atieno-Adhiambo, *Burying SM: The Politics of Knowledge and the Sociology of Power in Africa* (London, 1992).

Cole, Catherine M., *Ghana's Concert Party Theatre* (Bloomington IN, 2001).

Coleman, James S., *Nigeria: Background to Nationalism* (Berkeley CA, 1958).

Cole, Henry B., 'The grievances behind the Gold Coast riots: Position of the ex-servicemen', *African World* (April 1948).

Collins, John E., 'Comic opera in Ghana', *African Arts*, 9, 2 (1976), pp. 50–57.

Collins, John E., 'Ghanaian highlife', *African Arts* 10, 1 (1976), pp. 62–68.

Collins, John E., *West African Pop Roots* (Philadelphia, 1992).

Cookson, C. E., 'The Gold Coast hinterland and the Negroid races', *Journal of the Royal African Society*, 60 (April 1915), pp. 298–307.

Cooper, Frederick, *Decolonization and African Society: The Labor Question in French and British Africa* (Cambridge, 1996).

Cooper, Frederick, *Africa since 1940: The Past of the Present* (Cambridge, 2002).

Crabb, Brian James, *Passage to Destiny: The sinking of the SS Khedive Ismail in the Sea War against Japan* (Stamford, 1997).

Crocker, W. R., *Nigeria: A Critique of Colonial Administration* (London, 1936).

Crowder, Michael, 'The 1939–45 war and West Africa', in J. F. A. Ajayi and Michael Crowder, eds, *History of West Africa. Vol. 2* (London, 2nd edn, 1987), pp. 665–92.

Crowder, Michael, ed., *The Cambridge History of Africa. Vol. 8: From c. 1940 to c. 1975* (Cambridge, 1984).

Crowder, Michael, 'Introduction', and 'The Second World War: Prelude to decolonization', in Michael Crowder, ed., *The Cambridge History of Africa. Vol. 8: From c. 1940 to c. 1975* (Cambridge, 1984), pp. 8–51.

Crwys-Williams, Jennifer, *A Country at War 1939–1945: The Mood of a Nation* (Rivonia, 1992).

Daly, M. W., *Imperial Sudan: The Anglo–Egyptian Condominium 1934–1956* (Cambridge, 2003).

Daniels, Karen, 'Life in Claremont: An interview with May Santon', *African Studies* 60, 1 (2001), pp. 39–64.

Danquah, Moses, 'African soldiers and what they will want in their post-war life', *West African Review* (December 1945), pp. 36–37.

Danquah, Moses, 'Tragedy of Burma: British failure in Burma before the war', *West African Review* (December 1945), pp. 33–34.

Danquah, Moses, 'Chaplain was a jungle wallah', *Ghana World Magazine*, 1 (Jan–Feb 1959), pp. 33–39.

Darwin, John, *Britain and Decolonisation: The Retreat from Empire in the Post-War World* (Basingstoke, 1988).

Datta, Kusum, 'Farm labour, agrarian capital and the state in colonial Zambia: The African Labour Corps 1942–1952', *Journal of Southern African Studies* 14, 3 (1988), pp. 371–92.

Davidson, Basil, *Africa in Modern History: The Search for a New Society* (London, 1978).

Dickson, Alec, 'Army education in Africa', *Overseas Education* 17, 1 (1945).

Doig, Andrew B., 'The Christian Church and demobilization in Africa', *International Review of Missions*, 35 (1946), pp.174–82.

Dower, Kenneth Gandar, *Into Madagascar* (Harmondsworth, 1943).

Dower, Kenneth Gandar, *Askaris at War in Abyssinia/Askari Vitani kwa Abyssinia* (Nairobi, 1943).

Dower, Kenneth Gandar, *KAR in Madagascar* (Nairobi: East African Command and Ministry of Information, nd. *c.* 1943).

Dower, Kenneth Gandar, *Abyssinian Patchwork: An Anthology* (London, 1949).

Duder, J. D., 'An army of one's own: The politics of the Kenya Defence Force', *Canadian Journal of African Studies*, 25, 2 (1991), pp. 207–25.

East African Command, *The Story of the East African Army Service* Corps (Nairobi, nd. *c.* 1944).

Echenberg, Myron, 'Tragedy at Thiaroye: The Senegalese soldiers' uprising of 1944', in Robin Cohen, Jean Copans and Peter Gutkind, eds, *African Labor History* (Berkeley CA, 1978), pp. 109–28.

Echenberg, Myron, *Colonial Conscripts: The Tirailleurs Sénégalais in French West Africa, 1857–1960* (London, 1991).

Elgood, P. G., *Egypt and the Army* (Oxford, 1924).

Enahoro, Anthony, *Fugitive Offender* (London, 1956).

Enloe, Cynthia M., *Ethnic Soldiers: State Security in a Divided Society* (Harmondsworth, Penguin edn, 1980).

Fadoyebo, Isaac, *A Stroke of Unbelievable Luck*, edited and with an introduction by David Killingray (African Studies Program, University of Wisconsin-Madison, 1999).

Fairlie, Michael, *No Time Like the Past* (Edinburgh, 1992).

Fane, R., 'The return of the soldier: East Africa', *Journal of the Royal African Society*, 42 (1944), pp. 56–60.

Fetter, Bruce, 'Luluabourg revolt at Elizabethville', *African Historical Studies*, 2, 2 (1969), pp. 269–77.

Fogarty, Richard, *Race and War in France: Colonial Subjects in the French Army 1914–1918* (Baltimore MD, 2008).

Fortes, Meyer, 'The impact of the war on British West Africa', *International Affairs*, 21, 2 (April 1945), pp. 206–19.

Foucault, Michel, *Discipline and Punish: The Birth of the Prison* (Harmondsworth, Penguin edn, 1977).

Frederiksen, Bodil Folke, '"The present battle is the brain battle": Writing and publishing a Kikuyu newspaper in the pre-Mau Mau period in Kenya', in Karin Barber, ed.,

Africa's Hidden Histories: Everyday Literacy and Making the Self (Bloomington IN, 2006), pp. 278–313.

Furedi, Frank, 'The African crowd in Nairobi: Popular movements and élite politics', *Journal of African History* 14, 2 (1973), pp. 275–90.

Furedi, Frank, *The Mau Mau War in Perspective* (London, 1989).

Furedi, Frank, *The New Ideology of Imperialism: Renewing the Moral Imperative* (London, 1994).

Furedi, Frank, 'The demobilised African soldier and the blow to white prestige', in David Killingray and David Omissi, eds, *Guardians of Empire* (Manchester, 1999), pp. 179–97.

Fursdon, F. W. E., 'Draft conductor to Togoland: "The West African goes home"', *Army Quarterly* 57, 1 (1948), pp. 101–10.

Furse, Ralph, *Aucuparius: Recollections of a Recruiting Officer* (Oxford, 1962).

Gatheru, Mugo, *Child of Two Worlds* (London, 1964).

Gerhart, Gail M., *Black Power in South Africa: The Evolution of an Ideology* (Berkeley CA, 1978).

Gicaru, Muga, *Land of Sunshine: Scenes of Life in Kenya before Mau Mau* (London, 1958).

Gleeson, Ian, *The Unknown Force: Black, Indian and Coloured Soldiers Throughout Two World Wars* (Rivonia, 1994).

Glinga, Werner, '*Tirailleurs sénégalais*: A protagonist of African colonial society', in P. F. de Moraes Farias and Karen Barber, eds, *Self-Assertion and Brokerage: Early Cultural Nationalism in West Africa* (Birmingham, 1990), pp. 149–71.

Glover, John, 'The Volta expedition during the late Ashantee campaign', *Journal of the Royal United Service Institute* 18 (1874), pp. 317–30.

Gold Coast Government, *The Gold Coast Handbook 1937* (London, 1937).

Goldin, Ian, *Making Race: The Politics and Economics of Coloured Identity in South Africa* (Harlow, 1987).

Gordon, R. J., 'Impact of the Second World War on Namibia', *Journal of Southern African Studies* 19, 1 (1993), pp. 147–65.

Graham, Ronald W., compiler and editor. 'There was a soldier: The Life of Hama Kim MM', *Africana Marburgensia* 10 (1985).

Gray, B. *Basuto Soldiers in Hitler's War* (Maseru, 1953).

Great Britain, Ministry of Information, *The Abyssinian Campaign* (London, 1942).

Greenhalgh, Peter, *West African Diamonds 1919–83* (Manchester, 1985).

Grundlingh, Albert, *Fighting Their Own War: South African Blacks in the First World War* (Johannesburg, 1987).

Grundlingh, Albert, '"The King's Afrikaners"? Enlistment and ethnic identity in the Union of South Africa's Defence Force during the Second World War,' 1939–45 *Journal of African History* 40, 3 (1999), pp. 351–65.

Grundlingh, Louis, 'The recruitment of South African blacks for participation in the Second World War,' in David Killingray and Richard Rathbone, eds, *Africa and the Second World War* (Basingstoke, 1986), pp. 181–203.

Grundlingh, Louis, 'Aspects of the impact of the Second World War on the lives of Black South African and British colonial soldiers', *Transafrican Journal of History* 21, (1992), pp. 19–35.

Grundy, Kenneth W., *Soldiers Without Politics: Blacks in the South African Armed Forces* (Berkeley CA, 1983).

Hailey, Lord, *An African Survey* (London, 1938), republished as *An African Survey Revised 1956* (London, 1957).

Hailey, Lord, *Native Administration and Political Development in British Tropical Africa* (London, 1941). Reprinted with an introduction by A. H. M. Kirk-Greene (Nendeln, 1979).

Hailey, Lord, 'Post-war changes in Africa', *Journal of the Royal Society of Arts*, 103, 4955 (July 1955).

Hamilton, J., 'African colonial forces', in D. Smurthwaite, ed., *The Forgotten War: The British Army in the Far East 1941–1945* (London, 1992), pp. 66–77.

Hamilton, John A. L., *War Bush: 81 (West African) Division in Burma* (London, 2001).

Hammer, Mary, 'Black and white? Viewing Cleopatra in 1862', in Shearer West, ed., *The Victorians and Race* (Aldershot, 1996).

Hanley, Gerald, *Monsoon Victory* (London, 2001).

Hargreaves, John D., *Decolonization in Africa* (London, 2nd edn, 1996).

Harrison, J. F. C., *Scholarship Boy: A Personal History of the Mid-Twentieth Century* (London, 1995).

Harrison, Mark, *Medicine and Victory: British Military Medicine in the Second World War* (Oxford, 2004).

Hastings, Max, *Retribution: The Battle for Japan, 1944–45* (New York, 2008).

Hatch, John, *A History of Postwar Africa* (London, 1965).

Havinden, M., and D. Meredith, *Colonialism and Development: Britain and its Tropical Colonies, 1850–1960* (London, 1993).

Hawkins, T. H., and L. J. F. Brimble, *Adult Education: The Record of the British Army* (London, 1947).

Haywood, A. and F. A. S. Clarke, *The History of the Royal West African Frontier Force* (Aldershot, 1964).

Headrick, Rita, 'African soldiers in World War II', *Armed Forces and Society* 4, 3 (1978), pp. 501–26.

Henderson, K. D. D., *The Making of the Modern Sudan: The Life and Letters of Sir Douglas Newbold* (London, 1953).

Henley, Paul, 'Fly in the soup', *London Review of Books*, 21 June 2001, p. 37.

Higginson, John, *A Working Class in the Making: Belgian Colonial Labour Policy, Private Enterprise and the African Mineworkers* (Madison WI, 1989).

Hirson, Baruch, *Yours for the Union: Class and Community Struggles in South Africa, 1930–1947* (London, 1989).

Hodges, G. W. T., 'African manpower statistics for the British forces in East Africa, 1914–18', *Journal of African History* 19, 1 (1978), pp. 101–16.

Hodges, Geoffrey, *The Carrier Corps: Military Labor in the East African Campaign, 1914–1918* (Westport CT, 1986).

Hodgkin, Thomas, *Nationalism in Colonial Africa* (London, 1956).

Holbrook, Wendell P., 'Oral history and the nascent historiography for Africa and World War II: A focus on Ghana', *International Journal of Oral History* 3, 3 (1982), pp. 148–66.

Holderness, G., 'A chaplain with the West African Division in Burma', *Journal of the United Services Institute of India* 74, 315 (April 1944), pp. 1–5.

Horwitz, S., 'The non–European war record in South Africa', in Ellen Hellman, ed., *Handbook on Race Relations in South Africa* (Cape Town, 1949), pp. 534–38.

Hudson, E. V. H., 'The East African Education Corps', *Army Education* 25, 2 (1951), pp. 76–80.

Hyam, Ronald, *Britain's Declining Empire: The Road to Decolonization 1918–1968* (Cambridge, 2006).

Iliffe, John, *A Modern History of Tanganyika* (Cambridge, 1979).

Iliffe, John, *The African Poor: A History* (Cambridge, 1987).

Iliffe, John, *Africans: The History of a Continent* (Cambridge, 1995).

Iliffe, John, *East African Doctors* (Cambridge, 1998).

Iliffe, John, *Honour in African History* (Cambridge, 2005).

Irving, David, *The Trail of the Fox* (London, 1977).

Israel, Adrienne M., 'Measuring the war experience: Ghanaian soldiers in World War II', *Journal of Modern African Studies* 25 (1987), pp. 159–68.

Israel, Adrienne M., 'Ex-servicemen at the crossroads: Protest and politics in post-war Ghana', *Journal of Modern African Studies* 30, 2 (1992), pp. 359–68.

Itote, Waruhiu, *'Mau Mau' General* (Nairobi, 1967).

Jackson, Ashley, 'Motivation and mobilization for war: Recruitment for the British Army in the Bechuanaland Protectorate, 1941–42', *African Affairs* 96 (1997), pp. 399–417.

Jackson, Ashley, *Botswana 1939–1945: An African Country at War* (Oxford, 1999).

Jackson, Ashley, 'African soldiers and Imperial authorities: Tensions and unrest during the service of High Commission Territories soldiers in the British Army 1941–46', *Journal of Southern African Studies* 25, 4 (1999), pp. 645–65.

Jackson, Ashley, *War and Empire in Mauritius and the Indian Ocean* (Basingstoke, 2001).

Jackson, Ashley, 'Supplying war: The High Commission Territories' military-logistical contribution in the Second World War', *The Journal of Military History* 66 (2002), pp. 719–60.

Jackson, Ashley, *The British Empire and the Second World* War (London, 2006).

Jackson, H. D., *The Fighting Sudanese* (London, 1954).

James, Lawrence, *Mutiny in the British Commonwealth Forces 1797–1956* (London, 1987).

Jeffries, Richard, *Class, Power and Ideology in Ghana: The Railwaymen of Sekondi* (Cambridge, 1978).

Johnson, David, 'Settlers, farmers and coerced African labour in Southern Rhodesia, 1936–46', *Journal of African History* 33, 1 (1992), pp. 111–28.

Johnson, David, *World War II and the Scramble for Labour in Colonial Zimbabwe* (Harare, 2000).

Jolobe, James Ranisi, *Poems of an African* (Lovedale, 1946).

Jones, Arthur Creech. 'British colonial policy with particular reference to Africa', *International Affairs* 27, 2 (1951), pp. 176–83.

Kaggia, Bildad, *Roots of Freedom, 1921–1963: The Autobiography of Bildad Kaggia* (Nairobi, 1975).

Kakembo, R. H., *An African Soldier Speaks* (Edinburgh, 1946).

Kanogo, Tabitha, *Squatters and the Roots of Mau Mau* (London, 1987).

Kanogo, Tabitha, *Dedan Kimathi: Makers of Kenya's History, No. 3* (Nairobi, 1992).

Kariuke Josiah Mwangi, *Mau Mau Detainee* (Oxford, 1963; Harmondsworth, 1964).

Keene, John, ed., *South Africa in World War Two* (Johannesburg, 1995).

Kennedy, Greg, ed., *Imperial Defence: The Old World Order 1856–1956* (London, 2008).

Kent, J., 'The Foreign Office and defence of the Empire', in Greg Kennedy, ed., *Imperial Defence: The Old World Order 1856–1956* (London, 2008).

Kenyatta, Jomo, *Kenya: The Land of Conflict* (Manchester, 1945).

Kerslake, R. T., *Time and the Hour: Nigeria, East Africa and the Second World War* (London, 1997).

Kilby, Peter, *African Enterprise: The Nigerian Bread Industry* (Stanford CA, 1965).

Killingray, David, and James Matthews, '"Beasts of burden": British West African carriers in the First World War', *Canadian Journal of African Studies* 13, 1–2 (1979), pp. 5–23.

Killingray, David, 'The idea of a British Imperial African army', *Journal of African History* 20 (1979), pp. 421–36.

Killingray, David, 'Military and labour recruitment in the Gold Coast during the Second World War', *Journal of African History* 23, 1 (1982), pp. 83–95.

Killingray, David, 'The mutiny of the West African Regiment in the Gold Coast, 1901', *International Journal of African Historical Studies* 16, 3 (1983), pp. 441–54.

Killingray, David, 'Soldiers, ex-servicemen, and politics in the Gold Coast, 1939–50', *Journal of Modern African Studies* 21, 3 (1983), pp. 523–34.

Killingray, David, and R. Rathbone, eds, *Africa and the Second World War* (Basingstoke, 1986).

Killingray, David, 'Labour mobilization in British colonial Africa for the war effort, 1939–46', in David Killingray and R. Rathbone, eds, *Africa and the Second World War* (Basingstoke, 1986), pp. 68–96.

Killingray, David, 'Race and rank in the British Army in the twentieth century', *Ethnic and Racial Studies* 10, 3 (1987), pp. 278–90.

Killingray, David, 'Labour exploitation for military campaigns in British colonial Africa, 1870–1945', *Journal of Contemporary History* 24, 3 (1989), pp. 483–501.

Killingray, David, 'Imagined martial communities: Recruiting for the military and police in colonial Ghana, 1860–1960', in Carola Lentz and Paul Nugent, eds, *Ethnicity in Ghana: The Limits of Invention* (Basingstoke, 1999), pp. 119–36.

Killingray, David, 'The "Rod of Empire": The debate over corporal punishment in the British African Colonial Forces, 1888–1946', *Journal of African History*, 35, 2 (1994), pp. 201–16.

Killingray, David, ed., *Africans in Britain* (London, 1994).

Killingray, David, 'Africans and African-Americans in enemy hands', in Kent Fedorowich and Robert Moore, eds, *Prisoners-of-War and their Captors in World War II* (Leicester, 1996), pp. 181–204.

Killingray, David, 'Gender issues and African colonial armies', in David Killingray and David Omissi, eds, *Guardians of Empire* (Manchester, 1999), pp. 221–48.

Kilson, Martin, *Political Change in a West African State: A Study of the Modernization Process in Sierra Leone* (Cambridge MA, 1966).

Kirby, S. Woodburn, ed., *The War Against Japan: Vol. III and IV* (London, 1962 and 1965).

Kirk-Greene, A. H. M., '"Damnosa Hereditas": ethnic ranking and martial race imperative in Africa', *Ethnic and Racial Studies* 3, 4 (1980), pp. 393–414.

Kirk-Greene, Anthony, *On Crown Service: A History of HM Colonial and Overseas Civil Service* (London, 1999).

Kiyaga-Mulindwa, D., 'The Bechuanaland Protectorate and the Second World War', *Journal of Imperial and Commonwealth History* 12 (1984), pp. 33–53.

Knapp, Steven, 'Collective memory and the actual past', *Representations* 26 (1989), pp. 123–49.

Knott, A. J., 'East Africa and the returning askari', *Quarterly Review* 285 (1947), pp. 98–111.

Kolk, Mario, *Can You Tell Me Why I Went to War? A Story of a Young King's African Rifle, Reverend Father John E. A. Mandambwe* (Zomba, 2008).

Krikler, Jeremy, *White Rising: The 1922 Insurrection and Racial Killing in South Africa* (Manchester, 2005).

Ladouceur, Paul, *Chiefs and Politicians: The Politics of Regionalism in Northern Ghana* (London, 1979).

Lamb, Christina, *The Africa House: The True Story of an English Gentleman and his African Dream* (New York, 1999; London, 2000).

Lambo, Roger, 'Achtung! The Black Prince: West Africans in the Royal Air Force, 1939–46', in David Killingray, ed., *Africans in Britain* (London, 1994), pp. 145–63.

Langley, J. Ayodele, *Pan Africanism and Nationalism in West Africa 1900–1945* (Oxford, 1973).

Lawler, Nancy, *Soldiers of Misfortune: Ivoirien Tirailleurs of World War II* (Athens OH, 1992).

Lawler, Nancy, *Soldiers, Airmen, Spies and Whisperers: The Gold Coast in World War II* (Athens OH, 2002).

Leakey, Louis, *By the Evidence: Memoirs, 1932–1951* (New York, 1974).

Lee, Rebekah, and Megan Vaughan, 'Death and dying in the history of Africa since 1800', *Journal of African History* 49, 3 (2008), pp. 341–59.

Lee, Ulysses, *United States Army in World War II: Employment of Negro Troops* (Washington DC, 1966).

Lewis, Joanna, *Empire State-Building: War and Welfare in Kenya 1925–52* (Oxford, 2000).

Liebenow, J. Gus, *Colonial Rule and Political Development in Tanzania: The Case of the Makonde* (Nairobi, 1971).

Listowel, Judith, *The Making of Tanganyika* (London, 2nd edn, 1968).

Loolo, Godwin, *A History of Ogoni* (Port Harcourt, 1980).

Lovering, Timothy J., 'Military service, nationalism and race: The experience of Malawians in the Second World War', in R. Ahuja, *et al.*, eds, *The World in World Wars: Experience, Perception and Perspectives from the South* (Leiden, forthcoming).

Lugard, F. D., *The Dual Mandate in British Tropical Africa* (London, 1922).

McCaskie, T. C., *Asante Identities: Modernity in an African Village 1850–1950* (Edinburgh, 2000).

MacDonald, J. F., *The War History of Southern Rhodesia: Vol. 1* (Salisbury, 1947).

McMahon, V. R., 'The Military Police in West Africa', *The Red Cap: Journal of the Corps of Military Police (BAOR)* 1, 7 (1946), pp. 12–13.

Macmillan, W. M., *Warning from the West Indies: A Tract for the Empire* (London, 1936).

Maddox, Gregory H., 'Gender and famine in central Tanzania, 1916–1961', *African Studies Review* 39, 1 (1996), pp. 83–101.

Makonnen, Ras, *Pan Africanism from Within* (Nairobi 1973).

Makopakgosi III, Brian, 'The impact of the Second World War: The case of Kweneng in the then Bechuanaland Protectorate, 1939–1950,' in David Killingray and Richard Rathbone, eds, *Africa and the Second World War* (London, 1986), pp. 160–80.

Mamdani, Mahmood, *Citizen and Subject: Contemporary Africa and the Legacy of Late Colonialism* (Princeton NJ, 1996).

Mann, Gregory, *Native Sons: West African Veterans and France in the Twentieth Century* (Durham NC, 2006).

Marjomaa, Risto, 'The martial spirit: Yao soldiers in British service in Nyasaland (Malawi), 1895–1939', *Journal of African History* 44, 3 (2004), pp. 413–32.

Martin, H. J., and Neil D. Orpen, *South Africa at War: Military and Industrial Organization and Operations in Connection with the Conduct of the War, 1939–1945* (Cape Town, 1975).

Martin, H. J., and Neil D. Orpen, *South African Forces in World War II. Vol. VI: The SADF in Italy and the Mediterranean 1942–5* (Cape Town, 1977).

Martin, H. J., and Neil D. Orpen, *South African Forces in World War II. Vol. VII* (Cape Town, 1979).

Martin, Phyllis M., and Patrick O'Meara, eds, *Africa* (Bloomington IN, 2nd edn, 1986).

Matson, J. N., *A Digest of the Minutes of the Ashanti Confederacy Council 1935–1949* (Cape Coast, nd, *c.* 1951).

Matthews, H. C. G., and Brian Harrison, eds, *The Oxford Dictionary of National Biography* (Oxford, 2004).

Matthews, Z. K., *Freedom for My People: The Autobiography of Z. K. Matthews. Southern Africa 1901–1968* (Cape Town, 2nd edn, 1968).

Maxwell, Leigh, *Captives Courageous: South African Prisoners of War, World War II* (Johannesburg, 1992).

Mazrui, Ali A., *Towards a Pax Africana: A Study of Ideology and Ambition* (London, 1967).

Mazrui, Ali A., *Soldiers and Kinsmen in Uganda: The Making of a Military Ethnocracy* (London 1975)

Mazrui, Ali, *The Warrior Tradition in Modern Africa* (London, 1977).

Mazrui, Ali, 'Africa entrapped: Between the Protestant ethic and the legacy of Westphalia', in Hedley Bull and Adam Watson, eds, *The Expansion of International Society* (Oxford, 1984), pp. 289–308.

Mazrui, Ali, and Michael Tidy, *Nationalism and New States in Africa* (London, 1984).

Mazrui, Ali A., ed., *UNESCO General History of Africa. VIII: Africa since 1935* (London, 1999).

Michel, Marc, *L'appel à l'Afrique: Contributions et réactions à l'effort de guerre en A.O.F. 1914–1919* (Paris, 1982).

Miller, Daisy M., 'Raising the tribes: British policy in Italian East Africa, 1938–41', *Journal of Strategic Studies* 22, 1 (1999), pp. 96–123.

Miners, N. J., *The Nigerian Army 1956–1966* (London, 1971).

Mockler, Anthony, *Haile Selassie's War* (Oxford, 1984).

Mohamed, Jama, 'The 1944 Somaliland Camel Corps mutiny and popular politics', *History Workshop Journal* 50 (2000), pp. 93–113.

Moor, J. A. de, and H. L. Wesseling, eds, *Imperialism and War: Essays on Colonial Wars in Asia and Africa* (Leiden, 1989).

Moradi, Alexander, 'Towards an objective account of nutrition and health in colonial Kenya: A study of stature in African army recruits and civilians, 1880–1980', *Journal of Economic History* 96 (2009), pp. 720–55.

Morewood, Steven, 'Protecting the jugular vein of Empire: The Suez Canal in British defence strategy, 1919–1941', *War and Society* 10, 1 (1992), pp. 81–107.

Morley, John, *Colonial Postscript: Diary of a District Officer 1935–56* (London, 1992).

Moyse–Bartlett, H., *The King's African Rifles: A Study in the Military History of East and Central Africa* (Aldershot, 1956).

Muchai, Kango, *The Hard Core: The Story of Kango Muchai* (New York, 1966).

Mutongi, Kenda, '"Worries of the heart": Widowed mothers, daughters and masculinities in Maragoli, Western Kenya, 1940–60', *Journal of African History* 40, 1 (1999), pp. 67–86.

Mutonya, Mungai, and Timothy H. Parsons, 'KiKAR: A Swahili variety in Kenya's colonial army', *Journal of African Languages and Linguistics* 25 (2004), pp. 111–25.

Myrick, Bismarck, David L. Easterbrook and Jack R. Roelker, eds, *Three Aspects of Crisis in Colonial Kenya* (Syracuse NY, 1975).

Nasson, Bill, *Abraham Esau's War: A Black South African's War in the Cape, 1899–1902* (Cambridge, 1991).

Negash, Tekeste, *Italian Colonialism in Eritrea, 1882–1941: Policies, Praxis and Impact* (Stockholm, 1987).

Ngũgĩ wa Thiong'o, *Petals of Blood* (London, 1977).

Nicolini, Beatrice, ed., *Studies in Witchcraft, Magic, War and Peace in Africa* (Lampeter, 2006).

Niebuhr, Reinhold, *Moral Man and Immoral Society – a Study in Ethics and Political Philosophy* (New York, 1932).

Nigerian Army Education Corps and School, *History of the Nigerian Army 1863–1992* (Abuja, 1992).

Nissen, Margaret, *An African Church is Born: The Story of Adamawa and Central Province in Nigeria* (Dashen, 1984).

Nkrumah, Kwame, *Ghana: the Autobiography of Kwame Nkrumah* (London, 1957).

Nogaga, Nzamo, 'An African soldier's experiences as a prisoner-of-war', *South African Outlook* (1 October 1945), pp. 150–51.

Ntabeni, Mary Nombulelo, 'Military labour mobilisations in colonial Lesotho during World War II: 1940–1943', *Scientia Militaria: The South African Journal of Military Studies* 36, 2 (2008), pp. 36–59.

Nunneley, John, *Tales from the KAR* (London, 1998).

Oakes, D., ed., *Reader's Digest Illustrated History of South Africa: The Real Story* (Pleasantville NY, 1988).

Obama, Barack, *Dreams from my Father* (New York, 1995; London paperback edn, 2007).

Obiechina, E. N., ed., *Onitsha Market Literature* (London, 1972).

Odhiambo, E. S. Atieno and John Lonsdale, eds, *Mau Mau and Nationhood* (Oxford, 2003).

Ofusu-Appiah, L. H., ed., *The Encyclopaedia Africana Dictionary of African Biography. Vol. 1: Ethiopia–Ghana* (New York, 1977).

Ogot, Bethwell O., 'Mau Mau and nationhood: The untold story', in E. S. Atieno Odhiambo and John Lonsdale, eds, *Mau Mau and Nationhood* (Oxford, 2003), pp. 8–36.

Okoye, Mokwugo, *Storms on the Niger: A Study of Nigeria's Struggle* (Enugu, nd., *c*. 1981).

Oliver, Roland, and Anthony Atmore, *Africa Since 1800* (Cambridge, 3rd edn, 1981).

Olomola, Isola, 'The demobilization of Nigerian troops 1946–50: Problems and consequences', *Odu* New Series 13 (1976), pp. 40–59.

Olomola, Isola, 'The history of Nigeria's military barracks', *Nigeria Magazine* (1980), pp. 112–19.

Olukoju, Ayodeji, 'The cost of living in Lagos 1914–45', in David M. Anderson and Richard Rathbone, eds, *Africa's Urban Past* (Oxford, 2000), pp. 134–40.

Olusanya, G. O., *The Second World War and Politics in Nigeria 1939–1953* (Lagos, 1973).

Olusanya, G. O., 'The role of ex-servicemen in Nigerian politics', *Journal of Modern African Studies* 6, 2 (1968), pp. 221–32.

Omara-Otunnu, Amii, *Politics and the Military in Uganda 1890–1985* (London, 1987).

O'Meara, J., and A. Rodolph, *Springbok Legion: The History and Policy* (Johannesburg, 1944).

Omissi, David, *The Sepoy and the Raj: The Indian Army, 1860–1940* (London, 1994).

Opala, Joseph A., *Sierra Leone Heroes* (Freetown, 1987).

Orlebar, John, *Tales of the Sudan Defence Force* (privately printed, 1981).

Orpen, N., and H. T. Martin, *Salute the Sappers: Part I* (Johannesburg, 1981).

Owen, Christopher, *The Rhodesian African Rifles* (London, 1970).

Owen, Nicholas, 'Critics of Empire in Britain', in Judith M. Brown and Wm. Roger Louis, eds, *The Oxford History of the British Empire. Volume IV: The Twentieth Century* (Oxford, 1999), pp. 188–211.

Owino, Meshack. '*Vifo na Mazishi*: The impact of war on Kenya African soldiers' beliefs and attitudes towards death and burials in colonial Kenya', in Beatrice Nicolini, ed., *Studies in Witchcraft, Magic, War and Peace in Africa* (Lampeter, 2006), pp. 151–70.

Owusu, Maxwell, *Uses and Abuses of Political Power: A Case Study of Continuity and Change in the Politics of Ghana* (Chicago, 1970).

Page, Melvin E., 'The war of *thangata*: Nyasaland and the East African campaign, 1914–1918', *Journal of African History* 19, 1 (1978), pp. 87–100.

Paice, Edward, *Tip and Run: The Untold Tragedy of the Great War in Africa* (London, 2007).

Palmer, Annette, 'Black American soldiers in Trinidad 1942–44: Wartime politics in a colonial society', *Journal of Imperial and Commonwealth History* 14, 3 (1986), pp. 203–18.

Parker, John, and Richard Rathbone, *African History: A Very Short Introduction* (Oxford, 2007).

Parsons, Neil, Thomas Tlou and Willie Henderson, *Seretse Khama 1921–80* (Gaberone, 1995).

Parsons, Timothy H., *The African Rank-and-File: Social Implications of Colonial Military Service in the King's African Rifles, 1902–1964* (Oxford, 1999).

Parsons, Timothy, '"Wakamba warriors are soldiers of the Queen": The evolution of the Kamba as a martial race, 1890–1970', *Ethnohistory* 46 (1999), pp. 671–701.

Parsons, Timothy H., 'Dangerous education? The army as school in colonial East Africa', *Journal of Imperial and Commonwealth History* 8, 1 (2000), pp. 112–34.

Parsons, Timothy H., *The 1964 Army Mutinies in the Making of Modern East Africa* (Westport CT, 2003).

Paton, Alan, *Hofmeyr* (Cape Town, 1964).

Pearce, Robert D., *Sir Bernard Bourdillon: The Biography of a Twentieth-Century Colonialist* (Oxford, 1987).

Perry, F. W., *The Commonwealth Armies: Manpower and Organization in Two World War* (Manchester, 1988).

Peterson, Derek R., *Creative Writing: Translation, Bookkeeping and the Use of Imagination in Colonial Kenya* (Portsmouth NH, 2004).

Phillips, Anne, *The Enigma of Colonialism: British Policy in West Africa* (London, 1989).

Platt, Gen Sir William, 'The East African forces in the War and their future', *Journal of the Royal United Services Institute* 93 (1948), pp. 403–16.

Platt, Gen Sir William, *The Campaign Against Italian East Africa, 1940–41* (Khartoum, 1951).

Playfair, S. O., ed., *The Mediterranean and the Middle East: Vol. I: The Early Successes against Italy* (London, 1954).

Pope, Rex, 'British demobilization after the Second World War', *Journal of Contemporary History* 30, 1 (1985), pp. 65–81.

Pratten, David, *The Man-Leopard Murders: History and Society in Colonial Nigeria* (Edinburgh, 2007).

Prichard, James Cowles, *Researches into the Physical History of Man* (2nd edn, London, 1826).

Prosser, Gifford, and Wm Roger Louis, eds, *The Transfer of Power in Africa: Decolonization 1940–1960* (New Haven CT, 1982).

Pugliese, Christina, *Author, Publisher and Gikuyu Nationalist: The Life and Writings of Gakaaru wa Wanaju* (Bayreuth, 1995).

Ranger, T. O., *Dance and Society in Eastern Africa* (London, 1975).

Ranger, T. O., 'The invention of tradition revisited: The case of Africa', in T. O. Ranger and Olafemi Vaughan, eds, *Legitimacy and the State in Twentieth-Century Africa* (London, 1993), pp. 62–111.

Ranger, Terence, and Paul Slack, eds, *Epidemics and Ideas: Essays in the Historical Perceptions of Pestilence* (Cambridge, 1992).

Rathbone, Richard, 'Businessmen in politics: Party struggles in Ghana, 1947–57', *Journal of Development Studies* 9, 2 (1973), pp. 391–402.

Ray, Deborah W., 'The Takoradi route: Roosevelt's prewar venture beyond the Western hemisphere', *Journal of American History* 62, 3 (1975), pp. 340–58.

Richards, Audrey, *Land, Labour and Diet in Northern Rhodesia: An Economic Study of the Bemba Tribe* (Oxford, 1939).

Richards, A. I., and E. M. Widdowson, 'A dietary study in north-east Rhodesia', *Africa* 9, 2 (1936), pp. 166–96.

Richards, Jeffrey, and Anthony Algate, *Best of British* (Oxford, 1983).

Roberts, Andrew, ed., *The Colonial Moment in Africa: Essays on the Movement of Minds and Materials, 1900–1940* (Cambridge, 1990).

Rodseth, F., *Ndabazabantu: The Life of a Native Affairs Administrator* (Volda, 1984).

Rohdie, Samuel, 'The Gold Coast aborigines abroad', *Journal of African History* 6, 3 (1965), pp. 389–411.

Roos, Neil, *Ordinary Springboks: White Servicemen and Social Justice in South Africa 1939–1961* (Aldershot, 2005).

Rosberg, Carl G., and John Nottingham, *The Myth of 'Mau Mau': Nationalism in Kenya* (Stanford CA, 1966).

Roth, M., "'If you give us our rights we will fight": Black involvement in the Second World War', *South African Historical Journal* 15, 15 (1983), pp. 85–104;

Rubin, Gerry R., *Durban 1942: A British Troopship Revolt* (London, 1992).

St John, Robert, *Through Malan's Africa* (Garden City NY, 1954).

Sabben-Clare, E. E., 'African troops in Asia', *African Affairs* 44 (1945), pp. 151–57.

Sadleir, Randal, *Tanzania: Journey to Republic* (London, 1999).

Said, Mohamed, *The Life and Times of Abdulwahid Sykes (1924–1968): The Untold Story of the Muslim Struggle against British Colonialism in Tanganyika* (London, 1998).

Said, Mohamed, 'Founder of a political movement: Abdulwahid K. Sykes (1924–1968)', *Africa Events* 4, 9 (September, 1988), pp. 38–41.

Salmon, E. Marling, *Beyond the Call of Duty: African Deeds of Bravery* (London, 1952).

Sandilands, A., 'About the Bechuana of the AAPC', *Chaplains' Magazine* (January 1943).

Savage, D. C., and J. Forbes Munro, 'Carrier recruitment in the British East African Protectorate, 1914–18', *Journal of African History* 7, 2 (1966), pp. 313–42.

Sbacchi, Alberto, *Ethiopia under Mussolini: Fascism and Colonial Experience* (London, 1985).

Schapera, Isaac, *Migrant Labour and Tribal Life* (London, 1947).

Scheck, Raffael, *Hitler's African Victims: The German Army Massacres of Black French Soldiers in 1940* (Cambridge, 2006).

Schildkrout, Enid, 'The ideology of regionalism in Ghana', in W. Schack and E. P. Skinner, eds, *Strangers in African Societies* (Berkeley CA, 1979), pp. 183–207.

Schleh, Eugene P. A. , 'The post-war careers of ex-servicemen in Ghana and Uganda', *Journal of Modern African Studies* 6, 2 (1968), pp. 203–20.

Schmitt, Deborah Ann, *The Bechuanaland Pioneers and Gunners* (Westport CT, 2005).

Seirlis, J. K., 'Undoing the United Front? Coloured soldiers in Rhodesia 1939–1980', *African Studies* 63, 1 (2004), pp. 73–94.

Seychelles, Republic of: Ministry of Education and Information, *Histoire des Seychelles* (Paris, 1983).

Shepperson, George, 'The obsequies of Lance-Corporal Amidu', *Phylon: The Atlanta University Review of Race and Culture* 12, 1 (1951), pp. 54–64.

Shepperson, George A., 'External factors in the development of African nationalism, with particular reference to British Central Africa', *Phylon: The Atlantic University Review of Race and Culture* 22, 3 (1961), pp. 207–25.

Shepperson, George, and Thomas Price, *Independent African: John Chilembwe and the Origins, Setting and Significance of the Nyasaland Native Rising of 1915* (Edinburgh, 1958).

Shirley, W. R., *A History of the Nigerian Police* (Lagos, 1950).

Shiroya, O. J. E., *Kenya and World War II: African Soldiers in the European War* (Nairobi, 1985).

Shirreff, David, *Bare Feet and Bandoliers: Wingate, Sandford, the Patriots and the Part they Played in the Liberation of Ethiopia* (London, 1995).

Simelane, Hamilton Sipho, 'Landlessness and Imperial response in Swaziland, 1938–59', *Journal of Southern African Studies* 17, 4 (1991), pp. 717–41.

Simelane, Hamilton Sipho, 'Labour mobilization for the war effort in Swaziland, 1940–1942', *International Journal of African Historical Studies* 26, 3 (1993), pp. 541–74.

Simelane, Hamilton Sipho, 'Veterans, politics and poverty: the case of Swazi veterans in the Second World War', *South African Historical Journal* 38 (1998), pp. 144–70.

Simons, H. J. and Simons, R. E., *Class and Colour in South Africa 1850–1950* (Harmondsworth, 1969).

Sithole, Ndabaningi, *African Nationalism* (London, 1959; 2nd edn, London, 1968).

Smyth, Rosaleen, 'War propaganda during the Second World War in Northern Rhodesia', *African Affairs* 83 (1984), pp. 345–58.

Smyth, Rosaleen, 'Britain's African colonies and British propaganda during the Second World War', *Journal of Imperial and Commonwealth History* 14, 1 (1985), pp. 176–85.

Sobott, Gaele, 'Experiences of Batswana women during the Second World War', *Pula: Botswana Journal of African Studies* 13, 1/2 (1999), pp. 93–107.

Somerville, Christopher, *Our War: How the British Commonwealth Fought the Second World War* (London, 1998).

Spear, Thomas, 'Neo-traditionalism and the limits of invention in British colonial Africa', *Journal of African History* 44, 1 (2003), pp. 3–27.

Spencer, John, *James Beauttah Freedom Fighter* (Nairobi, 1983).

Stadler, W., '"Birds in the cornfield": Squatter movements in Johannesburg, 1944–1947', *Journal of Southern African Studies* 6, 1 (1979), pp. 93–123.

Staniland, Martin, 'The "military participation" of Ghanaian ethnic groups', *Research Review* (Legon, Ghana) 8, 2 (1972), pp. 29–31.

Stewart, Andrew, *Empire Lost: Britain, the Dominions and the Second World War* (London, 2008).

Stigand, C. H., *Administration in Tropical Africa* (London 1914).

Stocking Jnr, George, *Victorian Anthropology* (New York, 1987).

Stoler, Ann Laura, and Frederick Cooper, 'Between metropole and colony', in Frederick Cooper and Ann Laura Stoler, eds, *Tensions of Empire: Colonial Cultures in a Bourgeois World* (Berkeley CA, 1997).

Sullivan, Brian R., 'The Italian–Ethiopian war, October 1935–November 1941: Causes, conduct and consequences', in A. Hamish Ion and E. J. Errington, eds, *Great Powers and Little Wars: The Limits of Power* (Westport CT, 1993), pp. 167–201.

Sundkler, Bengt, and Christopher Steed, *A History of the Church in Africa* (Cambridge, 2000).

Tabili, Laura, *'We Ask For British Justice': Workers and Racial Difference in Late Imperial Britain* (Ithaca NY, 1994).

Tait, David, *The Konkomba of Northern Ghana* (London, 1961).

Thomas, Lynn M., 'Schoolgirl pregnancies, letter-writing and "modern" persons in late colonial East Africa', in Karen Barber, ed., *Africa's Hidden Histories: Everyday Literacy and Making the Self* (Bloomington IN, 2006).

Thomas, Martin, *The French Empire at War 1939–45* (Manchester, 1991).

Thomas, Ralph, 'Indian malcontents and West African soldiers: Some thoughts on the Indian problem', *West African Review* (November 1944), pp. 55–57

Thompson, Gardner, *Governing Uganda: British Colonial Rule and its Legacy* (Kampala, 2003).

Thompson, Leonard, *A History of South Africa* (New Haven CT, 1990).

Throup, David W., *Economic & Social Origins of Mau Mau* (London, 1987).

Tomalin, H. A., 'Physical and recreational training in West Africa', *Mind, Body and Spirit: Journal of the Army Physical Training Corps* 21 (June 1946), pp. 21–22.

Tournay, A. A., 'Payments to dependants of Gold Coast soldiers overseas, 1944–45'; and 'How the soldier's wife gets paid', *The Empire at War* (26 September 1945).

Turrey, E. D. A., and A. Abrahams, *The Sierra Leone Army: A Century of History* (London, 1987).

UNESCO, *History of Africa and the Second World* War (Paris, 1985).

Union of South Africa, *Official Year Book of the Union, No. 17: 1934–1935* (Pretoria, 1936).

Vail, Leroy, ed., *The Creation of Tribalism in Southern Africa* (London, 1989).

Valuslay, Chantal, *Le soldat occulté: Les malgaches de l'Armée Française, 1884–1920* (Paris, 1995).

Vambe, Lawrence, *From Rhodesia to Zimbabwe* (London, 1976).

Vandewalle, F. A., 'Mutineries au Congo Belge', *Zaïre* 11, 5 (1957), pp. 487–514.

Vaughan, Megan, *Curing Their Ills: Colonial Power and African Illness* (Cambridge, 1991).

Vaughan, Megan, 'Syphilis in colonial east and central Africa: The social construction of an epidemic', in Ranger, Terence, and Paul Slack, eds, *Epidemics and Ideas: Essays in the Historical Perceptions of Pestilence* (Cambridge, 1992), pp. 290–98.

Vickery, Kenneth P., 'The Second World War revival of forced labour in the Rhodesias', *International Journal of African Historical Studies* 22, 3 (1989), pp. 423–37.

Walshe, Peter, *The Rise of African Nationalism in South Africa: The African National Congress 1912–1952* (London, 1970).

Ward, Kevin, 'Archbishop Janani Luwum: The dilemmas of loyalty, opposition and witness in Amin's Uganda', in David Maxwell and Ingird Lowrie, eds, *Christianity and the African Imagination: Essays in Honour of Adrian Hastings* (Leiden, 2002).

Warwick, Peter, *Black People and the South African War 1899–1902* (Cambridge, 1983).

Weinberg, Gerhard L., *A World at Arms: A Global History of World War II* (Cambridge, 1994).

West, Shearer, ed., *The Victorians and Race* (Aldershot, 1996).

White, Luise, *The Comforts of Home: Prostitution in Colonial Nairobi* (Chicago, 1990).

Wigg, George, *Lord Wigg* (London, 1972).

Willan, B. P., 'The South African Native Labour Contingent, 1916–1918', *Journal of African History* 19, 1 (1978), pp. 61–86.

Williams, David, 'English–speaking West Africa', in M. Crowder, ed., *The Cambridge History of Africa. Vol. 8: c. 1940–c. 1975* (Cambridge, 1984), pp. 331–82.

Williams, Susan, *Colour Bar: The Triumph of Tshekedi Khama and his Nation* (London, 2006).

Willis, Justin, *Potent Brews: A Social History of Alcohol in East Africa 1850–1999* (Oxford, 2002).

Wolseley, Sir Garnet, 'The Negro as soldier', *Fortnightly Review* (December 1888), pp. 699–700.

Worboys, Michael, 'The discovery of colonial malnutrition between the wars', in David Arnold, ed., *Imperial Medicine and Indigenous Societies* (Manchester 1988), pp. 208–25.

Wrong, Margaret, 'British policy in Africa', *Christian Newsletter* (Oxford, 1942).

Wrong, Margaret, *West African Journey* (London, 1946).

Wylie, Diana, *A Little God: the Twilight of Patriarchy in a Southern African Chiefdom* (Hanover NH, 1990).

Young, Crawford, *The African Colonial State in Comparative Perspective* (New Haven CT, 1994).

Youell, George, *Africa Marches* (London, 1949).

Index

Printed in the USA
CPSIA information can be obtained
at www.ICGtesting.com
JSHW011454050624
64359JS00010B/184

9 781847 010476